Land Rover Defender Diesel
Owners Workshop Manual

Peter T Gill

(6398 - 288)

Models covered

Defender 90, 110 & 130 models, including Chassis Cab, Pick-up, Double Cab, Station Wagon, Soft Top and Hard Top versions with 2.2 litre (2198cc) & 2.4 litre (2402cc) turbo-diesel engines

Does NOT cover petrol models, or specialist options or conversions

© Haynes Publishing 2017

ABCDE
FGHIJ
KLMNO
PQRST

A book in the **Haynes Owners Workshop Manual Series**

ISBN **978 1 78521 398 4**

British Library Cataloguing in Publication Data
A catalogue record for this book is available from the British Library.

Printed in Malaysia

Haynes Publishing
Sparkford, Yeovil, Somerset BA22 7JJ, England

Haynes North America, Inc
859 Lawrence Drive, Newbury Park, California 91320, USA

Printed using NORBRITE BOOK 48.8gsm (CODE: 40N6533) from NORPAC; procurement system certified under Sustainable Forestry Initiative standard. Paper produced is certified to the SFI Certified Fiber Sourcing Standard (CERT - 0094271)

Contents

Contents

First introduced in 1948 at the Amsterdam motor show, the Land Rover was primarily designed for use by farmers as a combined tractor/pick-up truck, and only a limited production run was anticipated. However, the vehicle became a phenomenal success, and by 1951 the Land Rover was outselling Rover saloon cars.

The Land Rover 110 range was introduced to the UK market in 1983, and is basically a more refined development of the previous Land Rover Series III. The 110 name is derived from the 110-inch wheelbase. The 110 models were initially introduced with the 2286 cc normally-aspirated indirect-injection diesel engine, and were available in Pick-Up, Hard-Top and Station Wagon body styles.

In 1984, the 90 range was introduced (90-inch wheelbase), and the 2495 cc normally-aspirated diesel engine superseded the previous smaller-capacity unit across the 90 and 110 ranges.

In 1986, a more powerful turbocharged version of the 2495 cc engine superseded the normally-aspirated engine across the range.

For the 1991 model year, the 90 and 110 ranges were re-christened Defender, and received a heavily-revised 200 TDi turbocharged direct-injection engine, providing a significant improvement in performance over the previous indirect-injection engines. Engine development continued in 1994, when the 300 TDi engine was introduced, to meet revised engine emissions regulations. In November 1998 the TD5 engine was introduced, replacing the 300 TDi engine.

In February 2007, the Defender was revised, and the TD5 engine was replaced with a modified Ford 2.4 litre (Duratorq) diesel engine, which was used in the Ford Transit models. Later in July 2011, this engine was reduced to a 2.2 litre, but kept the same power output and improved the emissions to comply with latest regulations.

Land Rover 90 Hard-Top

The drive from the main gearbox is picked up by a transfer gearbox, which provides drive to the front and rear axles, via propeller shafts.

A wide range of standard and optional equipment is available within the model ranges, to suit most requirements.

Due to the rugged construction of the vehicle, the number of items requiring regular maintenance (mainly the need for regular lubrication checks) is higher than that found on many smaller vehicles, but the Defender is a straightforward vehicle to maintain, and most of the items requiring frequent attention are easily accessible.

Your Land Rover manual

The aim of this manual is to help you get the best value from your vehicle. It can do so in several ways. It can help you decide what work must be done (even should you choose to get it done by a garage). It will also provide information on routine maintenance and servicing, and give a logical course of action and diagnosis when random faults occur. However, it is hoped that you will use the manual by tackling the work yourself. On simpler jobs it may even be quicker than booking the vehicle into a garage and going there twice, to leave and collect it. Perhaps most important, a lot of money can be saved by avoiding the costs a garage must charge to cover its labour and overheads.

The manual has drawings and descriptions to show the function of the various components so that their layout can be understood. Tasks are described and photographed in a clear step-by-step sequence. The illustrations are numbered by the Section number and paragraph number to which they relate – if there is more than one illustration per paragraph, the sequence is denoted alphabetically.

References to the 'left' and 'right' of the vehicle are in the sense of a person in the driver's seat, facing forwards.

Acknowledgements

Thanks are due to Draper Tools Limited, who provided some of the workshop tools, and to all those people at Sparkford who helped in the production of this manual.

We take great pride in the accuracy of information given in this manual, but car manufacturers make alterations and design changes during the production run of a particular car of which they do not inform us. No liability can be accepted by the authors or publishers for loss, damage or injury caused by any errors in, or omissions from, the information given.

Land Rover Defender 110

Working on your car can be dangerous. This page shows just some of the potential risks and hazards, with the aim of creating a safety-conscious attitude.

General hazards

Scalding

• Don't remove the radiator or expansion tank cap while the engine is hot.
• Engine oil, transmission fluid or power steering fluid may also be dangerously hot if the engine has recently been running.

Burning

• Beware of burns from the exhaust system and from any part of the engine. Brake discs and drums can also be extremely hot immediately after use.

Crushing

• When working under or near a raised vehicle, always supplement the jack with axle stands, or use drive-on ramps.
Never venture under a car which is only supported by a jack.
• Take care if loosening or tightening high-torque nuts when the vehicle is on stands. Initial loosening and final tightening should be done with the wheels on the ground.

Fire

• Fuel is highly flammable; fuel vapour is explosive.
• Don't let fuel spill onto a hot engine.
• Do not smoke or allow naked lights (including pilot lights) anywhere near a vehicle being worked on. Also beware of creating sparks (electrically or by use of tools).
• Fuel vapour is heavier than air, so don't work on the fuel system with the vehicle over an inspection pit.
• Another cause of fire is an electrical overload or short-circuit. Take care when repairing or modifying the vehicle wiring.
• Keep a fire extinguisher handy, of a type suitable for use on fuel and electrical fires.

Electric shock

• Ignition HT and Xenon headlight voltages can be dangerous, especially to people with heart problems or a pacemaker. Don't work on or near these systems with the engine running or the ignition switched on.

• Mains voltage is also dangerous. Make sure that any mains-operated equipment is correctly earthed. Mains power points should be protected by a residual current device (RCD) circuit breaker.

Fume or gas intoxication

• Exhaust fumes are poisonous; they can contain carbon monoxide, which is rapidly fatal if inhaled. Never run the engine in a confined space such as a garage with the doors shut.
• Fuel vapour is also poisonous, as are the vapours from some cleaning solvents and paint thinners.

Poisonous or irritant substances

• Avoid skin contact with battery acid and with any fuel, fluid or lubricant, especially antifreeze, brake hydraulic fluid and Diesel fuel. Don't syphon them by mouth. If such a substance is swallowed or gets into the eyes, seek medical advice.
• Prolonged contact with used engine oil can cause skin cancer. Wear gloves or use a barrier cream if necessary. Change out of oil-soaked clothes and do not keep oily rags in your pocket.
• Air conditioning refrigerant forms a poisonous gas if exposed to a naked flame (including a cigarette). It can also cause skin burns on contact.

Asbestos

• Asbestos dust can cause cancer if inhaled or swallowed. Asbestos may be found in gaskets and in brake and clutch linings. When dealing with such components it is safest to assume that they contain asbestos.

Special hazards

Hydrofluoric acid

• This extremely corrosive acid is formed when certain types of synthetic rubber, found in some O-rings, oil seals, fuel hoses etc, are exposed to temperatures above 400OC. The rubber changes into a charred or sticky substance containing the acid. *Once formed, the acid remains dangerous for years. If it gets onto the skin, it may be necessary to amputate the limb concerned*.
• When dealing with a vehicle which has suffered a fire, or with components salvaged from such a vehicle, wear protective gloves and discard them after use.

The battery

• Batteries contain sulphuric acid, which attacks clothing, eyes and skin. Take care when topping-up or carrying the battery.
• The hydrogen gas given off by the battery is highly explosive. Never cause a spark or allow a naked light nearby. Be careful when connecting and disconnecting battery chargers or jump leads.

Air bags

• Air bags can cause injury if they go off accidentally. Take care when removing the steering wheel and trim panels. Special storage instructions may apply.

Diesel injection equipment

• Diesel injection pumps supply fuel at very high pressure. Take care when working on the fuel injectors and fuel pipes.

 Warning: Never expose the hands, face or any other part of the body to injector spray; the fuel can penetrate the skin with potentially fatal results.

Remember...

DO

• Do use eye protection when using power tools, and when working under the vehicle.

• Do wear gloves or use barrier cream to protect your hands when necessary.

• Do get someone to check periodically that all is well when working alone on the vehicle.

• Do keep loose clothing and long hair well out of the way of moving mechanical parts.

• Do remove rings, wristwatch etc, before working on the vehicle – especially the electrical system.

• Do ensure that any lifting or jacking equipment has a safe working load rating adequate for the job.

DON'T

• Don't attempt to lift a heavy component which may be beyond your capability – get assistance.

• Don't rush to finish a job, or take unverified short cuts.

• Don't use ill-fitting tools which may slip and cause injury.

• Don't leave tools or parts lying around where someone can trip over them. Mop up oil and fuel spills at once.

• Don't allow children or pets to play in or near a vehicle being worked on.

The following pages are intended to help in dealing with common roadside emergencies and breakdowns. You will find more detailed fault finding information at the back of the manual, and repair information in the main chapters.

If your car won't start and the starter motor doesn't turn

☐ Remove the front passenger seat cushion, then open the battery compartment cover and make sure that the battery terminals are clean and tight.
☐ Switch on the headlights and try to start the engine. If the headlights go very dim when you're trying to start, the battery is probably flat. Try jump starting (see next page) using another vehicle.

If your car won't start even though the starter motor turns as normal

☐ Is there fuel in the tank?
☐ Is there moisture on electrical components under the bonnet? Switch off the ignition, and then wipe off any obvious dampness with a dry cloth. Spray a water-repellent aerosol product (WD-40 or equivalent) on engine and fuel system electrical connectors like those shown in the photos.

A Check the security and condition of the battery connections.

B Check the wiring connectors to the starter motor solenoid for security.

C Remove the cover and check that all fuses are still in good condition and none have blown.

Jump starting

Jump starting will get you out of trouble, but you must correct whatever made the battery go flat in the first place. There are three possibilities:

1 *The battery has been drained by repeated attempts to start, or by leaving the lights on.*

2 *The charging system is not working properly (alternator drivebelt slack or broken, alternator wiring fault or alternator itself faulty).*

3 *The battery itself is at fault (electrolyte low, or battery worn out).*

The battery on this vehicle is located under the passenger seat, inside the vehicle. To access the battery, remove the passenger seat cushion and remove the cover from the top of the battery compartment.

When jump-starting a vehicle using a booster battery, observe the following precautions:

✓ Before connecting the booster battery, make sure that the ignition is switched off.
✓ Ensure that all electrical equipment (lights, heater, wipers, etc) is switched off.
✓ Take note of any special precautions printed on the battery case.
✓ Make sure that the booster battery is the same voltage as the one required, for the one in the vehicle being jump started.
✓ If the battery is being jump-started from the battery in another vehicle, the two vehicles MUST NOT TOUCH each other.
✓ Make sure that the transmission is in neutral (or PARK, in the case of automatic transmission).

Caution: If the vehicle does not start after a few attempts, investigate further for the fault. Continuous cranking of the engine and the vehicle not starting, could result in damage to the catalytic converter.

1 Remove the red plastic terminal cover and connect the red jump lead to the positive terminal (Ensure all electrical consumers are switched off).

2 Connect the other end of the red lead to the positive (+) terminal of the booster battery.

3 Connect one end of the black jump lead to the battery negative (-) terminal of the booster battery.

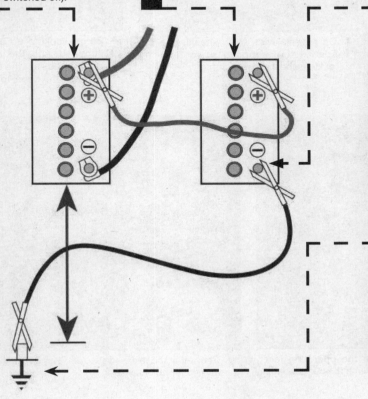

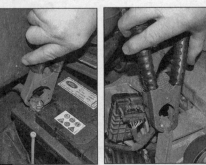

4 Connect the other end of the black jump lead to the negative (-) terminal of the battery, or preferably a bolt/bracket on the engine block.

5 Make sure that the jump leads will not come into contact with the fan, drive-belts or other moving parts of the engine.

6 Start the engine using the booster battery and run it at idle speed. Switch on the lights, rear window demister and heater blower motor, then disconnect the jump leads in the reverse order of connection. Turn off the lights etc.

Wheel changing

Preparation

☐ The jack should always be used on firm, level ground.

☐ If not already done, apply the handbrake, switch on the ignition, then engage first gear, and select the Low range in the transfer gearbox.

☐ Engage the differential lock, and check that the appropriate warning light on the instrument panel is illuminated. Switch off the ignition, and remove the key.

☐ Ensure that any occupants get out of the vehicle before jacking.

⚠️ *Warning: The handbrake acts on the transmission, not the rear wheels, and may not hold the vehicle stationary when jacking, unless the following procedure is followed precisely. If one front wheel and one rear wheel are raised, no vehicle holding or braking effect is possible using the handbrake, therefore the wheels must always be chocked (using the chock supplied in the tool kit). If the vehicle is coupled to a trailer, disconnect the trailer from the vehicle before commencing jacking. This is to prevent the trailer pulling the vehicle off the jack and causing personal injury.*

1 Remove the jacking up tools (and wheel chock)...

2 ... and the bottle jack from inside the battery compartment under the passenger front seat.

3 Using the wheel nut wrench supplied in the tool kit, initially slacken the nuts on the wheel to be removed.

4 On models with alloy wheels, use the special tool supplied to remove the locking wheel nut.

5 Before jacking up a wheel, the chock supplied with the tool kit should be positioned at the wheel diagonally opposite the wheel to be raised.

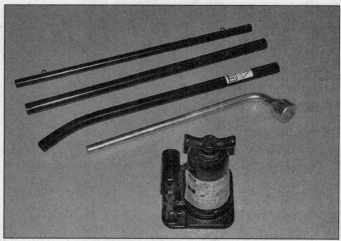

6 With the chock(s) in position, assemble the operating lever, ensuring that the locking clips engage fully with the corresponding slots.

7 Check that the release valve (arrowed) is fully closed before jacking (turned fully clockwise)

8 If jacking up a front wheel, slide the jack into position from the front of the vehicle (not from the side). Position the jack head so that when raised, it will engage with the front axle casing immediately below the coil spring, between the flange at the end of the axle casing, and the bracket to which the front suspension components are attached.

9 If raising a rear wheel, slide the jack into position from the rear of the vehicle (not from the side). Position the jack head so that when raised, it will engage with the rear axle casing immediately below the coil spring and the shock absorber mounting bracket.

10 Engage the operating lever with the jack, then pump the lever up and down to raise the vehicle.

Finally . . .

☐ Locate the spare wheel on the studs, then refit the original wheel nuts, and tighten as firmly as possible using the wrench.

☐ Lower the vehicle to the ground, and withdraw the jack.

☐ Finally tighten the wheel nuts using the wrench, with hand pressure only. Do not use foot pressure or an extension tube on the wheel wrench, as this could overstress the wheel studs, as well as making them difficult to remove subsequently.

☐ Fit the removed wheel to the spare wheel carrier, and where applicable, refit the cover.

☐ Stow the jack, chocks and tools in their correct locations.

☐ On completion, disengage the differential lock and select the High range in the transfer gearbox.

☐ At the earliest opportunity, check the that the wheel nuts have been tightened to the specified torque.

11 Once the wheel is clear of the ground, remove the wheel nuts, and lift off the wheel

12 Again using the wheel nut wrench, remove the nuts securing the spare wheel to the carrier, and lift off the wheel (2-door pick-up shown).

Towing

Front towing eye

Tow with all four wheels on the ground

☐ Turn the ignition key to position II to release the steering lock, and to ensure that the direction indicators and brake lights will work.

☐ Select Neutral in the main gearbox, and in the transfer gearbox. Ensure that the differential lock is disengaged.

☐ Secure the tow rope/chain (as applicable) to the front towing eye **(see illustration)**.

☐ Release the handbrake.

Note: *Greater than usual pedal pressure will be required to operate the brakes, since the vacuum servo unit is only operational with the engine running. Similarly, greater-than-usual steering effort will be required, as the power steering system will not be operational.*

Suspended tow by breakdown vehicle

⚠️ *Warning: To prevent damage to the vehicle, the propeller shaft MUST be removed (see Chapter 8), according to which wheels are in contact with the road.*

☐ If the front wheels are to be left in contact with the road, the ignition key should be turned to position I to release the steering lock. The steering wheel and/or linkage must be secured in the straight-ahead position – do not use the steering lock for this purpose.

Identifying leaks

Puddles on the garage floor or drive, or obvious wetness under the bonnet or underneath the car, suggest a leak that needs investigating. It can sometimes be difficult to decide where the leak is coming from, especially if an engine undershield is fitted. Leaking oil or fluid can also be blown rearwards by the passage of air under the car, giving a false impression of where the problem lies.

 Warning: Most automotive oils and fluids are poisonous. Wash them off skin, and change out of contaminated clothing, without delay.

 The smell of a fluid leaking from the car may provide a clue to what's leaking. Some fluids are distinctively coloured. It may help to remove the engine undershield, clean the car carefully and to park it over some clean paper overnight as an aid to locating the source of the leak. Remember that some leaks may only occur while the engine is running.

Sump oil

Engine oil may leak from the drain plug...

Oil from filter

...or from the base of the oil filter.

Gearbox oil

Gearbox oil can leak from the seals at the inboard ends of the driveshafts.

Antifreeze

Leaking antifreeze often leaves a crystalline deposit like this.

Brake fluid

A leak occurring at a wheel is almost certainly brake fluid.

Power steering fluid

Power steering fluid may leak from the pipe connectors on the steering rack.

Introduction

There are some very simple checks which need only take a few minutes to carry out, but which could save you a lot of inconvenience and expense.

These weekly checks require no great skill or special tools, and the small amount of time they take to perform could prove to be very well spent, for example:

☐ Keeping an eye on tyre condition and pressures, will not only help to stop them wearing out prematurely, but could also save your life.

☐ Many breakdowns are caused by electrical problems. Battery-related faults are particularly common, and a quick check on a regular basis will often prevent the majority of these.

☐ If your vehicle develops a brake fluid leak, the first time you might know about it is when your brakes don't work properly. Checking the level regularly will give advance warning of this kind of problem.

☐ If the oil or coolant levels run low, the cost of repairing any engine damage will be far greater than fixing the leak, for example.

Underbonnet check points

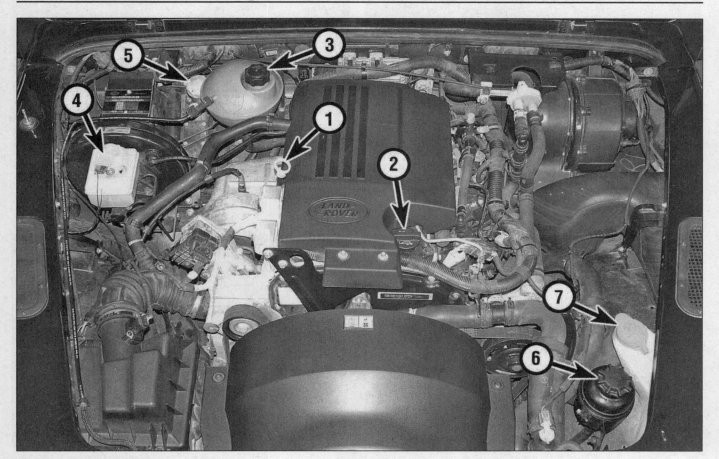

▲ 2.2 litre engine

1 *Engine oil level dipstick*

2 *Engine oil filler cap*

3 *Coolant reservoir (expansion tank)*

4 *Brake fluid reservoir*

5 *Clutch fluid reservoir*

6 *Power steering fluid reservoir*

7 *Washer fluid reservoir*

Engine oil level

HAYNES HiNT *If the oil is checked immediately after driving the vehicle, some of the oil will remain in the upper engine components and oil galleries, resulting in an inaccurate reading on the dipstick.*

Before you start

✔ The oil level should be checked with the vehicle standing on level ground.
✔ Check the oil level before it is driven, or wait at least 5 minutes after the engine has been switched off.

The correct oil

Modern engines place great demands on their oil. It is very important that the correct oil for your vehicle is used (see *Lubricants and fluids*).

Vehicle care

● If you have to add oil frequently, you should check whether you have any oil leaks. Place some clean paper under the vehicle overnight, and check for stains in the morning. If there are no leaks, the engine may be burning oil.
● Always maintain the level between the upper and lower dipstick marks. If the level is too low, severe engine damage may occur. Oil seal failure may result if the engine is overfilled by adding too much oil.

1 The engine oil level is checked with a dipstick which extends through a tube and into the sump at the bottom of the engine. The dipstick is located on the right-hand side of the engine. Withdraw the dipstick.

2 Withdraw the dipstick from the tube, and wipe all the oil from the end with a clean rag or paper towel. Insert the clean dipstick back into the tube as far as it will go, then withdraw it once more.

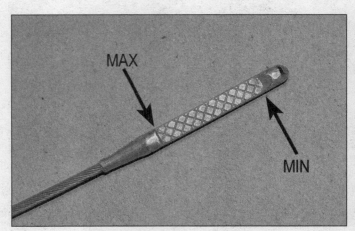

MAX

MIN

3 Check that the oil level is between the lower and upper marks at each end of the cross-hatching on the dipstick. Take the appropriate action as follows, according to the reading on the dipstick.

⚠ *Warning: The oil level should never be above the upper mark on the dipstick, as engine damage may be caused.*

a) If the oil level is nearer the upper mark than the lower mark take no action.
b) If the oil level is nearer, or below, the lower mark, add oil to bring the level to the upper mark.
c) The amount of oil needed to raise the level from the lower mark to the upper mark is approx. 2.0 litres.

4 To top-up the oil level, remove the oil filler cap from the front of the camshaft cover, and add fresh oil as required. If the level is allowed to fall below the lower mark/notch, oil starvation may result, which could lead to severe engine damage. If the engine is overfilled by adding too much oil, this may result in oil leaks or oil seal failures. An oil can spout or funnel may help to reduce spillage when adding oil to the engine. Always use the correct grade and type of oil, as shown in *Lubricants and fluids*.

Coolant level

⚠️ **Warning: DO NOT attempt to remove the expansion tank pressure cap when the engine is hot, as there is a very great risk of scalding. Do not allow antifreeze to come in contact with your skin, or with the painted surfaces of the vehicle. Rinse off spills immediately with plenty of water. Never leave antifreeze lying around in an open container, or in a puddle on the floor. Children and pets are attracted by its sweet smell, but antifreeze can be fatal if ingested.**

Before you start

✔ All vehicles covered by this manual have a pressurised cooling system. An expansion tank is located on the right-hand side of the engine compartment. The expansion tank has a continual flow of coolant passing through it, in order to purge air from the cooling system.
✔ The coolant level in the expansion tank should be checked regularly, and the level should always be checked with the engine cold.

Vehicle care

● With a sealed cooling system, the addition of coolant should only be necessary at very infrequent intervals. If frequent topping-up is required, it is likely there is a leak in the system. Check the radiator, all hoses and joint faces for any sign of staining or actual wetness, and rectify as necessary. Coolant leaks usually show up as a white or antifreeze-coloured stain in the area of the leak. If no leaks can be found, it is advisable to have the pressure cap and the entire system pressure-tested by a dealer or suitably-equipped garage, as this will often show up a small leak not previously visible.

● It is important that antifreeze is used in the cooling system all year round, not just during the winter months. Don't top-up with water alone, as the antifreeze will become too diluted.

1 With the engine cold, the expansion tank should be approximately half-full, ie, so that the coolant level is up to the ridge cast into the front edge of the tank. The cold level is indicated on the side of the expansion tank

2 If topping-up is necessary, wait until the engine is cold, then slowly unscrew the pressure cap on the expansion tank. Allow any remaining pressure to escape, then fully unscrew the cap. Add a mixture of water and antifreeze (see below) through the expansion tank filler neck until the coolant level is correct. Refit and tighten the pressure cap.

Power steering fluid level

Before you start

✔ Park the vehicle on level ground.
✔ Set the steering wheel straight-ahead.
✔ The engine should be cold and turned off.

HAYNES HINT *For the check to be accurate, the steering must not be turned while the level is being checked.*

Safety first!

● The need for frequent topping-up indicates a leak, which should be investigated immediately.

1 The reservoir is mounted at the front left-hand side of the engine compartment, in front of the washer fluid reservoir.

2 If topping-up is necessary, first wipe clean the area around the filler cap to prevent dirt entering the system, then unscrew the reservoir cap.

3 The fluid level can be checked on a dipstick fitted to the inside of the reservoir cap, and should be between the upper and lower marks (engine cold). Use the specified type of fluid for topping up and do not overfill the reservoir, when the level is correct, securely refit the cap.

Brake fluid level

Warning: Hydraulic fluid is poisonous; wash off immediately and thoroughly in the case of skin contact, and seek immediate medical advice if any fluid is swallowed, or gets into the eyes. Certain types of hydraulic fluid are inflammable, and may ignite when allowed into contact with hot components. When servicing any hydraulic system, it is safest to assume that the fluid IS inflammable, and to take precautions against the risk of fire as though it is petrol that is being handled. Finally, it is hygroscopic (it absorbs moisture from the air) – old fluid may be contaminated, and unfit for further use. When topping-up or renewing the fluid, always use the recommended type (see 'Lubricants and fluids'), and ensure that it comes from a freshly-opened, previously-sealed container.

Before you start

✔ Make sure that your car is on level ground.

HAYNES HINT *The fluid level in the reservoir will drop slightly as the brake pads wear down, but the fluid level must never be allowed to drop below the MIN mark.*

Safety first!

● If the reservoir requires repeated topping-up, this is an indication of a fluid leak somewhere in the brake system, which should be investigated immediately.
● If a leak is suspected, the vehicle should not be driven until the braking system has been checked. Never take any risks where brakes are concerned.
● Hydraulic fluid is an effective paint stripper, and will attack plastics; if any is spilt, it should be washed off immediately using copious quantities of fresh water.

1 The brake fluid reservoir is mounted on top of the brake master cylinder, which is attached to the front of the vacuum servo unit on the engine compartment bulkhead.

2 The brake fluid inside the reservoir is readily visible. With the vehicle on level ground, the level should be above the MIN (Danger) mark, and preferably on or near the MAX mark.

3 If topping-up is necessary, first wipe the area around the filler cap with a clean rag ...

4 ...and remove the filler cap.

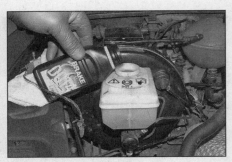

5 When adding fluid, pour it carefully into the reservoir, to avoid spilling it on surrounding painted surfaces. Be sure to use only the specified brake hydraulic fluid, since mixing different types of fluid can cause damage to the system. see *Recommended fluids and lubricants*. When adding fluid, it is a good idea to inspect the reservoir for contamination. The system should be drained and refilled if deposits, dirt particles or contamination are seen in the fluid. After filling the reservoir to the proper level, make sure that the cap is refitted securely, to avoid leaks and the entry of foreign matter.

Electrical systems

✔ Check the operation of all the electrical equipment, ie, lights, direction indicators, horn, etc. Refer to the appropriate Sections of Chapter 13 for details if any of the circuits are found to be inoperative.

✔ Note that stop-light switch adjustment is described in Chapter 10.

✔ Visually check all accessible wiring connectors, harnesses and retaining clips for security, and for signs of chafing or damage. Rectify any faults found.

✔ There are two separate fuse/relay boxes on Defender models. One is located on the under the facia panel on the drivers side of the vehicle, and another is located under the driver's seat (see illustrations). Refer to Chapter 13 for detailed information.

 HAYNES HiNT *If you need to check your brake lights and indicators unaided, back up to a wall or garage door and operate the lights. The reflected light should show if they are working properly.*

1 Fuse box under facia

2 Fuse box under drivers seat

3 If a single indicator light, stop-light or headlight has failed, it is likely that a bulb has blown and will need to be replaced. Refer to Chapter 13, Section 5 for details. If both stop-lights have failed, it is possible that the switch has failed (see Chapter 9, Section 4).

4 If more than one indicator light or headlight has failed, it is likely that either a fuse has blown or that there is a fault in the circuit. Refer to the wiring diagrams at the end of Chapter 13 for details of the fuse locations and circuits protected.

5 To renew a blown fuse, remove it, where applicable, using the plastic tool provided or needle nosed pliers. Fit anew fuse of the same rating, available from car accessory shops. It is important that you find the reason that the fuse blew (see Electrical fault finding in Chapter 13)

Wiper blades

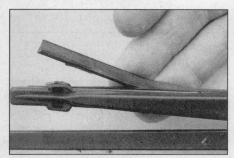

1 Check the condition of the wiper blades. If they are cracked, or show any signs of deterioration, or if they fail to clean the glass effectively, renew the blades. Ideally, the wiper blades should be renewed annually as a matter of course.

2 To remove a wiper blade, pull the arm away from the glass and swivel the blade through 90°…

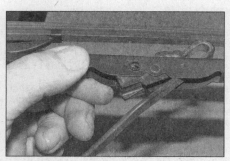

3 …then squeeze the locking clips, and detach the blade from the arm. When fitting the new blade, make sure that the blade locks securely into the arm, and that the blade is orientated correctly.

Battery

Caution: Before carrying out any work on the vehicle battery, read through the precautions given in 'Safety first!' at the beginning of this manual.

✔ Make sure that the battery tray is in good condition, and that the retaining clamp is tight.

✔ Corrosion on the tray, retaining clamp and the battery itself can be removed with a solution of water and baking soda. Thoroughly rinse all cleaned areas with plain water. Dry the battery and its surroundings with rags or tissues, which should then be discarded.

✔ Any metal parts damaged by corrosion should be covered with a zinc-based primer, then painted.

✔ Further information on the battery, charging and jump starting can be found in Chapter 5.

✔ A 'maintenance-free' battery is fitted, so topping-up is not possible. On some batteries, a charge indicator is fitted to the top of the battery. When the indicator shows green the battery is in a good state of charge, if the indicator is dark (or black) the battery requires charging, and if the indicator is clear, the battery requires renewing.

1 The battery is located beneath a cover panel under the left-hand front seat. The exterior of the battery should be inspected for damage such as a cracked case or cover.

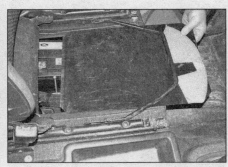

2 For access to the battery, remove the seat cushion, then release the retaining clip and slide out the cover panel.

3 Check the tightness of the battery cable clamp nuts to ensure good electrical connections, and check the entire length of each cable for cracks and frayed conductors.

4 If corrosion (visible as white, fluffy deposits) is evident, remove the cables from the battery terminals, clean them with a small wire brush, then refit them. Automotive stores sell a tool for cleaning the battery posts...

5 ...as well as cleaning the battery cable clamps

6 Corrosion can be kept to a minimum by applying a thin layer of petroleum jelly to the clamps and terminals after they have been reconnected.

Screen washer fluid level

● The windscreen/tailgate/headlight washer fluid reservoir is located at the left-hand front corner of the engine compartment. On models with headlight washers, an additional reservoir may also be fitted in the left-hand rear corner of the engine compartment.

Warning: On no account use coolant antifreeze in the washer system – this could discolour or damage paintwork

1 Check that the fluid level is within approximately 25.0 mm of the bottom of the filler neck, and top-up if necessary. When topping-up the reservoir, a screenwash additive should be added in the quantities recommended on the bottle.

Tyre condition and pressure

The original tyres on this vehicle have tread wear safety bands, which will appear when the tread depth reaches approximately 1.6 mm. Tread wear can be monitored with a simple, inexpensive device known as a tread depth indicator gauge **(see illustration)**.

Wheels and tyres should give no real problems in use, provided that a close eye is kept on them with regard to excessive wear or damage. To this end, the following points should be noted.

Ensure that tyre pressures are checked regularly, and maintained correctly. Checking should be carried out with the tyres cold, not immediately after the vehicle has been in use **(see illustration)**. If the pressures are checked with the tyres hot, an apparently-high reading will be obtained, owing to heat expansion. Under no circumstances should an attempt be made to reduce the pressures to the quoted cold reading in this instance, or effective underinflation will result.

Note any abnormal tread wear **(see illustration)**. Tread pattern irregularities such as feathering, flat spots, and more wear on one side than the other, are indications of front wheel alignment and/or balance problems. If any of these conditions are noted, they should be rectified as soon as possible.

Underinflation will cause overheating of the tyre owing to excessive flexing of the casing, and the tread will not sit correctly on the road surface. This will cause a consequent loss of adhesion and excessive wear, not to mention the danger of sudden tyre failure due to heat build-up.

Overinflation will cause rapid wear of the centre part of the tyre tread, coupled with reduced adhesion, harsher ride, and the danger of shock damage occurring in the tyre casing.

Regularly check the tyres for damage

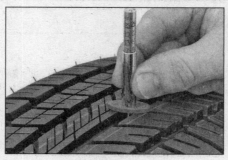

Measuring the tyre tread depth

Checking a tyre pressure

in the form of cuts or bulges, especially in the sidewalls. Remove any nails or stones embedded in the tread, before they penetrate the tyre to cause deflation. If removal of a nail reveals that the tyre has been punctured, refit the nail so that its point of penetration is marked. Then immediately change the wheel, and have the tyre repaired by a tyre dealer. Do not drive on a tyre in such a condition. If in any doubt as to the possible consequences of any damage found, consult your local tyre dealer for advice.

Periodically remove the wheels, and clean any dirt or mud from the inside and outside surfaces. Examine the wheel rims for signs of rusting, corrosion or other damage. Light alloy wheels are easily damaged by "kerbing" whilst parking, and similarly, steel wheels may become dented or buckled. Renewal of the wheel is very often the only course of remedial action possible.

The balance of each wheel and tyre assembly should be maintained to avoid excessive wear, not only to the tyres but also to the steering and suspension components. Wheel imbalance is normally signified by vibration through the vehicle's bodyshell, although in many cases it is particularly noticeable through the steering wheel. Conversely, it should be noted that wear or damage in suspension or steering components may cause excessive tyre wear. Out-of-round

or out-of-true tyres, damaged wheels and wheel bearing wear/ maladjustment also fall into this category. Balancing will not usually cure vibration caused by such wear.

Wheel balancing may be carried out with the wheel either on or off the vehicle. If balanced on the vehicle, ensure that the wheel-to-hub relationship is marked in some way prior to subsequent wheel removal, so that it may be refitted in its original position.

General tyre wear is influenced to a large degree by driving style – harsh braking and acceleration, or fast cornering, will all produce more rapid tyre wear. Interchanging of tyres may result in more even wear; however, if this is completely effective, a complete set of tyres will have to be renewed at once, which may prove financially restrictive for many owners.

Front tyres may wear unevenly as a result of wheel misalignment. The front wheels should always be correctly aligned according to the settings specified by the vehicle manufacturer (see Chapter 11).

Legal restrictions apply to many aspects of tyre fitting and usage, and in the UK, this information is contained in the Motor Vehicle Construction and Use Regulations. It is suggested that a copy of these regulations is obtained from your local police, if in doubt as to current legal requirements with regard to tyre type and condition, minimum tread depth, etc.

Tyre tread wear patterns

Shoulder Wear

Underinflation (wear on both sides)
Check and adjust pressures.
Incorrect wheel camber (wear on one side)
Repair or renew suspension parts
Hard cornering
Reduce speed!

Centre Wear

Overinflation
Check and adjust pressures.
If you sometimes have to inflate your car's tyres to the higher pressures specified for maximum load or sustained high speed, don't forget to reduce the pressures to normal afterwards.

Toe wear

Adjust front wheel alignement
Note: *The feathered edge of the thread which characterises toe wear is best checked by feel.*

Uneven Wear

Incorrect camber or castor
Repair or renew suspension parts
Malfunctioning suspension
Repair or renew suspension parts
Unbalanced wheel
Balance tyres
Out-of-round brake disc/drum
Machine or renew

Lubricants and fluids

Engine oil	
2.2 litre engine	
With DPF	Multigrade engine oil, viscosity SAE 5W/30 – WSS-M2C934-B
Without DPF	Multigrade engine oil, viscosity SAE 5W/30 – WSS-M2C913-B or C
2.4 litre engine	Multigrade engine oil, viscosity SAE 5W/30 – WSS-M2C913-B
Cooling system	Texaco XLC antifreeze or any Ethylene glycol-based antifreeze with OAT (Organic Acid Technology) corrosion inhibitors
Manual gearbox – MT82 6-speed	WSD-M2C200-C
Transfer gearbox	SAE 75W/90 or SAE 80W/90, API GL5, MIL-L-2015 – including B, C and D
Front and rear axles	Molytex EP90. Hypoid gear oil, viscosity SAE 90EP to API GL4, MIL-L-2105, or better
Swivel pin housings	Molytex EP90 or EP80. Hypoid gear oil, viscosity SAE 80EP or SAE 90EP to API GL4, MIL-L-2105, or better
Manual steering box	Hypoid gear oil, viscosity SAE 80EP or SAE 90EP to API GL4, MIL-L-2105, or better
Propeller shaft joints	Multi-purpose lithium-based grease to NLGI-2
Brake fluid reservoir	Hydraulic fluid DOT 4 – Shell ESL Donax EB
Clutch fluid reservoir	Hydraulic fluid DOT 4 – Shell ESL Donax EB
Power steering fluid reservoir	Texaco cold climate 14315 or 33270
Fuel	Commercial Diesel fuel for road vehicles (DERV)
Sealant (for sump, timing chain cover and camshaft carrier)	WSE-M4G323-A4, or equivalent
Sealant (for transmission)	WSS-M2G348-A10, or equivalent)

Tyre pressures (tyres cold)

Note: *Pressures apply only to original-equipment tyres, and may vary if any other make of tyre is fitted; check with the tyre manufacturer or supplier for correct pressures if necessary.*

	Front	Rear
90 models:		
205/80 R16	1.9 bar (28 psi)	2.6 bar (38 psi)
265/75 R16	1.9 bar (28 psi)	2.4 bar (35 psi)
7.50 R16	1.9 bar (28 psi)	2.6 bar (38 psi)
110 models (except Japan):		
7.50 R16	1.9 bar (28 psi)	2.6 bar (38 psi)
110 models (Japan):		
7.50 R16C	2.2 bar (32 psi)	4.1 bar (60 psi)
130 models:		
7.50 R16	3.0 bar (44 psi)	4.5 bar (65 psi)

Tyre pressure information plate on drivers side B-pillar.

Note: *Vehicle speed must not exceed 25 mph whilst off-road pressures are being used*

Chapter 1
Routine maintenance and servicing

Contents

Degrees of difficulty

Easy, suitable for novice with little experience		**Fairly easy,** suitable for beginner with some experience		**Fairly difficult,** suitable for competent DIY mechanic		**Difficult,** suitable for experienced DIY mechanic		**Very difficult,** suitable for expert DIY or professional	

1 Servicing specifications

Capacities

Engine oil:
Capacity (drain and refill, including oil filter) . . . . 7.0 litres
from MIN to MAX on dipstick . . . . 2.0 litres
Cooling system:
2.2 litre engines . . . . 8.2 litres
2.4 litre engines . . . . 10.0 litres
Fuel tank:
90 models. . . . . 56.0 litres (13.2 gallons)
110 models. . . . . 70.0 litres (16.2 gallons)
Main gearbox:
MT82 6-speed . . . . 2.20 litres
Transfer gearbox:
LT230Q type gearbox. . . . . 2.30 litres
Front axle . . . . 1.70 litres
Rear axle:
90 models. . . . . 1.70 litre
110 models. . . . . 2.26 litres
Power steering box and fluid reservoir. . . . . 3.40 litres
Swivel pin housing oil (each) . . . . 0.35 litre

Cooling system

Antifreeze mixture:
Minimum strength. . . . . 25% antifreeze, 75% water
Maximum strength . . . . 60% antifreeze, 40% water
Protection to -36°C. . . . . 50% antifreeze, 50% water

Brakes

Minimum brake disc pad thickness . . . . 3.0 mm
Minimum brake shoe lining thickness . . . . 1.5 mm (typical value)

Torque wrench settings

	Nm	lbf ft
Transmission (main gearbox) oil drain plug	50	37
Transmission (main gearbox) oil filler/level plug.	35	26
Oil filter element cover	35	26
Propeller shaft and rubber coupling securing bolts	47	35
Roadwheel nuts:		
Steel wheels.	108	80
Alloy wheels	130	96
Heavy duty wheel	170	125
Sump drain plug.	23	17
Transfer gearbox oil drain plug.	30	22
Transfer gearbox oil filler/level plug	30	22

2 Maintenance schedules

1 The maintenance intervals in this manual are provided with the assumption that you, not the dealer, will be carrying out the work. These are the minimum maintenance intervals recommended by the manufacturers for vehicles driven daily under normal operating conditions. If you wish to keep your vehicle in peak condition at all times, you may wish to perform some of these procedures more often. This applies especially if the vehicle is used in particularly hot or dusty climates, or if the vehicle is regularly used for towing. We encourage frequent maintenance because it enhances the efficiency, performance and resale value of your vehicle.

2 When the vehicle is new, it should be serviced by a dealer service department (or other workshop recognised by the vehicle manufacturer as providing the same standard of service) in order to preserve the warranty. The vehicle manufacturer may reject warranty claims if you are unable to prove that servicing has been carried out as and when specified, using only original equipment parts or parts certified to be of equivalent quality.

Every 250 miles or weekly
☐ Refer to Weekly checks

Every 7500 miles
☐ Renew the engine oil and filter (Section 5)

Every 15 000 miles
☐ Check the clutch fluid level (Section 6)
☐ Check the power steering fluid level (Section 7)
☐ Check the condition of the brake pads and discs (Section 8)
☐ Check the brake calipers for leaks (Section 8)
☐ Check the operation of the handbrake (Section 9)
☐ Check the handbrake adjustment (Section 9)
☐ Lubricate the handbrake linkage (Section 9)
☐ Check the operation of all door, bonnet and tailgate locks (Section 10)
☐ Lubricate all hinges and locks (including the fuel filler) (Section 10)
☐ Check the condition of the crankcase breather system hoses (Section 11)
☐ Check the condition of the auxiliary drivebelt(s) and adjust if necessary (Section 12)
☐ Check the main gearbox oil level (Section 13)
☐ Check the cooling and heater system hoses for security and leaks (Section 17)
☐ Check all underbody brake, fuel and clutch pipes and hoses for leaks and condition (Section 18)
☐ Check the steering and suspension components, including all hydraulic pipes and hoses for leaks and condition (Section 19)
☐ Check the front and rear axle breathers for obstructions (Section 20)
☐ Carry out a road test (Section 21)

Every 30 000 miles
In addition to all the items listed above, carry out the following:
☐ Check the transfer gearbox oil level (Section 14)
☐ Check the front and rear axle oil levels (Section 15)
☐ Drain water from fuel filter (Section 22)
☐ Renew the fuel filter element (Section 23)
☐ Renew the air cleaner element (Section 24)
☐ Clean the engine breather filter (Section)
☐ Check the brake vacuum servo hose for security (Section 25)
☐ Check the condition and security of the glow plug wiring (Section 26)
☐ Check the radiator and intercooler (where applicable) for obstructions, and clean if necessary (Section 27)
☐ Check the security of the jack and tools (Section 29)
☐ Lubricate the propeller shaft universal joints and sliding joints (Section 30)
☐ Check the exhaust system for security and condition (Section 31)
☐ Check the tightness of the propeller shaft coupling bolts (Section 32)
☐ Check the security of the fuel tank (Section 34)
☐ Check the security of the towing bracket (Section 35)
☐ Check and if necessary adjust the headlight and auxiliary light adjustment (Section 36)
☐ Check the front wheel alignment (Section 37)
☐ Check the condition of the spare wheel (Section 38)
☐ Check the condition and operation of all seat belts (Section 39)
☐ Renew the main gearbox oil (Section 40)
☐ Renew the brake fluid (Section 42)

Every 100 000 miles
In addition to all the items listed above, carry out the following:
☐ Renew the transfer gearbox oil (Section 43)
☐ Renew the front and rear axle oil (Section 44)
☐ Check the fuel injectors for leaks (Section 46)

Every 2 years
☐ Renew the coolant (Section 47)
☐ Check and if necessary adjust the steering gear backlash (Section 28)
☐ Remove all shock absorbers, and check their operation (Section 48)
☐ Renew the brake vacuum servo air filter (Section 49)
☐ Renew all braking system hydraulic fluid seals, the vacuum servo filter, and all flexible brake fluid hoses (Section 50)
☐ Clean the intercooler element (Section 51)

Underbonnet view of a TD5 engine model

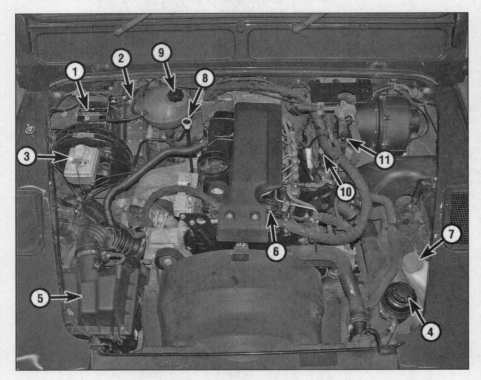

1 VIN plate
2 Clutch fluid reservoir
3 Brake fluid reservoir
4 Power steering fluid reservoir
5 Air filter housing
6 Engine oil filler flap
7 Screenwash reservoir
8 Engine oil level dipstick
9 Coolant expansion reservoir
10 Fuel pressure release valve
11 Coolant bleed screw

Front underbody view

1 Cooling fan cowl
2 Exhaust
3 Sump
4 Flywheel housing
5 Drag link
6 Track rod
7 Panhard rod
8 Oil filter
9 Steering box
10 Swivel pin housing
11 Radius arm

Centre underbody view

1 Chassis crossmember
2 Main transmission casing
3 Exhaust
4 Handbrake drum
5 Transfer gearbox
6 Rear propeller shaft

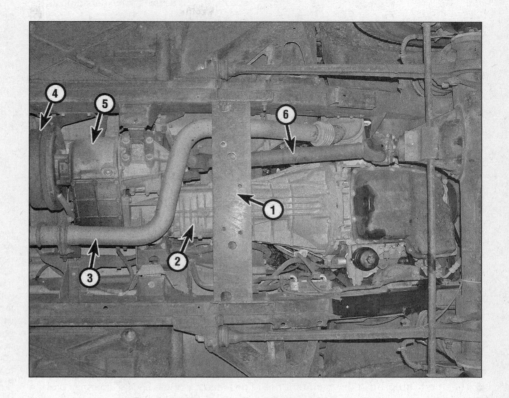

Rear underbody view

1 Exhaust
2 Lower link
3 Shock absorber
4 Rear axle
5 Upper link
6 Differential unit
7 Fuel filter

3 Introduction

1 This Chapter is designed to help the home mechanic maintain his/her vehicle for safety, economy, long life and peak performance.

2 The Chapter contains a master maintenance schedule, followed by Sections dealing specifically with each task on the schedule. Visual checks, adjustments, component renewal and other helpful items are included. Refer to the accompanying illustrations of the engine compartment and the underside of the vehicle for the locations of the various components.

3 Servicing of your vehicle in accordance with the mileage/time maintenance schedule and the following Sections will provide a planned maintenance programme, which should result in a long and reliable service life. This is a comprehensive plan, so maintaining some items but not others at the specified service intervals, will not produce the same results.

4 As you service your vehicle, you will discover that many of the procedures can – and should – be grouped together, because of the particular procedure being performed, or because of the close proximity of two otherwise-unrelated components to one another. For example, if the vehicle is raised for any reason, the exhaust can be inspected at the same time as the suspension and steering components.

5 The first step in this maintenance programme is to prepare yourself before the actual work begins. Read through all the Sections relevant to the work to be carried out, then make a list and gather together all the parts and tools required. If a problem is encountered, seek advice from a parts specialist, or a dealer service department.

4 Regular maintenance

1 If, from the time the vehicle is new, the routine maintenance schedule is followed closely, and frequent checks are made of fluid levels and high-wear items, as suggested throughout this manual, the engine will be kept in relatively good running condition, and the need for additional work will be minimised.

2 It is possible that there will be times when the engine is running poorly, due to the lack of regular maintenance. This is even more likely if a used vehicle, which has not received regular and frequent maintenance checks, is purchased. In such cases, additional work may need to be carried out, outside of the regular maintenance intervals.

3 If engine wear is suspected, a compression or leakdown test (Chapter 2A Section 2 or Chapter 2B Section 2) will provide valuable information regarding the overall performance of the main internal components. Such a test can be used as a basis to decide on the extent of the work to be carried out. If for example a compression or leakdown test indicates serious internal engine wear, conventional maintenance as described in this Chapter will not greatly improve the performance of the engine, and may prove a waste of time and money, unless extensive overhaul work is carried out first.

4 The following series of operations are those most often required to improve the performance of a generally poor-running engine:

a) *Clean, inspect and test the battery (Weekly checks).*
b) *Check the levels of all the engine-related fluids (Weekly checks).*
c) *Check the condition and tension of the auxiliary drivebelt (Section 12).*
d) *Check the fuel sedimenter – drain off any water, and renew the filter if necessary (Section 4).*
e) *Check the condition of the air cleaner element, and renew if necessary (Section 24).*
f) *Check the condition of all hoses, and check for fluid leaks.*

5 Engine oil and filter renewal

1 Before starting this procedure, gather together all the necessary tools and materials. Also, make sure that you have plenty of clean rags and newspapers handy, to mop up any spills. Ideally, the engine oil should be warm, as it will drain more easily and more built-up sludge will be removed with it. Take care not to touch the exhaust or any other hot parts of the engine when working under the vehicle. To avoid any possibility of scalding and to protect yourself from possible skin irritants and other harmful contaminants in used engine oils, it is advisable to wear gloves when carrying out this work.

2 Access to the underside of the vehicle will be greatly improved if it can be raised on a lift, driven onto ramps, or jacked up and supported on axle stands (see *Jacking and vehicle support*). Whichever method is chosen, make sure that the vehicle remains level, or if it is at an angle, that the drain plug is at the lowest point.

3 Remove the oil filler cap, then unscrew the engine oil drain plug (located at the rear of the sump) about half a turn **(see illustration)**. Position the draining container under the drain plug, then remove the plug completely – recover the sealing washer.

 HAYNES HiNT *As the drain plug threads release, move it sharply away so the stream of oil issuing from the sump runs into the container, not up your sleeve.*

4 Allow some time for the oil to drain, noting that it may be necessary to reposition the container as the oil flow slows to a trickle.

5 After all the oil has drained, discard the drain plug as a new one will be required for refitting. Clean the area around the drain plug opening, and fit a new drain plug, which comes complete with seal **(see illustration)**. Tighten the plug to the specified torque.

6 Move the container into position under the oil filter, which is located on the left-hand side of the cylinder block.

7 Unscrew the oil filter plastic cover from the bottom of the oil filter housing, then remove and discard the paper element **(see illustrations)**.

5.3 Slackening engine oil drain plug

5.5 Fit new drain plug

5.7a Unscrew the oil filter housing plastic cover...

5.7b ...and discard the paper element inside

5.8 Removing the O-ring seal

5.9a Insert the new filter element

5.9b Lubricate the O-ring seal with a little engine oil

8 Remove the O-ring seal and obtain a new one **(see illustration)**. Clean inside the filter housing and plastic cover.

9 Locate the new paper element inside the plastic cover, then fit the new O-ring seal and lubricate the seal with a little engine oil **(see illustrations)**.

10 Screw the filter cover complete with new filter element into the filter housing **(see illustration)**, and tighten it to the specified torque setting.

11 Remove the old oil and all tools from under the vehicle, then lower the vehicle to the ground.

12 Remove the dipstick and unscrew the oil filler cap (if not already removed) from the camshaft cover. Fill the engine, using the correct grade and type of oil (see Lubricants 0 Section 6). An oil can spout or funnel may help to reduce spillage **(see illustration)**. Pour in half the specified quantity of oil first, then wait a few minutes for the oil to fall to the sump. Continue adding oil, a small quantity at a time, until the level is just over the lower mark on the dipstick. Refit the filler cap.

13 Start the engine and run it for a few minutes, then check for leaks. Note that there may be a delay of a few seconds before the oil pressure warning light goes out when the engine is first started, as the oil circulates through the engine oil galleries and the new oil filter before the pressure builds up.

14 Switch off the engine, and wait a few minutes for the oil to settle in the sump once more. With the new oil circulated and the filter completely full, recheck the level on the dipstick, and add more oil as necessary, until the oil level is at the upper mark on the dipstick.

5.10 Fit the filter element and cover

15 Dispose of the used engine oil and filter safely, with reference to General repair procedures. Do not discard the old filter with domestic household waste. The facility for waste oil disposal provided by many local council refuse tips and/or recycling centers generally has a filter receptacle alongside.

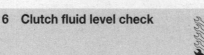
6 Clutch fluid level check

1 The clutch fluid reservoir is attached to the master cylinder, which is located on the right-hand side of the engine compartment on right-hand-drive models, or on the left-hand side of the engine compartment on left-hand-drive models.

2 The fluid level should be upto the line around the outside of the reservoir,

5.12 Using a funnel and oil jug with spout to refill engine

approximately 10mm down from the top of the reservoir **(see illustrations)**.

3 There should be no significant drop in fluid level during normal operation of the clutch.

4 Any significant loss of fluid is likely to be due to a leak in the hydraulic system, which should be investigated and corrected.

7 Power steering fluid level check

1 The power steering fluid level is checked with a dipstick attached to the reservoir filler cap.

2 The fluid level should be checked with the engine stopped, and the front wheels set in the straight-ahead position.

3 Unscrew the filler cap from the top of the reservoir, and wipe all fluid from the cap dipstick with a clean rag **(see illustration)**.

6.2a Check the fluid level in the reservoir

6.2b Using a funnel and hose to top-up the clutch fluid level

7.3a Remove the filler cap and check fluid level

7.3b Fluid level dipstick upper and lower markings

Refit the filler cap, then remove it again. Note the fluid level on the dipstick **(see illustration)**. When the engine is cold, the fluid level should be between the upper and lower marks on the dipstick. When the engine is at normal operating temperature, the fluid level should be up to the upper mark on the dipstick. **Note:** *Do not start the engine if the fluid level is below the minimum mark, as serious damage could be caused to the power steering pump.*

4 If necessary, top-up using the specified type of fluid, and then refit the filler cap.
5 If frequent topping-up of the system proves to be necessary, this indicates that there is a leak in the hydraulic system, which should be traced and rectified without delay.

8 Brake pad, disc and caliper check

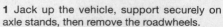

1 Jack up the vehicle, support securely on axle stands, then remove the roadwheels.
2 For a quick check, the thickness of friction material remaining on each pad can be measured through the slot in the caliper body. If any pad is worn to the specified minimum thickness or less, all four pads must be renewed (see Chapter 10 Section 4, 5).
3 For a comprehensive check, the brake pads should be removed and cleaned. This will allow the operation of the caliper to be

checked, and the condition of the brake disc itself to be fully examined on both sides.

9 Handbrake adjustment check

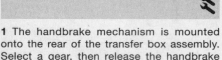

1 The handbrake mechanism is mounted onto the rear of the transfer box assembly. Select a gear, then release the handbrake lever and chock the front wheels.
2 Jack up the rear of the vehicle and support it on axle stands so that the wheels are clear of the ground.
3 Slacken the adjuster, situated at the lever end of the cable, to obtain some freeplay in the cable.
4 From underneath the vehicle, using a suitable spanner, rotate the adjuster on the rear of the handbrake assembly clockwise until both shoes are fully expanded against the drum (approx. 25Nm).
5 With the shoes in full contact with the drum, rotate the handbrake adjuster one and a half turns in an anti-clockwise direction. Check that the handbrake drum is free to rotate easily.
6 Applying normal, moderate pressure, pull the handbrake lever to the fully-applied position, counting the number of clicks emitted from the handbrake ratchet mechanism. The handbrake should be fully-applied on the third click of the ratchet mechanism. If necessary, adjust the cable setting using the adjuster nut **(see illustration)**, access to this adjuster nut, will need to be from under the vehicle.
7 When adjustment is correct, release the handbrake lever, and check the drum is free to rotate easily. If all is well, lower the vehicle to the ground.

10 Hinge and lock check and lubrication

1 Lubricate the hinges of the bonnet, doors and tailgate with a light general-purpose oil. Similarly, lubricate all latches, locks and lock strikers. At the same time, check the security

and operation of all the locks, adjusting them if necessary (see Chapter 12).
2 Lightly lubricate the bonnet release mechanism and cable with a suitable grease.

11 Crankcase breather hose check

1 Check all the engine breather hoses for signs of cracking, leaks, and general deterioration.
2 It is advisable to loosen the hose clips, and remove each hose to check for a build-up of deposits, which may cause restrictions or even a blockage. If necessary, clean the hose using paraffin, but ensure that the hose is completely dry before refitting.

12 Auxiliary drivebelt check

General

1 A single, flat, multi-ribbed drivebelt is used and is located on the front of the engine **(see illustration)**. The belt drives the alternator, power steering pump, coolant pump, radiator cooling fan, brake servo vacuum pump (2.4 litre engines) and, where fitted, the air conditioning compressor, from the engine's crankshaft pulley. The belt is tensioned by an automatic tensioner.
2 The good condition and proper tension of the auxiliary drivebelts are critical to the operation of the engine. They must, therefore, be regularly inspected.

Check

3 With the engine switched off, open and support the bonnet.
4 Undo the six retaining screws and remove the upper cover from the front of the engine compartment **(see illustration)**.
5 Using an inspection light or a small electric torch, and rotating the engine with a spanner applied to the crankshaft pulley bolt, check the whole length of the drivebelt for cracks, separation of the rubber, and torn or worn ribs. Also, check for fraying and glazing, which gives the drivebelt a shiny appearance.

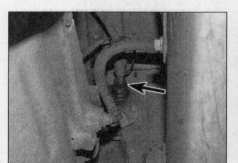

9.6 Handbrake cable adjuster nut

12.1 Auxiliary drivebelt routing with cooling fan removed – 2.4 litre engine

12.4 Remove the upper cover

6 Both sides of the drivebelt should be inspected, which means you will have to twist the drivebelt slightly to check the underside. Use your fingers to feel the drivebelt where you can't see it. If you are in any doubt as to the condition of the drivebelt, renew it as described in Section 52.

Drivebelt tension

7 The auxiliary drivebelt is tensioned by an automatic tensioner; regular tension checks are not required, and manual 'adjustment' is not possible.

8 If you suspect that a drivebelt is slipping and/or running slack, or that the tensioner is otherwise faulty, it must be renewed.

Drivebelt renewal

9 Refer to Section 52.

13 Transmission (main gearbox) oil level check

Note: *There is no requirement in the manufacturer's service schedule for the main gearbox oil level to be checked. However, it may be prudent for owners to perform this task at least once between gearbox oil changes.*

1 Ensure that the vehicle is on level ground.

2 Locate the oil filler/level plug on the right-hand side of the gearbox casing (see illustration), and place a suitable container beneath the hole to catch any escaping oil.

3 Unscrew the filler/level plug, and check the oil level. The level should be up to the lower edge of the filler/level plug hole.

4 If necessary, add oil of the specified type (see *Lubricants and fluids*) until the oil overflows from the filler/level hole (see illustration).

5 Clean and refit the filler/level plug, and tighten to the specified torque. Do not overtighten the plug, as it has tapered threads.

6 Wipe any spilt oil from the gearbox casing, and refit the engine undershield (where applicable).

13.2 Oil filler/level plug on side of casing – viewed from inside passenger compartment

14.1a Unscrewing the transfer box filler/level plug

14 Transfer gearbox oil level check

1 Proceed as described for the main gearbox in Section 13, noting that the filler/level plug is located in the rear of the transfer gearbox casing, to the side of the handbrake drum (see illustrations).

15 Axle oil level check

Note: *A 13 mm square-section wrench will be required to undo the axle filler/level plug. These wrenches can be obtained from most*

13.4 Topping up the transmission – viewed from under the vehicle

14.1b Topping up the transfer box

motor factors, or from your Land Rover dealer.

1 Ensure that the vehicle is standing on level ground, and apply the handbrake.

2 Working underneath the vehicle, unscrew the front axle oil filler/level plug (see illustration), which is located in the differential housing.

3 The oil level should be up to the lower edge of the filler/level plug hole.

4 If necessary, top-up with the specified grade of oil, until oil just begins to run from the plug hole. Do not overfill – if too much oil is added, wait until the excess has run out of the plug hole (see illustration).

5 Once the level is correct, refit the filler/level plug and tighten it securely.

6 Repeat the procedure for the rear axle (see illustration).

15.2 Front axle filler level plug

15.4 Topping-up the axle oil level

15.6 Rear axle filler level plug

16.2 Swivel pin housing filler/level plug

16 Swivel pin housing oil level check

Note: *Later vehicles do not have any level or drain plugs, as the swivel pin housing is filled for life with grease, so does not require any maintenance.*

1 Ensure that the vehicle is standing on level ground, and apply the handbrake.
2 Working underneath the vehicle, unscrew the left-hand swivel pin housing filler/level plug. The level plug has a square-section, and is situated at the front upper part of the housing **(see illustration)**.
3 The oil level should be up to the lower edge of the filler/level plug hole.
4 If topping-up is necessary, using the specified grade of oil, pour the oil into the housing until it just begins to run from the plug hole. Do not overfill – if too much oil is added, wait until the excess has run out of the level plug hole.
5 Once the level is correct, refit the filler/level plugs and tighten securely.
6 Repeat the above procedure on the right-hand swivel pin housing.

17 Cooling system and heater system hose check

1 Check the security and condition of all the engine-related coolant pipes and hoses. Ensure that all cable-ties or securing clips are in place, and in good condition. Clips which are broken or missing can lead to chafing of the hoses, pipes or wiring, which could cause more serious problems in the future.
2 Carefully check the radiator hoses and heater hoses along their entire length. Renew any hose which is cracked, swollen or deteriorated. Cracks will show up better if the hose is squeezed. Pay close attention to the hose clips that secure the hoses to the cooling system components. Hose clips can pinch and puncture hoses, resulting in cooling system leaks. If wire-type hose clips are used, it may be a good idea to update them with screw-type clips.
3 Inspect all the cooling system components

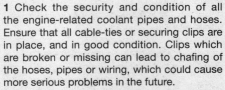

A leak in the cooling system will usually show up as white or antifreeze-coloured deposits on the area adjoining the leak.

(hoses, joint faces, etc) for leaks. Where any problems of this nature are found on system components, renew the component or gasket with reference to Chapter 3.

18 Underbody component, pipe, hose and wiring check

1 Visually inspect the engine joint faces, gaskets and seals for any signs of water or oil leaks. Pay particular attention to the areas around the valve cover, cylinder head, oil filter and sump joint faces. Bear in mind that, over a period of time, some very slight seepage from these areas is to be expected; what you are really looking for is any indication of a serious leak. Should a leak be found, renew the offending gasket or oil seal by referring to the appropriate Chapter(s) in this manual.
2 Similarly, check the transmission components for oil leaks, and investigate and rectify and problems found.
3 Check the security and condition of all the engine-related pipes and hoses. Ensure that all cable-ties or securing clips are in place, and in good condition. Clips which are broken or missing can lead to chafing of the hoses, pipes or wiring, which could cause more serious problems in the future.
4 Carefully check the condition of all coolant, fuel and brake hoses. Renew any hose which is cracked, swollen or deteriorated. Cracks will show up better if the hose is squeezed. Pay close attention to the hose clips that secure the hoses to the system components. Hose clips can pinch and puncture hoses, resulting in leaks. If wire-type hose clips are used, it may be a good idea to update them with screw-type clips.
5 With the vehicle raised, inspect the fuel tank and filler neck for punctures, cracks and other damage. The connection between the filler neck and tank is especially critical. Sometimes a rubber filler neck or connecting hose will leak, due to loose retaining clamps or deteriorated rubber.

6 Similarly, inspect all brake hoses and metal pipes. If any damage or deterioration is discovered, do not drive the vehicle until the necessary repair work has been carried out. Renew any damaged sections of hose or pipe.
7 Carefully check all rubber hoses and metal fuel lines leading away from the petrol tank. Check for loose connections, deteriorated hoses, crimped lines, and other damage. Pay particular attention to the vent pipes and hoses, which often loop up around the filler neck and can become blocked or crimped. Follow the lines to the front of the vehicle, carefully inspecting them all the way. Renew damaged sections as necessary.
8 From within the engine compartment, check the security of all fuel hose attachments and pipe unions, and inspect the fuel hoses and vacuum hoses for kinks, chafing and deterioration.
9 Check the condition of the oil cooler hoses and pipes.
10 Where applicable, check the condition of the power steering fluid hoses and pipes.
11 Check the condition of all exposed wiring harnesses.
12 Also check the engine and transmission components for signs of fluid leaks.

19 Steering and suspension component check

1 Apply the handbrake, then raise the front of the vehicle and securely support it on axle stands.
2 Visually inspect the balljoint dust covers for splits, chafing or deterioration. Any damage will cause loss of lubricant, together with dirt and water entry, resulting in rapid deterioration of the balljoints.
3 Where applicable, check the power steering fluid hoses for chafing or deterioration, and the pipe and hose unions for fluid leaks. Also check for signs of fluid leakage under pressure from the steering box, which would indicate failed fluid seals within the steering box assembly.
4 Grasp the roadwheel at the 12 o'clock and 6 o'clock positions, and try to rock it. Very slight freeplay may be felt, but if the movement is appreciable, further investigation is necessary to determine the source. Continue rocking the wheel while an assistant depresses the footbrake. If the movement is now eliminated or significantly reduced, it is likely that the hub bearings are at fault. If the freeplay is still evident with the footbrake depressed, then there is wear in the suspension joints or mountings.
5 Now grasp the wheel at the 9 o'clock and 3 o'clock positions, and try to rock it as before. Any movement felt now may again be caused by wear in the hub bearings, or the steering track rod and drag link balljoints. If a balljoint is worn, the visual movement will be obvious.
6 Using a large screwdriver or flat bar, check for wear in the suspension mounting bushes

by levering between the relevant suspension component and its attachment point. Some movement is to be expected, as the mountings are made of rubber, but excessive wear should be obvious. Also check the condition of any visible rubber bushes, looking for splits, cracks or contamination of the rubber.

7 With the vehicle standing on its wheels, have an assistant turn the steering wheel back-and-forth. There should be very little, if any, lost movement between the steering wheel and roadwheels. If this is not the case, closely observe the joints and mountings previously described, but in addition, check the steering column universal joints for wear. The steering box backlash is adjustable, but adjustment should be entrusted to a Land Rover dealer (see Section).

20 Axle breather check

1 Ensure that the vehicle is standing on level ground, and apply the handbrake.

2 Check that both the front and rear axle breather tubes **(see illustration)** are securely retained by all the relevant retaining clips, and show no signs of damage or deterioration.

3 If renewal is necessary, unscrew the union bolt/nut securing the breather pipe to the top of the axle, and recover the sealing washers (where fitted) from the union. Free the pipe from its retaining clips, and remove it from the vehicle.

4 Position a new sealing washer on each side of the union (where applicable), and refit the union bolt/nut. Ensure that the pipe is correctly routed and retained by all the necessary clips, then securely tighten the union bolt/nut.

21 Road test

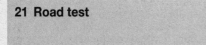

Instruments and electrical equipment

1 Check the operation of all instruments and electrical equipment.

2 Make sure that all instruments read correctly, and switch on all electrical equipment in turn, to check that it functions properly.

Steering and suspension

3 Check for any abnormalities in the steering, suspension, handling or road 'feel'.

4 Drive the vehicle, and check that there are no unusual vibrations or noises.

5 Check that the steering feels positive, with no excessive 'sloppiness', or roughness, and check for any suspension noises when cornering and driving over bumps.

Drivetrain

6 Check the performance of the engine, clutch and propeller shafts.

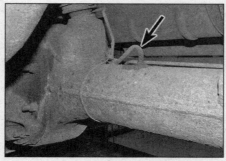

20.2 Breather pipe on top of rear axle...

7 Listen for any unusual noises from the engine, clutch and transmission.

8 Make sure that the engine runs smoothly when idling, and that there is no hesitation when accelerating.

9 Check that the clutch action is smooth and progressive, that the drive is taken up smoothly, and that the pedal travel is not excessive. Also listen for any noises when the clutch pedal is depressed.

10 Check that all gears can be engaged smoothly without noise, and that the gear lever action is smooth and not abnormally vague or 'notchy'. This check applies to both the main gearbox and the transfer gearbox.

Braking system

11 Make sure that the vehicle does not pull to one side when braking, and that the wheels do not lock prematurely when braking hard.

12 Check that there is no vibration through the steering when braking.

13 Check that the handbrake operates correctly without excessive movement of the lever, and that it holds the vehicle stationary on a slope.

14 Test the operation of the brake servo unit as follows. With the engine switched off, depress the footbrake four or five times to exhaust the vacuum. Start the engine, keeping the footbrake depressed. As the engine starts, there should be a noticeable 'give' in the brake pedal as vacuum builds-up. Allow the engine to run for at least two minutes, and then switch it off. If the brake pedal is depressed again, it should be possible to detect a hiss from the servo. After about four or five applications, no further hissing should be heard, and the pedal should feel considerably firmer.

22.3 Undo the drain tap and drain the water

22.2 Undo the fastener to remove the filter cover

22 Fuel filter water draining

Note: *This procedure is covered when the fuel filter is renewed, as the water drain tap is fitted on the base of the filter housing.*

1 The water drain tap is fitted to the base of the fuel filter, which is mounted on the longitudinal chassis member below the right-hand rear wheel arch.

2 Rotate the fastener on the left-hand side of the cover, and then remove the filter cover, releasing the locating pegs on the right-hand side of the cover **(see illustration)**.

3 Fit a length of tube to the drain tap, then place a container under the filter and rotate the drain tap on the base of the filter to allow any water to run out **(see illustration)**. When clean, uncontaminated fuel runs from the drain, tighten the tap.

4 Refit the cover around the filter, securing the locating pegs at the front and then tighten the fastener.

23 Fuel filter element renewal and bleeding

1 The fuel filter is mounted on the longitudinal chassis member below the right-hand rear wheel arch **(see illustration)**.

2 Rotate the fastener on the left-hand side of the cover, and then remove the filter cover,

23.1 Fuel filter location

23.2 Remove the cover releasing the locating pegs

23.4 Unscrew the element from the filter head

23.6a Apply a little clean diesel fuel to the filter sealing ring

23.6b Fitting instructions on side of filter

23.7a Disconnect the fuel line quick release coupling

23.7b Using a priming pump to draw fuel through filter

releasing the locating pegs on the right-hand side of the cover**(see illustration)**.

3 Place a container under the filter, then unscrew and remove the drain tap. Allow the fuel to drain out **(see illustration 22.3)**.

4 Unscrew the filter from the filter head. If necessary, use a filter removal tool or strap wrench **(see illustration)**.

5 Thoroughly clean the inside of the filter head.

6 Smear a little clean diesel fuel on the rubber sealing rings on the top of the new filter, then screw into position in the filter head **(see illustrations)**. Tighten the filter by hand only, fitting instructions are usually on the side of the filter also. Check the water drain tap at the base of the filter is tight, to prevent any leaks.

7 A priming pump or fuel vacuum pump will be required to draw the fuel up through the new filter. Disconnect the quick release connector at the fuel line by the fuel pressure valve, and then fit the bleeding equipment to the fuel line. Operate the fuel priming pump or vacuum pump and draw the fuel through until there is a steady flow of fuel is drawn through **(see illustrations)**. Disconnect the bleeding equipment from the fuel line and then re-connect the quick release fuel line. Use a rag to clean up any spilt fuel.

8 Start the engine and check for leaks around the fuel filter and the fuel lines, clean off any spilt fuel. Refit the cover around the filter, securing the locating pegs at the front and then tighten the fastener.

24 Air cleaner element renewal

1 Release the two securing clips (one at the front and one at the rear of the filter housing), then lift the air cleaner cover from the lower housing, releasing the locating pegs from the outer edge of the lower housing, under the wing panel **(see illustrations)**.

2 Lift the old element from its position in the lower half of the filter housing, then clean the inside of the lower housing and cover, removing any dirt, leaves and debris, that has been drawn up into the filter housing.

23.7c Using a vacuum pump to draw fuel through filter

24.1a Releasing the securing clips...

24.1b ...and unclip the cover

24.3 Fit new element with the seal uppermost

3 Fit the new element into the housing (see illustration).
4 Refit the cover into position, making sure the locating pegs fit correctly into the outer edge of the lower housing, then secure the cover in place with the clips.

25 Brake vacuum servo hose check

1 Working from the vacuum pump back to the servo unit, examine the vacuum hose for signs of damage or deterioration. At the same time, also check the servo unit check valve rubber grommet (see illustration). If necessary renew the hose/ grommet, referring to the information given in Chapter 3.

26 Glow plug wiring check

1 Where applicable, to improve access, undo the two retaining bolts and remove the plastic trim cover from the camshaft cover.
2 Check all the glow plug wiring for signs of fraying, chafing and general deterioration.
3 Check that the nuts securing the wiring to the glow plugs are secure. Where applicable (on 2.2 litre engines), also check the security of the wiring connector at the preheating system relay/timer unit (see illustration).

29.1 Make sure Jack and tools are secured

25.1 Check the valve and rubber grommet

27 Radiator and intercooler check

1 Check that the radiator and (where fitted) intercooler matrixes are clean, and free from obstructions which would reduce the airflow through them. Remove any debris, taking great care not to damage either component.

28 Steering gear backlash check

Steering gear backlash check

1 If at any time it is noted that the steering action has become stiff or sloppy, the vehicle should be taken to a Land Rover dealer for the steering components to be checked. Adjustments of the steering components and steering box are possible, but specialist knowledge and equipment are needed. Therefore, this task must be entrusted to a Land Rover dealer.

29 Jack and tools security check

1 Check that the jack and tools are securely stowed in the compartment under the passenger front seat (see illustration), check

30.3a Greasing a propeller shaft universal joint – nipple arrowed

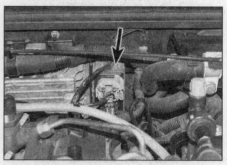

26.3 Relay fitted to the rear of the engine compartment

that the jack and tools are in good condition and they operate correctly. The tools share the compartment with the battery, so the jack and tools need to be secured in position to prevent any damage to the battery or cables.

30 Propeller shaft joint lubrication

Note: *A low-pressure grease gun will be required for this operation.*
1 Working under the vehicle, locate the grease nipples on the front and rear propeller shafts universal joint spiders, and on the shaft sliding joints (where applicable).
2 Thoroughly clean the around each nipple.
3 Fill a suitable grease gun with the recommended type of grease (see *Lubricants and fluids*), then apply the grease gun to each of the nipples in turn, and pump grease into the joints (see illustrations). Apply grease until it emerges from the end of the nipple, then wipe away the excess.

31 Exhaust system check

1 With the engine cold (at least an hour after the vehicle has been driven), check the complete exhaust system from the engine to the end of the tailpipe. Ideally, the inspection should be carried out with the vehicle raised.

30.3b Greasing a propeller shaft sliding joint – nipple arrowed

2 Check the exhaust pipes and connections for evidence of leaks, severe corrosion and damage. Make sure that all brackets and mountings are in good condition, and tight. Leakage at any of the joints or in other parts of the system will usually show up as a black sooty stain in the vicinity of the leak..

3 Rattles and other noises can often be traced to the exhaust system, especially the brackets and mountings **(see illustration)**. Try to move the pipes and silencers. If the components can come into contact with the body or suspension parts, secure the system with new mountings. If possible, separate the joints, and twist the pipes as necessary to provide additional clearance.

4 Run the engine at idle speed, then temporarily place a cloth rag over the rear end of the exhaust pipe, and listen for any escape of exhaust gases that would indicate a leak.

5 On completion, where applicable, lower the vehicle to the ground.

32 Propeller shaft securing bolt check

1 Working under the vehicle, use a torque wrench to check the tightness of the bolts securing the propeller shafts to the transfer gearbox and axle drive flanges **(see illustration)**.

33 ABS wheel speed sensor harness check

1 Working underneath the vehicle, check each sensor harness for chafing and damage, and that they are correctly routed.

2 The front sensor wiring harness, passes up through into the engine compartment and has a connector on the inner wing panel **(see illustration)**.

3 The rear sensor wiring harness, runs along the inside of the chassis along side the brake pipes and has a connector **(see illustration)**.

34 Fuel tank security check

1 Working under the vehicle, check the fuel tank for any signs of damage or corrosion.

2 If there is any sign of significant damage or corrosion, remove the fuel tank (see Chapter) and take it to a professional for repair. Do not under any circumstances attempt to weld or solder a fuel tank.

35 Towing bracket check

1 Where applicable, check the security of the towbar bracket mountings. Also check that all wiring is intact, and that the trailer electrical systems function correctly.

36 Headlight and auxiliary light adjustment check

1 Accurate adjustment of the headlight beam is only possible using optical beam-setting equipment, and this work should therefore be carried out by a Land Rover dealer, or a service station with the necessary facilities.

2 Basic adjustments can be carried out in an emergency, and further details are given in Chapter 13

37 Front wheel alignment check

1 Check the front wheel alignment as described in Chapter 11.

38 Spare wheel check

1 Refer to *Weekly checks*.

39 Seat belt check

1 Carefully examine the seat belt webbing for cuts, or any signs of serious fraying or deterioration. If the seat belt is of the retractable type, pull the belt all the way out, and examine the full extent of the webbing.

2 Fasten and unfasten the belt, ensuring that the locking mechanism holds securely, and releases properly when intended. If the

32.1 Check the propshaft retaining bolts

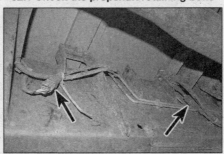

33.3 Connector on inside of chassis

31.3 Check the condition of the exhaust mountings

belt is of the retractable type, check also that the retracting mechanism operates correctly when the belt is released.

3 Check the security of all seat belt mountings and attachments which are accessible (without removing any trim or other components) from inside the vehicle.

4 Renew any worn components as described in Chapter 12.

40 Transmission (main gearbox) oil renewal

Caution: If this procedure is to be carried out on a hot transmission unit, take care not to burn yourself on the hot exhaust or the transmission/engine unit.

1 Ideally, the oil should be drained shortly after the vehicle has been driven, when the oil will be warm (take care as the exhaust system may still be hot). Park the vehicle on level ground.

2 Working under the vehicle, locate the main gearbox casing drain plug **(see illustration)**,

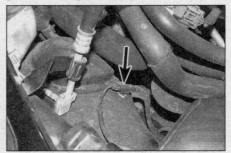

33.2 Connector on inner wing panel

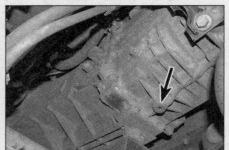

40.2 Oil drain plug

40.3a Slacken using an Allen key and bar...

40.3b ...then remove the drain plug

40.3c Allow plenty of time for the oil to drain fully

and place a suitable container beneath the plug to catch the escaping oil.

3 Unscrew the drain plug, and allow the oil to drain. If the oil is hot, take precautions against scalding. Allow at least ten minutes to allow time for all the oil to drain **(see illustrations)**.

4 Whilst the oil is draining, unscrew the oil filler/level plug from the right-hand side of the transmission casing **(see illustration 13.2)**. Take care not to touch any hot components whilst working up at the side of the transmission.

5 Renew the drain plug sealing washer regardless of their apparent condition.

6 When all the oil has drained from the gearbox, clean, refit and tighten the drain plug, using a new washer. Tighten the plug to the specified torque.

7 Fill the gearbox with the specified grade of oil (see *Lubricants and fluids*), until the oil flows from the filler/level plug hole **(see illustration 13.4)**. It is advisable to fill the gearbox slowly, to avoid a sudden spillage!

8 On completion, fit a new sealing washer and refit the filler/level plug, then tighten to the specified torque. For further information on checking oil level see Section 13

9 Wipe any split oil from the gearbox casing.

41 Alarm handset battery renewal

Warning: Do not remove the battery until you are ready to install a new one. The engine will

immobilise 5 minutes after the ignition key is removed from the switch (or 30 seconds after the engine has been switched off and the driver's door opened). If the battery renewal procedure is not completed in this time, the emergency key access code will have to be entered (refer to your Owners Handbook or Dealer/Specialist) before the handset can be synchronised.

1 Unlock the vehicle/disable the alarm system using the unlock button on the remote handset.

2 Insert the ignition key and turn the key to position II, then back to position 0 and remove the key.

3 Using a coin or small flat-bladed screwdriver, carefully prise apart the two halves of the handset and slide the battery from the retaining clip **(see illustration)**. Do not touch the circuit board or contact surfaces of the clip with bare skin.

4 Press and hold any one of the handset buttons for at least 5 seconds to drain any residual electrical energy.

5 Fit the new battery (type CR2032), into the clip with the positive (+) side facing upwards **(see illustration)**. Avoid touching the flat surfaces of the battery with bare skin as this may reduce the life of the battery.

6 Clip the two halves of the handset back together.

7 Press the padlock symbol button on the handset at least 4 times whilst next to the vehicle to resynchronise the handset, then press the unlock button once. The handset should now be ready for use.

42 Brake fluid renewal

1 The procedure is similar to that for the bleeding of the hydraulic system as described in Chapter, except that the brake fluid reservoir should be emptied before starting. Either syphon off the fluid, using a (clean) old battery hydrometer or similar, or open the first bleed screw in the sequence, and pump the fluid from the reservoir. Allowance should be made for all the old fluid to be expelled from the circuit when bleeding each section of the circuit. Used brake fluid is usually much darker in colour than fresh fluid, making it easy to distinguish the two.

43 Transfer gearbox oil renewal

1 Park the vehicle on level ground. Undo the fasteners and remove the transmission undershield (where applicable).

2 Locate the filler/level plug in the side of the transfer gearbox casing, then unscrew the plug (see Section 14).

3 Place a container beneath the drain plug in the bottom of the gearbox casing, then unscrew the drain plug and allow the oil to drain **(see illustration)**. Recover the sealing washer (where applicable).

4 When the oil has finished draining, refit and tighten the drain plug to the specified torque setting.

41.3 Carefully prise apart the two halves of the handset

41.5 Fit the new battery with the positive side upwards

43.3 Transfer gearbox oil drain plug

43.5 Refilling the transfer box

5 Refill the gearbox with oil of the specified type through the filler/level hole **(see illustration)**, until the oil level reaches the lower edge of the hole (place a container beneath the hole, to catch any escaping oil).

6 Clean and refit the filler/level plug, and tighten to the specified torque.

7 Wipe any split oil from the gearbox casing.

44 Axle oil renewal

Note: *A 13 mm square-section wrench will be required to undo the axle filler/level plug and drain plug. These wrenches can be obtained from most motor factors, or from your Land Rover dealer.*

1 This operation is much quicker and more efficient if the car is first taken on a journey of sufficient length to warm the axle oil up to normal operating temperature. Allow time, however, for the exhaust system to cool.

2 Park the car on level ground, switch off the ignition, and apply the handbrake firmly.

3 Wipe clean the area around the front axle filler/level plug **(see illustration)**, which is on the differential housing (see Section 15). Unscrew the plug, and clean it.

4 Position a suitable container under the drain plug situated on the base of the differential housing.

5 Unscrew the drain plug, and allow the oil to drain completely into the container. If the oil is hot, take precautions against scalding. Examine the sealing washer for signs of damage, renewing it if necessary, and clean both the filler/level and the drain plugs.

44.10 Rear axle drain and filler/level plugs

44.3 Front axle drain and filler/level plugs

6 When the oil has finished draining, clean the drain plug threads and those of the differential casing, then refit the drain plug and washer, tightening it securely.

7 Allow plenty of time for the oil level to settle properly before checking it. Note that the car must be parked on level ground when checking the oil level.

8 Refill the axle with the exact amount of the specified type of oil (see *Lubricants and fluids*), then check the oil level as described in Section 15. If the correct amount was poured into the transmission, and a large amount flows out on checking the level, refit the filler/level plug; take the vehicle on a short journey so that the new oil is distributed fully around the axle components, then check the level again on your return.

9 When the level is correct, refit the filler/level plug, tightening it securely, and wash off any spilt oil.

10 Repeat the procedure for the rear axle **(see illustration)**.

45 Swivel pin housing oil renewal

Note: *Later vehicles do not have any level or drain plugs, as the swivel pin housing is filled for life with grease, so does not require any maintenance.*

1 This operation is much quicker and more efficient if the car is first taken on a journey of sufficient length to warm the swivel pin housing oil up to normal operating temperature. Allow time, however, for the exhaust system to cool.

45.5 Removing the swivel pin housing drain plug

2 Park the car on level ground, switch off the ignition, and apply the handbrake firmly.

3 Working underneath the vehicle, unscrew the left-hand swivel pin housing level and filler plugs.

4 Position a suitable container under the drain plug situated on the base of the swivel pin housing.

5 Unscrew the drain plug, and allow the oil to drain completely into the container **(see illustration)**. If the oil is hot, take precautions against scalding. Examine the sealing washer for signs of damage, renewing it if necessary, and clean the threads of all removed plugs.

6 When the oil has finished draining, clean the drain plug threads and those of the housing, then refit the drain plug and washer, tightening it securely.

7 Allow plenty of time for the oil level to settle properly before checking it. Note that the car must be parked on level ground when checking the oil level.

8 Refill the housing with the exact amount of the specified type of oil (see), then check the oil level as described in Section 16. If the correct amount was poured into the swivel pin housing, and a large amount flows out on checking the level, refit the filler and level plugs; take the car on a short journey so that the new oil is distributed fully around the swivel pin housing components, then check the level again on your return.

9 When the level is correct, refit the filler and level plugs, tightening them securely, and wash off any spilt oil.

10 Repeat the above operation on the right-hand swivel pin housing.

46 Fuel injector leak check

1 Check the fuel injector seating areas in the cylinder head for any signs of fuel leakage.

2 Similarly, check the fuel supply pipe unions and the fuel leak-off pipe unions.

3 Rectify any leaks without delay. Do not overtighten the fuel unions in an attempt to cure leaks.

47 Coolant renewal

⚠ *Warning: Wait until the engine is cold before starting this procedure. Do not allow antifreeze to come in contact with your skin, or with the painted surfaces of the vehicle. Rinse off spills immediately with plenty of water. Never leave antifreeze lying around in an open container, or in a puddle in the driveway or garage floor. Children and pets are attracted by its sweet smell, but antifreeze is fatal if ingested. Refer to the 'Antifreeze mixture' sub-Section below before proceeding.*

Cooling system draining

1 To drain the cooling system, first cover the expansion tank cap with a wad of rag, and slowly turn the cap anti-clockwise to relieve the pressure in the cooling system (a hissing sound will normally be heard). Wait until any pressure remaining in the system is released, then continue to turn the cap until it can be removed. Set the heater controls inside the vehicle to hot.

2 Slacken the cooling system bleed screw in the heater hose, from the heater control valve **(see illustration)**.

3 Position a suitable container beneath the fuel cooler on the inside of the left-hand side chassis leg. Release the quick release hose clips and disconnect the two lower coolant hoses from the cooler **(see illustration)**. Allow the coolant to drain into the container. When the flow of coolant has stopped, wipe clean the area around the fuel cooler and refit the hoses.

4 To fully drain the system, also release the hose clip and remove the coolant hose from the oil thermostat on the oil filter housing **(see illustration)**, and allow any residual coolant to drain from the cylinder block into a container. When the flow of coolant has stopped, wipe clean the area around the filter housing and refit the hose, securing it in place with the retaining clip.

5 If the coolant has been drained for a reason other than renewal, then provided it is clean and less than two years old, it can be re-used.

Cooling system flushing

6 If coolant renewal has been neglected, or if the antifreeze mixture has become diluted, then in time, the cooling system may gradually lose efficiency, as the coolant passages become restricted due to rust, scale deposits, and other sediment. The cooling system efficiency can be restored by flushing the system clean.

7 The radiator should be flushed independently of the engine, to avoid unnecessary contamination.

8 To flush the radiator, disconnect the top and bottom hose at the radiator, then insert a garden hose into the radiator top inlet. Direct a flow of clean water through the radiator, and continue flushing until clean water emerges from the radiator bottom outlet. If after a reasonable period, the water still does not run clear, the radiator can be flushed with a good proprietary cleaning agent. It is important that the cleaning agent manufacturer's instructions are followed carefully. If the contamination is particularly bad, insert the hose in the radiator bottom outlet, and flush the radiator in reverse (reverse-flushing).

9 Remove the thermostat as described in Chapter 3, then temporarily refit the thermostat cover.

10 With the radiator top and bottom hoses disconnected from the radiator, insert a hose into the radiator bottom hose. Direct a clean flow of water through the engine, and

47.2 Slacken the bleed screw

47.3a Release the locking clips...

47.3b ...and disconnect the coolant hoses

47.4 Remove the oil thermostat coolant hose on the filter housing

continue flushing until clean water emerges from the radiator top hose.

11 On completion of flushing, refit the thermostat with reference to Chapter 3, and reconnect the hoses.

Cooling system filling

12 Before attempting to fill the cooling system, make sure that all hoses and clips are in good condition, and that the clips are tight. Note that an antifreeze mixture must be used all year round, to prevent corrosion of the alloy engine components.

13 If not already done, remove the expansion tank cap and slacken the bleed screw in the top of the heater hose **(see illustration 47.2)**.

14 Set the cabin heater controls to maximum heat.

15 Fill the system with the correct antifreeze mixture, by slowly pouring the coolant into the expansion tank to prevent airlocks from forming.

16 When coolant emerges from the bleed screw in the heater hose, free of air bubbles, the bleed screw can then be tightened.

17 Top-up the expansion tank to the correct level (see *Weekly checks*), then refit the expansion tank cap.

18 Start the engine, run it until it reaches normal operating temperature, then stop the engine and allow it to cool.

 Warning: DO NOT remove the cap from the expansion tank, whilst the engine is hot

19 Check for leaks, particularly around disturbed components. Check the coolant

level in the expansion tank, and top-up if necessary. Note that the system must be cold before an accurate level is indicated in the expansion tank. If the expansion tank cap is removed while the engine is still warm, cover the cap with a thick cloth. Unscrew the cap slowly, to gradually relieve the system pressure (a hissing sound will normally be heard). Wait until any pressure remaining in the system is released, then continue to turn the cap until it can be removed.

Antifreeze mixture

20 Always use an ethylene-glycol based antifreeze which is suitable for use in mixed-metal cooling systems (see *Weekly checks*). The quantity of antifreeze and levels of protection are indicated in the Specifications.

21 Before adding antifreeze, the cooling system should be completely drained, preferably flushed, and all hoses and clips checked for condition and security.

22 After filling with the correct antifreeze mixture, a label should be attached to the radiator or expansion tank, stating the type and concentration of antifreeze used, and the date installed. Any subsequent topping-up should be made with the same type and concentration of antifreeze.

23 Do not use engine antifreeze in the windscreen/tailgate washer system, as it will cause damage to the vehicle paintwork. A screenwash should be added to the washer system, in the quantities recommended on the bottle.

48 Shock absorber check

1 Check for any signs of fluid leakage around the shock absorber body, or from the rubber gaiter around the piston rod. Should any fluid be noticed, the shock absorber is defective internally, and should be renewed. **Note:** *Shock absorbers should always be renewed in pairs on the same axle – never renew just one, or abnormal handling characteristics may result.*
2 The efficiency of the shock absorber may be checked by bouncing the vehicle at each corner. Generally speaking, the body will return to its normal position and stop after being depressed. If it rises and returns on a rebound, the shock absorber is probably suspect. Examine also the shock absorber upper and lower mountings for any signs of wear.

49 Brake vacuum servo air filter renewal

1 Remove the servo unit (see Chapter 10).
2 Peel back the dust cover from the rear of the servo unit, to gain access to the air filter. Release the end cap from the servo unit, then carefully hook the old filters out of the servo, and release them from the pushrod.
3 Remove all traces of dirt from the servo unit, then install both new filters, making sure that they are correctly seated. Note that it will be necessary to cut a slot in each filter, to allow them to be slid into position.
4 Make sure that both filters are correctly seated, then clip the end cap back into position.
5 Slide the dust cover back into position, then refit the servo unit (Chapter 10).

50 Braking system seal, vacuum servo filter and hose renewal

1 At this interval, Land Rover recommend that all the brake wheel cylinder/caliper seals and flexible rubber hoses are renewed, and the hydraulic system filled with fresh fluid. At the same time, the vacuum servo unit filter should also be renewed. Refer to the relevant Sections of Chapter 10 for renewal information.

51 Intercooler element cleaning

1 Remove the intercooler as described in Chapter 4A Section 17.

52.2 Remove the trim cover

2 Check the element for damage and deterioration, and renew if necessary.
3 If the original element is to be refitted, flush the element with Unicorn Chemicals C Solve or a suitable alternative (check with your Land Rover dealer or specialist), following the instructions supplied with the cleaner.
4 Dry the element thoroughly, then refit as described in Chapter 4A.

52 Auxiliary drivebelt renewal

1 Before removing the auxiliary drive belt, disconnect the battery negative terminal (refer to Disconnecting the battery 5 Section 4).
2 Open the bonnet, undo the six retaining screws and lift off the viscous fan cover from the front of the engine compartment **(see illustration)**.
3 If the existing drivebelt is to be refitted, mark it, or note the maker's markings on its flat surface, so that it can be installed the same way round. Make an accurate note of the drivebelt arrangement as an aid to fitting.
4 Using a 3/8 square drive breaker bar or ratchet, rotate the tensioner pulley bracket clockwise to release its pressure on the drivebelt **(see illustration)**, and then slip the drivebelt from around the pulleys, noting its fitted position.
5 To remove the drivebelt completely from the engine, undo the retaining bolt and remove

52.5a Undo the tensioner retaining bolt...

52.4 Releasing the tension on the belt – viscous fan removed for clarity

the belt tensioner from the cylinder block **(see illustrations)**.
6 Check all the pulleys, ensuring that their grooves are clean, and removing all traces of oil and grease. Check that the tensioner works properly, with strong spring pressure being felt when its pulley is rotated clockwise, and a smooth return to the limit of its travel when released.
7 If the original drivebelt is being refitted, use the marks or notes made on removal, to ensure that it is installed to run in the same direction as it was previously.
8 Refit the drivebelt around the tensioner pulley bracket and refit the retaining bolt, tightening to the specified torque setting.
9 To fit the drivebelt, arrange it on the grooved pulleys so that it is centred in their grooves, and not overlapping their raised sides (note that the flat surface of the drivebelt is engaged on one or more pulleys) and routed correctly. Start at the bottom, and work up to finish at the idler pulley.
10 Rotate the tensioner clockwise and refit the drivebelt around the pulleys, then gently release the pressure on the belt anti-clockwise to tension the belt.
11 Rotate the crankshaft clockwise, by means of the crankshaft pulley, through at least two full turns to settle the drivebelt on the pulleys, then check that the drivebelt is properly installed.
12 Refit the viscous fan upper cover and reconnect the battery.

52.5b ...and remove it to free the drivebelt

Chapter 2 Part A
2.2 litre engine in-vehicle repair procedures

Contents

Degrees of difficulty

Easy, suitable for novice with little experience	**Fairly easy,** suitable for beginner with some experience	**Fairly difficult,** suitable for competent DIY mechanic	**Difficult,** suitable for experienced DIY mechanic	**Very difficult,** suitable for expert DIY or professional

Specifications

General

Engine type	Four-cylinder, in-line, double overhead camshaft
Designation	DuraTorq-TDCi
Engine code	DT224
Power output	90kW/121bhp
Capacity	2198 cc
Bore	86.0 mm
Stroke	94.6 mm
Compression ratio	15.5 : 1
Firing order	1-3-4-2 (No 1 cylinder at timing chain end)
Direction of crankshaft rotation	Clockwise (seen from the front of vehicle)

Cylinder head

Piston protrusion:

	Thickness of cylinder head gasket
0.310 to 0.400 mm	1.10 mm (1 hole/tooth)
0.401 to 0.450 mm	1.15 mm (2 holes/teeth)
0.451 to 0.500 mm	1.20 mm (3 holes/teeth)
Maximum permissible gasket surface distortion	0.2 mm

Lubrication

Engine oil type/specification	See *Lubricants, fluids and tyre pressures*
Engine oil capacity	7.0 litres

Oil pressure – minimum (engine at operating temperature):

At idle	1.25 bars
At 2000 rpm	2.00 bars

Torque wrench settings

	Nm	lbf ft
Alternator mounting bracket bolts	23	17
Auxiliary drivebelt idler pulley bolt	47	35
Big-end bearing cap bolts: *		
Stage 1	25	19
Stage 2	37	27
Stage 3	Angle-tighten a further 90°	
Camshaft carrier bolts:		
Stage 1 – bolts 1 to 22	23	17
Stage 2 – bolts 23 and 24	10	7
Camshaft cover	10	7
Camshaft position sensor	10	7
Camshaft sprocket bolts	33	24
Coolant outlet elbow bolts	23	17

Torque wrench settings (continued)	Nm	lbf ft
Coolant pump bolts	23	17
Cooling fan pulley bracket bolts	47	35
Crankshaft oil seal carrier bolts	10	7
Crankshaft position sensor	7	5
Crankshaft position sensor mounting bracket bolts	25	19
Crankshaft pulley bolts: *		
Stage 1	45	33
Stage 2	Angle-tighten a further 120°	
Cylinder head bolts: *		
Stage 1:		
Bolts 1 to 10	10	7
Bolts 11 to 18	5	4
Stage 2:		
Bolts 1 to 10	20	15
Bolts 11 to 18	10	7
Stage 3:		
Bolts 1 to 10	35	26
Bolts 11 to 18	20	15
Stage 4:		
Bolts 1 to 10	45	33
Bolts 11 to 18	26	19
Stage 5:		
Bolts 1 to 10	Angle-tighten a further 90°	
Bolts 11 to 18	Angle-tighten a further 90°	
Stage 6:		
Bolts 1 to 10	Angle-tighten a further 90°	
Bolts 11 to 18	Angle-tighten a further 90°	
Stage 7:		
Bolt 19	10	7
Engine crossmember bolts	70	52
Engine/transmission mountings:		
Engine mounting-to-engine bracket	103	76
Engine mounting-to-engine crossmember	40	30
Transmission mounting-to-subframe	55	41
Transmission mounting-to-transmission	80	59
Flywheel bolts:		
Stage 1	25	18
Stage 2	45	33
Stage 3	Angle-tighten a further 45°	
Fuel injection pump sprocket	55	41
Fuel rail-to-camshaft carrier	23	17
Lower crankcase/ladder to cylinder block	23	17
Main bearing cap bolts: *		
Stage 1	15	11
Stage 2	20	15
Stage 3	35	26
Stage 4	80	59
Stage 5	Angle-tighten a further 90°	
Oil filter housing bolts	23	17
Oil pump bolts	10	7
Oil pump pick-up pipe	10	7
Power steering pump bolts	23	17
Rocker arm carrier bolts:		
Stage 1	10	7
Stage 2	Angle-tighten a further 30°	
Sump bolts:		
Stage 1	7	5
Stage 2	14	10
Sump oil drain plug	23	17
Timing chain cover:		
Nuts	10	7
Bolts	14	10
Timing chain guide retaining bolts:		
Fixed guides	15	11
Tensioner guide	36	27
Timing chain tensioner	15	11
Transmission-to-engine bolts	40	30

* *Use new nuts/bolts*

1 General Information

How to use this Chapter

1 This Part of Chapter 2 is devoted to repair procedures possible while the engine is still installed in the vehicle. Since these procedures are based on the assumption that the engine is installed in the vehicle, if the engine has been removed and mounted on a stand, some of the preliminary dismantling steps outlined will not apply.

2 Information concerning engine/transmission removal and refitting and engine overhaul can be found in Part C of this Chapter.

Engine description

3 The 2.2 litre diesel engines covered in this Part of Chapter 2 are all in-line four-cylinder, turbocharged units, with a 16-valve, double overhead camshaft (DOHC) arrangement. The engine and transmission are mounted in-line at the front of the vehicle, driving the rear wheels via propeller shafts and transfer box to the front axle.

4 The engine cylinder block casting is of cast-iron and has a lower aluminium crankcase which is bolted to the underside of the cylinder block, with a pressed steel sump bolted under that.

5 The crankshaft runs in five main bearings, the centre main bearing's upper half incorporating thrust washers to control crankshaft endfloat. The connecting rods rotate on horizontally split bearing shells at their big-ends. The pistons are attached to the connecting rods by gudgeon pins which are a floating fit in the connecting rod small-end eyes, secured by circlips. The aluminium alloy pistons are fitted with three piston rings – two compression rings and an oil control ring.

6 The inlet and exhaust valves are each closed by coil springs. They operate in guides which are shrink-fitted into the cylinder head, as are the valve seat inserts.

7 The double overhead camshaft sprockets and the high-pressure fuel injection pump sprocket are driven by a chain from a sprocket on the crankshaft. The camshafts operate the 16 valves via roller-rocker arms with hydraulic clearance adjusters. The rocker arms and clearance adjusters are located in an aluminium carrier bolted to the cylinder head. Each camshaft rotates in five bearings that are machined directly in the cylinder head and the (bolted on) bearing caps. This means that the bearing caps are not available separately from the cylinder head, and must not be interchanged with caps from another engine.

8 The vacuum pump (used for the brake servo and other vacuum actuators) is located on the transmission end of the cylinder head, driven by a slot in the end of the exhaust camshaft.

9 Lubrication is by means of a chain driven oil pump driven from a sprocket on the crankshaft. The oil pump is mounted below the lower crankcase, and draws oil through a strainer located in the sump. The pump forces oil through an externally-mounted full-flow cartridge-type filter. From the filter, the oil is pumped into a main gallery in the cylinder block/crankcase, from where it is distributed to the crankshaft (main bearings) and cylinder head. An oil cooler is above the oil filter, at the side of the block. The cooler is supplied with coolant from the engine cooling system.

10 While the crankshaft and camshaft bearings receive a pressurised supply, the camshaft lobes and valves are lubricated by splash, as are all other engine components. The undersides of the pistons are cooled by oil, sprayed from nozzles fitted above the upper main bearing shells. The turbocharger receives its own pressurised oil supply.

Repairs with the engine in the vehicle

11 The following major repair operations can be accomplished without removing the engine from the vehicle. However, owners should note that any operation involving the removal of the timing chain, camshafts or cylinder head require careful forethought, depending on the level of skill and the tools and facilities available. Refer to the relevant text for details.

a) Compression pressure – testing.
b) Camshaft cover – removal and refitting.
c) Timing chain cover – removal and refitting.
d) Timing chain – renewal.
e) Timing chain tensioner and sprockets – removal and refitting.
f) Camshafts and hydraulic rockers – removal and refitting.
g) Cylinder head – removal, overhaul and refitting.
h) Crankshaft pulley – removal and refitting.
i) Sump – removal and refitting.
j) Pistons, connecting rods and big-end bearings – removal and refitting*.
k) Oil filter housing and oil cooler – removal and refitting.
l) Crankshaft oil seals – renewal.
m) Oil pump – removal and refitting.
n) Flywheel – removal and refitting.
o) Engine/transmission mountings – removal and refitting.

12 *Although the operation marked with an asterisk can be carried out with the engine in the vehicle (after removal of the sump), it is preferable for the engine to be removed, in the interests of cleanliness and improved access. For this reason, the procedure is described in Chapter 2C Section 9.

2 Compression and leakdown tests – description and interpretation

Compression test

Note: *A compression tester suitable for use with diesel engines will be required for this test.*

Note: *The following procedure is likely to log a fault code in the powertrain control module memory. If the engine management warning light is illuminated after the test, it will be necessary to have the fault code cleared by a Land Rover dealer or suitably equipped garage using specialist diagnostic equipment.*

1 When engine performance is down, or if misfiring occurs which cannot be attributed to the fuel or emissions systems, a compression test can provide diagnostic clues as to the engine's condition. If the test is performed regularly, it can give warning of trouble before any other symptoms become apparent.

2 The engine must be fully warmed-up to normal operating temperature and the battery must be fully charged. The aid of an assistant will also be required.

3 Remove the glow plugs as described in Section.

4 Fit a compression tester to the No 1 cylinder glow plug hole. The type of tester which screws into the plug thread is preferred.

5 Crank the engine for several seconds on the starter motor. After one or two revolutions, the compression pressure should build up to a maximum figure and then stabilise. Record the highest reading obtained.

6 Repeat the test on the remaining cylinders, recording the pressure in each.

7 The cause of poor compression is less easy to establish on a diesel engine than on a petrol engine. The effect of introducing oil into the cylinders (wet testing) is not conclusive, because there is a risk that the oil will sit in the recess on the piston crown, instead of passing to the rings. However, the following can be used as a rough guide to diagnosis.

8 An actual compression pressure value is not stated by Land Rover, however all cylinders should produce very similar pressures. Any significant difference indicates the existence of a fault. Note that the compression should build-up quickly in a healthy engine. Low compression on the first stroke, followed by gradually increasing pressure on successive strokes, indicates worn piston rings. A low compression reading on the first stroke, which does not build-up during successive strokes, indicates leaking valves or a blown head gasket (a cracked head could also be the cause).

9 A low reading from two adjacent cylinders is almost certainly due to the head gasket having blown between them and the presence of coolant in the engine oil will confirm this.

10 On completion, remove the compression tester, and refit the glow plugs as described in Section.

Leakdown test

11 A leakdown test measures the rate at which compressed air fed into the cylinder is lost. It is an alternative to a compression test, and in many ways it is better, since the escaping air provides easy identification of where pressure loss is occurring (piston rings, valves or head gasket).

12 The equipment required for leakdown testing is unlikely to be available to the home mechanic. If poor compression is suspected, have the test performed by a suitably equipped garage.

3 Engine timing – setting

Note: *Only turn the engine in the normal direction of rotation – clockwise viewed from the right-hand side of the vehicle.*

General information

1 Top Dead Centre (TDC) is the highest point in the cylinder that each piston reaches as it travels up and down when the crankshaft turns. Each piston reaches TDC at the end of the compression stroke and again at the end of the exhaust stroke, but TDC generally refers to piston position on the compression stroke. No 1 piston is at the timing chain end of the engine.

2 Setting No 1 piston at 50° before top dead centre (BTDC) is an essential part of many procedures, such as timing chain removal, cylinder head removal and camshaft removal.

3 The design of the engines covered in this Chapter is such that piston-to-valve contact may occur if the camshaft or crankshaft is turned with the timing chain removed. For this reason, it is important to ensure that the camshaft and crankshaft do not move in relation to each other once the timing chain has been removed from the engine.

Setting

Note: *Service tool 303-698, obtainable from the vehicle manufacturer or a tool supplier, will be required to set the timing at 50° BTDC.*

Note: *A new crankshaft position sensor will be required for refitting.*

4 Disconnect the battery negative terminal (refer to Chapter 5, Section 4).

5 Firmly apply the handbrake then jack up the front of the vehicle and support it securely on axle stands (see *Jacking and vehicle support*).

6 A timing hole is provided on the top of the transmission, to permit the crankshaft position sensor to be located.

7 Undo the retaining bolt and remove the

3.8 Undo the retaining bolt and withdraw the crankshaft position sensor

crankshaft position sensor heat shield from the top of the transmission.

8 Disconnect the wiring connector from the crankshaft position sensor, undo the retaining bolt and withdraw the sensor from the bellhousing **(see illustration)**. Note that a new sensor will be required for refitting.

9 The special tool can now be inserted into the sensor hole to set the timing at 50° BTDC **(see illustration)**.

10 Turn the crankshaft (by means of the crankshaft pulley) in the direction of engine rotation, until the end of the tool drops into a recess in the outer toothed part of the flywheel. This is the 50° BTDC position.

11 If the engine is being set to 50° BTDC as part of the timing chain removal/renewal procedure, further confirmation of the position can be gained once the timing chain outer cover has been removed. At 50° BTDC, 6 mm timing pins are inserted into the camshaft sprockets, see Section 7.

12 If the holes in the sprockets do not align, remove the special tool from the flywheel and rotate the engine one full turn, then re-install the tool.

13 Before rotating the crankshaft again, make sure that the special tool (and, where applicable, the sprocket timing pins) are removed. When operations are complete, fit the new crankshaft position sensor as described in Chapter 4A Section 9. Refit all other components removed for access. Do not use the crankshaft timing setting tool to prevent the crankshaft from rotating.

3.9 Timing tool inserted into the crankshaft sensor bracket (transmission removed for clarity)

4 Camshaft cover – removal and refitting

Caution: Do not carry out any work on the fuel system with the engine running. Wait for at least 2 minutes after the engine has been stopped before any work is carried out on the fuel system, to make sure the fuel pressure and temperature has dropped sufficiently. Make sure that all the fuel lines are kept clean. Fit blanking plugs to the end of the fuel lines when they are disconnected, to prevent foreign matter entering the components.

Removal

1 Disconnect the battery negative terminal (refer to Chapter 5 Section 4).

2 Refer to Chapter 4A Section 11 and remove the fuel injectors.

3 Undo the bolts securing the fuel supply pipe clamp to the camshaft cover and timing chain housing **(see illustration)**.

4 Undo the retaining nut and disconnect the engine oil dipstick tube bracket from the cover **(see illustration)**.

5 Disconnect the crankcase ventilation hose from the rear of the camshaft cover **(see illustration)**.

6 Note the locations of the different bolt types, then unscrew the twelve retaining bolts (one was securing the fuel pipe bracket) and lift the camshaft cover off the cylinder head.

4.3 Undo the fuel pipe bracket securing bolts

4.4 Undo the bracket securing nut

4.5 Disconnect breather hose

4.8a Remove the fuel injector seals from the camshaft cover...

4.8b ...and press new seals into position

4.9 Locate a new gasket on the camshaft cover ensuring that it fits correctly in the cover groove

Note that the bolts are captive in the camshaft cover and cannot be completely removed. Recover the gasket and discard it – a new gasket and fuel injector seals will be required for refitting.

Refitting

7 Thoroughly clean the sealing surfaces of the camshaft cover and the cylinder head.

8 Using a screwdriver, remove the fuel injector seals from the camshaft cover and press new seals into position **(see illustrations)**.

9 Locate a new gasket on the camshaft cover ensuring that it fits correctly in the cover groove **(see illustration)**.

10 The remainder of refitting is a reversal of removal, noting the following points:

a) *Renew all seals, gaskets and supply pipes as noted on removal.*

b) *Ensure the gasket is correctly seated on the cylinder head, and take care to avoid displacing it as the camshaft cover is lowered into position.*

c) *Refit the fuel injectors as described in Chapter 4A Section 11.*

5 Timing chain cover – removal and refitting

Note: *Land Rover technicians use special tools for removing the oil seal and aligning the timing chain cover – see text. A new timing*

chain cover will be required for refitting, as the cover will be irreparably distorted during removal.

Removal

1 Disconnect the battery negative terminal (refer to Chapter 5 Section 4).

2 Firmly apply the handbrake then jack up the front of the vehicle and support it securely on axle stands (see *Jacking and vehicle support*).

3 Undo the two retaining bolts, then lift the engine trim cover from the top of the camshaft cover, releasing the rear of the cover from the locating peg at the rear of the camshaft cover **(see illustrations)**.

4 Drain the cooling system as described in Chapter 1 Section 47.

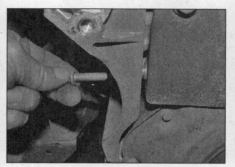

5.3a Lift up the front of the trim cover...

5 Remove the radiator cooling fan shroud as described in Chapter 3 Section 5.

6 Remove the auxiliary drivebelt as described in Chapter 1 Section 52.

7 Undo the retraining bolts and remove the mounting bracket from the top of the timing chain cover **(see illustration)**.

8 Remove the alternator, as described in Chapter 5 Section 6. With the alternator removed, slacken and remove the lower bolt from the mounting bracket **(see illustration)**.

9 Undo the remainder of the bolts from the accessory drive component bracket, and remove it from the front of the timing chain cover **(see illustration)**.

10 Undo the nut and two bolts and remove the coolant outlet elbow from the front of the

5.3b ...and release the rear from the locating peg

5.7 Remove the mounting bracket

5.8 Remove the lower bolt from the mounting bracket

5.9 Remove the accessory drive bracket

5.10 Remove the coolant outlet elbow

cylinder head **(see illustration)**, the upper hose can remain fitted to the housing and position it to one side. Remove and discard the outlet elbow O-ring seal as a new seal must be used for refitting.

11 To make access easier it may be necessary to undo the bolts securing the power steering pump to the cylinder block, then move it to one side and suitably support it.

12 Remove the crankshaft pulley as described in Section 6.

13 Remove the crankshaft timing chain end oil seal as described in Section 15.

14 Undo the retaining bolts and nuts securing the timing chain cover to the cylinder block and cylinder head.

15 Using a couple of well lubricated scrapers or similar, carefully work your way around the timing chain cover and prise it away from the engine. The cover will become distorted on removal, so discard it as a new cover must be used on refitting. Recover the coolant outlet elbow gasket.

Refitting

16 To aid installation of the timing chain cover, screw in two M10 x 60 mm locating studs into the holes on the centre of the cylinder block. Locate a new coolant outlet elbow gasket over the studs **(see illustration)**.

17 Make sure that the mating surfaces of the cover and the engine casing are clean. Apply a 3 mm bead of sealant (Land Rover recommend WSE-M4G323-A4, or equivalent) around the mating surface of the cylinder block and cylinder head, ensuring that the sealant bead passes around the inside of the retaining bolt holes **(see illustration)**. Apply a line of sealant also, where the cylinder block mates with the cylinder head and the sump.

Caution: Install the timing chain cover within 5 minutes of applying the sealer to the engine casing. Make sure the cover does not come into contact with the engine casing, until the correct position for fitting is obtained.

18 Fit the new timing chain cover remove the locating studs and install the retaining nuts and bolts hand tight **(see illustration)**.

19 Using a cover aligning tool (Special tool 303-682), insert the tool over the end of the crankshaft to align the cover **(see illustration)**, then tighten all the timing chain cover retaining nuts and bolts to the specified torque. Remove the tool once the cover is in position.

5.16 Locate a new coolant outlet elbow gasket over the studs

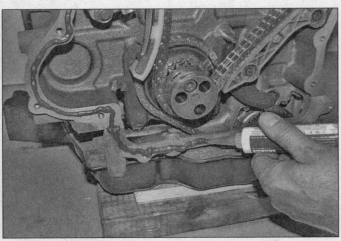

5.17 Apply a 3 mm bead of sealant around the mating surface of the cylinder block and cylinder head

5.18 Fit the new timing chain cover...

5.19 ...then insert the aligning tool over the end of the crankshaft before tightening the retaining bolts

6.5 Crankshaft pulley retaining bolts

6.9a Mark the pulley bolts with quick-drying paint then similarly mark the pulley two flats further on

6.9b Tighten the bolts until the marks align

20 Further refitting is a reversal of removal, noting the following points:
a) *Fit a new crankshaft oil seal as described in Section 15.*
b) *Refit the crankshaft pulley as described in Section 6.*
c) *Use a new O-ring seal when refitting the coolant outlet elbow.*
d) *Refit the cooling fan shroud as described in Chapter 3 Section 5.*
e) *Refit the auxiliary drivebelt as described in Chapter 1 Section 52.*
f) *Refill the cooling system as described in Chapter 1 Section 47.*

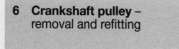

6 Crankshaft pulley – removal and refitting

Removal

Note: *New crankshaft pulley retaining bolts will be required for refitting.*

1 Disconnect the battery negative terminal (refer to Chapter 5 Section 4).
2 Remove the auxiliary drivebelt, as described in Chapter 1 Section 52.
3 The three bolts which secure the crankshaft pulley must now be slackened. If the vehicle is up on stands, ensure it is adequately supported, as considerable effort may be needed to slacken the bolts.
4 Technicians use a special holding tool (303-1310) which locates over two of the three

pulley retaining bolts and prevents it from turning. If this is not available, select a gear, and have an assistant firmly apply the handbrake and footbrake as the bolts are loosened. If this method is unsuccessful, remove the starter motor as described in Chapter 5 Section 9, and lock the flywheel ring gear, using a suitable tool, to prevent the crankshaft from rotating.
5 Unscrew the bolts securing the pulley to the crankshaft, and remove the pulley **(see illustration)**. Discard the bolts and obtain new bolts for refitting.
6 With the pulley removed, it is advisable to check the crankshaft oil seal for signs of oil leakage. If necessary, fit a new seal as described in Section 15.

Refitting

7 Refit the pulley to the end of the crankshaft, then fit the new pulley securing bolts and tighten them as far as possible before the crankshaft starts to rotate.
8 Holding the pulley against rotation as for removal, first tighten the bolts to the specified Stage 1 torque.
9 Stage 2 involves tightening the bolts though an angle, rather than to a torque. The bolts must be rotated through the specified angle – special angle gauges are available from tool outlets. As a guide, a 120° angle is equivalent to two flats on the retaining bolt, and this is easily judged by marking each bolt with quick-drying paint then similarly marking the pulley two flats further on. Tighten the bolts until the marks align **(see illustrations)**.

10 Refit the auxiliary drivebelt as described in Chapter 1 Section 52. If removed, refit the starter motor as described in Chapter 5 Section 9.
11 Lower the vehicle to the ground, and reconnect the battery negative lead.

7 Timing chain – removal, inspection and refitting

Note: *Only turn the engine in the normal direction of rotation – clockwise viewed from the front of the vehicle.*

Removal

1 Remove the timing chain cover, as described in Section 5.
2 Referring to the information in Section 3, set the engine to 50° BTDC on No 1 cylinder. In this position, insert a 6 mm timing pin (6 mm drill bit) in each camshaft sprocket and into the corresponding hole in the cylinder head **(see illustration)**.
3 Slacken the timing chain tensioner by inserting a small screwdriver into the access hole in the tensioner and releasing the pawl mechanism. Press against the timing chain guide to depress the piston into the tensioner housing. When fully depressed, insert a locking pin (approximately 2 mm diameter) to lock the piston in its compressed position **(see illustration)**.
4 To remove the tensioner, undo the two retaining bolts and remove the timing chain tensioner from the cylinder block **(see illustration)**. Note that a new tensioner will be required for refitting.

7.2 Insert 6 mm timing pins (6 mm drill bits), to align the camshaft sprockets

7.3 Insert a pin to lock the tensioner piston in its compressed position

7.4 Remove the timing chain tensioner from the cylinder block, taking care not to remove the locking pin

7.5a Undo the retaining bolts and remove the tensioner timing chain guide ...

7.5b ... then remove the upper fixed chain guide bolts (arrowed) ...

7.5c ... the middle fixed chain guide bolts (arrowed) ...

7.5d ... and the lower fixed timing chain guide bolts (arrowed)

7.7 Undo the sprocket retaining bolts and remove the camshaft sprockets and timing chain

5 Undo the retaining bolts and remove the tensioner timing chain guide and the fixed timing chain guides from the cylinder block **(see illustrations)**.

6 Holding the fuel injection pump sprocket in position, undo the retaining bolt and remove the sprocket.

7 With the camshafts held in position, undo the camshaft sprocket retaining bolts and remove the camshaft sprockets and timing chain **(see illustration)**. Do not rotate the crankshaft until the timing chain is refitted. **Note:** *Do not rely on the timing pins (6 mm drill bit) to hold the sprockets in position.*

8 To remove the timing chain sprocket from the crankshaft, the oil pump drive chain will need to be removed first. Lift the tensioner

arm and insert a suitable drill bit through the hole in the arm and behind the spring blade. With the tensioner now locked in the released position, slide the tensioner off the pivot stud. The chain can now be removed from the sprocket. Undo the retaining bolt and withdraw the sprocket from the crankshaft. Collect the spacer plate (where fitted) from inside the sprocket **(see illustrations)**.

Inspection

Note: *Keep all components identified for position to ensure correct refitting.*

9 Clean all components thoroughly and wipe dry.

10 Examine the fixed chain guides and tensioner guide for excessive wear or other

damage. Check the guides for deep grooves made by the timing chain.

11 Examine the timing chain for excessive wear. Hold it horizontally and check how much movement exists in the chain links. If there is any doubt, compare it to a new chain. Renew as necessary.

12 Examine the teeth of the camshaft, crankshaft and fuel injection pump sprockets for excessive wear and damage.

Refitting

13 Ensure that the crankshaft and camshaft are still set to 50° BTDC on No 1 cylinder, as described in Section 3.

14 If not already fitted, refit the crankshaft drive sprocket onto the crankshaft and securely tighten the retaining bolt. Refit the oil pump drive chain and tensioner, then hold pressure against the tensioner arm and withdraw the tensioner locking pin (see Section 12, for further information on refitting the oil pump).

15 Refit the fuel pump sprocket and the exhaust camshaft sprocket, however DO NOT tighten the retaining bolts at this stage.

16 With the timing chain around the inlet camshaft sprocket, and with the coloured link on the chain aligned with the timing mark on the sprocket, refit the timing chain and sprocket. Feed the timing chain around the crankshaft drive sprocket, fuel pump sprocket and exhaust camshaft sprocket.

17 With the timing pins (6 mm drill bits)

7.8a Lift the tensioner arm and insert a drill bit (arrowed) through the hole in the arm and behind the spring blade...

7.8b ...then slide the tensioner off the pivot stud

7.8c Collect the spacer plate from inside the crankshaft sprocket

7.17a The coloured links on the timing chain must line up with the timing marks (arrowed) on the camshaft sprockets...

7.17b ...and fuel injection pump sprocket

inserted into the sprockets to re-align them, the coloured links on the timing chain must line up with the timing marks on the sprockets **(see illustrations)**.

18 Fit the new timing chain tensioner to the cylinder block and tighten the retaining bolts to the specified torque. Take care not to remove the locking pin.

19 Refit the timing chain tensioner guide on the upper pivot pin and tighten the retaining bolt to the specified torque setting. Hold pressure against the bottom of the tensioner guide and withdraw the tensioner locking pin. This will then tension the timing chain.

20 Refit the three fixed timing chain guides and tighten the retaining bolts to the specified torque setting.

21 Tighten the camshaft sprocket retaining bolts, and the fuel injection pump sprocket retaining bolts, to the specified torque setting.

Note: *Do not rely on the timing pins (6 mm drill bits) to hold the sprockets in position.*

22 Check that the engine is still set to 50° BTDC (as described in Section 3), and remove the timing pins (6 mm drill bits) from the sprockets and the timing peg from the crankshaft sensor hole.

23 Turn the engine (in the direction of engine rotation) two full turns. Refit the timing pins

and crankshaft timing peg to make sure the engine timing is still set at 50° BTDC (see Section 3 for further information).

24 Check the tension of the chain then remove the timing pins (6 mm drill bits) from the sprockets and the timing peg from the crankshaft sensor hole. Fit the new crankshaft position sensor as described in Chapter 4A Section 9.

25 Refit the timing chain cover as described in Section 5.

8 Timing chain tensioner and sprockets – removal, inspection and refitting

Timing chain tensioner

1 The timing chain tensioner is removed as part of the timing chain renewal procedure, in Section 7.

Camshaft sprockets

2 The camshaft sprockets are removed as part of the timing chain renewal procedure, in Section 7.

Crankshaft sprocket

3 The crankshaft sprocket is removed as

part of the timing chain renewal procedure, in Section 7.

Fuel injection pump sprocket

4 Removal of the injection pump sprocket is described as part of the timing chain renewal procedure, in Section 7

9 Camshafts and hydraulic rockers – removal and refitting

Note: *New rocker arm carrier retaining bolts will be required for refitting.*
Note: *Only turn the engine in the normal direction of rotation – clockwise viewed from the front of the vehicle.*

Removal

1 Remove the timing chain cover, as described in Section 5.

2 Referring to the information in Section 3, set the engine to 50° BTDC on No 1 cylinder. In this position, insert a 6 mm timing pin (6 mm drill bit) in each camshaft sprocket and into the corresponding hole in the cylinder head **(see illustration 7.2)**.

3 Remove the camshaft cover, as described in Section 4.

4 Remove the fuel rail as described in Chapter 4A Section 12.

5 Remove the brake servo vacuum pump as described in Section.

6 Progressively slacken and remove the retaining bolts and lift off the rocker arm carrier **(see illustrations)**. Note that new retaining bolts will be required for refitting. Note also that further dismantling of the rocker arm carrier is not possible as the rocker arms and hydraulic clearance adjusters are not available separately.

7 Working as described in Section 7, remove the timing chain tensioner, timing chain guides and camshaft sprockets.

8 Slacken the camshaft carrier retaining bolts

9.6a Progressively slacken and remove the retaining bolts arrowed...

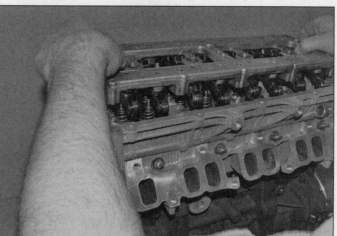

9.6b ...and lift off the rocker arm carrier

9.11a Lubricate the camshafts and cylinder head bearing journals...

9.11b ...then carefully lower the camshafts into position

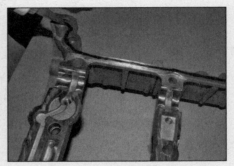

9.12a Apply a 2.5 mm bead of sealant around the outer mating surface of the camshaft carrier...

in the reverse of the sequence shown **(see illustration 9.13)**, and then lift the camshaft carrier from the cylinder head.

9 Carefully lift out the camshafts, and place them somewhere clean and safe – the lobes must not be scratched.

Refitting

10 Make sure that the top surfaces of the cylinder head, and in particular the camshaft bearing surfaces and the mating surfaces for the camshaft carrier, are completely clean.

11 Lubricate the camshafts and cylinder head bearing journals with clean engine oil then carefully lower the camshafts into position in the cylinder head **(see illustrations)**.

12 Apply a 2.5 mm bead of sealant (Land Rover recommend WSE-M4G323-A4, or equivalent) around the outer mating surface of the camshaft carrier, then place the carrier in position on the cylinder head **(see illustrations)**. Note: *Install the camshaft carrier within 5 minutes of applying the sealer to the mating surface. Make sure the carrier does not come into contact with the cylinder head, until the correct position for fitting is obtained.*

13 Install the camshaft carrier retaining bolts and tighten them to the specified torque in the sequence shown **(see illustration)**.

14 Refit the timing chain, sprockets, guides and tensioner as described in Section 7.

15 Install the rocker arm carrier using new retaining bolts, then tighten the bolts to the specified torque.

16 Refit the timing chain cover, as described in Section 5.

17 Refit the camshaft cover, as described in Section 4.

18 Refit the fuel rail as described in Chapter 4A Section 12.

19 Refit the brake servo vacuum pump as described in Section.

10 Cylinder head – removal, inspection and refitting

Removal

1 Disconnect the battery negative terminal (refer to Chapter 5 Section 4).

2 Drain the cooling system as described in Chapter 1 Section 47.

3 Remove the camshafts and hydraulic rockers as described in Section 9.

4 Remove the exhaust manifold as described in Chapter 4A Section 16.

5 Remove the inlet manifold as described in Chapter 4A Section 15.

6 Remove the EGR cooler as described in Chapter 4B Section 2.

7 Remove the alternator as described in Chapter 5 Section 6.

8 Undo the four bolts and remove the alternator mounting bracket from the cylinder head.

9 Undo the retaining nuts and disconnect the glow plug wiring harness from the glow plugs and cylinder head.

10 Check around the head and the engine bay that there is nothing still attached to the cylinder head, nor anything which would prevent it from being lifted away.

11 Working in the reverse order of the tightening sequence **(see illustration 10.35a)**, loosen the cylinder head bolts by half a turn at a time, until they are all loose. Remove the head bolts, and discard them – Land Rover state that they must not be re-used, even if they appear to be serviceable.

12 Lift the cylinder head away, and use assistance if possible, as it is a heavy assembly. Do not, under any circumstances, lever the head between the mating surfaces, as this will certainly damage the sealing surfaces for the gasket, leading to leaks.

9.12b ...then place the carrier in position on the cylinder head

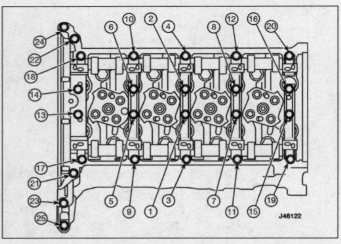

9.13 Tightening sequence for the camshaft carrier retaining bolts

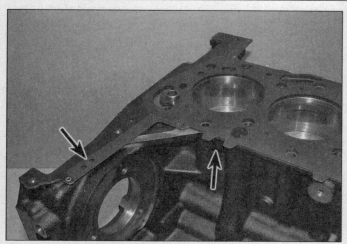

10.15 Teeth and holes in the gasket (arrowed), which indicate the gasket's thickness

10.18 Using a dial test indicator to measure the piston protrusion

13 Once the head has been removed, recover the gasket from the two dowels and discard the gasket, as a new one will be required on refitting, see paragraph 15.

Inspection

14 If required, dismantling and inspection of the cylinder head is covered in Chapter 2C Section 6 and Chapter 2C Section 7.

Cylinder head gasket selection

15 Examine the old cylinder head gasket for manufacturer's identification markings. These will be in the form of teeth (one, two or three) on the front edge of the gasket and/or holes in the gasket, which indicate the gasket's thickness **(see illustration)**.

16 Unless new components have been fitted, or the cylinder head has been machined (skimmed), the new cylinder head gasket must be of the same type as the old one. Purchase the required gasket, and proceed to paragraph 22.

17 If the head has been machined, or if new pistons have been fitted, it is likely that a head gasket of different thickness to the original will be needed. Gasket selection is made on the basis of the measured piston protrusion above the cylinder head gasket surface (the protrusion must fall within the range specified at the start of this Chapter).

18 To measure the piston protrusion, anchor a dial test indicator (DTI) to the top face (cylinder head gasket mating face) of the cylinder block, and zero the gauge on the gasket mating face **(see illustration)**.

19 Rest the gauge probe above No 1 piston crown, and turn the crankshaft slowly by hand until the piston reaches TDC (its maximum height). Measure and record the maximum piston projection at TDC.

20 Repeat the measurement for the remaining pistons, and record the results.

21 If the measurements differ from piston to piston, take the highest figure, and use this to determine the thickness of the head gasket

required. See Specifications at the start of this Chapter.

Preparation for refitting

22 The mating faces of the cylinder head and cylinder block must be perfectly clean before refitting the head. Use a hard plastic or wooden scraper to remove all traces of gasket and carbon; also clean the piston crowns. **Note:** *The new head gasket has rubber-coated surfaces, which could be damaged from sharp edges or debris left by a metal scraper.*

23 Take particular care when cleaning the piston crowns, as the soft aluminium alloy is easily damaged.

24 Make sure that the carbon is not allowed to enter the oil and water passages. This is particularly important for the lubrication system, as carbon could block the oil supply to the engine's components. Using adhesive tape and paper, seal the water, oil and bolt holes in the cylinder block.

25 To prevent carbon entering the gap between the pistons and bores, smear a little grease in the gap. After cleaning each piston, use a small brush to remove all traces of grease and carbon from the gap, then wipe away the remainder with a clean rag. Clean all the pistons in the same way.

26 Check the mating surfaces of the cylinder block and the cylinder head for nicks, deep scratches and other damage (refer to the Note in paragraph 22). If slight, they may be removed carefully with a file, but if excessive, machining may be the only alternative to renewal.

27 If warpage of the cylinder head gasket surface is suspected, use a straight-edge to check it for distortion. Refer to Chapter 2C Section 7 if necessary.

28 Ensure that the cylinder head bolt holes in the crankcase are clean and free of oil. Syringe or soak up any oil left in the bolt holes. This is most important in order that the correct bolt tightening torque can be applied, and to prevent the possibility of the block

being cracked by hydraulic pressure when the bolts are tightened.

Refitting

29 Make sure the timing is still set at 50° BTDC (see Section 3). This will eliminate any risk of piston-to-valve contact as the cylinder head is refitted.

30 To guide the cylinder head into position, screw two long studs (or old cylinder head bolts with the heads cut off, and slots cut in the ends to enable the bolts to be unscrewed) into the end cylinder head bolt locations on the manifold side of the cylinder block.

31 Ensure that the cylinder head locating dowels are in place in the cylinder block, then fit the new cylinder head gasket over the dowels **(see illustration)**. The gasket can only be fitted one way, with the teeth to determine the gasket thickness at the front **(see illustration 10.15)**. Take care to avoid damaging the gasket's rubber coating.

32 Lower the cylinder head into position on the gasket, ensuring that it engages correctly over the guide studs and dowels.

33 Fit the new cylinder head bolts to the remaining bolt locations and screw them in as far as possible by hand.

34 Unscrew the two guide studs from

10.31 Locate the new cylinder head gasket over the dowels correctly

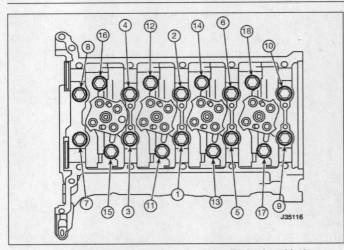

10.35a Tightening sequence for the cylinder head bolts

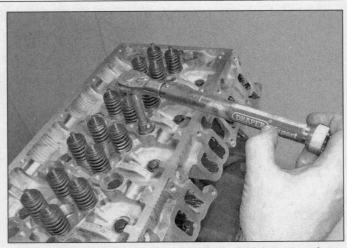

10.35b Tighten the cylinder head bolts in the initial stages using a torque wrench

the cylinder block, then screw in the two remaining new cylinder head bolts as far as possible by hand.

35 Working in the sequence shown, tighten all the cylinder head bolts through the specified Stages as given in the Specifications at the beginning of this Chapter **(see illustrations)**.

36 The last stage involves tightening the bolts through an angle, rather than to a torque. Each bolt in sequence must be rotated through the specified angle – special angle gauges are available from tool outlets **(see illustration)**. As a guide, a 180° angle is equivalent to half a turn, and this is easily judged by assessing the start and end positions of the socket handle.

37 The remainder of the refitting procedure is a reversal of the removal procedure, bearing in mind the following points:

a) Refit the alternator as described in Chapter 5 Section 6.
b) Refit the EGR cooler as described in Chapter 4B Section 2.
c) Refit the inlet manifold as described in Chapter 4A Section 15.
d) Refit the exhaust manifold as described in Chapter 4A Section 16.
e) Refit the camshafts and hydraulic rockers as described in Section 9.
f) Refit the timing chain as described in Section 7.

g) Refit the camshaft cover as described in Section 4.
h) Refill the cooling system as described in Chapter 1 Section 47.
i) Check and if necessary top-up the engine oil level as described in Weekly checks.
j) Before starting the engine, read through the section on engine restarting after overhaul, in Chapter 2C Section 17.

11 Sump – removal and refitting

Removal

Note: A new sump (oil pan) will be required for refitting, as the oil pan will be irreparably distorted during removal.

1 Firmly apply the handbrake, then jack up the front of the vehicle and support it securely on axle stands (see Jacking and vehicle support).

2 Drain the engine oil and then refit the drain plug and tighten. Although not strictly necessary as part of the dismantling procedure, owners are advised to remove and discard the oil filter, so that it can be renewed

with the oil (refer to Chapter 1 Section 5 if necessary).

3 Progressively unscrew and remove the sump retaining bolts/nuts. There are eleven bolts and five nuts/studs securing the sump in position (Land Rover recommend that the five nuts and studs are removed first, noting there fitted position for refitting).

4 A conventional sump gasket is not used, and sealant is used instead. Unfortunately, the use of sealant can make removal of the sump more difficult. If care is taken not to damage the surfaces, the sealant can be cut around using a scraper or a sharp knife. On no account lever between the mating faces, as this will almost certainly damage them, resulting in leaks when finished.

5 Once the sump is free, lower it down and discard it, as a new one will be required for refitting (**Note:** If the old sump is re-used it is likely to leak, as it will be distorted on removal).

Refitting

6 On reassembly, thoroughly clean and degrease the mating surfaces of the lower crankcase, removing all traces of sealant, then use a clean rag to wipe out the underside of the engine.

7 To aid installation of the new sump, screw in the five locating studs (if removed) into lower crankcase.

8 Apply a 3 mm bead of sealant (Land Rover recommend WSE-M4G323-A4, or equivalent) to the new sump flange, making sure the bead is around the inside edge of the bolt holes **(see illustration)**. **Note:** The sump must be refitted within 5 minutes of applying the sealant.

9 Fit the sump over the locating studs, and fit the retaining nuts. Refit the remaining bolts and tighten all the bolts hand tight only at this stage.

10 Working in a progressive diagonal sequence, tighten all the bolts/nuts to the specified torque, in the two Stages given in the Specifications.

10.36 Using an angle tightening gauge to tighten the cylinder head bolts through the final stages

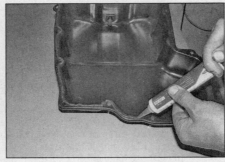

11.8 Apply a 3 mm bead of sealant to the sump flange

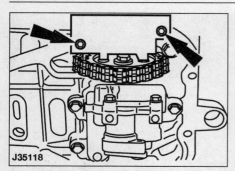

12.2 Aligning the oil pump sprocket using the Land Rover special tool bolted to the lower crankcase

12.3 Undo the retaining bolts and remove the pick-up pipe from the oil pump

12.4 Disengage the oil pump sprocket from the chain and remove the oil pump

11 Check that the new sump drain plug, fitted to the new sump, is tightened to the correct torque.

12 Lower the vehicle to the ground, and refill the engine with oil. If removed, fit a new oil filter with reference to Chapter 1 Section 5.

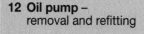
12 Oil pump – removal and refitting

Note: *The following procedure is for removal and refitting of the oil pump. If the oil pump drive chain or tensioner requires renewal, the engine timing chain will need to be removed (see Section 7).*

Removal

1 Remove the sump as described in Section 11.

2 Special tool (303-705) is used to align the oil pump sprocket. Bolt the tool/plate to the sump flange so that it sits flush with the oil pump drive sprocket (see illustration).

3 Undo the retaining bolts and remove the pick-up pipe from the oil pump (see illustration). Remove and discard the O-ring seal and obtain a new O-ring for refitting.

4 Undo the retaining bolts and release the oil pump from the lower crankcase. Push or pull on the oil pump drive chain to compress the tensioner, then disengage the oil pump sprocket from the chain and remove the oil pump (see illustration).

Refitting

Caution: *The oil pump sprocket and crankshaft sprocket must be kept in line with each other, so that the chain runs straight. Use manufacturers special tool or a DTI gauge to make sure they are aligned correctly.*

5 Refit the oil pump to the lower crankcase, installing the drive chain to the sprocket on the oil pump. Only finger-tighten the oil pump retaining bolts at this stage.

6 Slide the oil pump until the drive sprocket sits flush with the special tool, as aligned on removal (see illustration 12.2). With the oil pump in position, tighten the retaining bolts to the specified torque.

7 Ensuring that the alignment of the pump is correct, undo the retaining bolts and remove the special tool from the sump flange.

8 If the oil pump has been removed as part of an engine overhaul procedure, and the timing chain cover has been removed, the oil pump sprocket alignment can be checked with a DTI gauge.

9 Mount the gauge on the cylinder block with the probe against the inner teeth of the crankshaft sprocket (see illustrations). Zero the gauge in this position.

10 Without moving the gauge body, move the probe to the oil pump sprocket (see illustration). Move the oil pump as necessary until the two gauge readings are the same,

12.9a Mount the DTI gauge on the cylinder block...

12.10 Move the probe to the oil pump sprocket and move the pump as necessary until the two gauge readings are the same

then tighten the pump retaining bolts to the specified torque.

11 Fit a new O-ring seal to the pick-up pipe, then refit the pick-up pipe to the oil pump (see illustration).

12 Refit the sump with reference to Section 11.

13 Oil pressure warning light switch – removal and refitting

Removal

1 The oil pressure warning light switch is screwed into the housing in front of the oil

12.9b ...with the probe against the inner teeth of the crankshaft sprocket, then zero the gauge

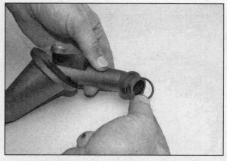

12.11 Fit a new O-ring seal to the pick-up pipe

13.1 Oil pressure warning light switch location

14.4 Disconnect the coolant hoses from the top of the housng...

filter on the left-hand side of the engine **(see illustration)**.

2 To improve access to the switch, it may be necessary to apply the handbrake, then jack up the front of the vehicle and support it on axle stands (see *Jacking and vehicle support*).

3 Unplug the wiring from the switch and unscrew it from the filter housing. Be prepared for some oil loss.

Refitting

4 Refitting is the reverse of the removal procedure. Apply a thin smear of suitable sealant to the switch threads, and tighten it securely.

5 Check the engine oil level and top-up as necessary (see *Weekly checks*).

6 Check for correct warning light operation and for signs of oil leaks, once the engine has been restarted and warmed-up to normal operating temperature.

14 Oil filter housing and cooler – removal and refitting

Removal

1 The oil filter housing is mounted on the left-hand side of the cylinder block, with the oil cooler bolted to its upper face.

2 Firmly apply the handbrake, then jack up the front of the vehicle and support it securely on axle stands (see *Jacking and vehicle support*).

3 Position a container beneath the oil filter to catch escaping oil and coolant.

4 Drain the cooling system as described in Chapter 1 Section 47, or clamp the two oil cooler coolant hoses to minimise spillage, then remove the clips, and disconnect the hoses from the oil cooler housing **(see illustration)**. Be prepared for coolant spillage.

5 Disconnect the oil pressure warning light switch wiring connector **(see illustration 13.1)**.

6 Unscrew the six retaining bolts and withdraw the oil filter housing and cooler from the cylinder block. Collect the gasket and note a new gasket must be used on refitting **(see illustrations)**.

7 With the filter housing removed, if required, undo the four bolts and separate the oil cooler from the filter housing. Collect the gasket noting a new gasket must be used on refitting.

Refitting

8 Refitting is a reversal of removal, bearing in mind the following points:

a) Use new gaskets.
b) Fit the oil cooler mounting bolts, and tighten them securely.
c) Tighten the oil filter housing retaining bolts to the specified torque.
d) On completion, lower the vehicle to the ground. Check and if necessary top-up the oil and coolant levels, then start the engine and check for signs of oil or coolant leakage.

15 Crankshaft oil seals – renewal

Timing chain end seal

1 Remove the crankshaft pulley with reference to Section 6.

2 Land Rover technicians use a special seal-removing and refitting tool (303-679), but an adequate substitute can be achieved using a three-legged puller and three bolts. Turn the seal anticlockwise, using the tool, to remove the crankshaft oil seal from the timing chain cover **(see illustrations)**.

3 Wipe clean the oil seal contact surfaces and seating, and clean up any sharp edges or burrs which might damage the new seal as it

14.6a Unscrew the bolts (arrowed)...

14.6b ...withdraw the oil filter housing from the cylinder block...

14.6c ...and collect the rubber gasket

15.2a Tool for removing the oil seal, using a three-legged puller and three bolts...

15.2b ...insert the bolts into the recesses (arrowed) in the seal...

15.2c ...and rotate the seal anticlockwise to remove

is fitted, or which might cause the seal to leak once in place.

4 The new oil seal will be supplied fitted with a locating sleeve, which must not be removed prior to fitting.

5 Locate the new seal (lips facing inwards) over the end of the crankshaft, press the seal squarely and fully into position in the cover, then remove the locating sleeve **(see illustrations)**.

6 Using the special tool used on removal, turn the seal clockwise until it is located securely into the timing chain cover.

7 Refit the crankshaft pulley with reference to Section 6.

Flywheel end seal

8 Remove the transmission as described in Chapter 7A Section 5, and the clutch assembly as described in Chapter 6 Section 2.

9 Remove the flywheel as described in Section 16.

10 Unbolt and remove the oil seal carrier, noting that the seal is renewed complete with the carrier, and is not available separately. A complete set of new carrier retaining bolts should also be obtained for reassembly.

11 Clean the end of the crankshaft, polishing off any burrs or raised edges, which may have caused the seal to fail in the first place. Clean also the seal carrier mating face on the engine block, using a suitable solvent for degreasing if necessary.

12 The new oil seal is supplied fitted with a locating sleeve, which must not be removed prior to fitting. It should also have a centring sleeve supplied with the seal **(see illustration)**.

13 Apply suitable sealant (Loctite 510, or equivalent) to the oil seal carrier, at the cylinder block-to-lower crankcase jointing point **(see illustration)**.

14 Offer up the carrier into position, feeding the locating sleeve over the end of the crankshaft **(see illustration)**. Insert the new seal carrier retaining bolts, and tighten them all by hand. Remove the locating sleeve.

15 Using the special centring sleeve supplied with the seal, centre the oil seal carrier around the end of the crankshaft **(see illustration)**.

16 Ensuring that the correct alignment of the carrier is maintained, work in a diagonal sequence, tightening the retaining bolts to the specified torque. Remove the seal centring sleeve.

17 The remainder of the reassembly procedure is the reverse of dismantling, referring to the relevant text for details where required. Check for signs of oil leakage when the engine is restarted.

15.5a Locate the new seal over the end of the crankshaft using the locating sleeve...

15.5b ...press the seal into position and remove the locating sleeve

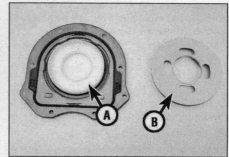

15.12 Flywheel end oil seal locating sleeve (A) and centering sleeve (B)

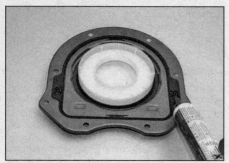

15.13 Apply sealant to the oil seal carrier, at the cylinder block-to-lower crankcase jointing point

15.14 Offer up the oil seal carrier, feeding the locating sleeve over the end of the crankshaft

15.15 Using the centering sleeve, centre the oil seal carrier around the end of the crankshaft

16.2 Locating dowel (arrowed) to align the flywheel when refitting

16.3a Use a tool like this (arrowed) to lock the flywheel …

16.3b … while the retaining bolts (arrowed) are slackened

16 Flywheel – removal, inspection and refitting

Removal

1 Remove the transmission as described in Chapter 7A Section 5, and the clutch assembly as described in Chapter 6 Section 2.

2 There is a locating dowel in the end of the crankshaft, to ensure correct alignment during refitting **(see illustration)**.

3 Prevent the flywheel from turning by locking the ring gear teeth, or by bolting a strap between the flywheel and the cylinder block/crankcase. Slacken the bolts evenly until all are free **(see illustrations)**.

4 Remove each bolt in turn and ensure that new replacements are obtained for reassembly. These bolts are subjected to severe stresses and so must be renewed, regardless of their apparent condition, whenever they are disturbed.

5 Withdraw the flywheel, remembering that it is very heavy – do not drop it.

Inspection

6 A conventional solid flywheel or a dual-mass flywheel may be fitted, depending on engine power output and year of manufacture.

Single-mass (solid) flywheel

7 Examine the flywheel for wear or chipping of the ring gear teeth. Renewal of the ring gear is not possible and if the wear or chipping is significant, a new flywheel will be required.

16.17 Use a torque wrench to tighten the flywheel retaining bolts to the initial settings

8 Examine the flywheel for scoring of the clutch face. If the clutch face is scored significantly, a new flywheel will be required.

9 If there is any doubt about the condition of the flywheel, seek the advice of a Land Rover dealer or engine reconditioning specialist.

Dual-mass flywheel

10 A dual-mass flywheel has the effect of reducing engine and transmission vibrations and harshness. The flywheel consists of a primary mass and a secondary mass constructed in such a way that the secondary mass is allowed to rotate slightly in relation to the primary mass. Springs within the assembly restrict this movement to set limits.

11 Dual-mass flywheels have earned an unenviable reputation for unreliability and have been known to fail at quite low mileages (sometimes as low as 20 000 miles). As well as the checks described above in paragraphs 7 and 8, some additional checks should be performed as follows.

12 Look through the bolt hole and inspection openings in the secondary mass and check for any visible damage in the area of the centre bearing.

13 Place your thumbs on the clutch face of the secondary mass at the 3 o'clock and 9 o'clock positions and try to rock it. The maximum movement should not exceed 3 mm. Repeat this check with your thumbs at the 12 o'clock and 6 o'clock positions.

14 Rotate the secondary mass clockwise and anti-clockwise. It should move freely in both directions until spring resistance is felt, with no abnormal grating or rattling noises. The maximum rotational movement should not exceed a distance of five teeth of the ring gear.

15 If there is any doubt about the condition of the flywheel, seek the advice of your local Land Rover dealer or engine reconditioning specialist. They will be able to advise if the flywheel is an acceptable condition, or whether renewal is necessary.

Refitting

16 Fit the flywheel to the crankshaft so that all bolt holes align (it will fit only one way) check the dowel is located correctly. Apply suitable locking compound to the threads of the new bolts, then insert them.

17 Lock the flywheel by the method used on dismantling. Working in a diagonal sequence, tighten the bolts to the specified Stage 1 torque wrench setting **(see illustration)**.

18 Then working in the same diagonal sequence, tighten them to the specified Stage 2 torque wrench setting.

19 Stage 3 involves tightening the bolts though an angle, rather than to a torque. Each bolt must be rotated through the specified angle – special angle gauges are available from tool outlets.

20 The remainder of reassembly is the reverse of the removal procedure, referring to the relevant text for details where required.

17 Engine/transmission mountings – inspection and renewal

General

1 The engine/transmission mountings seldom require attention, but broken or deteriorated mountings should be renewed immediately, or the added strain placed on the driveline components may cause damage or wear.

2 While separate mountings may be removed and refitted individually, if more than one is disturbed at a time (such as if the engine/transmission unit is removed from its mountings), they must be reassembled and their nuts/bolts tightened in the position marked on removal.

3 On reassembly, the complete weight of the engine/transmission unit must not be taken by the mountings until all are correctly aligned with the marks made on removal. Tighten the engine/transmission mounting nuts and bolts to their specified torque settings.

Inspection

4 During the check, the engine/transmission unit must be raised slightly, to remove its weight from the mountings.

5 Firmly apply the handbrake, then jack up the front of the vehicle and support it securely on axle stands (see *Jacking and vehicle support*). Position a jack under the sump, or under the transmission, with a large block of wood between the jack head and the sump/transmission, then carefully raise the engine/

17.10 Undo the two lower mounting bolts...

17.11 Undo the upper securing nut

transmission just enough to take the weight off the mountings.

 Warning: Do not place any part of your body under the engine when it is supported only by the jack.

6 Check the mountings to see if the rubber is cracked, hardened or separated from the metal components. Sometimes the rubber will split right down the centre.

7 Check for relative movement between each mounting bracket and the engine/transmission or body (use a large screwdriver or lever to attempt to move the mountings). If movement is noted, lower the engine and check the tightness of the mounting nuts/bolts.

Renewal

Engine mountings

8 If not already done, firmly apply the handbrake, then jack up the front of the vehicle and support it securely on axle stands (see *Jacking and vehicle support*).

9 Either support the weight of the engine assembly from underneath, using a trolley jack and a suitable flat piece of wood between

the jack head and the sump, or preferably, from above by attaching a suitable hoist to the engine.

10 With the engine securely supported, undo the bolts securing the lower part of the engine mounting to the chassis **(see illustration)**.

11 Undo the nut securing the top of the mounting to the mounting bracket on the cylinder block **(see illustration)**.

12 Carefully raise the engine slightly, taking care not to damage any hoses or cables, and withdraw the mounting from between the engine mounting bracket and the chassis.

17.15a Right-hand transmission mounting

13 Refitting is a reversal of removal, tightening all nuts and bolts to the specified torque. Tighten the nut securing the mounting to the engine bracket finger tight initially, then finally tighten them once the weight of the engine is again taken by the mounting.

Transmission mounting

14 If not already done, firmly apply the handbrake, then jack up the front of the vehicle and support it securely on axle stands (see *Jacking and vehicle support*).

15 Undo the upper and lower retaining nuts securing the mounting to the transmission bracket and chassis **(see illustrations)**. Note the left-hand mounting has a heat shield around it, to prevent the rubber getting damaged, as it is close to the exhaust pipe.

16 Position a trolley jack under the transmission with a suitable flat piece of wood between the jack head and transmission casing. Raise the jack just sufficiently to withdraw the mounting from between the mounting brackets. Take great care not to place undue strain on surrounding components.

17 Refitting is a reversal of removal, tightening all bolts to the specified torque, where given.

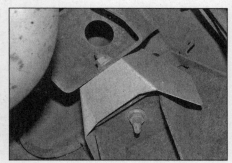

17.15b Left-hand transmission mounting (with heat shield)...

Notes

Chapter 2 Part B
2.4 litre engine in-vehicle repair procedures

Contents

Degrees of difficulty

Easy, suitable for novice with little experience	Fairly easy, suitable for beginner with some experience	Fairly difficult, suitable for competent DIY mechanic	Difficult, suitable for experienced DIY mechanic	Very difficult, suitable for expert DIY or professional

Specifications

General

Engine type.	Four-cylinder, in-line, double overhead camshaft
Designation	DuraTorq-TDCi
Engine code	DT244
Power output	90kW/121bhp
Capacity	2402 cc
Bore	89.9 mm
Stroke	94.6 mm
Compression ratio	17.5 : 1
Firing order.	1-3-4-2 (No 1 cylinder at timing chain end)
Direction of crankshaft rotation	Clockwise (seen from front of vehicle)

Cylinder head

Piston protrusion:	Thickness of cylinder head gasket
0.310 to 0.400 mm	1.10 mm (1 hole/tooth)
0.401 to 0.450 mm	1.15 mm (2 holes/teeth)
0.451 to 0.500 mm	1.20 mm (3 holes/teeth)
Maximum permissible gasket surface distortion	0.10 mm

Lubrication

Engine oil type/specification	See Lubricants, fluids and tyre pressures
Engine oil capacity	7.0 litres
Oil pressure – minimum (engine at operating temperature):	
At idle	1.25 bars
At 2000 rpm	2.00 bars

Torque wrench settings

	Nm	lbf ft
Auxiliary drivebelt idler pulley bolt	47	35
Big-end bearing cap bolts: *		
Stage 1	25	18
Stage 2	60	44
Stage 3	Angle-tighten a further 90°	

Torque wrench settings (continued)

	Nm	lbf ft
Camshaft carrier bolts:		
Stage 1 – bolts 1 to 22	23	17
Stage 2 – bolts 23 and 24.	10	7
Camshaft cover	10	7
Camshaft position sensor	10	7
Camshaft sprocket bolts	33	24
Coolant outlet elbow bolts	23	17
Coolant pump bolts	23	17
Cooling fan pulley bracket bolts.	47	35
Crankshaft oil seal carrier bolts	10	7
Crankshaft position sensor	7	5
Crankshaft position sensor mounting bracket bolts	25	18
Crankshaft pulley bolts: *		
Stage 1	45	33
Stage 2	Angle-tighten a further 120°	
Cylinder head bolts: *		
Stage 1:		
Bolts 1 to 10	20	15
Bolts 11 to 18	10	7
Stage 2:		
Bolts 1 to 10	40	29
Bolts 11 to 18	20	15
Stage 3:		
Bolts 1 to 10	Angle-tighten a further 180°	
Bolts 11 to 18	Angle-tighten a further 180°	
Bolt 19	10	7
Engine crossmember bolts.	70	52
Engine/transmission mountings:		
Engine mounting-to-engine bracket.	103	76
Engine mounting-to-engine crossmember.	40	30
Transmission mounting-to-subframe:		
5-speed transmissions	40	30
6-speed transmissions	55	41
Transmission mounting-to-transmission:		
5-speed transmissions	55	41
6-speed transmissions	80	59
Flywheel bolts: *		
Stage 1	15	11
Stage 2	30	22
Stage 3	75	55
Stage 4	Angle-tighten a further 45°	
Fuel injection pump sprocket bolts	32	24
Lower crankcase/ladder to cylinder block	23	17
Main bearing cap bolts: *		
Stage 1	15	11
Stage 2	20	15
Stage 3	35	26
Stage 4	80	59
Stage 5	Angle-tighten a further 90°	
Oil filter housing bolts.	23	17
Oil pump bolts	10	7
Oil pump pick-up pipe	10	7
Power steering pump and alternater mounting bracket bolts	22	16
Power steering pump bolts	23	17
Rocker arm carrier bolts:		
Stage 1	10	7
Stage 2	Angle-tighten a further 30°	
Sump bolts:		
Stage 1	7	5
Stage 2	14	10
Sump oil drain plug	23	17
Timing chain cover:		
Nuts	10	7
Bolts	14	10
Timing chain guide retaining bolts	15	11
Timing chain tensioner	15	11
Transmission-to-engine bolts.	40	30

Use new nuts/bolts

1 General Information

How to use this Chapter

1 This Part of Chapter 2 is devoted to repair procedures possible while the engine is still installed in the vehicle. Since these procedures are based on the assumption that the engine is installed in the vehicle, if the engine has been removed and mounted on a stand, some of the preliminary dismantling steps outlined will not apply.

2 Information concerning engine/transmission removal and refitting and engine overhaul can be found in Part C of this Chapter.

Engine description

3 The 2.4 litre diesel engines covered in this Part of Chapter 2 are all in-line four-cylinder, turbocharged units, with a 16-valve, double overhead camshaft (DOHC) arrangement. The engine and transmission are mounted in-line at the front of the vehicle, driving the rear wheels via propeller shafts and transfer box to the rear axle.

4 The engine cylinder block casting is of cast-iron and has a lower aluminium crankcase which is bolted to the underside of the cylinder block, with a pressed steel sump bolted under that.

5 The crankshaft runs in five main bearings, the centre main bearing's upper half incorporating thrust washers to control crankshaft endfloat. The connecting rods rotate on horizontally split bearing shells at their big-ends. The pistons are attached to the connecting rods by gudgeon pins which are a floating fit in the connecting rod small-end eyes, secured by circlips. The aluminium alloy pistons are fitted with three piston rings – two compression rings and an oil control ring.

6 The inlet and exhaust valves are each closed by coil springs. They operate in guides which are shrink-fitted into the cylinder head, as are the valve seat inserts.

7 The double overhead camshaft sprockets and the high-pressure fuel injection pump sprocket are driven by a chain from a sprocket on the crankshaft. The camshafts operate the 16 valves via roller-rocker arms with hydraulic clearance adjusters. The rocker arms and clearance adjusters are located in an aluminium carrier bolted to the cylinder head. Each camshaft rotates in five bearings that are machined directly in the cylinder head and the (bolted on) bearing caps. This means that the bearing caps are not available separately from the cylinder head, and must not be interchanged with caps from another engine.

8 The vacuum pump (used for the brake servo and other vacuum actuators) is located on top of the coolant pump, at the left-hand side front of the engine and driven by the auxiliary drivebelt.

9 Lubrication is by means of a chain driven oil pump driven from a sprocket on the crankshaft. The oil pump is mounted below the lower crankcase, and draws oil through a strainer located in the sump. The pump forces oil through an externally-mounted full-flow cartridge-type filter. From the filter, the oil is pumped into a main gallery in the cylinder block/crankcase, from where it is distributed to the crankshaft (main bearings) and cylinder head. An oil cooler is above the oil filter, at the side of the block. The cooler is supplied with coolant from the engine cooling system.

10 While the crankshaft and camshaft bearings receive a pressurised supply, the camshaft lobes and valves are lubricated by splash, as are all other engine components. The undersides of the pistons are cooled by oil, sprayed from nozzles fitted above the upper main bearing shells. The turbocharger receives its own pressurised oil supply.

Repairs with the engine in the vehicle

11 The following major repair operations can be accomplished without removing the engine from the vehicle. However, owners should note that any operation involving the removal of the timing chain, camshafts or cylinder head require careful forethought, depending on the level of skill and the tools and facilities available. Refer to the relevant text for details.

a) *Compression pressure – testing.*
b) *Camshaft cover – removal and refitting.*
c) *Timing chain cover – removal and refitting.*
d) *Timing chain – renewal.*
e) *Timing chain tensioner and sprockets – removal and refitting.*
f) *Camshafts and hydraulic rockers – removal and refitting.*
g) *Cylinder head – removal, overhaul and refitting.*
h) *Crankshaft pulley – removal and refitting.*
i) *Sump – removal and refitting.*
j) *Pistons, connecting rods and big-end bearings – removal and refitting*.*
k) *Oil filter housing and oil cooler – removal and refitting.*
l) *Crankshaft oil seals – renewal.*
m) *Oil pump – removal and refitting.*
n) *Flywheel – removal and refitting.*
o) *Engine/transmission mountings – removal and refitting.*

12 *Although the operation marked with an asterisk can be carried out with the engine in the vehicle (after removal of the sump), it is preferable for the engine to be removed, in the interests of cleanliness and improved access. For this reason, the procedure is described in Chapter 2C Section 9.

2 Compression and leakdown tests – description and interpretation

Compression test

Note: *A compression tester suitable for use with diesel engines will be required for this test.*

Note: *The following procedure is likely to log a fault code in the powertrain control module memory. If the engine management warning light is illuminated after the test, it will be necessary to have the fault code cleared by a Land Rover dealer or suitably equipped garage using specialist diagnostic equipment.*

1 When engine performance is down, or if misfiring occurs which cannot be attributed to the fuel or emissions systems, a compression test can provide diagnostic clues as to the engine's condition. If the test is performed regularly, it can give warning of trouble before any other symptoms become apparent.

2 The engine must be fully warmed-up to normal operating temperature and the battery must be fully charged. The aid of an assistant will also be required.

3 Remove the glow plugs as described in Section.

4 Fit a compression tester to the No 1 cylinder glow plug hole. The type of tester which screws into the plug thread is preferred.

5 Crank the engine for several seconds on the starter motor. After one or two revolutions, the compression pressure should build up to a maximum figure and then stabilise. Record the highest reading obtained.

6 Repeat the test on the remaining cylinders, recording the pressure in each.

7 The cause of poor compression is less easy to establish on a diesel engine than on a petrol engine. The effect of introducing oil into the cylinders (wet testing) is not conclusive, because there is a risk that the oil will sit in the recess on the piston crown, instead of passing to the rings. However, the following can be used as a rough guide to diagnosis.

8 An actual compression pressure value is not stated by Land Rover, however all cylinders should produce very similar pressures. Any significant difference indicates the existence of a fault. Note that the compression should build-up quickly in a healthy engine. Low compression on the first stroke, followed by gradually increasing pressure on successive strokes, indicates worn piston rings. A low compression reading on the first stroke, which does not build-up during successive strokes, indicates leaking valves or a blown head gasket (a cracked head could also be the cause).

9 A low reading from two adjacent cylinders is almost certainly due to the head gasket having blown between them and the presence of coolant in the engine oil will confirm this.

10 On completion, remove the compression tester, and refit the glow plugs as described in Section.

Leakdown test

11 A leakdown test measures the rate at which compressed air fed into the cylinder is lost. It is an alternative to a compression test, and in many ways it is better, since the escaping air provides easy identification of where pressure loss is occurring (piston rings, valves or head gasket).

3.8 Undo the retaining bolt and withdraw the crankshaft position sensor

12 The equipment required for leakdown testing is unlikely to be available to the home mechanic. If poor compression is suspected, have the test performed by a suitably equipped garage.

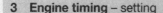

3 Engine timing – setting

Note: *Only turn the engine in the normal direction of rotation – clockwise viewed from the front of the vehicle.*

General information

1 Top Dead Centre (TDC) is the highest point in the cylinder that each piston reaches as it travels up and down when the crankshaft turns. Each piston reaches TDC at the end of the compression stroke and again at the end of the exhaust stroke, but TDC generally refers to piston position on the compression stroke. No 1 piston is at the timing chain end of the engine.

2 Setting No 1 piston at 50° before top dead centre (BTDC) is an essential part of many procedures, such as timing chain removal, cylinder head removal and camshaft removal.

3 The design of the engines covered in this Chapter is such that piston-to-valve contact may occur if the camshaft or crankshaft is turned with the timing chain removed. For this reason, it is important to ensure that the camshaft and crankshaft do not move in relation to each other once the timing chain has been removed from the engine.

Setting

Note: *Service tool 303-698, obtainable from the vehicle manufacturer or a local tool supplier, will be required to set the timing at 50° BTDC.*

Note: *A new crankshaft position sensor will be required for refitting.*

4 Disconnect the battery negative terminal (refer to Chapter 5 Section 4).

5 Firmly apply the handbrake then jack up the front of the vehicle and support it securely on axle stands (see *Jacking and vehicle support*).

3.9 Timing tool inserted into the crankshaft sensor bracket (transmission removed for clarity)

6 A timing hole is provided on the top of the transmission, to permit the crankshaft position sensor to be located.

7 Unclip and remove the crankshaft position sensor heat shield from the top of the transmission.

8 Disconnect the wiring connector from the crankshaft position sensor, undo the retaining bolt and withdraw the sensor from the bellhousing **(see illustration)**. Note that a new sensor will be required for refitting.

9 The special tool can now be inserted into the sensor hole to set the timing at 50° BTDC **(see illustration)**.

10 Turn the crankshaft (by means of the crankshaft pulley) in the direction of engine rotation, until the end of the tool drops into a recess in the outer toothed part of the flywheel. This is the 50° BTDC position.

11 If the engine is being set to 50° BTDC as part of the timing chain removal/renewal procedure, further confirmation of the position can be gained once the timing chain outer cover has been removed. At 50° BTDC, 6 mm timing pins are inserted into the camshaft and fuel pump sprockets, see Section 7.

12 If the holes in the camshaft sprockets do not align, remove the timing pin from the crankshaft and rotate the engine one full turn, then re-install the timing pin.

13 Before rotating the crankshaft again, make sure that the timing pin and where fitted the camshaft sprocket timing pins are

removed. When operations are complete, fit the new crankshaft position sensor as described in Chapter 4A Section 9. Refit all other components removed for access. Do not use the crankshaft timing setting tool to prevent the crankshaft from rotating.

4 Camshaft cover – removal and refitting

Caution: Do not carry out any work on the fuel system with the engine running. Wait for at least 2 minutes after the engine has been stopped before any work is carried out on the fuel system, to make sure the fuel pressure and temperature has dropped sufficiently. Make sure that all the fuel lines are kept clean. Fit blanking plugs to the end of the fuel lines when they are disconnected, to prevent foreign matter entering the components.

Removal

1 Disconnect the battery negative terminal (refer to Chapter 5 Section 4).

2 Refer to Chapter 4A Section 11 and remove the fuel injectors.

3 Undo the bolts securing the fuel supply pipe clamp to the camshaft cover and timing chain housing **(see illustration)**.

4 Disconnect the crankcase ventilation hose from the rear of the camshaft cover **(see illustration)**.

5 Note the locations of the different bolt types, then unscrew the twelve retaining bolts (one was securing the fuel pipe bracket) and lift the camshaft cover off the cylinder head. Note that the bolts are captive in the camshaft cover and cannot be completely removed. Recover the gasket and discard it – a new gasket and fuel injector seals will be required for refitting.

Refitting

6 Thoroughly clean the sealing surfaces of the camshaft cover and the cylinder head.

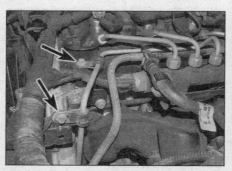

4.3 Undo the fuel pipe bracket securing bolts

4.4 Disconnect breather hose

4.7a Remove the fuel injector seals from the camshaft cover…

4.7b …and press new seals into position

4.8 Locate a new gasket on the camshaft cover ensuring that it fits correctly in the cover groove

7 Using a screwdriver, remove the fuel injector seals from the camshaft cover and press new seals into position (see illustrations).

8 Locate a new gasket on the camshaft cover ensuring that it fits correctly in the cover groove (see illustration).

9 The remainder of refitting is a reversal of removal, noting the following points:

a) Renew all seals, gaskets and supply pipes as noted on removal.

b) Ensure the gasket is correctly seated on the cylinder head, and take care to avoid displacing it as the camshaft cover is lowered into position.

c) Refit the fuel injectors as described in Chapter 4A Section 11.

5 Timing chain cover – removal and refitting

Note: Land Rover technicians use special tools for removing the oil seal and aligning the timing chain cover – see text. A new timing chain cover will be required for refitting, as the cover will be irreparably distorted during removal.

Removal

1 Disconnect the battery negative terminal (refer to Chapter 5 Section 4).

2 Firmly apply the handbrake then jack up the front of the vehicle and support it securely on axle stands (see Jacking and vehicle support).

3 Undo the two retaining bolts, then lift the engine trim cover from the top of the camshaft cover, releasing the locating peg at the rear of the cover from the rear of the cylinder head (see illustrations).

4 Drain the cooling system as described in Chapter 1 Section 47.

5 Remove the radiator cooling fan shroud as described in Chapter 3 Section 5.

6 Remove the auxiliary drivebelt as described in Chapter 1 Section 52.

7 Undo the retraining bolts and remove the mounting bracket from the top of the timing chain cover (see illustration).

8 Remove the alternator, as described in Chapter 5 Section 6. With the alternator removed, slacken and remove the lower bolt

from the mounting bracket (see illustration).

9 Undo the remainder of the bolts from the accessory drive component bracket, and remove it from the front of the timing chain cover (see illustration).

5.3a Lift up the front of the trim cover…

5.7 Remove the mounting bracket

5.9 Remove the accessory drive bracket

10 Undo the nut and two bolts and remove the coolant outlet elbow from the front of the cylinder head (see illustration), the upper hose can remain fitted to the housing and position it to one side. Remove and discard

5.3b …and release the locating peg from the cylinder head

5.8 Remove the lower bolt from the mounting bracket

5.10 Remove the coolant outlet elbow

5.16 Locate a new coolant outlet elbow gasket over the studs

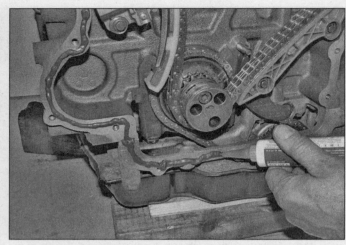

5.17 Apply a 3 mm bead of sealant around the mating surface of the cylinder block and cylinder head

the outlet elbow O-ring seal as a new seal must be used for refitting.

11 To make access easier it may be necessary to undo the bolts securing the power steering pump to the cylinder block, then move it to one side and suitably support it.

12 Remove the crankshaft pulley as described in Chapter 2A Section 6.

13 Remove the crankshaft timing chain end oil seal as described in Chapter 2A Section 15.

14 Undo the retaining bolts and nuts securing the timing chain cover to the cylinder block and cylinder head.

15 Using a couple of well lubricated scrapers or similar, carefully work your way around the timing chain cover and prise it away from the engine. The cover will become distorted on removal, so discard it as a new cover must be used on refitting. Recover the coolant outlet elbow gasket.

Refitting

16 To aid installation of the timing chain

cover, screw in two M10 x 60 mm locating studs into the holes on the centre of the cylinder block. Locate a new coolant elbow gasket over the studs **(see illustration)**.

17 Make sure that the mating surfaces of the cover and the engine casing are clean. Apply a 3 mm bead of sealant (Land Rover recommend WSE-M4G323-A4, or equivalent) around the mating surface of the cylinder block and cylinder head, ensuring that the sealant bead passes around the inside of the retaining bolt holes **(see illustration)**. Apply a line of sealant also, where the cylinder block mates with the cylinder head and the sump.

Caution: Install the timing chain cover within 5 minutes of applying the sealer to the engine casing. Make sure the cover does not come into contact with the engine casing, until the correct position for fitting is obtained.

18 Fit the new timing chain cover remove the

locating studs and install the retaining nuts and bolts hand tight **(see illustration)**.

19 Using a cover aligning tool (Special tool 303-682), insert the tool over the end of the crankshaft to align the cover **(see illustration)**, then tighten all the timing chain cover retaining nuts and bolts to the specified torque. Remove the tool once the cover is in position.

20 Further refitting is a reversal of removal, noting the following points:

a) Fit a new crankshaft oil seal as described in Chapter 2A Section 15.

b) Refit the crankshaft pulley as described in Chapter 2A Section 6.

c) Use a new O-ring seal when refitting the coolant outlet elbow.

d) Refit the cooling fan shroud as described in Chapter 3 Section 5.

e) Refit the auxiliary drivebelt as described in Chapter 1 Section 52.

f) Refill the cooling system as described in Chapter 1 Section 47.

5.18 Fit the new timing chain cover...

5.19 ...then insert the aligning tool over the end of the crankshaft before tightening the retaining bolts

6.5 Crankshaft pulley retaining bolts

6.9a Mark the pulley bolts with quick-drying paint then similarly mark the pulley two flats further on

6.9b Tighten the bolts until the marks align

6 Crankshaft pulley – removal and refitting

Removal

Note: *New crankshaft pulley retaining bolts will be required for refitting.*

1 Disconnect the battery negative terminal (refer to Chapter 5 Section 4).
2 Remove the auxiliary drivebelt, as described in Chapter 1 Section 52.
3 The three bolts which secure the crankshaft pulley must now be slackened. If the vehicle is up on stands, ensure it is adequately supported, as considerable effort may be needed to slacken the bolts.
4 Technicians use a special holding tool (303-1310) which locates over two of the three pulley retaining bolts and prevents it from turning. If this is not available, select a gear, and have an assistant firmly apply the handbrake and footbrake as the bolts are loosened. If this method is unsuccessful, remove the starter motor as described in Section, and lock the flywheel ring gear, using a suitable tool, to prevent the crankshaft from rotating.
5 Unscrew the bolts securing the pulley to the crankshaft, and remove the pulley **(see illustration)**. Discard the bolts and obtain new bolts for refitting.
6 With the pulley removed, it is advisable to check the crankshaft oil seal for signs of oil leakage. If necessary, fit a new seal as described in Chapter 2A Section 15.

Refitting

7 Refit the pulley to the end of the crankshaft, then fit the new pulley securing bolts and tighten them as far as possible before the crankshaft starts to rotate.
8 Holding the pulley against rotation as for removal, first tighten the bolts to the specified Stage 1 torque.
9 Stage 2 involves tightening the bolts though an angle, rather than to a torque. The bolts must be rotated through the specified angle – special angle gauges are available from tool outlets. As a guide, a 120° angle is equivalent to two flats on the retaining bolt, and this is easily judged by marking each bolt with quick-drying paint then similarly marking the pulley two flats further on. Tighten the bolts until the marks align **(see illustrations)**.
10 Refit the auxiliary drivebelt as described in Chapter 1 Section 52.
11 Lower the vehicle to the ground, and reconnect the battery negative lead.

7 Timing chain – removal, inspection and refitting

Note: *Only turn the engine in the normal direction of rotation – clockwise viewed from the front of the vehicle.*

Removal

1 Remove the timing chain cover, as described in Chapter 2A Section 5.
2 Referring to the information in Chapter 2A Section 3, set the engine to 50° BTDC on No 1 cylinder. In this position, insert a 6 mm timing pin (6 mm drill bit) in each camshaft sprocket and into the corresponding hole in the cylinder head **(see illustration)**.
3 Slacken the timing chain tensioner by inserting a small screwdriver into the access hole in the tensioner and releasing the pawl mechanism. Press against the timing chain guide to depress the piston into the tensioner housing. When fully depressed, insert a locking pin (approximately 2 mm diameter) to lock the piston in its compressed position **(see illustration)**.
4 To remove the tensioner, undo the two retaining bolts and remove the timing chain

7.2 Insert 6 mm timing pins (6 mm drill bits), to align the camshaft sprockets

7.3 Insert a pin to lock the tensioner piston in its compressed position

7.4 Remove the timing chain tensioner from the cylinder block, taking care not to remove the locking pin

7.5a Undo the retaining bolts and remove the tensioner timing chain guide ...

tensioner from the cylinder block (see illustration). Note that a new tensioner will be required for refitting.

5 Undo the retaining bolts and remove the tensioner timing chain guide and the fixed timing chain guides from the cylinder block (see illustrations).

6 Holding the fuel injection pump sprocket in position, undo the retaining bolt and remove the sprocket.

7 With the camshafts held in position, undo the camshaft sprocket retaining bolts and remove the camshaft sprockets and timing chain (see illustration). Do not rotate the crankshaft until the timing chain is refitted.

7.5b ... then remove the upper fixed chain guide bolts (arrowed) ...

7.5c ... the middle fixed chain guide bolts (arrowed) ...

7.5d ... and the lower fixed timing chain guide bolts (arrowed)

7.7 Undo the sprocket retaining bolts and remove the camshaft sprockets and timing chain

7.8a Lift the tensioner arm and insert a drill bit (arrowed) through the hole in the arm and behind the spring blade...

7.8b ...then slide the tensioner off the pivot stud

7.8c Collect the spacer plate from inside the crankshaft sprocket

7.17a The coloured links on the timing chain must line up with the timing marks (arrowed) on the camshaft sprockets...

7.17b ...and fuel injection pump sprocket

Note: *Do not rely on the timing pins (6 mm drill bit) to hold the sprockets in position.*

8 To remove the timing chain sprocket from the crankshaft, the oil pump drive chain will need to be removed first. Lift the tensioner arm and insert a suitable drill bit through the hole in the arm and behind the spring blade. With the tensioner now locked in the released position, slide the tensioner off the pivot stud. The chain can now be removed from the sprocket. Undo the retaining bolt and withdraw the sprocket from the crankshaft. Collect the spacer plate (where fitted) from inside the sprocket **(see illustrations)**.

Inspection

Note: *Keep all components identified for position to ensure correct refitting.*

9 Clean all components thoroughly and wipe dry.

10 Examine the fixed chain guides and tensioner guide for excessive wear or other damage. Check the guides for deep grooves made by the timing chain.

11 Examine the timing chain for excessive wear. Hold it horizontally and check how much movement exists in the chain links. If there is any doubt, compare it to a new chain. Renew as necessary.

12 Examine the teeth of the camshaft,

crankshaft and fuel injection pump sprockets for excessive wear and damage.

Refitting

13 Ensure that the crankshaft and camshaft are still set to 50° BTDC on No 1 cylinder, as described in Chapter 2A Section 3.

14 If not already fitted, refit the crankshaft drive sprocket onto the crankshaft and securely tighten the retaining bolt. Refit the oil pump drive chain and tensioner, then hold pressure against the tensioner arm and withdraw the tensioner locking pin (see Chapter 2A Section 12, for further information on refitting the oil pump).

15 Refit the fuel pump sprocket and the exhaust camshaft sprocket, however DO NOT tighten the retaining bolts at this stage.

16 With the timing chain around the inlet camshaft sprocket, and with the coloured link on the chain aligned with the timing mark on the sprocket, refit the timing chain and sprocket. Feed the timing chain around the crankshaft drive sprocket, fuel pump sprocket and exhaust camshaft sprocket.

17 With the timing pins (6 mm drill bits) inserted into the sprockets to re-align them, the coloured links on the timing chain must line up with the timing marks on the sprockets **(see illustrations)**.

18 Fit the new timing chain tensioner to the cylinder block and tighten the retaining bolts to the specified torque. Take care not to remove the locking pin.

19 Refit the timing chain tensioner guide on the upper pivot pin and tighten the retaining bolt to the specified torque setting. Hold pressure against the bottom of the tensioner guide and withdraw the tensioner locking pin. This will then tension the timing chain.

20 Refit the three fixed timing chain guides and tighten the retaining bolts to the specified torque setting.

21 Tighten the camshaft sprocket retaining bolts, and the fuel injection pump sprocket retaining bolts, to the specified torque setting.

Note: *Do not rely on the timing pins (6 mm drill bits) to hold the sprockets in position.*

22 Check that the engine is still set to 50° BTDC (as described in Chapter 2A Section 3), and remove the timing pins (6 mm drill bits) from the sprockets and the timing peg from the crankshaft sensor hole.

23 Turn the engine (in the direction of engine rotation) two full turns. Refit the timing pins and crankshaft timing peg to make sure the engine timing is still set at 50° BTDC (see Chapter 2A Section 3 for further information).

24 Check the tension of the chain then remove the timing pins (6 mm drill bits) from

9.6a Progressively slacken and remove the retaining bolts arrowed…

9.6b …and lift off the rocker arm carrier

9.11a Lubricate the camshafts and cylinder head bearing journals…

the sprockets and the timing peg from the crankshaft sensor hole. Fit the new crankshaft position sensor as described in Chapter 4A Section 9.

25 Refit the timing chain cover as described in Chapter 2A Section 5.

8 Timing chain tensioner and sprockets – removal, inspection and refitting

Timing chain tensioner

1 The timing chain tensioner is removed as part of the timing chain renewal procedure, in Chapter 2A Section 7.

Camshaft sprockets

2 The camshaft sprockets are removed as part of the timing chain renewal procedure, in Chapter 2A Section 7.

Crankshaft sprocket

3 The crankshaft sprocket is removed as part of the timing chain renewal procedure, in Chapter 2A Section 7.

Fuel injection pump sprocket

4 Removal of the injection pump sprocket is described as part of the timing chain renewal procedure, in Chapter 2A Section 7

9 Camshafts and hydraulic rockers – removal and refitting

Note: *New rocker arm carrier retaining bolts will be required for refitting.*
Note: *Only turn the engine in the normal direction of rotation – clockwise viewed from the front of the vehicle.*

Removal

1 Remove the timing chain cover, as described in Chapter 2A Section 5.
2 Referring to the information in Chapter 2A Section 3, set the engine to 50° BTDC on No 1 cylinder. In this position, insert a 6 mm timing pin (6 mm drill bit) in each camshaft sprocket and into the corresponding hole in the cylinder head **(see illustration 7.2)**.
3 Remove the camshaft cover, as described in Chapter 2A Section 4.
4 Remove the fuel rail as described in Chapter 4A Section 12.
5 Remove the brake servo vacuum pump as described in Chapter 10 Section 19.
6 Progressively slacken and remove the retaining bolts and lift off the rocker arm carrier **(see illustrations)**. Note that new retaining bolts will be required for refitting. Note also that further dismantling of the rocker arm carrier is not possible as the rocker arms and

hydraulic clearance adjusters are not available separately.
7 Working as described in Chapter 2A Section 7, remove the timing chain tensioner, timing chain guides and camshaft sprockets.
8 Slacken the camshaft carrier retaining bolts in the reverse of the sequence shown **(see illustration 9.13)**, and then lift the camshaft carrier from the cylinder head.
9 Carefully lift out the camshafts, and place them somewhere clean and safe – the lobes must not be scratched.

Refitting

10 Make sure that the top surfaces of the cylinder head, and in particular the camshaft bearing surfaces and the mating surfaces for the camshaft carrier, are completely clean.
11 Lubricate the camshafts and cylinder head bearing journals with clean engine oil then carefully lower the camshafts into position in the cylinder head **(see illustrations)**.
12 Apply a 2.5 mm bead of sealant (Land Rover recommend WSE-M4G323-A4, or equivalent) around the outer mating surface of the camshaft carrier, then place the carrier in position on the cylinder head **(see illustrations)**. **Note:** *Install the camshaft carrier within 5 minutes of applying the sealer to the mating surface. Make sure the carrier does not come into contact with the cylinder head, until the correct position for fitting is obtained.*
13 Install the camshaft carrier retaining bolts

9.11b …then carefully lower the camshafts into position

9.12a Apply a 2.5 mm bead of sealant around the outer mating surface of the camshaft carrier…

9.12b …then place the carrier in position on the cylinder head

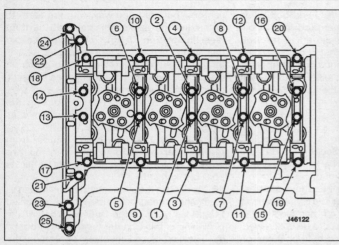

9.13 Tightening sequence for the camshaft carrier retaining bolts

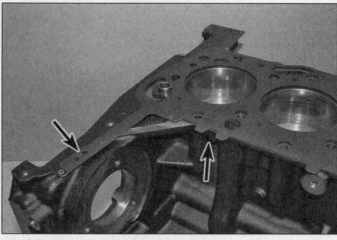

10.15 Teeth and holes in the gasket (arrowed), which indicate the gasket's thickness

and tighten them to the specified torque in the sequence shown (see illustration).

14 Refit the timing chain, sprockets, guides and tensioner as described in Chapter 2A Section 7.

15 Install the rocker arm carrier using new retaining bolts, then tighten the bolts to the specified torque.

16 Refit the timing chain cover, as described in Chapter 2A Section 5.

17 Refit the camshaft cover, as described in Chapter 2A Section 4.

18 Refit the fuel rail as described in Chapter 4A Section 12.

19 Refit the brake servo vacuum pump as described in Chapter 10 Section 19.

10 Cylinder head – removal, inspection and refitting

Removal

1 Disconnect the battery negative terminal (refer to Chapter 5 Section 4).

2 Drain the cooling system as described in Chapter 1 Section 47.

3 Remove the camshafts and hydraulic rockers as described in Chapter 2A Section 9.

4 Remove the exhaust manifold as described in Chapter 4A Section 16.

5 Remove the inlet manifold as described in Chapter 4A Section 15.

6 Remove the EGR cooler as described in Chapter 4B Section 2.

7 Remove the alternator as described in Chapter 5 Section 6.

8 Undo the four bolts and remove the alternator mounting bracket from the cylinder head.

9 Undo the retaining nuts and disconnect the glow plug wiring harness from the glow plugs and cylinder head.

10 Check around the head and the engine bay that there is nothing still attached to the cylinder head, nor anything which would prevent it from being lifted away.

11 Working in the reverse order of the tightening sequence (see illustration 10.35a), loosen the cylinder head bolts by half a turn at a time, until they are all loose. Remove the head bolts, and discard them – Land Rover state that they must not be re-used, even if they appear to be serviceable.

12 Lift the cylinder head away, and use assistance if possible, as it is a heavy assembly. Do not, under any circumstances, lever the head between the mating surfaces, as this will certainly damage the sealing surfaces for the gasket, leading to leaks.

13 Once the head has been removed, recover the gasket from the two dowels and discard the gasket, as a new one will be required on refitting, see paragraph 15.

Inspection

14 If required, dismantling and inspection of the cylinder head is covered in Chapter 2C Section 6 and Chapter 2C Section 7.

Cylinder head gasket selection

15 Examine the old cylinder head gasket for manufacturer's identification markings. These will be in the form of teeth (one, two or three) on the front edge of the gasket and/or holes in the gasket, which indicate the gasket's thickness (see illustration).

16 Unless new components have been fitted, or the cylinder head has been machined (skimmed), the new cylinder head gasket must be of the same type as the old one. Purchase the required gasket, and proceed to paragraph 22.

17 If the head has been machined, or if new pistons have been fitted, it is likely that a head gasket of different thickness to the original will be needed. Gasket selection is made on the basis of the measured piston protrusion above the cylinder head gasket surface (the protrusion must fall within the range specified at the start of this Chapter).

18 To measure the piston protrusion, anchor a dial test indicator (DTI) to the top face (cylinder head gasket mating face) of the cylinder block, and zero the gauge on the gasket mating face (see illustration).

19 Rest the gauge probe above No 1 piston crown, and turn the crankshaft slowly by hand until the piston reaches TDC (its maximum height). Measure and record the maximum piston projection at TDC.

20 Repeat the measurement for the remaining pistons, and record the results.

21 If the measurements differ from piston to piston, take the highest figure, and use this to determine the thickness of the head gasket required. See Specifications at the start of this Chapter.

Preparation for refitting

22 The mating faces of the cylinder head and cylinder block must be perfectly clean before refitting the head. Use a hard plastic or wooden scraper to remove all traces of gasket and carbon; also clean the piston crowns. **Note:** *The new head gasket has rubber-coated surfaces, which could be damaged from sharp edges or debris left by a metal scraper.*

23 Take particular care when cleaning the piston crowns, as the soft aluminium alloy is easily damaged.

10.18 Using a dial test indicator to measure the piston protrusion

24 Make sure that the carbon is not allowed to enter the oil and water passages. This is particularly important for the lubrication system, as carbon could block the oil supply to the engine's components. Using adhesive tape and paper, seal the water, oil and bolt holes in the cylinder block.

25 To prevent carbon entering the gap between the pistons and bores, smear a little grease in the gap. After cleaning each piston, use a small brush to remove all traces of grease and carbon from the gap, then wipe away the remainder with a clean rag. Clean all the pistons in the same way.

26 Check the mating surfaces of the cylinder block and the cylinder head for nicks, deep scratches and other damage (refer to the Note in paragraph 22). If slight, they may be removed carefully with a file, but if excessive, machining may be the only alternative to renewal.

27 If warpage of the cylinder head gasket surface is suspected, use a straight-edge to check it for distortion. Refer to Chapter 2C Section 7 if necessary.

28 Ensure that the cylinder head bolt holes in the crankcase are clean and free of oil. Syringe or soak up any oil left in the bolt holes. This is most important in order that the correct bolt tightening torque can be applied, and to prevent the possibility of the block being cracked by hydraulic pressure when the bolts are tightened.

Refitting

29 Make sure the timing is still set at 50° BTDC (see Chapter 2A Section 3). This will eliminate any risk of piston-to-valve contact as the cylinder head is refitted.

30 To guide the cylinder head into position, screw two long studs (or old cylinder head bolts with the heads cut off, and slots cut in the ends to enable the bolts to be unscrewed) into the end cylinder head bolt locations on the manifold side of the cylinder block.

31 Ensure that the cylinder head locating dowels are in place in the cylinder block, then fit the new cylinder head gasket over the dowels (**see illustration**). The gasket

can only be fitted one way, with the teeth to determine the gasket thickness at the front (**see illustration 10.15**). Take care to avoid damaging the gasket's rubber coating.

32 Lower the cylinder head into position on the gasket, ensuring that it engages correctly over the guide studs and dowels.

33 Fit the new cylinder head bolts to the remaining bolt locations and screw them in as far as possible by hand.

34 Unscrew the two guide studs from the cylinder block, then screw in the two remaining new cylinder head bolts as far as possible by hand.

35 Working in the sequence shown, tighten all the cylinder head bolts through the specified Stages as given in the Specifications at the beginning of this Chapter (**see illustrations**).

36 The last Stage involves tightening the bolts through an angle, rather than to a torque. Each bolt in sequence must be rotated through the specified angle – special angle gauges are available from tool outlets (**see illustration**). As a guide, a 180° angle

10.31 Locate the new cylinder head gasket over the dowels correctly

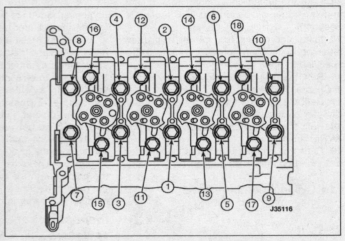

10.35a Tightening sequence for the cylinder head bolts

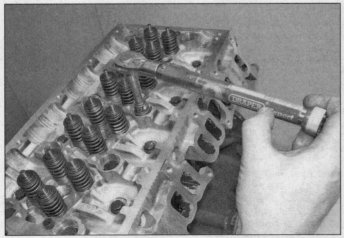

10.35b Tighten the cylinder head bolts in the initial stages using a torque wrench

10.36 Using an angle tightening gauge to tighten the cylinder head bolts through the final stages

is equivalent to half a turn, and this is easily judged by assessing the start and end positions of the socket handle.

37 The remainder of the refitting procedure is a reversal of the removal procedure, bearing in mind the following points:

a) *Refit the alternator as described in Chapter 5 Section 6.*

b) *Refit the EGR cooler as described in Chapter 4B Section 2.*

c) *Refit the inlet manifold as described in Chapter 4A Section 15.*

d) *Refit the exhaust manifold as described in Chapter 4A Section 16.*

e) *Refit the camshafts and hydraulic rockers as described in Chapter 2A Section 9.*

f) *Refit the timing chain as described in Chapter 2A Section 7.*

g) *Refit the camshaft cover as described in Chapter 2A Section 4.*

h) *Refill the cooling system as described in Chapter 1 Section 47.*

i) *Check and if necessary top-up the engine oil level as described in 'Weekly checks'.*

j) *Before starting the engine, read through the section on engine restarting after overhaul, in Chapter 2C Section 17.*

11 Sump – removal and refitting

Removal

Note: *A new sump (oil pan) will be required for refitting, as the oil pan will be irreparably distorted during removal.*

1 Firmly apply the handbrake, then jack up the front of the vehicle and support it securely on axle stands (see *Jacking and vehicle support*).

2 Drain the engine oil, then clean and refit the engine oil drain plug. Inspect the seal for damage, fit a new drain plug and seal if required. Tighten the drain plug to the specified torque. Although not strictly necessary as part of the dismantling procedure, owners are advised to remove and discard the oil filter, so that it can be renewed

with the oil (refer to Chapter 1 Section 5 if necessary).

3 Progressively unscrew and remove the sump retaining bolts/nuts. There are eleven bolts and five nuts/studs securing the sump in position (Land Rover recommend that the five nuts and studs are removed first, noting there fitted position for refitting).

4 A conventional sump gasket is not used, and sealant is used instead. Unfortunately, the use of sealant can make removal of the sump more difficult. If care is taken not to damage the surfaces, the sealant can be cut around using a scraper or a sharp knife. On no account lever between the mating faces, as this will almost certainly damage them, resulting in leaks when finished.

5 Once the sump is free, lower it down and discard it, as a new one will be required for refitting (**Note:** *If the old sump is re-used it is likely to leak, as it will be distorted on removal*).

Refitting

6 On reassembly, thoroughly clean and degrease the mating surfaces of the lower crankcase, removing all traces of sealant, then use a clean rag to wipe out the underside of the engine.

7 To aid installation of the new sump, screw in the five locating studs (if removed) into lower crankcase.

8 Apply a 3 mm bead of sealant (Land Rover recommend WSE-M4G323-A4, or equivalent) to the new sump flange, making sure the bead is around the inside edge of the bolt holes (**see illustration**). **Note:** *The sump must be refitted within 5 minutes of applying the sealant.*

9 Fit the sump over the locating studs, and fit the retaining nuts. Refit the remaining bolts and tighten all the bolts hand tight only at this stage.

10 Working in a progressive diagonal sequence, tighten all the bolts/nuts to the specified torque, in the two Stages given in the Specifications.

11 Lower the vehicle to the ground, and refill the engine with oil. If removed, fit a new oil filter with reference to Chapter 1 Section 5.

11.8 Apply a 3 mm bead of sealant to the sump flange

12 Oil pump – removal and refitting

Note: *The following procedure is for removal and refitting of the oil pump. If the oil pump drive chain or tensioner requires renewal, the engine timing chain will need to be removed (see Chapter 2A, Section 7).*

Removal

1 Remove the sump as described in Chapter 2A Section 11.

2 Special tool (303-705) is used to align the oil pump sprocket. Bolt the tool/plate to the sump flange so that it sits flush with the oil pump drive sprocket (**see illustration**).

3 Undo the retaining bolts and remove the pick-up pipe from the oil pump (**see illustration**). Remove and discard the O-ring seal and obtain a new O-ring for refitting.

4 Undo the retaining bolts and release the oil pump from the lower crankcase. Push or pull on the oil pump drive chain to compress the tensioner, then disengage the oil pump sprocket from the chain and remove the oil pump (**see illustration**).

Refitting

Caution: *The oil pump sprocket and crankshaft sprocket must be kept in line with each other, so that the chain runs straight. Use manufacturers special tool or a DTI gauge to make sure they are aligned correctly.*

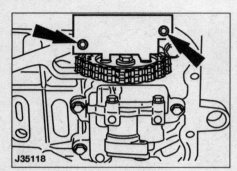

12.2 Aligning the oil pump sprocket using the Land Rover special tool bolted to the lower crankcase

12.3 Undo the retaining bolts and remove the pick-up pipe from the oil pump

12.4 Disengage the oil pump sprocket from the chain and remove the oil pump

12.9a Mount the DTI gauge on the cylinder block...

12.9b ...with the probe against the inner teeth of the crankshaft sprocket, then zero the gauge

5 Refit the oil pump to the lower crankcase, installing the drive chain to the sprocket on the oil pump. Only finger-tighten the oil pump retaining bolts at this stage.

6 Slide the oil pump until the drive sprocket sits flush with the special tool, as aligned on removal (see illustration 12.2). With the oil pump in position, tighten the retaining bolts to the specified torque.

7 Ensuring that the alignment of the pump is correct, undo the retaining bolts and remove the special tool from the sump flange.

8 If the oil pump has been removed as part of an engine overhaul procedure, and the timing chain cover has been removed, the oil pump sprocket alignment can be checked with a DTI gauge.

9 Mount the gauge on the cylinder block with the probe against the inner teeth of the crankshaft sprocket (see illustrations). Zero the gauge in this position.

10 Without moving the gauge body, move the probe to the oil pump sprocket (see illustration). Move the oil pump as necessary until the two gauge readings are the same, then tighten the pump retaining bolts to the specified torque.

11 Fit a new O-ring seal to the pick-up pipe,

then refit the pick-up pipe to the oil pump (see illustration).

12 Refit the sump with reference to Chapter 2A Section 11.

13 Oil pressure warning light switch – removal and refitting

Removal

1 The oil pressure warning light switch is screwed into the housing in front of the oil filter on the left-hand side of the engine (see illustration).

2 To improve access to the switch, it may be necessary to apply the handbrake, then jack up the front of the vehicle and support it on axle stands (see *Jacking and vehicle support*).

3 Unplug the wiring from the switch and unscrew it from the filter housing. Be prepared for some oil loss.

Refitting

4 Refitting is the reverse of the removal procedure. Apply a thin smear of suitable sealant to the switch threads, and tighten it securely.

5 Check the engine oil level and top-up as necessary (see *Weekly checks*).

6 Check for correct warning light operation and for signs of oil leaks, once the engine has been restarted and warmed-up to normal operating temperature.

14 Oil filter housing and cooler – removal and refitting

Removal

1 The oil filter housing is mounted on the left-hand side of the cylinder block, with the oil cooler bolted to its upper face.

2 Firmly apply the handbrake, then jack up the front of the vehicle and support it securely on axle stands (see *Jacking and vehicle support*).

3 Position a container beneath the oil filter to catch escaping oil and coolant.

4 Drain the cooling system as described in Chapter 1 Section 47, or clamp the two oil cooler coolant hoses to minimise spillage, then remove the clips, and disconnect the

12.10 Move the probe to the oil pump sprocket and move the pump as necessary until the two gauge readings are the same

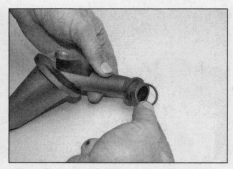

12.11 Fit a new O-ring seal to the pick-up pipe

13.1 Oil pressure warning light switch location

hoses from the oil cooler housing **(see illustration)**. Be prepared for coolant spillage.
5 Disconnect the oil pressure warning light switch wiring connector **(see illustration 13.1)**.
6 Unscrew the six retaining bolts and withdraw the oil filter housing and cooler from the cylinder block. Collect the gasket and note a new gasket must be used on refitting **(see illustrations)**.
7 With the filter housing removed, if required, undo the four bolts and separate the oil cooler from the filter housing. Collect the gasket noting a new gasket must be used on refitting.

Refitting

8 Refitting is a reversal of removal, bearing in mind the following points:
a) *Use new gaskets.*
b) *Fit the oil cooler mounting bolts, and tighten them securely.*
c) *Tighten the oil filter housing retaining bolts to the specified torque.*
d) *On completion, lower the vehicle to the ground. Check and if necessary top-up the oil and coolant levels, then start the engine and check for signs of oil or coolant leakage.*

15 Crankshaft oil seals – renewal

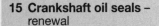

Timing chain end seal

1 Remove the crankshaft pulley with reference to Chapter 2A Section 6.
2 Land Rover technicians use a special seal-removing and refitting tool (303-679), but an adequate substitute can be achieved using a three-legged puller and three bolts. Turn the seal anticlockwise, using the tool, to remove the crankshaft oil seal from the timing chain cover **(see illustrations)**.
3 Wipe clean the oil seal contact surfaces and seating, and clean up any sharp edges or burrs which might damage the new seal as it is fitted, or which might cause the seal to leak once in place.
4 The new oil seal will be supplied fitted with a locating sleeve, which must not be removed prior to fitting.

14.4 Disconnect the coolant hoses from the top of the houisng…

14.6b …withdraw the oil filter housing from the cylinder block…

5 Locate the new seal (lips facing inwards) over the end of the crankshaft, press the seal squarely and fully into position in the cover, then remove the locating sleeve **(see illustrations)**.

15.2a Tool for removing the oil seal, using a three-legged puller and three bolts…

15.2c …and rotate the seal anticlockwise to remove

14.6a Unscrew the bolts (arrowed)…

14.6c …and collect the rubber gasket

6 Using the special tool used on removal, turn the seal clockwise until it is located securely into the timing chain cover.
7 Refit the crankshaft pulley with reference to Chapter 2A Section 6.

15.2b …insert the bolts into the recesses (arrowed) in the seal…

15.5a Locate the new seal over the end of the crankshaft using the locating sleeve…

15.5b …press the seal into position and remove the locating sleeve

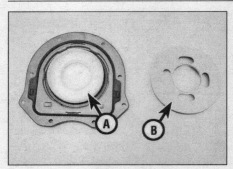

15.12 Flywheel end oil seal locating sleeve (A) and centering sleeve (B)

15.13 Apply sealant to the oil seal carrier, at the cylinder block-to-lower crankcase jointing point

15.14 Offer up the oil seal carrier, feeding the locating sleeve over the end of the crankshaft

15.15 Using the centering sleeve, centre the oil seal carrier around the end of the crankshaft

Flywheel end seal

8 Remove the transmission as described in Chapter 7A Section 5, and the clutch assembly as described in Chapter 6 Section 2.

9 Remove the flywheel as described in Chapter 2A Section 16.

10 Unbolt and remove the oil seal carrier, noting that the seal is renewed complete with the carrier, and is not available separately. A complete set of new carrier retaining bolts should also be obtained for reassembly.

11 Clean the end of the crankshaft, polishing off any burrs or raised edges, which may have caused the seal to fail in the first place. Clean also the seal carrier mating face on the engine block, using a suitable solvent for degreasing if necessary.

12 The new oil seal is supplied fitted with a locating sleeve, which must not be removed prior to fitting. It should also have a centring sleeve supplied with the seal **(see illustration)**.

13 Apply suitable sealant (Loctite 510, or equivalent) to the oil seal carrier, at the cylinder block-to-lower crankcase jointing point **(see illustration)**.

14 Offer up the carrier into position, feeding the locating sleeve over the end of the crankshaft **(see illustration)**. Insert the new seal carrier retaining bolts, and tighten them all by hand. Remove the locating sleeve.

15 Using the special centring sleeve supplied with the seal, centre the oil seal carrier around the end of the crankshaft **(see illustration)**.

16 Ensuring that the correct alignment of

the carrier is maintained, work in a diagonal sequence, tightening the retaining bolts to the specified torque. Remove the seal centring sleeve.

17 The remainder of the reassembly procedure is the reverse of dismantling, referring to the relevant text for details where required. Check for signs of oil leakage when the engine is restarted.

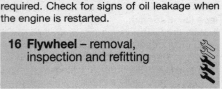

16 Flywheel – removal, inspection and refitting

Removal

1 Remove the transmission as described in, and the clutch assembly as described in Chapter 6 Section 2.

2 There is a locating dowel in the end of the crankshaft, to ensure correct alignment during refitting **(see illustration)**.

3 Prevent the flywheel from turning by locking the ring gear teeth, or by bolting a strap between the flywheel and the cylinder block/crankcase. Slacken the bolts evenly until all are free **(see illustrations)**.

4 Remove each bolt in turn and ensure that new replacements are obtained for reassembly. These bolts are subjected to severe stresses and so must be renewed, regardless of their apparent condition, whenever they are disturbed.

5 Withdraw the flywheel, remembering that it is very heavy – do not drop it.

Inspection

6 A conventional solid flywheel or a dual-mass flywheel may be fitted, depending on engine power output and year of manufacture.

Single-mass (solid) flywheel

7 Examine the flywheel for wear or chipping of the ring gear teeth. Renewal of the ring gear is not possible and if the wear or chipping is significant, a new flywheel will be required.

8 Examine the flywheel for scoring of the clutch face. If the clutch face is scored significantly, a new flywheel will be required.

9 If there is any doubt about the condition of the flywheel, seek the advice of a Land Rover dealer or engine reconditioning specialist.

16.2 Locating dowel (arrowed) to align the flywheel when refitting

16.3a Use a tool like this (arrowed) to lock the flywheel ...

16.3b ... while the retaining bolts (arrowed) are slackened

Dual-mass flywheel

10 A dual-mass flywheel has the effect of reducing engine and transmission vibrations and harshness. The flywheel consists of a primary mass and a secondary mass constructed in such a way that the secondary mass is allowed to rotate slightly in relation to the primary mass. Springs within the assembly restrict this movement to set limits.

11 Dual-mass flywheels have earned an unenviable reputation for unreliability and have been known to fail at quite low mileages (sometimes as low as 20 000 miles). As well as the checks described above in paragraphs 7 and 8, some additional checks should be performed as follows.

12 Look through the bolt hole and inspection openings in the secondary mass and check for any visible damage in the area of the centre bearing.

13 Place your thumbs on the clutch face of the secondary mass at the 3 o'clock and 9 o'clock positions and try to rock it. The maximum movement should not exceed 3 mm. Repeat this check with your thumbs at the 12 o'clock and 6 o'clock positions.

14 Rotate the secondary mass clockwise and anti-clockwise. It should move freely in both directions until spring resistance is felt, with no abnormal grating or rattling noises. The maximum rotational movement should not exceed a distance of five teeth of the ring gear.

15 If there is any doubt about the condition of the flywheel, seek the advice of your local Land Rover dealer or engine reconditioning specialist. They will be able to advise if the flywheel is an acceptable condition, or whether renewal is necessary.

Refitting

16 Fit the flywheel to the crankshaft so that all bolt holes align (it will fit only one way) check the dowel is located correctly. Apply suitable locking compound to the threads of the new bolts, then insert them.

17 Lock the flywheel by the method used on dismantling. Working in a diagonal sequence, tighten the bolts to the specified Stage 1 torque wrench setting **(see illustration)**.

18 Then working in the same diagonal sequence, tighten them to the specified Stage 2 torque wrench setting.

19 Stage 3 involves tightening the bolts though an angle, rather than to a torque. Each bolt must be rotated through the specified angle – special angle gauges are available from tool outlets.

20 The remainder of reassembly is the reverse of the removal procedure, referring to the relevant text for details where required.

---

17 Engine/transmission mountings – inspection and renewal

General

1 The engine/transmission mountings seldom require attention, but broken or deteriorated mountings should be renewed immediately, or the added strain placed on the driveline components may cause damage or wear.

2 While separate mountings may be removed and refitted individually, if more than one is disturbed at a time (such as if the engine/transmission unit is removed from its mountings), they must be reassembled and their nuts/bolts tightened in the position marked on removal.

3 On reassembly, the complete weight of the engine/transmission unit must not be taken by the mountings until all are correctly aligned with the marks made on removal. Tighten the engine/transmission mounting nuts and bolts to their specified torque settings.

Inspection

4 During the check, the engine/transmission unit must be raised slightly, to remove its weight from the mountings.

5 Firmly apply the handbrake, then jack up the front of the vehicle and support it securely on axle stands (see *Jacking and vehicle support*). Position a jack under the sump, or under the transmission, with a large block of wood between the jack head and the sump/transmission, then carefully raise the engine/transmission just enough to take the weight off the mountings.

 Warning: Do not place any part of your body under the engine when it is supported only by the jack.

6 Check the mountings to see if the rubber is cracked, hardened or separated from the metal components. Sometimes the rubber will split right down the centre.

7 Check for relative movement between each mounting bracket and the engine/transmission or body (use a large screwdriver or lever to attempt to move the mountings). If movement is noted, lower the engine and check the tightness of the mounting nuts/bolts.

Renewal

Engine mountings

8 If not already done, firmly apply the handbrake, then jack up the front of vehicle and support it securely on axle stands (see *Jacking and vehicle support*).

9 Either support the weight of the engine assembly from underneath, using a trolley jack and a suitable flat piece of wood between the jack head and the sump, or preferably, from above by attaching a suitable hoist to the engine.

10 With the engine securely supported, undo the bolts securing the lower part of the engine mounting to the chassis **(see illustration)**.

16.17 Use a torque wrench to tighten the flywheel retaining bolts to the initial settings

17.10 Undo the two lower mounting bolts...

17.11 Undo the upper securing nut

17.15a Right-hand transmission mounting

17.15b Left-hand transmission mounting (with heat shield)...

11 Undo the nut securing the top of the mounting to the mounting bracket on the cylinder block **(see illustration)**.

12 Carefully raise the engine slightly, taking care not to damage any hoses or cables, and withdraw the mounting from between the engine mounting bracket and the chassis.

13 Refitting is a reversal of removal, tightening all nuts and bolts to the specified torque. Tighten the nut securing the mounting to the engine bracket finger tight initially, then finally tighten them once the weight of the engine is again taken by the mounting.

Transmission mounting

14 If not already done, firmly apply the handbrake, then jack up the front of the vehicle and support it securely on axle stands (see *Jacking and vehicle support*).

15 Undo the upper and lower retaining nuts securing the mounting to the transmission bracket and chassis **(see illustrations)**. Note the left-hand mounting has a heat shield around it, to prevent the rubber getting damaged, as it is close to the exhaust pipe.

16 Position a trolley jack under the transmission with a suitable flat piece of wood between the jack head and transmission casing. Raise the jack just sufficiently to withdraw the mounting from between the mounting brackets. Take great care not to place undue strain on surrounding components.

17 Refitting is a reversal of removal, tightening all bolts to the specified torque, where given.

Chapter 2 Part C
Engine removal and overhaul procedures

Contents

Degrees of difficulty

Easy, suitable for novice with little experience	**Fairly easy,** suitable for beginner with some experience	**Fairly difficult,** suitable for competent DIY mechanic	**Difficult,** suitable for experienced DIY mechanic	**Very difficult,** suitable for expert DIY or professional

Specifications

Engine identification

Engine type.	Manufacturer's engine code
2.2 litre engine:	
90kW/121bhp.	DT224
2.4 litre engine:	
90kW/121bhp.	DT244

2.2 litre engines

Valve stem-to-guide clearance:

Inlet	0.045 mm
Exhaust	0.055 mm

Cylinder block

Cylinder bore diameter:

Class 1	86.000 to 86.010 mm
Class 2	86.010 to 86.020 mm
Class 3	86.020 to 86.030 mm

Pistons and piston rings

Piston diameter:

Class A	85.94 to 85.95 mm
Class B	85.95 to 85.96 mm
Class C	85.96 to 85.97 mm
Piston-to-cylinder bore clearance	0.05 to 0.07 mm

Piston ring end gaps*:

Top compression ring.	0.25 to 0.40 mm
Second compression ring.	0.85 to 1.10 mm
Oil scraper ring	0.20 to 0.40 mm

*Note: Piston ring end gaps should be offset at 120° to each other when fitted

Crankshaft and bearings

Crankshaft endfloat	0.090 to 0.305 mm
Big-end bearing journal standard diameter	52.980 to 53.000 mm
Big-end bearing shell running clearance	0.034 mm to 0.100 mm

Main bearing journals standard diameter:

1 to 4	64.950 to 64.970 mm
5	69.950 to 69.970 mm

Main bearing shell running clearance:

1 to 4	0.033 to 0.080 mm
5	0.034 to 0.083 mm
Torque wrench settings	Refer to Chapter 2A Specifications

2.4 litre engines

Valve stem-to-guide clearance:

Inlet	0.045 mm
Exhaust	0.055 mm

Cylinder block
Cylinder bore diameter:

Class 1	89.900 to 89.910 mm
Class 2	89.910 to 89.920 mm
Class 3	89.920 to 89.930 mm

Pistons and piston rings
Piston diameter:

Class A	89.84 to 89.85 mm
Class B	89.85 to 89.86 mm
Class C	89.86 to 89.87 mm
Piston-to-cylinder bore clearance	0.05 to 0.07 mm

Piston ring end gaps*:

Top compression ring	0.25 to 0.40 mm
Second compression ring	0.50 to 0.75 mm
Oil scraper ring	0.25 to 0.50 mm

***Note:** Piston ring end gaps should be offset at 120° to one another when fitted*

Crankshaft and bearings

Crankshaft endfloat	0.090 to 0.305 mm
Big-end bearing journal standard diameter	52.980 to 53.000 mm
Big-end bearing shell running clearance	0.034 mm to 0.100 mm

Main bearing journals standard diameter:

1 to 4	64.950 to 64.970 mm
5	69.950 to 69.970 mm

Main bearing shell running clearance:

1 to 4	0.005 to 0.051 mm
5	0.004 to 0.054 mm
Torque wrench settings	Refer to Chapter 2B Specifications

1 General Information

1 This Part of Chapter 2 is devoted to engine/transmission removal and refitting, to those repair procedures requiring the removal of the engine/transmission from the vehicle, and to the overhaul of engine components. It includes only the Specifications relevant to those procedures. Refer to Part A or B (depending on engine type) for additional Specifications and for all torque wrench settings.

2 The information ranges from advice concerning preparation for an overhaul and the purchase of new parts, to detailed step-by-step procedures covering removal and installation of internal engine components and the inspection of parts.

3 The following Sections have been written based on the assumption that the engine has been removed from the vehicle. For information concerning in-vehicle engine repair, as well as removal and installation of the external components necessary for the overhaul, see Part A or B of this Chapter.

Note: *Before carrying out any major engine dismantling, consult a Land Rover dealer or engine reconditioning specialist on the availability of replacement parts.*

Major components such as the crankshaft, pistons, connecting rods, camshafts etc are not available as separate items from Land Rover although they may be available from alternative sources.

2 Engine overhaul – general information

1 It's not always easy to determine when, or if, an engine should be completely overhauled, as a number of factors must be considered.

2 High mileage is not necessarily an indication that an overhaul is needed, while low mileage doesn't preclude the need for an overhaul. Frequency of servicing is probably the most important consideration. An engine that has had regular and frequent oil and filter changes, as well as other required maintenance, will most likely give many thousands of miles of reliable service. Conversely, a neglected engine may require an overhaul very early in its life.

3 Excessive oil consumption is an indication that piston rings, valve seals and/or valve guides are in need of attention. Make sure that oil leaks are not responsible before deciding that the rings and/or guides are worn. Perform a cylinder compression test (refer to Part A or B of this Chapter) to determine the likely cause of the problem.

4 Check the oil pressure with a gauge fitted in place of the oil pressure switch, and compare it with that specified in Chapter 2A Section 13 or Section, as applicable. If it is extremely low, the main and big-end bearings, and/or the oil pump, are probably worn out.

5 Loss of power, rough running, knocking or metallic engine noises, excessive valve gear noise, and high fuel consumption may also point to the need for an overhaul, especially if they are all present at the same time. If a complete service does not cure the situation, major mechanical work is the only solution.

6 A full engine overhaul involves restoring all internal parts to the specification of a new engine. During a complete overhaul, the pistons and the piston rings are renewed, and the cylinder bores are reconditioned. New main and big-end bearings are generally fitted. If necessary, the crankshaft may be reground, to compensate for wear in the journals. The valves are also serviced as well, since they are usually in less-than-perfect condition at this point. Always pay careful attention to the condition of the oil pump when overhauling the engine, and renew it if there is any doubt as to its serviceability. The end result should be an as-new engine that will give many trouble-free miles.

7 Critical cooling system components such as the hoses, thermostat and coolant pump should be renewed when an engine is overhauled. The radiator should also be checked carefully, to ensure that it is not clogged or leaking.

8 Before beginning the engine overhaul, read the entire procedure, to familiarise yourself with the scope and requirements of the job. Check on the availability of parts and make sure that any necessary special tools and equipment are obtained in advance. Most work can be done with typical hand tools, although a number of precision measuring tools are required for inspecting parts to determine if they must be renewed.

9 The services provided by an engineering machine shop or engine reconditioning specialist will almost certainly be required, particularly if major repairs such as crankshaft regrinding or cylinder reboring are necessary. Apart from carrying out machining operations, these establishments will normally handle the inspection of parts, offer advice concerning reconditioning or renewal and supply new components such as pistons, piston rings and bearing shells. It is recommended that the establishment used is a member of the Federation of Engine Re-Manufacturers, or a similar society.

10 Always wait until the engine has been completely dismantled, and until all components (especially the cylinder block/crankcase and the crankshaft) have been inspected before deciding what service and repair operations must be performed by an engineering works. The condition of these components will be the major factor to consider when determining whether to overhaul the original engine, or to buy a reconditioned unit. Do not, therefore, purchase parts or have overhaul work done on other components until they have been thoroughly inspected. As a general rule, time is the primary cost of an overhaul, so it does not pay to fit worn or sub-standard parts.

11 As a final note, to ensure maximum life and minimum trouble from a reconditioned engine, everything must be assembled with care, in a spotlessly clean environment.

3 Engine/transmission removal – methods and precautions

1 If you have decided that the engine must be removed for overhaul or major repair work, several preliminary steps should be taken.

2 Locating a suitable place to work is extremely important. Adequate work space, along with storage space for the vehicle, will be needed. If a workshop or garage isn't available, at the very least, a flat, level, clean work surface made of concrete or asphalt is required.

3 Cleaning the engine compartment and engine/transmission before beginning the removal procedure will help keep tools clean and organised.

4 The help of an assistant is essential. Apart from the safety aspects involved, there are many instances when one person cannot simultaneously perform all of the operations required during engine removal.

5 Plan the operation ahead of time. Arrange for (or obtain) all of the tools and equipment you'll need prior to beginning the job. Some of the equipment necessary to perform engine removal and installation safely and with relative ease, and which may have to be hired or borrowed, includes:

a) *Heavy duty trolley jacks.*
b) *A strong pair of axle stands.*
c) *An assortment of wooden blocks and assorted wooden strips.*
d) *A complete set of spanners and sockets.*
e) *Rags and cleaning solvent for mopping-up spilled oil, coolant and fuel.*

6 Plan for the vehicle to be out of use for quite a while. An engineering machine shop or engine reconditioning specialist will be required to perform some of the work which cannot be accomplished without special equipment. These places often have a busy schedule, so it would be a good idea to consult them before removing the engine, in order to accurately estimate the amount of time required to rebuild or repair components that may need work.

7 During the engine removal procedure, it is advisable to make notes of the locations of all brackets, cable ties, earthing points, etc, as well as how the wiring harnesses, hoses and electrical connections are attached and routed around the engine and engine compartment. An effective way of doing this is to take a series of photographs of the various components before they are disconnected or removed. The resulting photographs will prove invaluable when the engine is refitted.

8 Always be extremely careful when removing and refitting the engine. Serious injury can result from careless actions. Plan ahead and take your time, and a job of this nature, although major, can be accomplished successfully.

9 The engine is most easily removed by separating it from the transmission, and lifting the engine upwards and out from the engine compartment.

4 Engine – removal and refitting

Note: *An engine hoist and suitable lifting tackle will be required for this operation.*

Removal

1 Ensure that the vehicle is parked on level ground, and apply the handbrake.

2 Disconnect the battery negative lead (see Chapter 5 Section 4).

3 On models with air-conditioning, have the refrigerant discharged at a dealer service department or an automotive air conditioning repair facility. Refer to Chapter 3 Section 10, before working on the air-conditioning system.

4 To give better access and lighting, remove the bonnet as described in Chapter 12 Section 7

5 Undo the 2 bolts and remove the plastic trim cover from the top of the engine.

6 Drain the engine oil with reference to Chapter 1 Section 5.

7 Drain the cooling system as described in Chapter 1 Section 47.

8 Remove the radiator as described in Chapter 3 Section 3

9 Remove the coolant pump as described in Chapter 3 Section 7

10 Slacken the retaining clip and remove the coolant hose from the coolant elbow on the front of the engine.

11 Slacken the retaining clips and disconnect the heater hoses from the left-hand side of the engine compartment.

12 Release the locking clip and disconnect the upper connector from the ECU (Electronic Control Unit), at the rear of the engine compartment. Refer to Chapter 4A Section 9, for further information.

13 Remove the air cleaner housing as described in Chapter 4A Section 4, 14.

14 Remove the starter motor as described in Section.

15 Release the securing clips and disconnect the coolant hoses from the fuel cooler and oil filter cooler.

16 On 2.2 litre engines, disconnect the servo vacuum hose from the vacuum pump at the rear of the cylinder head. On 2.4 litre engines, disconnect the servo vacuum hose from the vacuum pump, which is positioned on top of the coolant pump and driven by the auxiliary drivebelt.

17 Undo the retaining bolts and remove the power steering pump, and move it to one side, without disconnecting the hoses – refer to Chapter 11 Section 26 if necessary.

18 Loosen the securing clips, and remove the air intake hoses from the intake manifold and the turbocharger.

19 Disconnect the fuel supply and return pipes from the fuel injection pump. Be prepared for fuel spillage.

> **HAYNES HiNT**
> *Cover the open ends of the pipes, and plug the openings in the injection pump, to keep dirt out.*

20 Disconnect the exhaust front section from the turbocharger, with reference to Chapter 4A Section 18.

21 Disconnect all relevant wiring from the engine ancillary components. Note that on most models, wiring harness connectors are provided, which eliminates the need to disconnect all the wiring from the individual components – the engine wiring harness can then be removed with the engine. Note the routing of all wiring, to ensure correct refitting. Make a check to ensure that all relevant wiring has been disconnected, to enable the engine to be removed. Undo the bolts/clips and move the harnesses away from the engine.

22 With the air-conditioning system discharged, unscrew the union bolts, and disconnect the refrigerant pipes from the air conditioning compressor. **Note:** *it is possible to unbolt the compressor and move it to one side without disconnecting the refrigerant pipes/discharging the refrigerant.*

⚠ **Warning: DO NOT attempt to discharge the system yourself – refer to the precautions given for models with air conditioning in Chapter 3 Section 10.**

23 Place a trolley jack under the gearbox, with an interposed block of wood to spread the load. Raise the jack to support the gearbox.

24 Connect a suitable hoist and lifting tackle to the front and rear engine lifting brackets.

25 Raise the hoist sufficiently to just take the weight of the engine.

26 Undo the bolt and remove the crankshaft position sensor from the right-hand side of the transmission bellhousing. Recover the sensor spacer where fitted.

27 Using two nuts locked together, remove the remaining stud each side securing the bonnet slam panel, then undo the panel support stays lower bolts and move the slam panel to one side.

28 Undo the bolts securing the transmission bellhousing to the engine.

29 Undo the nuts securing the left- and right-hand engine mounting brackets to the mountings.

30 Carefully raise the hoist, and lift the engine from the gearbox. It will be necessary to pull the engine forwards to disengage the gearbox input shaft from the clutch – take care not to allow the weight of the engine or gearbox to hang on the input shaft. If necessary, alter the position of the jack supporting the gearbox, and the hoist supporting the engine, until the engine is free.

31 Make a final check to ensure that all hoses, pipes and wires have been disconnected from the engine, and released from any brackets, to facilitate engine removal.

32 With the aid of an assistant, carefully raise the hoist to lift the engine from the vehicle, taking care not to damage surrounding components in the engine compartment.

 HAYNES HINT *Fasten a suitable hose clip around the gearbox input shaft to prevent the release bearing from being inadvertently pushed forwards on the shaft whilst the engine is removed from the vehicle.*

Refitting

33 Ensure that the clutch friction disc has been centralised, as described in Chapter 6 Section 2.

34 Where applicable, remove the hose clip from the gearbox input shaft.

35 Apply a little clutch assembly grease to the splines of the gearbox input shaft. Do not apply too much grease, as it may contaminate the clutch.

36 Attach the hoist and lifting tackle to the engine, as during the removal procedure, and lift the engine into position over the vehicle engine compartment.

37 Lower the engine into position, taking care not to damage the surrounding components.

38 Manipulate the engine and gearbox as necessary to enable the two assemblies to be mated together. Alter the position of the jack supporting the gearbox, and the hoist supporting the engine, until the two assemblies are correctly aligned. Ensure that the weight of the engine or gearbox is not allowed to hang on the gearbox input shaft, and ensure that the gearbox input shaft engages with the splines of the clutch friction disc.

39 Refit the transmission-to-engine bolts and tighten them to the specified torque.

40 Ensure the engine mounting brackets locate over the mountings, then refit the nuts and tighten them to the specified torque.

41 Disconnect the hoist and lifting tackle from the engine lifting brackets.

42 Further refitting is a reversal of removal, bearing in mind the following points:

a) *Reconnect all relevant engine harness wiring, and clip the harness into position, ensuring that it is routed as noted before removal.*

b) *Reconnect the exhaust front section to the manifold or turbocharger (as applicable), with reference to Chapter 4A.*

c) *Refit the starter motor as described in Section.*

d) *Where applicable, reconnect the fluid hoses to the power steering pump, using new O-ring seals.*

e) *Reconnect the oil cooler pipes to the oil filter adapter and the oil cooler, using new O-ring seals (where applicable).*

f) *Refit the radiator, cooling fan and cowl with reference to Chapter 3.*

g) *Refit the bonnet with reference to Chapter 12.*

h) *Where applicable, check the power steering fluid level, and top-up as necessary as described in Chapter 1.*

i) *Refill the cooling system as described in Chapter 1.*

j) *Refill the engine with oil as described in Chapter 1.*

k) *Where applicable, have the system recharged with refrigerant by a Land Rover dealer, or a suitably-equipped specialist.*

l) *Bleed the fuel system as described in Chapter 4A.*

5 Engine overhaul – dismantling sequence

Note: *Before carrying out any major engine dismantling, consult a Land Rover dealer or engine reconditioning specialist on the availability of replacement parts. Major components such as the crankshaft, pistons, connecting rods, camshafts etc are not available as separate items from Land Rover although they may be available from alternative sources.*

1 It is much easier to dismantle and work on the engine if it is mounted on a portable engine stand. These stands can often be hired from a tool hire shop. Before the engine is mounted on a stand, the flywheel should be removed so that the stand bolts can be tightened into the end of the cylinder block/crankcase.

2 If a stand is not available it is possible to dismantle the engine with it mounted on blocks, on a sturdy workbench or on the floor. Be extra careful not to tip or drop the engine when working without a stand.

3 If you are going to obtain a reconditioned engine, all external components must be removed first to be transferred to the new engine (just as they will if you are doing a complete engine overhaul yourself). **Note:** *When removing the external components from the engine, pay close attention to details that may be helpful or important during refitting. Note the fitted position of gaskets, seals, spacers, pins, washers, bolts and other small items. These external components include the following:*

a) *Alternator, starter and mounting brackets.*

b) *Glow plug/preheating system components.*

c) *Cooling system/thermostat housings.*

d) *Oil level dipstick and dipstick tube.*

e) *All fuel injection system components.*

f) *Brake vacuum pump.*

g) *All electrical switches and sensors and engine wiring harness.*

h) *Inlet and exhaust manifolds.*

i) *Engine/transmission mounting brackets.*

j) *Flywheel.*

4 If you are obtaining a 'short' engine (which consists of the engine cylinder block/crankcase, crankshaft, pistons and connecting rods all assembled), then the cylinder head, sump, oil pump, oil filter cooler/housing and timing chains will have to be removed also.

5 If you are planning a complete overhaul, the engine can be dismantled and the internal components removed in the following order.

a) *Inlet manifold (Chapter 4A Section 15).*

b) *Exhaust manifold (Chapter 4A Section 16).*

c) *Timing chain, tensioners and sprockets (Chapter 2A Section 8 and Chapter 2B Section 8).*

d) *Cylinder head (Chapter 2A Section 10 and Chapter 2B Section 10).*

e) *Flywheel (Chapter 2A Section 16 and Chapter 2B Section 16).*

f) *Sump (Chapter 2A Section 11 and Chapter 2B Section 11).*

g) *Oil pump (Chapter 2A Section 12 and Chapter 2B Section 12).*
h) *Piston/connecting rod assemblies (Section 9).*
i) *Crankshaft (Section 10).*

6 Before beginning the dismantling and overhaul procedures, make sure that you have all of the correct tools necessary. Refer to Tools and working facilities for further information.

6 Cylinder head – dismantling

Note: *New and reconditioned cylinder heads are available from the manufacturers and from engine overhaul specialists. Due to the fact that some specialist tools are required for the dismantling and inspection procedures and new components may not be readily available, it may be more practical and economical for the home mechanic to purchase a reconditioned head, rather than to dismantle, inspect and recondition the original head.*

1 With the cylinder head removed as described in the relevant Part of this Chapter, clean away all external dirt, and remove any remaining components as applicable.

2 With the cylinder head resting on one side, using a valve spring compressor compress each valve spring in turn until the split collets can be removed. A special valve spring compressor will be required to reach into the deep wells in the cylinder head without risk of damaging the tappet bores. Such compressors are widely available from most good motor accessory shops. Release the compressor and lift off the spring upper seat and spring **(see illustrations)**.

3 If, when the valve spring compressor is screwed down, the spring upper seat refuses to free and expose the split collets, gently tap the top of the tool, directly over the upper seat, with a light hammer. This will free the seat to remove the collets.

4 Withdraw the valve through the combustion chamber. If it binds in the guide (will not pull through), push it back in and deburr the area around the collet groove with a fine file or whetstone.

5 Use a pair of pliers or a special tool to extract the valve spring lower seat/stem oil seal from the valve guides **(see illustration)**.

6 It is essential that the valves are kept together with their collets, spring seats and springs, and in their correct sequence (unless they are so badly worn that they are to be renewed). If they are going to be kept and used again, place them in a labelled polythene bag or similar small container **(see illustration)**.

7 Cylinder head and valve components – cleaning and inspection

1 Thorough cleaning of the cylinder head and valve components followed by a detailed inspection, will enable you to decide how much valve service work must be carried out during the engine overhaul. **Note:** *If the engine has been severely overheated, it is best to assume that the cylinder head is warped, and to check carefully for signs of this.*

Cleaning

2 Using a degreasing agent, remove all traces of oil deposits from the cylinder head, paying particular attention to the journal bearings, camshaft bores, valve guides and oilways.

3 Scrape away all traces of old gasket material and sealing compound from the cylinder head, taking great care not to score or gouge the surfaces.

4 Scrape away the carbon from the combustion chambers and ports, then wash the cylinder head thoroughly with paraffin or a suitable solvent to remove the remaining debris.

5 Scrape off any heavy carbon deposits that may have formed on the valves, then use a power-operated wire brush to remove deposits from the valve heads and stems.

Inspection

Note: *Be sure to perform all the following inspection procedures before concluding that the services of a machine shop or engine overhaul specialist are required. Make a list of all items that require attention.*

Cylinder head

6 Inspect the head very carefully for cracks,

6.2a Compress the valve springs using a spring compressor tool…

6.2b …and remove the split collets

6.2c Release the tool and remove the upper spring seat…

6.2d …and the valve spring

6.5 Use a removal tool to extract the valve stem oil seal

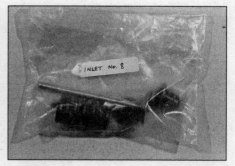

6.6 Use clearly marked containers to identify components and to keep matched assemblies together

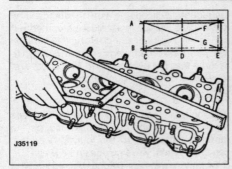

7.7 Check the cylinder head surface for warping in the planes indicated. Using feeler blades under the straight-edge

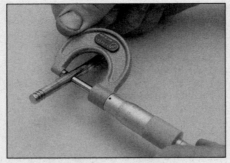

7.13 Measure the diameter of the valve stems with a micrometer

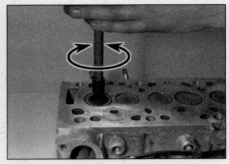

7.16 Grind-in the valves with a reciprocating rotary motion

evidence of coolant leakage, and other damage. If cracks are found, a new cylinder head should be obtained.

7 Use a straight-edge and feeler blade to check that the cylinder head gasket surface is not distorted, check the head across a number of different ways to find any distortion **(see illustration)**. If it is, it may be possible to resurface it.

8 Examine the valve seats in each of the combustion chambers. If they are severely pitted, cracked or burned, then they will need to be renewed or recut by an engine overhaul specialist. If they are only slightly pitted, this can be removed by grinding-in the valve heads and seats with fine valve-grinding compound as described below.

9 If the valve guides are worn, indicated by a side-to-side motion of the valve, new guides must be fitted. Measure the diameter of the existing valve stems (see below) and the bore of the guides, then calculate the clearance, and compare the result with the specified value. If the clearance is excessive, renew the valves or guides as necessary.

10 The renewal of valve guides is best carried out by an engine overhaul specialist.

11 If the valve seats are to be recut, this must be done only after the guides have been renewed.

Valves

12 Examine the head of each valve for pitting, burning, cracks and general wear, and check the valve stem for scoring and wear ridges. Rotate the valve, and check for any obvious indication that it is bent. Look for pits and excessive wear

on the tip of each valve stem. Renew any valve that shows any such signs of wear or damage.

13 If the valve appears satisfactory at this stage, measure the valve stem diameter at several points using a micrometer **(see illustration)**. Any significant difference in the readings obtained indicates wear of the valve stem. Should any of these conditions be apparent, the valve(s) must be renewed.

14 If the valves are in satisfactory condition, they should be ground (lapped) into their respective seats to ensure a smooth gas-tight seal. If the seat is only lightly pitted, or if it has been recut, fine grinding compound only should be used to produce the required finish. Coarse valve-grinding compound should not be used unless a seat is badly burned or deeply pitted. If this is the case, the cylinder head and valves should be inspected by an expert to decide whether seat recutting, or even the renewal of the valve or seat insert, is required.

15 Valve grinding is carried out as follows. Place the cylinder head upside-down on a bench, with a block of wood at each end to give clearance for the valve stems.

16 Smear a trace of the appropriate grade of valve-grinding compound on the seat face, and press a suction grinding tool onto the valve head. With a semi-rotary action, grind the valve head to its seat, lifting the valve occasionally to redistribute the grinding compound **(see illustration)**. A light spring placed under the valve head will greatly ease this operation.

17 If coarse grinding compound is being used, work only until a dull, matt even surface

is produced on both the valve seat and the valve, then wipe off the used compound and repeat the process with fine compound. When a smooth unbroken ring of light grey matt finish is produced on both the valve and seat, the grinding operation is complete. Do not grind in the valves any further than absolutely necessary, or the seat will be prematurely sunk into the cylinder head.

18 When all the valves have been ground-in, carefully wash off all traces of grinding compound, using paraffin or a suitable solvent, before reassembly of the cylinder head.

Valve components

19 Examine the valve springs for signs of damage and discolouration, and also measure their free length by comparing each of the existing springs with a new component.

20 Stand each spring on a flat surface and check it for squareness. If any of the springs are damaged, distorted, or have lost their tension, obtain a complete set of new springs.

21 Check the spring upper seats and collets for obvious wear and cracks. Any questionable parts should be renewed, as extensive damage will occur if they fail during engine operation. Any damaged or excessively-worn parts must be renewed. The valve spring lower seat/stem oil seals must be renewed as a matter of course whenever they are disturbed.

8 Cylinder head – reassembly

1 Regardless of whether or not the head was sent away for repair work of any sort, make sure that it is clean before beginning reassembly. Be sure to remove any metal particles and abrasive grit that may still be present from operations such as valve grinding or head resurfacing. Use compressed air, if available, to blow out all the oil holes and passages.

⚠️ *Warning: Wear eye protection when using compressed air.*

2 Beginning at one end of the head, fit the new valve spring lower seat/stem oil seal. Use a suitable socket or metal tube to press the seal firmly onto the guide **(see illustrations)**.

8.2a Fit the new valve spring lower seat/ stem oil seal...

8.2b ...then use a suitable socket or metal tube to press the seal firmly onto the guide

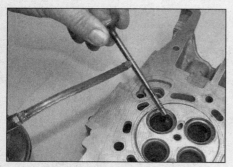

8.3 Apply clean engine oil to the valve stem, and refit the valve

8.4a Refit the valve spring...

8.4b ...and the upper spring seat

8.5 Compress the spring and install the collets. Use grease to hold the two halves of the split collet in the groove

9.2 Undo the retaining bolts and remove the pick-up pipe from the oil pump

9.3 Disengage the oil pump sprocket from the chain and remove the oil pump

3 Apply clean engine oil to the valve stem, and refit the valve **(see illustration)**. Where the original valves are being re-used, ensure that each is refitted in its original guide. If new valves are being fitted, insert them into the locations to which they have been ground.

4 Refit the valve spring and upper seat **(see illustrations)**.

5 Compress the spring with the valve spring compressor, and carefully install the collets in the stem groove. Apply a small dab of grease to each collet to hold it in place if necessary **(see illustration)**. Slowly release the compressor and make sure the collets seat properly.

6 When the valves are installed, use a hammer and interposed block of wood (to prevent the end of the valve stem being damaged), to tap the end of the valve stem gently in order to settle the components.

7 Repeat the procedure for the remaining valves. Be sure to return the valve assembly components to their original locations – don't mix them up!

---

9 Piston/connecting rod assemblies – removal and inspection

Note: *While this task is theoretically possible when the engine is in place in the vehicle, in practice it requires so much preliminary dismantling and is so difficult to carry out due to the restricted access, that owners are advised to remove the engine from the vehicle first. The following paragraphs assume that the engine has been removed.*

Removal

1 Remove the cylinder head and sump with reference to Part A or B of this Chapter.

2 Undo the retaining bolts and remove the pick-up pipe from the oil pump **(see illustration)**. Remove and discard the O-ring seal and obtain a new O-ring for refitting.

3 Undo the retaining bolts and release the oil pump from the lower crankcase. Push or pull on the oil pump drive chain to compress the tensioner, then disengage the oil pump sprocket from the chain and remove the oil pump **(see illustration)**.

4 Unscrew the bolts securing the lower crankcase to the cylinder block. Loosen the bolts gradually and evenly, then separate the lower crankcase from the cylinder block. Remove the gasket.

5 Temporarily refit the crankshaft pulley so

that the crankshaft can be rotated. Note that each piston/connecting rod assembly can be identified by its cylinder number (counting from the timing chain end of the engine) etched into the flat-machined surface of both the connecting rod and its cap. Furthermore, each piston has an arrow stamped into its crown, pointing towards the timing chain end of the engine. If no marks can be seen, make your own before disturbing any of the components so that you can be certain of refitting each piston/connecting rod assembly the right way round, and to its correct (original) bore, with the cap also the right way round **(see illustration)**.

6 Use your fingernail to feel if a ridge has formed at the upper limit of ring travel (about 6 mm down from the top of each cylinder). If carbon deposits or cylinder wear have produced ridges, they must be completely removed with a special tool called a ridge reamer **(see illustration)**.

9.5 If necessary, make your own marks (arrowed) to correspond with the connecting rod location

9.6 A ridge reamer may be required, to remove the ridge from the top of each cylinder

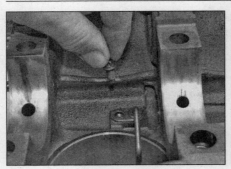

9.10a Remove the piston cooling jet-retaining screws...

9.10b ...and remove the jets from their mounting holes

Follow the manufacturer's instructions provided with the tool.

Caution: Failure to remove the ridges before attempting to remove the piston/connecting rod assemblies may result in piston ring breakage.

7 Slacken each of the big-end bearing cap bolts half a turn at a time, until they can be removed by hand. Remove the No 1 cap and bearing shell. Don't drop the shell out of the cap.

Caution: The connecting rod/bearing cap mating surfaces are not machined flat, since the big-end bearing caps are 'cracked' off from the rod during production and left untouched to ensure the cap and rod mate perfectly. Great care must be taken to ensure the mating surfaces of the cap and rod are not marked or damaged in anyway. Any damage to the mating surfaces will adversely affect the strength of the connecting rod and could lead to premature failure.

8 Remove the upper bearing shell, and push the connecting rod/piston assembly out through the top of the cylinder block. Use a wooden hammer handle to push on the connecting rod's bearing recess. If resistance is felt, double-check that all of the ridge was removed from the cylinder. Repeat the procedure for the remaining cylinders.

9 After removal, reassemble the big-end bearing caps and shells on their respective connecting rods, and refit the bolts finger-tight. Leaving the old shells in place until reassembly will help prevent the bearing

9.14a The piston ring grooves can be cleaned with a special tool as shown here...

recesses from being accidentally nicked or gouged. New shells should be used on reassembly.

10 Remove the retaining screws and withdraw the piston cooling jets from the bottom of the cylinder bores **(see illustrations)**.

Inspection

11 Before the inspection process can be carried out, the piston/connecting rod assemblies must be cleaned and the original piston rings removed from the pistons. The rings should have smooth, polished working surfaces, with no dull or carbon-coated sections and no traces of wear on their top and bottom surfaces. Any discoloured sections will show that the ring is not sealing correctly against the bore wall, so allowing combustion gases to blow by. The end gaps should be clear of carbon but not polished (indicating a too-small end gap), and all the rings (including the elements of the oil control ring) should be free to rotate in their grooves, but without excessive up-and-down movement. If the rings appear to be in good condition, they are probably fit for further use; if so, check the end gaps (in an unworn part of the bore) as described in Section 14. If any of the rings appears to be worn or damaged, or has an end gap significantly different from the specified value, the usual course of action is to renew all of them as a set. **Note:** *While it is usual to renew piston rings when an engine is overhauled, they may be re-used if in acceptable condition. If re-using the rings,*

9.14b ...or alternatively a section of a broken piston ring may be used, if available

make sure that each ring is marked during removal to ensure that it is refitted correctly.

12 Using a piston ring removal tool, carefully remove the rings from the pistons. Be careful not to nick or gouge the pistons in the process, and mark or label each ring as it is removed, so that its original top surface can be identified on reassembly, and so that it can be returned to its original groove. Take care also with your hands – piston rings are sharp! (see **Tool Tip**).

 TOOL TiP *If a piston ring removal tool is not available, the rings can be removed by hand, expanding them over the top of the pistons. The use of two or three old feeler blades will be helpful in preventing the rings dropping into empty grooves.*

13 Scrape all traces of carbon from the top of the piston. A hand-held wire brush or a piece of fine emery cloth can be used once the majority of the deposits have been scraped away. Do not under any circumstances use a wire brush mounted in a drill motor to remove deposits from the pistons as the piston material is soft, and may be eroded away by the wire brush.

14 Use a piston ring groove-cleaning tool to remove carbon deposits from the ring grooves. If a tool isn't available, but replacement rings have been found, a piece broken off the old ring will do the job. Be very careful to remove only the carbon deposits (don't remove any metal) and do not nick or scratch the sides of the ring grooves **(see illustrations)**. Protect your fingers as piston rings are sharp.

15 Once the deposits have been removed, clean the piston/rod assemblies with solvent and dry them with compressed air if available. Make sure the oil return holes in the back sides of the ring grooves and the oil hole in the lower end of each rod are clear.

16 If the pistons and cylinder walls are not damaged or worn excessively and if the cylinder block/crankcase is not rebored, new pistons will not be necessary. Normal piston wear appears as even vertical wear on the piston thrust surfaces, and slight looseness of the top ring in its groove.

17 Carefully inspect each piston for cracks around the skirt, at the pin bosses, and at the ring lands (between the ring grooves).

18 Look for scoring and scuffing on the thrust faces of the piston skirt, holes in the piston crown, and burned areas at the edge of the crown. If the skirt is scored or scuffed, the engine may have been suffering from overheating and/or abnormal combustion which caused excessively high operating temperatures. The cooling and lubrication systems should be checked thoroughly. A hole in the piston crown, or burned areas at the edge of the piston crown indicates that abnormal combustion (knocking or detonation) has been occurring. If any of the above problems exist, the causes must be investigated and corrected or the damage will occur again. The causes may include intake air leaks, incorrect fuel/air mixture, or EGR system malfunctions.

19 Corrosion of the piston in the form of small pits, indicates that coolant is leaking into the combustion chamber and/or the crankcase. Again, the cause must be corrected or the problem may persist in the rebuilt engine.

20 Check the piston-to-rod clearance by twisting the piston and rod in opposite directions. Any noticeable play indicates excessive wear which must be corrected. The piston/connecting rod assemblies should be taken to an engine reconditioning specialist to have the pistons, gudgeon pins and rods checked, and new components fitted as required.

21 Check the connecting rods for cracks and other damage. Temporarily remove the big-end bearing caps and the old bearing shells, wipe clean the rod and cap bearing recesses, and inspect them for nicks, gouges and scratches. After checking the rods, refit the old shells, slip the caps into place, and tighten the bolts finger-tight.

10 Crankshaft – removal and inspection

Removal

Note: *The crankshaft can be removed only after the engine/transmission has been removed from the vehicle. It is assumed that the transmission, flywheel, timing chain, lower crankcase, cylinder head, sump, oil pump, and piston/connecting rod assemblies, have already been removed. The crankshaft oil seal carrier must be unbolted from the cylinder block/crankcase before proceeding with crankshaft removal.*

1 Before the crankshaft is removed, check the endfloat. Mount a DTI (Dial Test Indicator, or dial gauge) with the probe in line with the crankshaft and just touching the crankshaft **(see illustration)**.

2 Push the crankshaft fully away from the

10.1 Measure the crankshaft endfloat using a DTI gauge

gauge, and zero the gauge. Next, lever the crankshaft towards the gauge as far as possible, and check the reading obtained. The distance that the crankshaft moved is its endfloat. If it is greater than specified, check the crankshaft thrust surfaces for wear. If no wear is evident, new thrustwashers (integral with No 3 main bearing upper shell) should correct the end-float.

3 If a dial gauge is not available, feeler gauges can be used. Gently lever or push the crankshaft all the way towards the right-hand end of the engine. Slip feeler gauges between the crankshaft and the right-hand face of No 3 (centre) main bearing to determine the clearance **(see illustration)**.

4 The main bearing caps are numbered consecutively from the timing chain end of the engine. The caps also have an embossed arrow pointing to the timing chain end of the engine **(see illustrations)**. Slacken the cap bolts a quarter-turn at a time each, starting with the end caps and working toward the centre, until they can be removed by hand.

5 Gently tap the caps with a soft-faced hammer, then separate them from the cylinder block/crankcase. If necessary, use the bolts as levers to remove the caps. Take care not to drop the bearing shells as the bearing caps are removed.

6 Carefully lift the crankshaft out of the engine **(see illustration)**. It may be a good idea to have an assistant available since the crankshaft is quite heavy. With the bearing shells in place in the cylinder block/crankcase and main bearing caps, return the caps to their

10.3 If a DTI gauge is not available, measure the endfloat using feeler gauges

respective locations on the block and tighten the bolts finger-tight. Leaving the old shells in place until reassembly will help prevent the bearing recesses from being accidentally nicked or gouged. New shells should be used on reassembly.

Inspection

7 Clean the crankshaft, and dry it with compressed air if available. Be sure to clean the oil holes with a pipe cleaner or similar probe.

⚠️ *Warning: Wear eye protection when using compressed air.*

8 Check the main and crankpin (big-end) bearing journals carefully. If uneven wear, scoring, pitting and cracking are evident then the crankshaft should be reground (where possible) by an engineering workshop, and refitted to the engine with new undersize bearings.

9 Rather than attempt to determine the crankshaft journal sizes and the bearing clearances, take the crankshaft to an automotive engineering workshop. Have them perform the necessary measurements, grind the journals if necessary, and supply the appropriate new shell bearings.

10 Check the oil seal journals at each end of the crankshaft for wear and damage. If either seal has worn an excessive groove in its journal, it may cause the new seals to leak when the engine is reassembled. Consult an engine overhaul specialist, who will be able to advise whether a repair is possible or whether a new crankshaft is necessary.

10.4a Note the main bearing caps are numbered to indicate their locations...

10.4b ...and the caps have an embossed arrow pointing to the timing chain end of the engine

10.6 Carefully remove the crankshaft from the cylinder block

11.2 Felt marker pens can be used as shown to identify bearing shells without damaging them

11 Cylinder block/crankcase – cleaning and inspection

Cleaning

1 For complete cleaning, make sure that all the external components have been removed, including mounting brackets, oil cooler and filter housing, piston cooling jets, fuel injection pump mounting bracket (where applicable) and all electrical switches/sensors. **Note:** *If the crankshaft position sensor mounting bracket is removed, its new fitted position will have to be established on reassembly (see Section 16).*

2 Remove the main bearing caps, and separate the bearing shells from the caps and the cylinder block. Mark or label the shells, indicating which bearing they were removed from, and whether they were in the cap or the block, then set them aside **(see illustration)**. Wipe clean the block and cap bearing recesses and inspect them for nicks, gouges and scratches.

3 Scrape all traces of gasket from the cylinder block, taking care not to damage the sealing surfaces.

4 Remove all oil gallery plugs (where fitted). The plugs are usually very tight and they may have to be drilled out and the holes retapped. Use new plugs when the engine is reassembled.

5 If any of the castings are extremely dirty, they should be steam-cleaned.

6 After the castings are returned from steam-cleaning, clean all oil holes and oil galleries one more time. Flush all internal passages with warm water until the water runs clear, then dry thoroughly and apply a light film of oil to all machined surfaces, to prevent rusting. If you have access to compressed air, use it to speed the drying process, and to blow out all the oil holes and galleries.

Warning: Wear eye protection when using compressed air.

7 If the castings are not very dirty, you can do an adequate cleaning job with hot soapy water and a stiff brush. Take plenty of time, and do a thorough job. Regardless of the

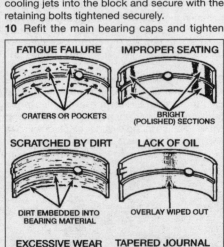

11.8 All bolt holes in the block, particularly the main bearing cap and head bolt holes, should be cleaned and restored with a tap

cleaning method used, be sure to clean all oil holes and galleries very thoroughly, and to dry all components completely. Protect the machined surfaces as described above to prevent rusting.

8 The threaded holes in the cylinder block must be clean to ensure accurate torque readings when tightening nuts/bolts during reassembly. Run the correct-size tap (which can be determined from the size of the relevant bolt) into each of the holes to remove rust, corrosion, thread sealant or other contamination, and to restore damaged threads **(see illustration)**. If possible, use compressed air to clear the holes of debris produced by this operation. Do not forget to clean the threads of all bolts and nuts which are to be re-used, as well.

9 Where applicable, apply suitable sealant to the new oil gallery plugs, and insert them into the relevant holes in the cylinder block. Tighten the plugs securely. Refit the piston cooling jets into the block and secure with the retaining bolts tightened securely.

10 Refit the main bearing caps and tighten

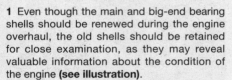

FATIGUE FAILURE	IMPROPER SEATING
CRATERS OR POCKETS	BRIGHT (POLISHED) SECTIONS
SCRATCHED BY DIRT	LACK OF OIL
DIRT EMBEDDED INTO BEARING MATERIAL	OVERLAY WIPED OUT
EXCESSIVE WEAR	TAPERED JOURNAL
OVERLAY WIPED OUT	RADIUS RIDE

H 28395

12.1 When inspecting the main and big end bearings, look for any of these problems

the bolts finger-tight. If the engine is not going to be reassembled right away, cover it with a large plastic bag to keep it clean. Apply a thin coat of engine oil to all machined surfaces to prevent rusting.

Inspection

11 Visually check the castings for cracks and corrosion. Look for stripped threads in the threaded holes. If there has been any history of internal coolant leakage, it may be worthwhile having an engine overhaul specialist check the cylinder block/crankcase for cracks with special equipment. If defects are found, have them repaired, if possible, or renew the assembly.

12 Check each cylinder bore for scuffing and scoring. Any evidence of this kind of damage should be double-checked with an inspection of the pistons (see Section 9). If the damage is in its early stages, it may be possible to repair the block by reboring it. Seek the advice of an engineering workshop.

13 Place the cylinder block on a level surface, crankcase downwards. Use a straight-edge and set of feeler blades to measure the distortion of the cylinder head mating surface in both planes. A maximum figure is not quoted by the manufacturer, but use the figure 0.05 mm as a rough guide. If the measurement exceeds this figure, repair may be possible by machining (consult an engineering workshop for advice).

14 To allow an accurate assessment of the wear in the cylinder bores to be made, take the cylinder block to an automotive engineering workshop, and have them carry out the measurement procedures. If necessary, they will be able to rebore the cylinders, and supply the appropriate piston kits.

15 Even if the cylinder bores are not excessively worn, the cylinder bores must be honed. This process involves using an abrasive tool to produce a fine, cross-hatch pattern on the inner surface of the bore. This has the effect of seating the piston rings, resulting in a good seal between the piston and cylinder. Again, an engineering workshop will be able to carry out the job for you at a reasonable cost.

16 Refit all the components removed in paragraph 1.

12 Main and big-end bearings – inspection

1 Even though the main and big-end bearing shells should be renewed during the engine overhaul, the old shells should be retained for close examination, as they may reveal valuable information about the condition of the engine **(see illustration)**.

2 Bearing failure occurs because of lack of lubrication, the presence of dirt or other foreign particles, overloading the engine, and corrosion. Regardless of the cause of bearing failure, it must be corrected before the engine is reassembled, to prevent it from happening again.

3 When examining the bearing shells, remove them from the cylinder block/crankcase and main bearing caps, and from the connecting rods and the big-end bearing caps, then lay them out on a clean surface in the same general position as their location in the engine. This will enable you to match any bearing problems with the corresponding crankshaft journal.

4 Dirt or other foreign matter gets into the engine in a variety of ways. It may be left in the engine during assembly, or it may pass through filters or the crankcase ventilation system. It may get into the oil and from there into the bearings. Metal chips from machining operations and normal engine wear are often present. Abrasives are sometimes left in engine components after reconditioning, especially when parts are not thoroughly cleaned using the proper cleaning methods. Whatever the source, these foreign objects often end up embedded in the soft bearing material and are easily recognized. Large particles will not embed in the material, and will score or gouge the shell and journal. The best prevention for this cause of bearing failure is to clean all parts thoroughly and to keep everything spotlessly clean during engine assembly. Frequent and regular engine oil and filter changes are also recommended.

5 Lack of lubrication (or lubrication breakdown) has a number of inter-related causes. Excessive heat which thins the oil, overloading which squeezes the oil from the bearing face and oil leakage (from excessive bearing clearances, worn oil pump or high engine speeds) all contribute to lubrication breakdown. Blocked oil passages which usually are the result of misaligned oil holes in a bearing shell, will also starve a bearing of oil and destroy it. When lack of lubrication is the cause of bearing failure, the bearing material is wiped or extruded from the steel backing of the shell. Temperatures may increase to the point where the steel backing turns blue from overheating.

6 Driving habits can have a definite effect on bearing life. Full-throttle, low-speed operation (labouring the engine) puts very high loads on bearings, which tends to squeeze out the oil film. These loads cause the shells to flex, which produces fine cracks in the bearing face (fatigue failure). Eventually, the bearing material will loosen in pieces, and tear away from the steel backing.

7 Short-distance driving leads to corrosion of bearings, because insufficient engine heat is produced to drive off condensed water and corrosive gases. These products collect in the engine oil forming acid and sludge. As the oil is carried to the engine bearings, the acid attacks and corrodes the bearing material.

8 Incorrect shell refitting during engine assembly will lead to bearing failure as well. Tight-fitting shells leave insufficient bearing running clearance and will result in oil starvation. Dirt or foreign particles trapped behind a bearing shell result in high spots on the bearing which lead to failure.

9 Do not touch the internal bearing surface of any shell with your fingers during reassembly, as there is a risk of scratching the delicate surface or of depositing particles of dirt on it.

10 As mentioned at the beginning of this Section, the bearing shells should be renewed as a matter of course during an engine overhaul. To do otherwise is false economy.

13 Engine overhaul – reassembly sequence

1 Before reassembly begins, ensure that all new parts have been obtained, and that all necessary tools are available. Read the entire procedure to familiarise yourself with the work involved, and to ensure that all items necessary for reassembly of the engine are at hand. In addition to all normal tools and materials, thread-locking compound will be needed. A suitable tube of sealant will also be required for certain joint faces that are without gaskets. It is recommended that the manufacturers own products are used, as these are specially formulated for the purpose.

2 In order to save time and avoid problems, engine reassembly can be carried out in the following order:

a) Crankshaft (Section 15).
b) Piston/connecting rod assemblies (Section 16).
c) Oil pump (Chapter 2A Section 12 and Chapter 2B Section 12).
d) Sump (Chapter 2A Section 11 and Chapter 2B Section 11).
e) Flywheel (Chapter 2A Section 16 and Chapter 2B Section 16).
f) Cylinder head (Chapter 2A Section 10 and Chapter 2B Section 10).
g) Timing chains, tensioners and sprockets (Chapter 2B Section 8, and Chapter 2A Section 8).
h) Inlet manifold (Chapter 4A Section 15).
i) Exhaust manifold (Chapter 4A Section 16).
j) Engine external components and ancillaries.

3 At this stage, all engine components should be absolutely clean and dry with all faults repaired. All components should be neatly arranged on a completely clean work surface or in individual containers.

14 Piston rings – refitting

1 Before installing new piston rings, check their end gaps. Lay out each piston set with a piston/connecting rod assembly, and keep them together as a matched set from now on.

2 Insert the top compression ring into the first cylinder, and square it up with the cylinder

14.2 When checking the piston ring end gap, the ring must be square in the cylinder bore. Push the ring down with the top of the piston

walls by pushing it in with the top of the piston **(see illustration)**. The ring should be near the bottom of the cylinder, at the lower limit of ring travel.

3 To measure the end gap, slip feeler gauges between the ends of the ring until a gauge equal to the gap width is found **(see illustration)**. The feeler gauge should slide between the ring ends with a slight amount of drag. Compare the measurement to the value given in the Specifications. If the gap is larger or smaller than specified, double-check to make sure you have the correct rings before proceeding. If you are assessing the condition of used rings, have the cylinder bores checked and measured by a Land Rover dealer or similar engine reconditioning specialist, so that you can be sure of exactly which component is worn, and seek advice as to the best course of action to take.

4 If the end gap is still too small, it must be opened up by careful filing of the ring ends using a fine file. If it is too large, this is not as serious, unless the specified limit is exceeded, in which case very careful checking is required of the dimensions of all components, as well as of the new parts.

5 Repeat the procedure for each ring that will be installed in the first cylinder, and for each ring in the remaining cylinders. Remember to keep rings, pistons and cylinders matched up.

6 Refit the piston rings as follows. Where the original rings are being refitted, use the marks or notes made on removal, to ensure

14.3 With the ring square in the bore, measure the end gap with a feeler gauge

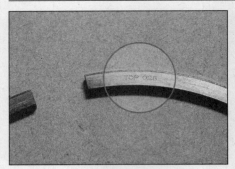

14.6 Piston ring TOP markings

15.3a Fitting the shells in each main bearing location

15.3b Note the thrustwashers integral with the No 3 (centre) upper main bearing shell

that each ring is refitted to its original groove and the same way up. New rings generally have their top surfaces identified by markings, often an indication of size (such as STD or the word TOP). The rings must be fitted with such markings uppermost **(see illustration)**. **Note:** *Always follow the instructions printed on the ring package or box as different manufacturers may require different approaches. Do not mix up the top and second compression rings as they usually have different cross-sections.*

7 The oil control ring (lowest one on the piston) is usually installed first. It is usually composed of three separate elements. Slip the spacer/expander into the groove. Next, install the lower side rail. Do not use a piston ring installation tool on the oil ring side rails, as they may be damaged. Instead, place one end of the side rail into the groove between the spacer/expander and the ring land, hold it firmly in place, then slide a finger around the piston while pushing the rail into the groove. Next, install the upper side rail in the same manner.

8 After all the oil ring components have been installed, check that both the upper and lower side rails can be turned smoothly in the ring groove.

9 The second compression (middle) ring is installed next, followed by the top compression ring. Make sure their marks are uppermost. Do not expand either ring any more than necessary to slide it over the top of the piston.

10 With all the rings in position, space the ring gaps (including the elements of the oil control ring) uniformly around the piston at 120° intervals. Repeat the procedure for the remaining pistons and rings.

15 Crankshaft – refitting

Note: *New main bearing cap retaining bolts must be used when refitting the crankshaft.*

1 Crankshaft refitting is the first major step in engine reassembly. It is assumed at this point that the cylinder block/crankcase and crankshaft have been cleaned, inspected and repaired or reconditioned as necessary. Where removed, the oil jets must be refitted at this stage and their mounting bolts tightened securely.

2 Place the cylinder block on a clean, level work surface, with the crankcase facing upwards. Wipe out the inner surfaces of the main bearing caps and crankcase with a clean cloth as they must be kept spotlessly clean.

3 Clean the rear surface of the new main bearing shells with a lint free cloth. Fit the shells with an oil groove in each main bearing location in the block. Note the thrustwashers integral with the No 3 (centre) upper main bearing shell **(see illustrations)**.

Fit the other shell from each bearing set in the corresponding main bearing cap. The oil holes in the block must line up with one of the oil holes in the bearing shell. Don't hammer the shells into place, and don't nick or gouge the bearing faces. It is critically important that the surfaces of the bearings are kept free from damage and contamination.

4 Clean the bearing surfaces of the shells in the block and the crankshaft main bearing journals with a clean, lint-free cloth. Check or clean the oil holes in the crankshaft, as any dirt will become embedded in the new bearings when the engine is first started.

5 Apply a thin, uniform layer of clean molybdenum disulphide-based grease, engine assembly lubricant, or clean engine oil to each surface **(see illustration)**. Coat the thrustwasher surfaces as well.

6 Making sure the crankshaft journals are clean, lay the crankshaft back in place in the block.

7 Lubricate the crankshaft oil seal journals with molybdenum disulphide-based grease, engine assembly lubricant, or clean engine oil.

8 Clean the bearing surfaces of the shells in the caps then lubricate them. Refit the caps in their respective positions, with the arrows pointing to the timing chain end of the engine.

9 Apply a smear of clean engine oil to the threads and underneath the heads of the new main bearing cap bolts. Fit the bolts tightening them all by hand.

10 Working on one cap at a time, from the centre main bearing outwards (and ensuring that each cap is tightened down squarely and evenly onto the block), tighten the main bearing cap bolts to the specified Stage 1 torque setting given in Chapter 2A or Chapter 2B **(see illustration)**.

11 When all the bolts have been tightened to the Stage 1 setting, go around again and tighten them to the Stage 2 setting, then Stage 3 and Stage 4.

12 Stage 5 involves tightening the bolts though an angle, rather than to a torque. The bolts must be rotated through the specified angle – special angle gauges are available

15.5 Ensure the bearing shells are absolutely clean and lubricate liberally

15.10 Tighten the main bearing cap bolts in the initial Stages using a torque wrench

15.12 Using an angle-tightening gauge to tighten the main bearing cap bolts to the final Stage

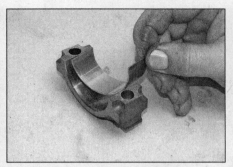

16.3 Press the bearing shells into the connecting rods and caps ensuring they sit centrally

16.6 Insert the piston/connecting rod assembly into the top of the cylinder

from tool outlets **(see illustration)**. As a guide, a 90° angle is equivalent to a quarter-turn, and this is easily judged by assessing the start and end positions of the socket handle.

13 Rotate the crankshaft a number of times by hand, to check for any obvious binding.

14 Check the crankshaft endfloat (see Section 10). It should be correct if the crankshaft thrust faces are not worn or damaged, and if the thrust control bearings have been renewed.

15 Referring to Part A or B of this Chapter, fit a new crankshaft oil seal, then refit the flywheel.

16 Refit the piston connecting rod assemblies as described in Section 16.

16 Piston/connecting rod assemblies – refitting

Note: *At this point, it is assumed that the crankshaft has been measured, renewed/reground as necessary, and has been fitted to the engine as described in Section 15.*

Note: *New retaining bolts must be used when refitting the big-end bearing caps.*

1 Before refitting the piston/connecting rod assemblies, the cylinder bores must be

perfectly clean, the top edge of each cylinder must be chamfered, and the crankshaft must be in place.

2 Remove the big-end bearing cap from No 1 cylinder connecting rod (refer to the marks noted or made on removal). Remove the original bearing shells, and wipe the bearing recesses of the connecting rod and cap with a clean, lint-free cloth. They must be kept spotlessly clean.

3 Ensure that all traces of the protective grease on the new bearing shells are cleaned off using paraffin, then wipe the shells dry with a lint-free cloth. Press the bearing shells into the connecting rods and caps ensuring they sit centrally within the rods and caps **(see illustration)**.

4 Lubricate the cylinder bores, the pistons, piston rings and upper bearing shells with clean engine oil. Lay out each piston/connecting rod assembly in order on a clean work surface. Take care not to scratch the crankpins and cylinder bores when the pistons are refitted.

5 Start with piston/connecting rod assembly No 1. Make sure that the piston rings are still spaced as described in Section 14, then clamp them in position with a piston ring compressor.

6 Insert the piston/connecting rod assembly into the top of cylinder No 1 **(see illustration)**. Lower the big-end in first, guiding it to protect the cylinder bores. Take particular care not to damage or break off the oil spray jets when guiding the connecting rods onto the crankpins.

7 Ensure that the orientation of the piston in its cylinder is correct. The piston crown, connecting rod and big-end bearing caps should have markings which must be aligned in the position noted on removal (see Section 9).

8 Using a block of wood or hammer handle against the piston crown, tap the assembly into the cylinder until the piston crown is flush with the top of the cylinder **(see illustration)**.

9 Ensure that the bearing shell is still correctly installed. Liberally lubricate the crankpin and both bearing shells with clean engine oil. Taking care not to mark the cylinder bores, tap the piston/connecting rod assembly down the bore and onto the crankpin. Oil the threads and underside of the new retaining bolt heads, then fit the big-end bearing cap, tightening its retaining bolts finger tight at first. Note that the orientation of the bearing cap with respect to the connecting rod must be correct when the two components are reassembled **(see illustration)**.

16.8 Using a hammer handle to tap the piston into its bore

16.9 Note the markings on the bearing cap with respect to the connecting rod on refitting

16.10a Tighten the big-end bearing cap bolts to the Stage 1 and Stage 2 torque settings using a torque wrench...

16.10b ...then tighten the bolts to the Stage 3 setting using an angle-tightening gauge

10 Tighten the retaining bolts to the specified Stage 1 torque setting, then to the Stage 2 setting. Stage 3 involves tightening the bolts though an angle rather than to a torque. The bolts must be rotated through the specified angle (special angle gauges are available from tool outlets). As a guide, a 90° angle is equivalent to a quarter-turn, and this is easily judged by assessing the start and end positions of the socket handle **(see illustrations)**.

11 Repeat the entire procedure for the remaining piston/connecting rod assemblies.

12 After all the piston/connecting rod assemblies have been properly installed, rotate the crankshaft a number of times by hand to check for any obvious binding or tight spots.

13 Fit the new lower crankcase-to-cylinder block gasket. Refit the lower crankcase to the cylinder block, then insert the bolts and hand-tighten **(see illustrations)**.

14 Place a straight-edge across the transmission mating surface of the cylinder block and the lower crankcase to check the lower crankcase-to-cylinder block alignment. The lower crankcase should be flush with the cylinder block. If not flush, the alignment should be within −0.01 mm overlap to a +0.2 mm gap at the rear of the cylinder block. Repeat this check by placing the straight-edge against the two projecting bosses on the side of the cylinder block **(see illustrations)**. In this instance the alignment should be −0.05 mm overlap to a +0.05 mm gap

15 Once the alignment is within tolerance, tighten the lower crankcase bolts to the specified torque.

16 Where applicable, set the position of the crankshaft position sensor mounting bracket, then refer to Part A or B of this Chapter (as applicable) and refit the relevant assemblies.

Setting the crankshaft position sensor mounting bracket

Note: *Land Rover service tool 303-698 obtainable from Land Rover dealers or a tool supplier, will be required for this procedure.*

17 If the crankshaft position sensor mounting bracket was removed from the cylinder block during the cleaning and reconditioning procedures described previously, its position in relation to the flywheel will need to be reset as follows.

18 Refit the crankshaft position sensor mounting bracket and install the bolts, tightened finger tight.

19 Make up an arrow pointer out of stiff tin plate or similar. Drill a hole in the plate and bolt it to the cylinder block using the upper left-hand transmission mounting bolt hole. Use suitable washers as necessary so that the pointer lies just flush with the flywheel periphery **(see illustration)**. Once the pointer

16.13a Fit the new lower crankcase-to-cylinder block gasket...

16.13b ...then refit the lower crankcase to the cylinder block

16.14a Place a straight-edge across the transmission mating surface of the cylinder block...

16.14b ...and against the two projecting bosses on the fuel injection pump side of the cylinder block

16.19 Make up an arrow pointer out of stiff tin plate and bolt it to the cylinder block using suitable washers as necessary

16.21a Rotate the crankshaft until No 1 piston is approximately 10 mm before top dead centre, then zero the dial gauge

16.21b Mark the position of the flywheel using a white marker pen (or similar) in relation to the arrow pointer

16.24 Measure the distance between the two marks made on the flywheel

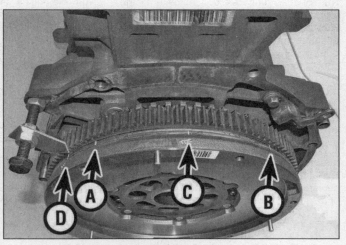

16.26 Arrangement of the flywheel markings

*A First mark   B Second mark   C Established TDC position
D Established 50° BTDC position*

is in place, do not move it during the setting procedure.

20 Mount a DTI (Dial Test Indicator, or dial gauge) on the cylinder head mating face of the cylinder block, with the probe in line with No 1 cylinder piston.

21 Rotate the crankshaft until No 1 piston is approximately 10 mm before top dead centre (TDC). Zero the dial gauge and mark the position of the flywheel using a white marker pen or similar, in relation to the arrow pointer **(see illustrations)**.

22 Turn the flywheel anti-clockwise until the dial gauge indicates 'O'. Again, mark the position of the flywheel, using a white marker pen or similar, in relation to the arrow pointer.

23 Repeat paragraphs 21 and 22 to make sure that the markings on the flywheel are correct.

24 Using a dressmaker's tape measure (or a suitable length of string) measure the distance between the two marks on the flywheel **(see illustration)**. Divide this measurement by 2 and mark that measurement on the flywheel. This will be the TDC position.

25 Again, using a tape measure or a suitable length of string, wrap it around the flywheel outer periphery to measure the flywheel circumference. Record this measurement.

26 Multiply the circumference measurement by 0.1388 and mark this new figure on the flywheel by measuring anti-clockwise from the previously marked TDC position. This new figure will be the 50° BTDC position **(see illustration)**.

27 Turn the flywheel to align the newly established 50° BTDC position with the arrow pointer **(see illustration)**.

28 Insert the manufacturers special tool into the crankshaft position sensor mounting bracket, and move the bracket within the

16.27 Turn the flywheel to align the newly established 50° BTDC position with the arrow pointer

16.28a Insert the special tool into the crankshaft position sensor mounting bracket...

16.28b ...and move the bracket until the tool drops into position in the flywheel

limit of the elongated bolt holes until the tool drops into position in the flywheel **(see illustrations)**. Now tighten the crankshaft position sensor mounting bracket retaining bolts to the specified torque. Remove the special tool on completion.

17 Engine –
initial start-up after overhaul

1 With the engine refitted in the vehicle, double-check the engine oil and coolant levels. Make a final check that everything has been reconnected, and that there are no tools or rags left in the engine compartment.

2 Turn the engine on the starter until the oil pressure warning light goes out. If the lamp fails to extinguish after several seconds of cranking, check the engine oil level and oil filter security. Assuming these are correct, check the security of the oil pressure switch wiring. Do not progress any further until you are satisfied that oil is being pumped around the engine at sufficient pressure.

3 Prime and bleed the fuel system as described in Chapter 4A Section 3, then start the engine, noting that this may take a little longer than usual.

4 While the engine is idling, check for fuel, water and oil leaks. Don't be alarmed if there are some odd smells and smoke from parts getting hot and burning off oil deposits.

5 Assuming all is well, run the engine until it reaches normal operating temperature, then switch off the engine.

6 After a few minutes, recheck the oil and coolant levels as described in *Weekly checks* and top-up as necessary.

7 Note that there is no need to retighten the cylinder head bolts once the engine has first run after reassembly.

8 If new pistons, rings or crankshaft bearings have been fitted, the engine must be treated as new and run-in for the first 600 miles. Do not operate the engine at full-throttle or allow it to labour at low engine speeds in any gear. It is recommended that the oil and filter be changed at the end of this period.

Chapter 3
Cooling, heating and ventilation systems

Contents

Degrees of difficulty

| **Easy,** suitable for novice with little experience | **Fairly easy,** suitable for beginner with some experience | **Fairly difficult,** suitable for competent DIY mechanic | **Difficult,** suitable for experienced DIY mechanic | **Very difficult,** suitable for expert DIY or professional |

Specifications

General

Cooling system capacity:
2.2 litre engine	8.2 litres
2.4 litre engine	10.0 litres
Radiator capacity	2.3 litres
Coolant expansion tank (up to cold level)	1.2 litres
Expansion tank cap opening pressure.	1.0 bar
Cooling fan type.	Viscous (with bi-metallic control)
Cooling fan diameter	475 mm (18.70 inches)

Thermostat

Opening temperatures:
Starts to open.	82°C
Fully open	96°C

Torque wrench setting

	Nm	lbf ft
Coolant pump bolts	23	17
Coolant pump outlet manifold	10	7
Cylinder head temperature sensor (2.4 litre engines)	10	7
Charge air cooler to radiator bolts	20	15
Charge air cooler bracket bolts	10	7

1 General information and precautions

General information

1 The cooling system is of pressurised type, comprising a coolant pump, a crossflow radiator, temperature-conscious thermo-viscous cooling fan, and thermostat. The coolant pump is bolted to the front of the engine cylinder block, and is driven by the auxiliary drivebelt off the crankshaft pulley. The thermo-viscous cooling fan is attached to a pulley bolted to the front of the engine cylinder block, and is also driven by the auxiliary drivebelt off the crankshaft pulley.

2 The thermostat is located between the upper and lower radiator hoses on the left-hand side front of the engine compartment, behind the radiator.

3 The system functions as follows. Cold coolant from the radiator passes to the coolant pump, where it is pumped around the cylinder block, head passages and heater matrix. After cooling the cylinder bores, combustion surfaces and valve seats, the coolant reaches the underside of the thermostat, which is initially closed. The coolant passes through the heater, and is returned to the coolant pump.

4 When the engine is cold, the coolant circulates only through the cylinder block, cylinder head and heater. When the coolant reaches a predetermined temperature, the thermostat opens and the coolant also passes through to the radiator. As the coolant circulates through the radiator, it is cooled by the inrush of air when the vehicle is in forward motion. Airflow is supplemented by the action of the cooling fan when necessary. Once the coolant has passed through the radiator, and has cooled, the cycle is repeated.

5 An expansion tank is fitted to the right-hand rear side of the engine compartment to accommodate expansion of the coolant when hot.

6 The thermo-viscous cooling fan is controlled by the temperature of air behind the radiator. When the air temperature reaches a predetermined level, a bi-metallic coil opens a valve within the unit, and silicon fluid is fed through a system of vanes. Half of the vanes are driven directly by the fan pulley by the auxiliary drivebelt, and the remaining half are connected to the fan blades. The vanes are arranged so that drive is transmitted to the fan blades in relation to the drag, or viscosity of the fluid, and this in turn depends on ambient temperature and engine speed. The fan is therefore only operated when required.

7 On models with air conditioning, a electric cooling fan is also fitted and is mounted on the front of the condenser. The electric fan is controlled by the engine management system powertrain control module according to air conditioning system demand.

Precautions

 Warning: Do not attempt to remove the expansion tank filler cap, nor disturb any part of the cooling system, while the engine is hot, as there is a high risk of scalding. If the expansion tank filler cap must be removed before the engine and radiator have fully cooled (even though this is not recommended) the pressure in the cooling system must first be relieved. Cover the cap with a thick layer of cloth, to avoid scalding, and slowly unscrew the filler cap until a hissing sound can be heard. When the hissing has stopped, indicating that the pressure has reduced, slowly unscrew the filler cap until it can be removed; if more hissing sounds are heard, wait until they have stopped before unscrewing the cap completely. At all times keep well away from the filler cap opening.

Warning: Do not allow antifreeze to come into contact with skin, or with the painted surfaces of the vehicle. Rinse off spills immediately with plenty of water. Never leave antifreeze lying around in an open container, or in a puddle in the driveway or on the garage floor. Children and pets are attracted by its sweet smell, but antifreeze can be fatal if ingested.

Warning: Refer to Section for precautions to be observed when working on models with air conditioning.

2 Cooling system hoses – disconnection and renewal

Note: *Refer to the warnings given in Section 1 of this Chapter before proceeding.*

1 If the checks described in Chapter 1 Section 17 reveal a faulty hose, it must be renewed as follows.

2 First drain the cooling system (see Chapter 1 Section 47). If the coolant is not due for renewal, it may be re-used if it is collected in a clean container.

3 To disconnect a hose, use a screwdriver to slacken the clips, then move them along the hose, clear of the relevant inlet/outlet union. On some models, the clips are released by squeezing together the tangs at the ends of the clips. This can be achieved using pliers/pipe grips, or using a tool specifically for this purpose **(see illustration)**. Carefully work the hose free. The hoses can be removed with relative ease when new – on an older vehicle, they may have stuck.

4 If a hose proves stubborn, try to release it by rotating it on its unions before attempting to work it off. Gently prise the end of the hose with a blunt instrument (such as a flat-bladed screwdriver), but do not apply too much force, and take care not to damage the pipe stubs or hoses. Note in particular that the radiator hose

2.3 Spring-type clips fitted to radiator hoses

unions are fragile; do not use excessive force when attempting to remove the hoses.

 HAYNES HINT *If all else fails, cut the hose with a sharp knife, then slit it so that it can be peeled off in two pieces. A new hose will be required, but this is preferable to buying a new radiator. Check first, however, that a new hose is readily available.*

5 When fitting a hose, first slide the clips onto the hose, then work the hose into position. If clamp-type clips were originally fitted, it is a good idea to update them with screw-type clips when refitting the hose. If the hose is stiff, use a little soapy water as a lubricant, or soften the hose by soaking it in hot water.

6 Work the hose into position, checking that it is correctly routed, then slide each clip along the hose until it passes over the flared end of the relevant inlet/outlet union, before tightening the clips securely.

7 Refill the cooling system with reference to Chapter 1 Section 47.

8 Check thoroughly for leaks as soon as possible after disturbing any part of the cooling system.

3 Radiator – removal, inspection and refitting

HAYNES HINT *If leakage is the reason for wanting to remove the radiator, bear in mind that minor leaks can be often be cured using a radiator sealant, with the radiator in situ.*

Removal

1 Disconnect the battery, as described in Chapter 5 Section 4.

2 Open the bonnet, then undo the six

3.2 Remove the upper fan shroud

3.6 Remove the two stay brackets

3.7a Remove the retaining nuts...

fasteners and remove the upper part of the cooling fan shroud **(see illustration)**.

3 Undo the retaining screws and remove the grille and support surround panel, as described in Chapter 12 Section 19.

4 On models with air-conditioning, remove the condenser, as described in Section 11.

5 Remove the bonnet, as described in Chapter 12 Section 7, as the bonnet support stay crossmember/latch panel needs to be removed.

6 Undo the retaining bolts and remove the two stay brackets from in front of the radiator/intercooler **(see illustration)**.

7 Working at each side of the crossmember/latch panel, undo the four retaining nuts (two at each side), and then remove the studs **(see illustrations)**. With the studs removed, the crossmember/latch panel can now be removed and moved to one side. Note the bonnet release cable is still attached to the latch panel, so position it to one side.

8 Remove the charge air cooler (intercooler), as described in Chapter 4A Section 17.

9 Drain the cooling system as described in Chapter 1 Section 47.

10 Release the securing clip and disconnect the small fuel cooler coolant hose from the right-hand lower part of the radiator **(see illustration)**.

11 Release the securing clip and disconnect the small coolant hose from the reservoir to the top left-hand part of the radiator, then unclip it from the along the top of the radiator **(see illustrations)**.

3.7b ...and lock two together to remove the studs

3.10 Disconnect the hose from the radiator

3.11a Disconnect the coolant hose...

3.11b ...and unclip it from the retaining clips

12 Release the clips and disconnect the upper and lower coolant hoses to the left-hand rear of the radiator, from the "T" piece and thermostat housing **(see illustrations)**.

13 On 2.2 litre engines, disconnect the coolant temp sensor wiring connector from the "T" piece to the left-hand side of the radiator **(see illustration)**.

3.12a Remove the two coolant hoses – 2.2 litre engine

3.12b Remove the three coolant hoses – 2.4 litre engine

3.13 Disconnect the sensor wiring connector

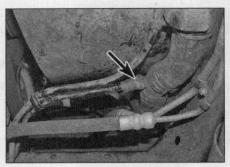

3.14 Disconnect the fuel cooler hose

3.15a Remove the radiator...

3.15b ...lifting it from the lower mountings

3.16 Check rubber mountings

side rear of the radiator, clipped to the lower fan shroud(see illustration).

2 Drain the cooling system as described in Chapter 1 Section 47. If the coolant is relatively new or in good condition, drain it into a clean container and re-use it.

3 Release the six fasteners and remove the upper shroud from the front of the engine compartment (see illustration 3.2).

4 To make access easier, undo the retaining bolts and move the power steering fluid reservoir and bracket to one side.

5 Release the securing clip and disconnect the hose from the left-hand side of the charge air cooler/intercooler, and move it to one side to access the thermostat housing (see illustration).

6 Slacken the securing clips and disconnect the three coolant hoses from the thermostat housing (see illustration).

7 Unclip the thermostat housing from the lower fan shroud and remove it from the engine compartment.

Refitting

8 Refitting is a reversal of removal, and refill the cooling system as described in Chapter 1 Section 47.

14 Working under the vehicle (below the lower part of the fan shroud), disconnect the small coolant hose from the radiator lower coolant hose (see illustration).

15 Lift the radiator assembly upwards, releasing it from the lower mounting pegs on the crossmember(see illustrations), as it is removed, unclip any hoses from the retaining clips under the lower fan shroud. The radiator will be removed, complete with lower part of the fan shroud, lower coolant hoses and thermostat housing.

Refitting

16 Refitting is the reverse of the removal procedure, noting the following points:
a) Ensure that the rubber mountings are

located correctly in the lower part of the radiator (see illustration).
b) Securely tighten all hose retaining clips.
c) On completion, refill the cooling system as described in Chapter 1 Section 47.

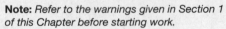

4 Thermostat –
removal and refitting

Note: Refer to the warnings given in Section 1 of this Chapter before starting work.

Removal

1 The thermostat is located to the left-hand

5 Cooling fans –
removal and refitting

Note: A viscous coupling is fitted to the cooling fan, and a large open-ended spanner will be required to unscrew the coupling assembly.

Removal

1 Disconnect the battery negative lead, as described in Chapter 5 Section 4.

2 Release the six fasteners and remove the upper shroud from the front of the engine compartment (see illustration 3.2).

3 Using the special open-ended spanner, unscrew the viscous coupling from the

4.1 Location of the thermostat

4.5 Disconnect the intercooler hose

4.6 Remove the hoses from the thermostat housing

5.3a Use a flat open-ended spanner...

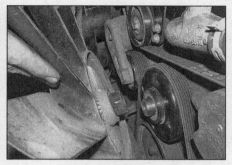

5.3b ...to remove the viscous fan – 2.4 litre shown

5.3c 2.2 litre has longer fan securing nut

5.3d Using special tool to prevent pulley from turning

5.5 Undo the four upper screws

5.6 Undo the screw at the side of the grille surround (one side shown)

pulley(see illustrations). If necessary, use a special tool to counterhold the pulley. **Note:** *The viscous coupling has a normal right-hand thread – ie, it unscrews anti-clockwise.*

Refitting

4 Refitting is the reverse of removal.

Condenser cooling fan (models with air-conditioning)

Removal

5 Open the bonnet and undo the four retaining screws from across the top of the grille panel (see illustration).
6 Undo the two retaining screws (one at each side) from the lower part of the front grill surround (see illustration). With all the screws removed the grille and surround can be withdrawn from the front of the vehicle.
7 Disconnect the wiring plug, then undo the

retaining nuts and remove the cooling fan assembly from the front of the condenser (see illustration).

Refitting

8 Refitting is a reversal of removal.

6 Coolant temperature sensor – removal and refitting

1 The coolant temperature sensor provides data to the engine management ECM, which uses the data to adjust the fuelling of the engine, glow plug operation, and control the operation of the temperature gauge/warning system. The sensor is an NTC (Negative Temperature Co-efficient) sensor, meaning that as the temperature rises, the resistance of the sensor decreases. Although no specific

values are given by Land Rover, it should be possible to check that the resistance of the sensor changes as the temperature changes using a digital multimeter. Should the sensor fail, a fault code should be stored in the ECM memory by the self-diagnosis system, which can be interrogated using a suitable fault code reader.
2 On 2.4 litre engines, the coolant temperature sensor is called a cylinder head temperature (CHT) sensor, and is screwed into the rear of the cylinder head. On 2.2 litre engines, the coolant temperature sensor is called an engine coolant temperature (ECT) sensor and is located in the coolant top hose to the radiator (see illustrations).

Removal

3 Either partially drain the cooling system to just below the level of the sensor (as described

5.7 Condenser cooling fan

6.2a CHT sensor – 2.4 litre engines

6.2b ECT sensor – 2.2 litre engines

6.4 Release the red locking clip and disconnect the wiring connector

6.5 Disconnect the wiring connector

7.4 Remove the hoses from the pump – 2.2 litre shown

in Chapter 1 Section 47), or have ready a suitable plug which can be used to plug the sensor aperture whilst it is removed. If a plug is used, take great care not to damage the sensor unit threads (where applicable), and do not use anything which will allow foreign matter to enter the cooling system.

4 On 2.4 litre engines, release the locking clip and disconnect the wiring connector on the top of the engine at the rear of the cylinder head **(see illustration)**. There is a short length of wire connected to the cylinder head temperature sensor, so a socket with a slot down the side (Land Rover tool no. 303-680), will be required to unscrew the sensor from the rear of the cylinder head.

5 On 2.2 litre engines, disconnect the wiring connector, then turn the sensor anti-clockwise and pull it out from the upper coolant hose **(see illustration)**. Check the sealing washer/O-ring and replace if required.

Refitting

6 On 2.4 litre engines, refit the sensor to the rear of the cylinder head and tighten to the specified torque, and then reconnect the wiring.

7 On 2.2 litre engines, refit the sender to the upper hose and turn clockwise to secure in place, and then reconnect the wiring.

8 Top-up the cooling system as described in Chapter 1 Section 47.

9 On completion, start the engine and check the operation of the temperature gauge. Also check for coolant leaks.

7 Coolant pump – removal and refitting

Note: *Refer to the warnings given in Section 1 of this Chapter before starting work.*

Removal

1 Drain the cooling system as described in Chapter 1 Section 47. If the coolant is relatively new or in good condition, drain it into a clean container and re-use it.

2 Remove the auxiliary drivebelt, as described in Chapter 1 Section 52.

3 On 2.4 litre engines, remove the braking system vacuum pump, from the top of the coolant pump, as described in Chapter 10 Section 19.

4 Release the clips and disconnect the accessible coolant hoses from the rear of the coolant pump **(see illustration)**.

5 Undo the three bolts (2.2 litre engines) or four bolts (2.4 litre engines) and detach the

coolant pump from the cylinder block. Release the clips and disconnect any remaining coolant hoses, then remove the pump from the engine **(see illustrations)**. Remove the gasket and discard it. Obtain a new gasket for refitting.

6 If required, undo the bolts and remove the coolant pipe block from the rear of the pump. Discard the O-ring seal and obtain a new O-ring for refitting.

Refitting

7 Refitting is a reversal of removal, but tighten the mounting bolts/nuts to the specified torque. Refill the cooling system as described in Chapter 1 Section 47.

8 Heating and ventilation system – general information

1 The heating/ventilation system consists of a multi-speed blower motor, face-level vents in the centre and at each end of the facia, and air ducts to the front footwells.

2 The control unit is located in the facia, and the controls operate flap valves to deflect and mix the air flowing through the various parts of the heating/ventilation system. The flap

7.5a Undo the three bolts/nut – 2.2 litre engine

7.5b Undo the four bolts – 2.4 litre engine

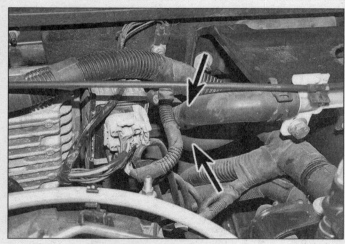

9.4 Disconnect the heater hoses

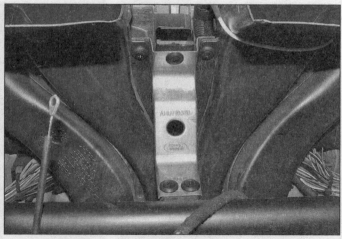

9.6 Remove the screws/fasteners from the support bracket

valves are contained in the air distribution housing, which acts as a central distribution unit, passing air to the various ducts and vents.

3 Cold air enters the system through the grille at the side of the engine compartment.

4 The airflow, which can be boosted by the blower, then flows through the various ducts, according to the settings of the controls. Stale air is expelled through ducts at the rear of the vehicle. If warm air is required, the cold air is passed through the heater matrix, which is heated by the engine coolant.

5 A recirculation lever enables the outside air supply to be closed off, while the air inside the vehicle is recirculated. This can be useful to prevent unpleasant odours entering from outside the vehicle, but should only be used briefly, as the recirculated air inside the vehicle will soon deteriorate in quality.

9	Heater/ventilation components – removal and refitting

Caution: On models with air conditioning, it is not possible to remove the heater unit assembly without first discharging the air conditioning system (see Section 10). Operations involving the heater unit assembly, should therefore be entrusted to a Land Rover dealer or specialist, if the system has not been discharged.

Heater unit assembly

1 Disconnect the battery negative terminal, as described in Chapter 5 Section 4. To improve access, remove the bonnet as described in Chapter 12 Section 7.

2 On models with air-conditioning, have the system discharged by a specialist. Remove the engine control module (ECM) from the rear of the engine compartment, and then disconnect the air-conditioning pipes from

the bulkhead. Make sure all the openings are sealed using blanking plugs, to prevent dirt and moisture entering the system.

3 Clamp the two heater hoses that connected to the heater matrix pipes, on the left-hand side of the bulkhead, to minimise coolant loss or drain the cooling system, as described in Chapter 1 Section 47.

4 Note the fitting of each hose, and then slacken the retaining clips, and disconnect the coolant hoses from the heater matrix unions on the bulkhead **(see illustration)**.

5 Remove the facia panel as described in Chapter 12 Section 24.

6 Undo the retaining screws and remove them from the support bracket at the centre of the air vents **(see illustration)**.

7 Release the fasteners and remove the air ducting from across the vehicle bulkhead **(see illustrations)**. As the ducting is removed, release any wiring or cable retaining clips from the ducting, noting the routing of any wiring/ cables and fasteners.

8 On models with air-conditioning, disconnect the wiring connector for the de-icing sensor at the left-hand side of the heater housing.

9 Slacken and remove the four retaining nuts, one to each side of the upper part of the

9.7a Remove the outer ducting...

9.7b ...the inner ducting...

9.7c ...the lower ducting...

9.7d ...and the centre ducting

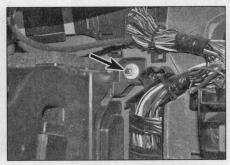

9.9a Remove the left-hand upper nut...

9.9b ...the upper right-hand nut...

9.9c ...and the two lower nuts

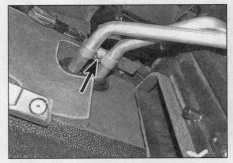

9.13 Undo the pipe support bracket screw

9.14 Undo the two pipe securing clamps

9.20 Disconnect the wiring connector

heater unit and two at the lower centre part of the heater housing (see illustrations).

10 Manoeuvre the heater assembly out of position, releasing the grommet where the heater pipes go through the bulkhead, and then remove it from the vehicle. Recover the seal fitted between the unit and bulkhead (where applicable).

HINT: Be prepared for some coolant spillage as the heater is removed; wash off any spilt coolant immediately with cold water.

11 Refitting is the reverse of removal.

Heater matrix

12 Remove the facia panel as described in Chapter 12 Section 24.

13 Working at the top of the coolant pipes, where the pipes go through the grommet in the bulkhead, slacken and remove the support bracket retaining screw (see illustration).

14 Slacken the two clamps, securing the

coolant pipes to the heater matrix (see illustration).

15 Carefully maneuver the coolant pipes out of position, and then withdraw the heater matrix from the housing. Where applicable, recover the seal fitted to the outside of the matrix. Examine the seals for signs of damage and deterioration, and renew if necessary.

16 On refitting, fit the seal to the heater matrix (where applicable), and slide the matrix into the housing.

17 Ensure that the matrix is correctly seated, then refit the coolant pipes back to the heater matrix, making sure they are secured in position correctly.

18 Refit the facia panel with reference to Chapter 12 Section 24.

Heater blower motor

19 According to Land Rover information the heater blower motor is easily removed from the engine compartment, complete with its housing. We found that the blower

motor housing could not be removed easily as the air inlet ducting could not easily be removed without any damage. There is not enough room between the housing and the wing to remove the blower motor alone. As the left-hand front wing is only bolted on, we found it easier to remove the wing, to gain access to the blower motor housing. Remove the front wing, as described in Chapter 12 Section 19.

20 Disconnect the wiring connector from the blower motor (see illustration).

21 Slacken and remove the three retaining screws, and withdraw the blower motor from the housing (see illustrations).

22 Refitting is the reverse of removal.

Heater blower motor resistor

23 Working down the left-hand side of the blower motor housing, disconnect the resistor wiring connector (see illustration).

9.21a Undo the retaining screws...

9.21b ...and withdraw the blower motor

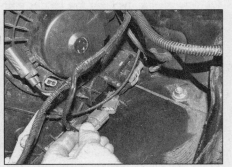

9.23 Disconnect the wiring connector

9.24 Remove the blower motor resistor

11.1a Air conditioning system high-pressure service point...

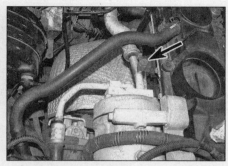

11.1b ...and low-pressure service point

24 Undo the two retaining screws and withdraw the resistor from the lower part of the blower motor housing **(see illustration)**.
25 Refitting is the reverse of removal.

---

10 Air conditioning system – general information and precautions

General information

1 An air conditioning system, where fitted, enables the temperature of incoming air to be lowered, and also dehumidifies the air, which makes for rapid demisting and increased comfort.
2 The cooling side of the system works in the same way as a domestic refrigerator. Refrigerant gas is drawn into a belt-driven compressor, and passes into a condenser mounted in front of the radiator, where it loses heat and becomes liquid. The liquid passes through an expansion valve to an evaporator, where it changes from liquid under high pressure to gas under low pressure. This change is accompanied by a drop in temperature, which cools the evaporator. The refrigerant returns to the compressor, and the cycle begins again.
3 Air blown through the evaporator passes to the air distribution unit, where it is mixed with hot air blown through the heater matrix, to achieve the desired temperature in the passenger compartment.
4 The heating side of the system works in the same way as on models without air conditioning (see Section 8).
5 The operation of the system is controlled electronically by the coolant temperature sensor, and the pressure switches which are screwed into the compressor high-pressure line.

Precautions

When an air conditioning system is fitted, it is necessary to observe special precautions whenever dealing with any part of the system, its associated components and any items which necessitate disconnection of the system. If for any reason the system must be disconnected, entrust this task to your Land Rover dealer or a refrigeration engineer.

⚠ *Warning: The refrigeration circuit contains a liquid refrigerant under pressure, and it is dangerous to disconnect any part of the system without specialised knowledge and equipment. The refrigerant should only be handled by qualified persons. If it is splashed onto the skin, it can cause frostbite. It is not itself poisonous, but in the presence of a naked flame (including a lighted cigarette) it forms a poisonous gas. Uncontrolled discharging of the refrigerant is dangerous and potentially damaging to the environment. Do not operate the air conditioning system if it is known to be short of refrigerant, as this may damage the compressor.*

---

11 Air conditioning system components – removal and refitting 🔧

⚠ *Warning: The air conditioning system is under high pressure. Do not loosen any fittings or remove any components until after the system has been discharged. Air conditioning refrigerant should be properly discharged into an approved type of container, at a dealer service department or an automotive air conditioning repair facility capable of handling R134a refrigerant. Cap or plug the pipe lines as soon as they are disconnected, to prevent the entry of moisture or dirt. Always wear eye protection when disconnecting air conditioning system fittings.*

11.5b ...from each side of the condenser

Condenser
Removal

1 Have the refrigerant discharged at a dealer service department or an automotive air conditioning repair facility **(see illustration)**.
2 Disconnect the battery negative terminal (refer to Chapter 5 Section 4).
3 Remove the front grille and surround, as described in Chapter 12 Section 19.
4 Disconnect the wiring connector to the condenser cooling fan.
5 Disconnect the refrigerant lines from each side of the condenser **(see illustrations)**, and immediately cap the openings to prevent the entry of dirt and moisture. Discard the O-ring seals and obtain new ones for refitting.
6 Undo the three bolts and lift the condenser. fan assembly from the front of the vehicle **(see illustration)**.
7 if required the cooling fan can be unbolted

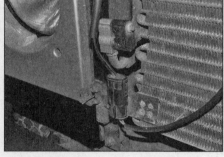

11.5a Disconnect the refrigerant pipe connections...

11.6 Undo the three bolts from the condenser frame

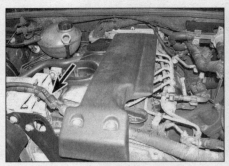

11.20 Disconnect the wiring connector

11.21 Undo the refrigerant pipe securing bolt

11.22 Undo the compressor securing bolts/nut

from the front of the condenser and the condenser unbolted from the support frame.

Refitting

8 Refitting is a reversal of removal, but fit new O-ring seals. The O-ring seals must be coated with clean refrigerant oil before refitting them. Have the system evacuated, charged and leak-tested by the specialist who discharged it.

Evaporator

Removal

9 Remove the air heater unit assembly, as described in Section 9.
10 Undo the three retaining screws and remove the cover from the right-hand side of the heater housing.
11 Release the de-icing sensor wiring from the evaporator and housing.
12 Undo the six retaining screws and remove the evaporator lower cover.
13 Undo the two retaining screws and withdraw the air flow deflector from the front of the evaporator.
14 Carefully remove the foam seal from around the expansion valve on the rear of the heater housing, then undo the two retaining bolts and remove the expansion valve from the housing. Discard the O-ring seals and obtain new ones for refitting.
15 Undo the remaining screws and split the heater unit housing into two halves, and then remove the evaporator.

Refitting

16 Refitting is a reversal of removal.

11.25 Undo the two bolts from the mounting bracket

Compressor

Removal

17 Have the refrigerant discharged at a dealer service department or an automotive air conditioning repair facility.
18 Disconnect the battery negative terminal (refer to Chapter 5 Section 4).
19 Remove the auxiliary drivebelt as described in Chapter 1 Section 52.
20 Disconnect the compressor wiring connector **(see illustration)**.
21 Unscrew the securing bolt and disconnect the pipe union block from the rear of the compressor **(see illustration)**. Discard the O-ring seals and obtain new ones for the refitting procedure. Tape over or plug the compressor apertures and line ends to prevent entry of moisture and dirt.
22 Support the compressor, then unscrew the three mounting bolts **(see illustration)**, and withdraw the compressor from mounting bracket on top of the engine.

Refitting

23 Refitting is a reversal of removal, but fit new O-ring seals after coating them with clean refrigerant oil, and tighten the mounting bolts to the specified torque. Have the system evacuated, charged and leak-tested by the specialist that discharged it.

Receiver drier

Removal

24 Have the refrigerant discharged at a

11.26 Undo the refrigerant pipe securing bolts

dealer service department or an automotive air conditioning repair facility.
25 Undo the two retaining bolts and disconnect the power steering reservoir from the mounting bracket **(see illustration)**.
26 Undo the retaining bolts and disconnect the refrigerant lines from the top of the receiver drier **(see illustration)**. Discard the O-ring seals and obtain new ones for refitting. Tape over or plug the accumulator apertures and line ends to prevent entry of dust and dirt.
27 Unscrew the clamp bolt, down the side of the mounting bracket, and then withdraw the receiver drier out from the engine compartment.

Refitting

28 Refitting is a reversal of removal, but fit new O-ring seals after coating them with clean refrigerant oil. Have the system evacuated, charged and leak-tested by the specialist who discharged it.

Expansion valve

Removal

29 Disconnect the battery negative terminal (refer to Chapter 5 Section 4).
30 Have the refrigerant discharged at a dealer service department or an automotive air conditioning repair facility.
31 Remove the engine control module (ECM) from the rear of the engine compartment, and then disconnect the air-conditioning pipes from the bulkhead. Discard the O-ring seals and obtain new ones for refitting. Make sure all the openings are sealed using blanking plugs, to prevent dirt and moisture entering the system.
32 Undo the two retaining bolts and remove the expansion valve from the bulkhead. Discard the O-ring seals and obtain new ones for refitting.

Refitting

33 Refitting is a reversal of removal, but fit new O-ring seals after coating them with clean refrigerant oil. Have the system evacuated, charged and leak-tested by the specialist who discharged it.

Chapter 4 Part A
Fuel and exhaust systems

Contents

Degrees of difficulty

Easy, suitable for novice with little experience	**Fairly easy,** suitable for beginner with some experience	**Fairly difficult,** suitable for competent DIY mechanic	**Difficult,** suitable for experienced DIY mechanic	**Very difficult,** suitable for expert DIY or professional

Specifications

General

System type	Turbocharged Direct Common-rail injection (TDCi), intercooled, controlled by engine management engine control module (ECM)
Firing order.	1 – 3 – 4 – 2 (No 1 at timing chain end)
Idle speed.	900 rpm (regulated by engine management system – no adjustment possible)
Fuel system operating pressure.	230 to 1600 bars (according to operating conditions)

Torque wrench settings

	Nm	lbf ft
Air conditioning compressor bolts	25	19
Alternator mounting bracket bolts	23	17
Camshaft sensor bolt	10	7
Catalytic converter support bracket bolts	25	19
Catalytic converter-to-turbocharger nuts*	48	35
Crankshaft position sensor bolt	7	5
Cylinder head temperature sensor	10	7
EGR pipe retaining nuts/bolts	10	7
Exhaust manifold heat shield bolts	10	7
Exhaust manifold-to-cylinder head*		
2.2 litre engines		
Stage 1	15	11
Stage 2	35	26
Stage 3 (stage 2 – repeated)	35	26
2.4 litre engines	40	30
Exhaust manifold-to-EGR cooler pipe*		
2.2 litre engines	25	19
2.4 litre engines	23	17
Exhaust system clamp nuts	43	32
Exhaust system flange nuts*	48	35
Fuel pump sender unit retaining ring	35	26
Fuel injection pump adaptor plate bolts	23	17
Fuel injection pump retaining bolts	23	17
Fuel injection pump sprocket retaining bolt:		
2.2 litre engines	55	41
2.4 litre engines:		
Retaining bolts	32	24
Retaining nut	64	47
Fuel injection pump support bracket bolts	23	17
Fuel injector clamp bracket bolts: *		
Stage 1	7	5
Stage 2	Angle-tighten a further 180°	
Fuel rail bolts	23	17
Fuel supply pipe union nuts	35	26
Inlet manifold-to-cylinder head bolts/nuts	15	11
Radiator support bracket bolts	10	7
Turbocharger oil return pipe nuts	10	7
Turbocharger oil supply pipe banjo union bolt	35	26
Turbocharger retaining nuts*	23	17
Turbocharger support bracket bolts	23	17

Use new nuts/bolts

1 General information and precautions

General information

1 The fuel system consists of a rear-mounted fuel tank, fuel pump sender unit mounted in the top of the fuel tank, fuel filter, high-pressure fuel injection pump, fuel rail, fuel pipes, injectors, and engine control module (ECM).

2 Fuel is pumped from the tank by the pump sender unit to the high-pressure fuel pump, which is bolted to the front left-hand side of the cylinder block. The fuel passes through the fuel filter, which is located on the chassis to the right-hand side of the fuel tank, in front of the off-side rear wheel, where foreign matter and water are removed.

3 The pump supplies fuel at very high pressure to a common rail (fuel rail) supplying all four injectors, which are then opened as signalled by the ECM. On reaching the high-pressure pump, the fuel is pressurised according to demand, and accumulates in the fuel rail, which acts as a fuel reservoir. The pressure in the rail is accurately maintained using a pressure sensor in the end of the rail and the pump's metering valve, with fuel return being controlled according to fuel temperature. The ECM determines the exact timing and duration of the injection period according to engine operating conditions. The four fuel injectors operate sequentially according to the firing order of the cylinders.

4 There are four pipes from the fuel rail (one for each of the injectors), and one from the fuel pump to the fuel rail. Each injector disperses the fuel evenly, and sprays fuel directly into the combustion chamber as its piston approaches TDC on the compression stroke.

5 Cold-starting performance is automatically controlled by the ECM. Under cold start conditions, the cylinder head temperature (CHT) sensor (2.4 litre engines) or engine coolant temperature (ECT) sensor (2.2 litre engines) informs the ECM on the engine temperature, this determines the preheat time. The glow plugs are located in the side of the cylinder head, one for each cylinder, and are electrically-heated. A warning light illuminates when the ignition is switched on, showing that the glow plugs are in operation. When the light goes out, preheating is complete and the engine can be started. On 2.2 litre engines there is a glow plug control module, which powers the glow plugs individually.

6 The fuel system has a built-in 'strategy' to prevent it from drawing in air should the vehicle run low on fuel. The ECM monitors the level of fuel in the tank, via the fuel pump sender unit. After switching on the low fuel level warning light, it will eventually induce a misfire as a further warning to the driver, and lower the engine's maximum speed until the engine stops (approximately 1 mile).

7 On 2.2 litre engines, there is an inertia switch fitted to the right-hand rear of the engine compartment on the bulkhead. In the event of any impact, the the inertia switch contacts open and disable the fuel injection system and fuel tank pump sender. To reset the inertia switch, press down on the rubber cap, this will close the contacts and voltage to system will be resumed.

8 The fuel system on common rail diesel engines is normally very reliable. Provided that clean fuel is used, that the specified maintenance is conscientiously carried out, and absolute cleanliness is observed during any maintenance or repair operation, no problems should be experienced. The injection pump and injectors may require overhaul after a high mileage has been covered, but this cannot be done on a DIY basis.

Precautions

⚠️ *Warning: It is necessary to take certain precautions when working on the fuel system components, particularly the high-pressure side of the system. Before carrying out any operations on the fuel system, refer to the precautions given in 'Safety first!' at the beginning of this manual, and to any additional warning notes at the start of the relevant Sections. Also refer to the additional information contained in Section 2.*

Caution: Do not operate the engine if any of air intake ducts are disconnected or the filter element is removed. Any debris entering the engine will cause severe damage to the turbocharger.

Caution: To prevent damage to the turbocharger, do not race the engine immediately after start-up, especially if it is cold. Allow it to idle smoothly to give the oil a few seconds to circulate around the turbocharger bearings. Always allow the engine to return to idle speed before switching it off – do not blip the throttle and switch off, as this will leave the turbo spinning without lubrication.

Caution: Observe the recommended intervals for oil and filter changing, and use a reputable oil of the specified quality. Neglect of oil changing, or use of inferior oil, can cause carbon formation on the turbo shaft, leading to subsequent failure.

2 Common rail diesel injection system – special information

Warnings and precautions

1 It is essential to observe strict precautions when working on the fuel system components, particularly the high-pressure side of the system. Before carrying out any operations on the fuel system, refer to the precautions given in Safety first! at the beginning of this manual, and to the following additional information.

a) Do not carry out any repair work on the high-pressure fuel system unless you are competent to do so, have all the necessary tools and equipment required, and are aware of the safety implications involved.

b) Before starting any repair work on the fuel system, wait at least 30 seconds after switching off the engine to allow the fuel circuit to return to atmospheric pressure.
c) Never work on the high-pressure fuel system with the engine running.
d) Keep well clear of any possible source of fuel leakage, particularly when starting the engine after carrying out repair work. A leak in the system could cause an extremely high-pressure jet of fuel to escape, which could result in severe personal injury.
e) Never place your hands or any part of your body near to a leak in the high-pressure fuel system.
f) Do not use steam cleaning equipment or compressed air to clean the engine or any of the fuel system components.

Repair procedures and general information

2 Strict cleanliness must be observed at all times when working on any part of the fuel system. This applies to the working area in general, the person doing the work, and the components being worked on.
3 Before working on the fuel system components, they must be thoroughly cleaned with a suitable degreasing fluid. Cleanliness is particularly important when working on the fuel system connections at the following components:
a) Fuel filter.
b) Fuel injection pump.
c) Fuel rail.
d) Fuel injectors.
e) High-pressure fuel pipes.
4 After disconnecting any fuel pipes or components, the open union or orifice must be immediately sealed to prevent the entry of dirt or foreign material. Plastic plugs and caps in various sizes are available in packs from motor factors and accessory outlets, and are particularly suitable for this application (see illustration). Fingers cut from disposable rubber gloves should be used to protect components such as fuel pipes, fuel injectors and wiring connectors, and can be secured in place using elastic bands. Suitable gloves of this type are available at no cost from most petrol station forecourts.
5 Whenever any of the high-pressure fuel

2.4 Typical plastic plug and cap set for sealing disconnected fuel pipes and components

pipes are disconnected or removed, a new pipe(s) must be obtained for refitting.
6 The torque wrench settings given in the Specifications must be strictly observed when tightening component mountings and connections. This is particularly important when tightening the high-pressure fuel pipe unions.

3 Fuel system – priming and bleeding

Note: *Refer to the warnings and precautions contained in Sections 1 and 2 before proceeding.*
1 After disconnecting any part of the fuel system or running out of fuel, it is necessary to prime the fuel system and bleed off any air which may have entered the system components.
2 In some circumstances, the system will self-bleed by operating the starter for a maximum of 10 seconds. If the engine does not start within this time, wait 30 seconds and repeat the procedure. If, after two or three attempts, the engine still will not start, proceed as follows.
3 It will be necessary to obtain the special priming hose (kit No. 310-110A) or a suitable alternative hand-priming pump, together with various adaptors to enable the pump to be connected to the fuel lines. Hand-priming pump and adaptor kits are readily available from motor factors and tool supply outlets at moderate cost (see illustration).
4 Disconnect the fuel return pipe at the quick-release connection to allow attachment of the hand-priming pump (see illustration).

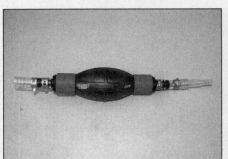
3.3 Typical hand-priming pump

3.4 Hand-priming pump connected to the fuel line

4.1 Remove the upper shroud...

4.2a Disconnect the breather hose

4.2b Remove air outlet rubber hose

5 Using the adaptors supplied with the hand priming pump, connect the pump into the fuel return pipe. Ensure that the arrow on the pump is pointing towards the fuel tank.

6 Squeeze and release the pump to draw fuel from the tank, through the filter, through the high-pressure fuel pump and back to the tank via the fuel return line. Continue to squeeze and release the pump until fuel without air bubbles can be seen flowing through the clear plastic adaptor on the pump. Note that it may take some time before the fuel flow is completely free of air bubbles.

7 When no more air bubbles can be seen, operate the starter for a maximum of 10 seconds, waiting 30 seconds between each attempt. If the engine does not start after two attempts, continue operating the priming pump as there may still be air in the system.

8 Once the engine starts and runs satisfactorily, switch it off, disconnect the priming pump and reconnect the fuel return pipe.

4 Air cleaner assembly – removal and refitting

Air cleaner assembly

1 Undo the six fasteners and remove the cooling fan upper shroud **(see illustration)**.

2 Disconnect the breather hose, then release the hose clips and remove the outlet rubber hose from the air cleaner cover **(see illustrations)**. As the hose is removed, release any wiring or cable securing clips.

3 Disconnect the wiring connector from the mass airflow sensor located on the air cleaner cover **(see illustration)**.

4 Release the two clips securing the air cleaner cover to the air cleaner lower housing, then lift it upwards and out from the engine compartment **(see illustrations)**.

5 Lift out the filter element, noting its direction of fitting **(see illustration)**.

6 On air-conditioning models, undo the retaining bolt from the refrigerant pipe bracket and move the refrigerant pipe to one side. DO NOT disconnect the pipe, unless the air-conditioning system has been discharged by an air-conditioning specialist.

7 Working under the right-hand front wing panel, undo the three retaining bolts securing the lower part of the air cleaner housing to the inner wing panel **(see illustration)**.

8 Lift the air cleaner housing up to release it from the retaining grommets and air intake ducting, then remove it from the engine compartment **(see illustration)**.

9 Refitting is the reverse of the removal procedure.

4.3 Disconnect the wiring connector from the mass airflow sensor

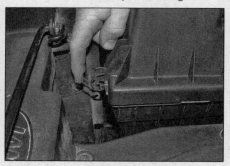

4.4a Release the two retaining clips...

4.4b ...and withdraw the filter cover

4.5 Remove the filter element

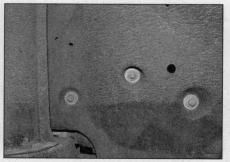

4.7 Undo the bolts securing the air cleaner housing

4.8 Lift the air cleaner housing and remove it from the engine compartment

5.1a Undo the three retaining bolts…

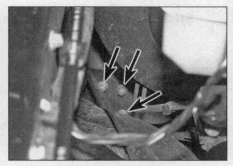

5.1b …whilst preventing the nuts from turning

5.2 Disconnect the wiring connector

5 Accelerator pedal – removal and refitting

Removal

1 Undo the three retaining bolts from the accelerator pedal and remove the pedal from the floor panel (see illustrations). The pedal is held to the floor panel with bolts and nuts, this will require an assistant to hold the nuts to prevent them from turning, whilst the bolts are removed. Access to the securing nuts is from inside the engine compartment below the brake servo.

2 Disconnect the wiring connector from the accelerator pedal position sensor, as the pedal is withdrawn from the floor panel (see illustration).

Refitting

3 Refitting is the reverse of the removal procedure. On completion, check the action of the pedal with the engine running.

6 Fuel tank – removal and refitting

Note: *Refer to the precautions given in Section 1 before proceeding.*

Removal

1 Disconnect the battery negative lead (see Chapter 5 Section 4)

2 Remove the fuel filler cap and drain the fuel tank, using a hand pump or syphoning equipment.

3 Disconnect the fuel filler hose and breather hose from under the right-hand rear wheel arch (see illustrations).

4 Disconnect the fuel tank vent pipe from the left-hand rear of the vehicle.

5 If the vehicle is fitted with a towing ball drop-plate with support bars, the bars must be removed (see illustration).

6 Where a rear anti-roll bar is fitted, undo the retaining bolts and pivot it forwards away from the fuel tank and secure to the rear trailing arms with a cable tie (see illustrations).

7 Working at the rear of the vehicle, undo the two retaining nuts through the holes in the rear crossmember (see illustration).

8 Place a jack and interposed block of wood under the tank.

9 On 110 models, unscrew the two tank front mounting bolts, and recover the washers

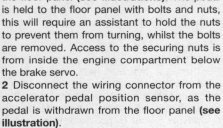

6.3a Disconnect the breather hose…

6.3b …and the filler hose

6.5 Remove the two support bars

6.6a Undo the bolts…

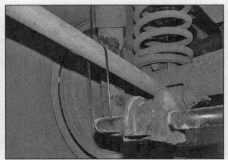

6.6b …and fasten the anti-roll bar away from the fuel tank

6.7 Undo the two fuel tank retaining nuts

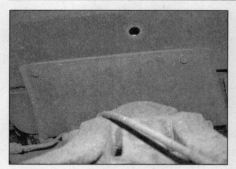

6.9 Undo the front mounting bolts

6.10 Undo the lower mounting bolts (one side shown)

and spacers, noting their locations to ensure correct refitting **(see illustration)**.

10 On 90 models, undo the four retaining bolts (two at each side) from under the fuel tank **(see illustration)**.

11 Carefully move the fuel tank forwards until the studs on the rear of the fuel tank are free from the rear crossmember. Lower the tank sufficiently for access to the fuel return hose connection on the top of the tank. Unscrew the union, and disconnect the fuel return hose from the tank. Plug or cover the open end of the hose, to prevent dirt ingress.

Note: *Although Land Rover information states that the fuel tank can be removed from under the vehicle, we found that on 90 models, there was not enough room to move the fuel tank forwards. The only way the tank could be removed was out through the top, which would mean raising the body up from the chassis to allow room for the fuel tank to be removed.*

12 Continue to lower the tank, and withdraw it from under the vehicle.

13 if required, the fuel pump sender unit can be removed from the tank. Unscrew the locking ring by turning it anti-clockwise, and recover the sender unit sealing ring.

Refitting

14 Refitting is a reversal of removal, bearing in mind the following points:

a) *Where applicable, refit the fuel pump sender and the fuel return pipe assembly, using a new gasket and a new sealing ring. Note that the lugs on the pump sender*

unit must engage with the corresponding cut-outs in the tank.

b) *Ensure that the washers and spacers are correctly positioned on the tank mounting bolts, as noted during removal.*

c) *Do not fully tighten any of the fixings until the completion of refitting.*

7 Fuel pump sender unit – removal and refitting

Note: *Refer to the warnings and precautions contained in Sections 1 and 2 before proceeding.*

Note: *Manufacturers special tool 310-118 (or a suitable alternative) will be required to unscrew the pump sender unit retaining ring.*

Removal

1 Remove the fuel tank as described in Section 6.

2 Using the special tool, unscrew and remove the sender unit retaining ring **(see illustration)**.

3 Lift the sender unit out of the fuel tank, taking care not to damage the float or bend the float arm. Remove and discard the O-ring seal, a new seal will be required for refitting.

Refitting

4 Refitting is the reverse of the removal procedure, using a new O-ring seal, and tightening the sender unit retaining ring to the specified torque.

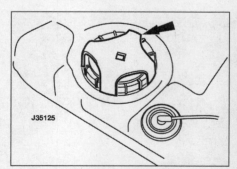

7.2 Special tool (arrowed) used to release the fuel gauge sender unit retaining ring

8.2 Diagnostic connector location

8 Diesel injection system – checking

Note: *Refer to the warnings and precautions contained in Sections 1 and 2 before proceeding.*

1 If a fault appears in the diesel injection system, first ensure that all the system wiring connectors are securely connected and free of corrosion. Then ensure that the fault is not due to poor maintenance; ie, check that the air cleaner filter element is clean, the cylinder compression pressures are correct, the fuel filter has been drained (or changed) and the engine breather hoses are clear and undamaged.

2 If these checks fail to reveal the cause of the problem, the vehicle should be taken to a suitably-equipped workshop for testing. A diagnostic connector (located under the facia on the driver's side inside the fusebox) is incorporated in the engine management system wiring harness, into which dedicated electronic test equipment can be plugged **(see illustration)**.

3 The test equipment is capable of 'interrogating' the engine control module (ECM) electronically and accessing its internal fault log (reading fault codes).

4 Fault codes can only be extracted from the ECM using a dedicated fault code reader. A Land Rover dealer will obviously have such a reader, but they are also available from other suppliers. It is unlikely to be cost-effective for the private owner to purchase a fault code reader, but a well-equipped local garage or auto-electrical specialist will have one.

5 Using this equipment, faults can be pinpointed quickly and simply, even if their occurrence is intermittent. Testing all the system components individually in an attempt to locate the fault by elimination is a time-consuming operation that is unlikely to be fruitful (particularly if the fault occurs dynamically), and carries a high risk of damage to the ECM's internal components.

6 Experienced home mechanics equipped with a diesel tachometer or other diagnostic equipment may be able to check the engine idle speed; if found to be out of specification, the vehicle must be taken to a suitably-equipped Land Rover dealer for assessment. The engine idle speed is not manually adjustable; incorrect test results indicate the need for maintenance (possibly, injector cleaning or re-calibration) or a fault within the injection system.

7 If excessive smoking or knocking is evident, it may be due to a problem with the fuel injectors. Proprietary treatments are available which can be added to the fuel, in order to clean the injectors. Injectors deteriorate with prolonged use, however, and it is reasonable to expect them to need reconditioning or renewal after 60 000 miles or so. Accurate testing, overhaul and calibration of the injectors must be left to a specialist.

9 Injection system electronic components – removal and refitting

Crankshaft position sensor

Note: *It is recommended by the manufacturer that the crankshaft position sensor is renewed, if the fitted position of the original sensor is disturbed.*

1 Disconnect the battery negative terminal (refer to *Disconnecting the battery*).

2 The sensor is located in the top of the bellhousing to the right-hand rear of the engine compartment.

3 Firmly apply the handbrake, then jack up the front of the vehicle and support it securely on axle stands (see *Jacking and vehicle support*).

4 Undo the retaining bolt and unclip the heat shield from over the top of the sensor.

5 Disconnect the wiring connector, then unscrew the mounting bolt and withdraw the sensor from the mounting bracket **(see illustrations)**.

6 Look down through the centre of the crankshaft position sensor mounting bracket and make sure that one of the trigger teeth on the flywheel is directly below the centre of the mounting bracket. If necessary turn the engine crankshaft, by means of the crankshaft pulley (only turn the engine in the direction of rotation), to align the trigger tooth.

7 Insert the new sensor into the mounting bracket and push it down until the pip on the underside of the sensor rests on the flywheel trigger tooth. Refit the retaining bolt and tighten it securely.

8 Reconnect the sensor wiring connector and heat shield.

9 Lower the vehicle to the ground and reconnect the battery.

Coolant temperature sensor

10 Proceed as described in Chapter 3 Section 6.

Temperature and manifold absolute pressure sensor

11 Disconnect the battery negative terminal (refer to Chapter 5 Section 4).

9.5a Undo the mounting bolt (arrowed)...

9.5b ...and withdraw the crankshaft sensor

9.12a Temperature and manifold absolute pressure sensor – 2.4 litre engines

9.12b Temperature and manifold absolute pressure sensor – 2.2 litre engines

12 Disconnect the wiring connector from the sensor which is located on the inlet manifold **(see illustrations)**.

13 Unscrew and remove the retaining screw, and withdraw the sensor from the manifold. Discard the O-ring seal, as a new one will be required for refitting.

14 Refitting is a reversal of removal. Where applicable, fit a new O-ring seal to the sensor.

EGR valve

15 Refer to Chapter 4B Section 2.

Accelerator pedal position sensor

16 The accelerator pedal sensor is integral with the pedal assembly, which is removed as described in Section 5.

Engine Control Module (ECM)

17 The engine control module is located at the rear of the engine compartment, bolted to the bulkhead. **Note:** *When a new ECM is installed it will need to be connected to Land Rover approved diagnostic equipment, to allow for the vehicle configuration to be uploaded to the new ECM.*

18 Disconnect the battery negative terminal (refer to Chapter 5 Section 4).

19 On earlier models, remove the shear bolt and remove the security bracket **(see illustration)** from around the wiring connectors on the side of the ECM.

20 Release the locking clips and disconnect the three wiring connectors **(see illustrations)**, from the side of the engine control module (ECM).

9.19 Remove the wiring security shield

9.20a Release the locking clips...

9.20b ...and disconnect the wiring connectors

9.21a Unclip the wiring loom retaining clips...

9.21b ...and remove the two retaining nuts

9.22 Remove the ECM

9.24 Disconnect the mass airflow sensor wiring connector

9.25 Undo the two securing screws

21 Release the wiring loom retaining clips from the ECM securing studs, and then undo the two retaining nuts from the upper part of the ECM **(see illustrations)**.

22 Tilt the ECM forwards and lift it upwards, and out from the mounting bracket on the bulkhead **(see illustration)**.

Mass airflow sensor

23 Disconnect the battery negative terminal (refer to *Disconnecting the battery*).

24 Disconnect the wiring connector from the sensor which is located in the air cleaner upper cover **(see illustration)**.

25 Undo the two sensor mounting bolts **(see illustration)** and remove the sensor from the air cleaner upper housing.

26 Refitting is a reversal of removal.

Camshaft sensor

Note: *If a fault occurs with the sensor when the engine is running, the engine will carry on running and may illuminate the malfunction indicator lamp (MIL) on the instrument panel. Depending on the fault, the engine may suffer a loss of power. Once the engine is switched off, If the fault is still present, the engine will just turn over and will not re-start.*

27 Disconnect the battery negative terminal (refer to *Disconnecting the battery*).

28 Disconnect the wiring connector from the camshaft sensor **(see illustration)**, located just below the fuel rail.

29 Undo the sensor retaining bolt and remove the sensor from the camshaft carrier.

30 Fit a new O-ring to the sensor, and lubricate it lightly.

31 Refit the sensor, tighten the retaining bolt securely and reconnect the wiring connector.

32 Reconnect the battery on completion.

Clutch pedal switch

Note: *When the clutch is operated, the contacts open and disconnect the negative (earth) feed to the ECM, which will then reduce engine torque. In the event of switch failure, there may be some loss in drive-ability with poor acceleration and less power.*

33 The clutch pedal pressure switch is located on the master cylinder inside the right-hand rear of the engine compartment **(see illustration)**.

34 Disconnect the wiring connector from the switch, then unscrew the switch from the master cylinder. Be prepared for some fluid spillage as the switch is removed. Discard the sealing washer, as a new one will be required for refitting.

35 Refitting is the reversal of removal, fitting a new sealing washer to the switch.

Brake pedal diagnostic switch

36 Refer to Chapter 10 Section 18.

Fuel pressure sensor

37 It is not possible to replace the sensor separately from the fuel rail. Land Rover advise that no attempt should be made to remove it from the fuel rail. If the sensor is faulty, renew the fuel rail as described in Section 12. **Note:** *On 2.2 litre engines the pressure sensor is fitted to the rear of the fuel rail, and on 2.4 litre engines the pressure sensor is fitted to the front of the fuel rail* **(see illustration)**.

9.28 Location of camshaft sensor

9.33 Clutch pedal pressure switch

9.37 Pressure senor – 2.4 litre engine

9.38 Pressure limiting valve –
2.4 litre engine

10.3 Remove the mounting bracket

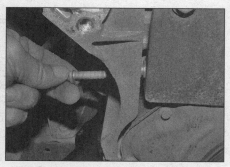

10.4 Remove the bolt from the mounting
bracket

Fuel pressure limiting valve (2.4 litre engines)

38 It is not possible to replace the pressure limiting valve separately from the fuel rail. Land Rover advise that no attempt should be made to remove it from the fuel rail. If the valve is faulty, renew the fuel rail as described in Section 12. The pressure limiting valve is fitted to the rear of the fuel rail (see illustration).

ABS wheel speed sensors

39 Refer to Section for removal and refitting details.

---

10 Fuel injection pump – removal and refitting

Caution: Be careful not to allow dirt into the injection pump or injector pipes during this procedure.

Note: Refer to the warnings and precautions contained in Sections 1 and 2 before proceeding.

Note: If a new injection pump is fitted, there is a possibility that the engine may not run properly (or even at all) until the engine control module (ECM) has been electronically reconfigured using Land Rover diagnostic equipment, or a compatible alternative.

All engines

Removal

1 Disconnect the battery negative terminal (refer to Disconnecting the battery 5 Section 4).

2 Remove the auxiliary drivebelt as described in Chapter 1 Section 52.

3 Undo the retraining bolts and remove the mounting bracket from the top of the timing chain cover (see illustration).

4 Remove the alternator, as described in Chapter 5 Section 6. With the alternator removed, slacken and remove the lower bolt from the mounting bracket (see illustration).

5 Undo the remainder of the bolts from the accessory drive component bracket, and remove it from the front of the timing chain cover (see illustration).

6 Remove the inlet manifold as described in Section 15.

7 Disconnect the wiring connectors from the fuel temperature sensor and from the metering valve on the rear of the fuel injection pump (see illustration). Suitably cover the connectors on the pump to prevent the entry of dirt and cleaning solvent.

8 Before proceeding further, use a brush and suitable solvent to clean the area around the pump's fuel supply pipe union and surrounding areas. It is essential that no dirt enters the pump. Allow time for any solvent used to dry.

9 Disconnect the quick-release connectors and disconnect the fuel return hose and the fuel supply hose from the fuel injection pump. Plug or suitably cover the open connections – dirt must not be allowed to enter the pump. Noting how they are routed, unclip the hoses and move them aside.

10 Undo the bolts and release the

pump-to-fuel rail fuel supply pipe clamp brackets.

11 Carefully loosen the fuel supply pipe union at the fuel pump and the one to the fuel rail. Once the unions are loose, wrap clean absorbent tissue or rag around them briefly, to soak away any dirt which may otherwise enter. If available, Land Rover recommend using a vacuum line to suck any dirt away from the opening union – do not use an airline, as this may blast dirt inwards, rather than cleaning it away.

12 Remove the fuel supply pipe, and discard it – a new one should be used when refitting. Plug or suitably cover the open connections.

2.2 litre engines

13 Using the manufacturers special tool (303-1619), remove the access cover from the timing chain cover. A suitable alternative tool was made up using a three-legged puller and three bolts (see illustration). Note that a new access cover will be required for refitting.

14 Fit special tool 303-1151 to the timing chain cover, and turn it clockwise to lock the fuel pump sprocket to the timing chain cover.

15 Undo the fuel pump sprocket retaining bolt. **Note:** The sprocket retaining bolt has a left-hand thread and is unscrewed by turning it clockwise.

16 Unbolt and remove the fuel injection pump rear support bracket from the pump and cylinder block.

17 Undo the three bolts securing the fuel injection pump to the cylinder block. It will now be necessary to free the fuel pump shaft

10.5 Remove the accessory drive
component bracket

10.7 Wiring and fuel pipes on the fuel
injection pump – 2.2 litre shown

10.13 Using a home-made tool to remove
the access cover from the timing chain
cover

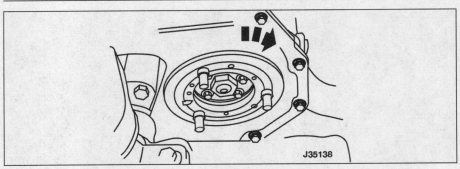

10.21 Special tool used to lock the pump sprocket in place

from the sprocket. The sprocket is a tapered fit on the shaft and manufacturer special tools 303-249 and 303-249-01 or suitable alternatives will be needed. Bolt the tools to the sprocket, then tighten the centre screw to force the pump shaft out of the sprocket.

18 Once the sprocket taper is released, remove the pump from the cylinder block. Recover and discard the O-ring seal – a new one will be required on refitting.

2.4 litre engines

19 Using the manufacturers special tool (303-679), remove the access cover from the timing chain cover, by turning it anti-clockwise. A suitable alternative tool was made up using a three-legged puller and three bolts **(see illustration 10.13)**. Note that a new access cover will be required for refitting.

20 Undo the fuel pump sprocket retaining bolts and the retaining nut.

21 Fit manufacturers special tool 303-1151 to the timing chain cover, and turn it clockwise to lock the sprocket to the timing chain cover **(see illustration)**.

22 Undo the two bolts securing the fuel injection pump to the cylinder block. It will now be necessary to free the fuel pump shaft from the sprocket. The sprocket is a tapered fit on the shaft and manufacturers special tool 303-1149/303-1333 or a suitable alternative will be needed. Bolt the tool to the sprocket, then tighten the centre screw to force the pump shaft out of the sprocket.

23 Once the sprocket taper is released, remove the pump from the cylinder block.

Recover and discard the O-ring seal – a new one will be required on refitting.

All engines

Refitting

24 If still in place, remove the manufacturers special tool from the sprocket.

25 Locate a new O-ring seal on the pump then offer the pump into position. Refit the pump retaining bolts and tighten them to the specified torque.

26 On 2.2 litre engines, refit the fuel injection pump rear support bracket to the pump and cylinder block and tighten the retaining bolts to the specified torque.

27 Refit the fuel pump sprocket retaining bolt/nut and tighten them to the specified torque.

28 Remove the special tool used to lock the fuel injection pump sprocket in place.

29 Using the special tool or the home-made tool, fit the new access cover to the timing chain cover.

30 Place the new fuel supply pipe in position and screw on the union nuts at the fuel injection pump and fuel rail. When refitting, do not bend or strain the pipe, and make sure it is kept clean.

31 Tighten the fuel supply pipe unions at the fuel injection pump and fuel rail to their specified torque setting.

32 Refit and tighten the bolts securing pump-to-fuel rail fuel supply pipe clamp brackets.

33 Reconnect the fuel return hose and the fuel supply hose to the fuel injection pump.

34 Reconnect the wiring connectors to the fuel temperature sensor and the metering valve on the rear of the fuel injection pump.

35 Refit the inlet manifold as described in Section 15.

36 Refit the accessory drive component bracket to the front of the engine.

37 Refit the mounting bracket to the top of the timing chain cover.

38 Refit the auxiliary drivebelt as described in Chapter 1 Section 52.

39 Where applicable, refit the plastic trim cover to the top of the engine.

40 Fit a new fuel filter as described in Chapter 1 Section 23.

41 Reconnect the battery negative terminal, then prime and bleed the fuel system as described in Section 3.

42 Once the engine starts, allow it to idle until it reaches normal operating temperature. As the engine warms-up, check for signs of leakage from the fuel unions.

11 Fuel injectors –
removal and refitting

Note: *Refer to the warnings and precautions contained in Sections 1 and 2 before proceeding.*
Caution: Be careful not to allow dirt into the injection system during this procedure.

Removal

1 Disconnect the battery negative terminal (refer to *Disconnecting the battery*).

2 Undo the two retaining bolts at the front of the engine trim cover and remove it from the top of the engine **(see illustration)**.

3 Before proceeding further, use a brush and suitable solvent to clean the area around the fuel supply pipe unions on the fuel rail and injectors. Allow time for any solvent used to dry.

4 Using a small screwdriver, lift the locking tab and disconnect the wiring connectors from the fuel injectors **(see illustrations)**.

5 Again using a small screwdriver, push back the retaining clip and disconnect the fuel return hose from the top of each injector **(see illustrations)**. Check the condition of

11.2 Remove the engine upper trim cover

11.4a Lift the locking tab...

11.4b ...and disconnect the wiring connectors from the fuel injectors

11.5a Push back the retaining clip...

11.5b ...and disconnect the fuel return hose from each injector – 2.4 litre shown

11.6 Carefully loosen the fuel pipe unions at the injectors and the fuel rail

the O-ring seal at each injector connection – renew if necessary.

6 Carefully loosen the fuel pipe unions at the injectors and the fuel rail **(see illustration)**. Where applicable, use a second spanner to counter-hold the unions at the injectors to prevent any damage. Once the unions are loose, wrap clean absorbent tissue or rag around them briefly, to soak away any dirt which may otherwise enter. If available, Land Rover recommend using a vacuum line to suck any dirt away from the opening union – do not use an airline, as this may blast dirt inwards, rather than cleaning it away.

7 Once the fuel pipe unions are loose, fully unscrew them and remove the fuel pipes **(see illustration)**. Discard the pipes – new ones should be used when refitting. Plug or suitably cover the open connections.

8 Where applicable, depress the retaining tabs and lift the plastic wiring harness support cover off the two injector clamp brackets **(see illustrations)**.

9 On 2.4 litre engines, use a forked tool, to remove the wiring harness support clips from the camshaft cover and move the wiring harness to one side **(see illustrations)**.

10 Undo the retaining bolt and lift the injector clamp bracket off each pair of injectors **(see illustrations)**. Discard the clamp bracket retaining bolts – new ones must be fitted.

11 Using an open-ended spanner, twist each injector from side-to-side until it becomes

11.7 Once the fuel pipe unions are loose, fully unscrew them and remove the fuel pipes

11.8a Depress the retaining tabs and lift the plastic wiring harness support cover...

11.8b ...off the injector clamp brackets – 2.4 litre engine

11.9a Using a forked tool, remove the wiring harness support clips...

11.9b ...and move the wiring harness to one side

11.10a Undo the retaining bolt (arrowed)...

11.10b ...and lift the injector clamp bracket off each pair of injectors

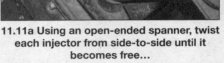

11.11a Using an open-ended spanner, twist each injector from side-to-side until it becomes free...

11.11b ...then lift it from its location in the cylinder head

11.12 Remove the fuel injector seals from the camshaft cover and discard them

free, then lift it from its location in the cylinder head **(see illustrations)**. Discard the injectors sealing washers – new ones must be fitted.

12 Using a screwdriver, remove the fuel injector seals from the camshaft cover and discard them – new ones must be fitted **(see illustration)**.

13 If the original injectors are to be refitted, it is absolutely essential that they are refitted in to their original positions. It is advisable to mount the injectors in a suitable stand, the right way up. This will help to prevent difficulties when priming and bleeding after refitting **(see illustration)**.

Refitting

14 If new injectors are being fitted, take a note of the identification numbers stamped on the top of the wiring connector location **(see illustration)**. These need to be uploaded

into the engine control module (ECM) on completion of the work.

15 Fit a new sealing washer onto each injector **(see illustration)**. If necessary, use a suitable deep socket to push the sealing washers fully into place.

16 Fit the new fuel injector seals to the camshaft cover and push them fully into place **(see illustration)**.

17 Fit the injectors and clamp brackets into the cylinder head, then tighten the new clamp bracket bolts finger-tight only at this stage.

18 Working on one fuel injector at a time, remove the blanking plugs from the fuel pipe unions on the fuel rail and the relevant injector. Locate a new fuel pipe over the unions and screw on the union nuts. Take care not to cross-thread the nuts or strain the fuel pipes

as they are fitted. Once the union nut threads have started, finger-tighten the nuts only at this stage, to the ends of the threads.

19 When all the fuel pipes are in place, tighten the injector clamp bracket retaining bolts to the specified torque and through the specified angle.

20 Tighten the fuel pipe union nuts to the specified torque using a torque wrench and crow's-foot adapter **(see illustration)**. Where applicable, use a second spanner to counter-hold the unions at the injectors to prevent any damage. Tighten all the disturbed union nuts in the same way.

21 If new injectors have been fitted, their classification numbers must be programmed into the engine management ECM using dedicated diagnostic equipment. If this equipment is not available, entrust this task to a Land Rover dealer or suitably-equipped repairer. Note that it should be possible to drive the vehicle, albeit with reduced performance/increased emissions, to a repairer for the numbers to be programmed.

22 The remainder of refitting is a reversal of removal.

23 On completion, fit a new fuel filter as described in Chapter 1 Section 23

24 With everything reassembled, reconnect the battery negative terminal, then prime and bleed the fuel system as described in Section 3.

25 Once the engine starts, allow it to idle until it reaches normal operating temperature. As the engine warms-up, check for signs of leakage from the fuel pipe unions.

11.13 It is advisable to mount the injectors the right way up in a suitable stand after removal

11.14 Injector identification numbers (arrowed) are stamped on the top of the wiring connector location

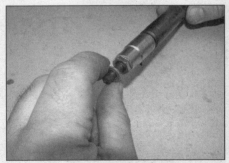

11.15 Fit a new sealing washer onto each injector

11.16 Fit the new fuel injector seals to the camshaft cover and push them fully into place

11.20 Tighten the fuel pipe union nuts to the specified torque using a torque wrench and crow's-foot adapter

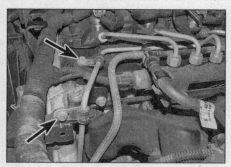

12.6 Undo the two fuel supply pipe clamp securing bolts

12.8 Disconnect the fuel pipe from the pressure limiting valve – 2.4 litre engines

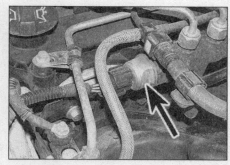

12.10 Fuel pressure sensor – 2.4 lite engine

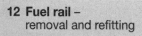

12 Fuel rail –
removal and refitting

Note: *Refer to the warnings and precautions contained in Sections 1 and 2 before proceeding.*
Caution: Be careful not to allow dirt into the injection system during this procedure.

Removal

1 Disconnect the battery negative terminal (refer to Chapter 5 Section 4).
2 Undo the two retaining bolts at the front of the engine trim cover and remove it from the top of the engine (see illustration 11.2).
3 Before proceeding further, use a brush and suitable solvent to clean the area around the fuel supply pipe unions on the fuel rail, fuel injection pump and injectors. Allow time for any solvent used to dry.
4 Carefully loosen the fuel pipe unions at the injectors and the fuel rail (see illustration 11.6). Where applicable, use a second spanner to counter-hold the unions at the injectors to prevent any damage. Once the unions are loose, wrap clean absorbent tissue or rag around them briefly, to soak away any dirt which may otherwise enter. If available, Land Rover recommend using a vacuum line to suck any dirt away from the opening union – do not use an airline, as this may blast dirt inwards, rather than cleaning it away.
5 Once the fuel pipe unions are loose, fully

unscrew them and remove the fuel pipes (see illustration 11.7). Discard the pipes – new ones should be used when refitting. Plug or suitably cover the open connections.
6 Carefully loosen the fuel supply pipe union at the fuel pump and the one at the centre of the fuel rail, undo the two fuel pipe clamp retaining bolts (see illustration).
7 Remove the fuel supply pipe, and discard it – a new one must be used when refitting. Plug or suitably cover the open connections.
8 On 2.4 litre engines, disconnect the fuel return hose union at the quick-release connector on rear of the fuel rail (see illustration).
9 On later 2.2 litre models, it will be necessary to undo the retaining bolts, release the retaining clips and move the fuel injector wiring harness clear of the fuel rail.
10 Disconnect the wiring connector from the fuel pressure sensor on the end of the fuel rail (see illustration). **Note:** *On 2.2 litre engines the pressure sensor is fitted to the rear of the fuel rail, and on 2.4 litre engines the pressure sensor is fitted to the front of the fuel rail*
11 Undo the two fuel rail mounting bolts and lift away the fuel rail (see illustration).

Refitting

12 Offer the fuel rail into position, then fit the mounting bolts, hand-tight only.
13 Fit new fuel pipes to the fuel rail, injectors and fuel pump, leaving the union nuts hand-tight only at this stage. Do not bend or strain the pipes, and make sure they are kept clean.

14 Tighten the fuel rail mounting bolts to the specified torque.
15 With all the fuel injection pipes in place, fully tighten the union nuts to the specified torque using a torque wrench and crow's-foot adapter (see illustration).
16 The remainder of refitting is a reversal of removal.
17 On completion, fit a new fuel filter as described in Chapter 1 Section 23.
18 With everything reassembled, reconnect the battery negative terminal, then prime and bleed the fuel system as described in Section 3.
19 Once the engine starts, allow it to idle until it reaches normal operating temperature. As the engine warms-up, check for signs of leakage from the fuel pipe unions.

13 Turbocharger –
general information

1 The turbocharger increases engine efficiency by raising the pressure in the inlet manifold above atmospheric pressure. Instead of the air simply being sucked into the cylinders, it is forced in. Additional fuel is supplied by the injection pump, in proportion to the increased amount of air.
2 Energy for the operation of the turbocharger comes from the exhaust gas. The gas flows through a specially-shaped housing (the turbine housing) and in so doing, spins the turbine wheel. The turbine wheel is attached to a shaft, at the end of which is another vaned wheel, known as the compressor wheel. The compressor wheel spins in its own housing, and compresses the inducted air on the way to the intake manifold.
3 Between the turbocharger and the inlet manifold, the compressed air passes through an intercooler. The purpose of the intercooler is to remove from the inducted air some of the heat gained in being compressed. Because cooler air is denser, removal of this heat further increases engine efficiency.
4 The turbo shaft is pressure-lubricated by its own dedicated oil feed pipe. The shaft 'floats' on a cushion of oil. Oil is returned to the sump via a return pipe that connects to the sump.
5 The turbocharger is either of fixed vane type,

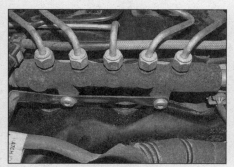

12.11 Fuel rail mounting bolts

12.15 Tighten the fuel pipe union nuts to the specified torque using a torque wrench and crow's-foot adapter

or variable vane type according to engine type. On the fixed vane type there is a wastegate control valve, which opens a flap at high engine speeds. On the variable vane type, as the engine speed increases the guide vanes in the turbine housing are progressively opened.

6 Refer to Section 1 for precautions to be observed with turbocharger operation.

14 Turbocharger – removal and refitting

Note: *The turbocharger should only be removed with the engine completely cool.*

Removal

1 Disconnect the battery negative terminal (refer to Chapter 5 Section 4).

2 Undo the two retaining bolts at the front of the engine trim cover and remove it from the top of the engine **(see illustration 11.2)**.

3 Release the securing clip and disconnect the breather hose from the camshaft cover **(see illustration)**.

4 Slacken the retaining clips and remove the air cleaner air outlet hose and breather pipe from the engine compartment **(see illustration)**.

5 Trace the wiring back from the oxygen sensors (where fitted), and disconnect the wiring connectors.

6 Disconnect the wiring connector from the turbocharger actuator motor **(see illustration)**.

14.3 Disconnect the breather hose

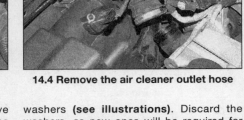
14.4 Remove the air cleaner outlet hose

7 Undo the retaining bolts and remove the heat shield from over the top of the turbocharger **(see illustrations)**. Where applicable, pass the oxygen sensor wiring through the heat shield as it is being removed.

8 To make access to the turbocharger easier, remove the alternator, as described in Chapter 5 Section 6.

9 If not already done, jack up the front of the vehicle, and support securely on axle stands (see Chapter 14 Section 5).

10 Working under the front of the turbocharger, slacken the retaining clip and disconnect the intercooler air hose from the turbocharger **(see illustration)**.

11 Undo the two bolts and separate the oil return pipe flange from under the turbocharger. Collect the flange gasket and discard, as a new one will be required for refitting.

12 Undo the turbocharger oil supply pipe banjo union bolt and collect the two copper

washers **(see illustrations)**. Discard the washers, as new ones will be required for refitting.

13 Remove the exhaust front pipe/catalytic converter/diesel particle filter (DPF), depending on model, with reference to Chapter 4B Section 3.

14 Undo the two nuts/bolts securing the turbocharger to the exhaust manifold. Lift the turbocharger up and off the manifold studs and recover the gasket. Discard the gasket, as a new one will be required for refitting.

15 No further dismantling of the turbocharger is recommended. Interfering with the wastegate setting may lead to a reduction in performance, or could result in engine damage. No parts appear to be available separately for the turbocharger.

16 If on inspection there are any signs of internal oil contamination on the turbine or compressor wheels, this indicates failure of the

14.6 Disconnect the wiring connector

14.7a Remove heat shield – 2.2 litre engine (with oxygen sensor)

14.7b Remove heat shield – 2.4 litre engine

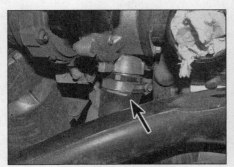
14.10 Disconnect the intercooler air hose

14.12a Oil supply banjo bolt – 2.2 litre engine

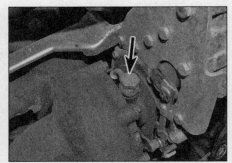
14.12b Oil supply banjo bolt – 2.4 litre engine

turbocharger oil seals. Renewing these seals is a job best left to a turbocharger specialist. In the event of any problem with the turbocharger, one of these specialists will usually be able to rebuild a defective unit, or offer a rebuilt unit on an exchange basis, either of which will prove cheaper than a new unit.

Refitting

17 Refitting is a reversal of removal, noting the following points:
a) *Tighten all nuts/bolts to the specified torque, where given.*
b) *Renew the turbocharger mounting studs in the exhaust manifold and the turbocharger mounting nuts.*
c) *Renew the nuts securing the catalytic converter to the turbocharger.*
d) *Use new gaskets/seals on all disturbed joints.*
e) *Renew the oil supply pipe banjo union copper washers.*

15 Inlet manifold – removal and refitting

2.2 litre models

Removal

1 Disconnect the battery negative terminal (refer to *Disconnecting the battery*).
2 To make access to the inlet manifold easier, drain the cooling system (see Chapter 1 Section 47), and remove the coolant hoses from around the inlet manifold **(see illustration)**.
3 Remove the EGR valve as described in Chapter 4B Section 2. Then, undo the two bolts securing the metal EGR pipe to the inlet manifold **(see illustration)**. Remove the EGR pipe and recover the gasket.
4 Before proceeding further, use a brush and suitable solvent to clean the area around the fuel supply pipe unions on the fuel rail and fuel injection pump. Allow time for any solvent used to dry.
5 Carefully loosen the fuel supply pipe union at the fuel pump and the one to the fuel rail. Once the unions are loose, wrap clean absorbent tissue or rag around them briefly, to soak away any dirt which may otherwise enter. If available, Land Rover recommend using a vacuum line

15.2 Coolant hoses restricting access to inlet manifold

to suck any dirt away from the opening union – do not use an airline, as this may blast dirt inwards, rather than cleaning it away.
6 Undo the bolt and the nut securing the fuel supply pipe clamps to the camshaft cover.
7 Remove the fuel supply pipe, and discard it – a new one must be used when refitting. Plug or suitably cover the open connections.
8 Disconnect the fuel return hose unions at the quick-release connectors and move the return hose clear of the inlet manifold.
9 Disconnect the wiring connectors from the throttle body, camshaft sensor and manifold absolute pressure sensor. Release the wiring harness from the retaining clips and move it clear of the manifold.
10 Undo the two bolts and move the support bracket clear of the fuel rail.
11 Slacken the securing clip and disconnect the air intake hose from the throttle body **(see illustration)**.
12 Undo the nine bolts securing the inlet manifold to the cylinder head. Remove the manifold and recover the rubber seals.

Refitting

13 Fit the new rubber seals to the inlet manifold then place the manifold in position on the cylinder head. Evenly and progressively tighten the retaining bolts to the specified torque.
14 Place the support bracket in position on the fuel rail and tighten the retaining bolts to the specified torque.
15 Reconnect the disconnected wiring connectors and clip the wiring harness back into place.

16 Reconnect the air inlet hose to the throttle body and tighten the securing clip.
17 Fit the new fuel pipe to the fuel rail and fuel pump and tighten the union nuts to the specified torque using a torque wrench and crow's-foot adapter.
18 Reconnect the fuel return hose unions and tighten the bolt and the nut securing the fuel supply pipe clamps to the camshaft cover.
19 Using a new gasket, refit the metal EGR pipe to the manifold and securely tighten the retaining bolts.
20 Refit the EGR valve as described in Chapter 4B Section 2.
21 With everything reassembled, reconnect the battery negative terminal, then prime and bleed the fuel system as described in Section 3.
22 Once the engine starts, allow it to idle until it reaches normal operating temperature. As the engine warms-up, check for signs of leakage from the fuel pipe unions.
23 If drained, refill the cooling system, as described in Chapter 1 Section 47. Refit the engine plastic trim cover on completion.

2.4 litre models

Removal

24 Disconnect the battery negative terminal (refer to *Disconnecting the battery*).
25 Disconnect the fuel return hose union at the quick-release connector, release the retaining clips and and move the return hose clear of the inlet manifold **(see illustration)**.
26 Disconnect the wiring connectors from the camshaft sensor **(see illustration)** and EGR valve. Release the wiring harness from

15.3 Undo the two EGR pipe securing bolts

15.11 Disconnect the air intake hose from the throttle body

15.25 Disconnect the fuel hose

15.26 Disconnect the camshaft wiring connector

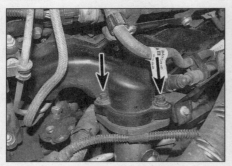

15.27 Undo the two retaining bolts

15.28 Disconnect the bracket from the manifold

the retaining clips and move it clear of the manifold.

27 Undo the two bolts securing the metal EGR outlet assembly to the inlet manifold **(see illustration)**. Remove the extension and recover the sealing ring.

28 Undo the retaining bolt(s) and move the support bracket clear of the fuel rail **(see illustration)**.

29 Undo the nine bolts securing the inlet manifold to the cylinder head. Remove the manifold and recover the eight rubber O-ring seals.

Refitting

30 Refitting is a reversal of removal, noting the following points:
a) *Tighten all nuts/bolts to the specified torque, where given.*
b) *Use new gaskets and/or sealing rings on all disturbed joints.*

16 Exhaust manifold – removal and refitting

Removal

1 Remove the turbocharger as described in Section 14. It may be possible to partially remove the turbocharger, so as to allow the exhaust manifold to be withdrawn from the cylinder head.

2 Undo the nut/bolt securing the engine oil level dipstick guide tube to the cylinder head cover **(see illustrations)**, and then pull the dipstick tube upwards to remove the guide tube from the cylinder block. Recover the O-ring seal from the lower part of the dipstick tube and renew.

3 Undo the retaining bolts and remove the heat shield mounting bracket from across the top of the exhaust manifold **(see illustration)**.

4 Undo the bolts securing the heat shields to the rear of the manifold, and the bolts/nuts securing the manifold to the EGR valve cooler pipe at the rear of the cylinder head **(see illustrations)**. Collect the heat shield.

5 Undo the six bolts and two nuts securing the manifold to the cylinder head.

6 Remove the manifold from the cylinder head and recover the gasket/heat shield.

7 Remove the two manifold retaining studs and obtain new gasket/heat shield, EGR valve cooler gasket, manifold retaining studs, six retaining bolts and two retaining nuts for refitting.

Refitting

8 Refitting is a reversal of removal, noting the following points:
a) *Renew all the items listed in paragraph 7.*
b) *Tighten all nuts/bolts to the specified torque, where given.*
c) *Refit the turbocharger as described in Section 14.*

17 Intercooler (charge air cooler) – removal and refitting

Removal

1 Open the bonnet, then undo the six fasteners and remove the upper fan shroud from the front of the engine compartment **(see illustration)**.

16.2a Undo the bracket retaining nut (2.2 litre engines)…

16.2b …and bolt (2.4 litre engines)

16.3 Remove heat shield mounting bracket – 2.4 litre engine shown

16.4a Remove the heat shields (2.2 litre engine)…

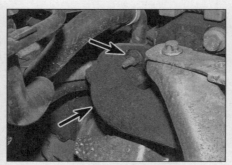

16.4b …and remove the EGR pipe nuts/ bolts (2.4 litre shown)

17.1 Remove the fan upper shroud

17.5 Remove the stay brackets

17.6a Remove the nuts…

17.6b …and lock two together to remove studs

2 On models with air-conditioning fitted, remove the condenser, as described in Chapter 3 Section 11.

3 Undo the retaining screws and remove the grille and support surround panel, as described in Chapter 12 Section 19.

4 Remove the bonnet, as described in Chapter 12 Section 7, as the bonnet support stay crossmember/latch panel needs to be removed.

5 Undo the retaining bolts and remove the two stay brackets from in front of the intercooler/charge air cooler **(see illustration)**.

6 Working at each side of the crossmember/latch panel, undo the four retaining nuts (two at each side), and then remove the studs **(see illustrations)**. With the studs removed, the crossmember/latch panel can now be removed and moved to one side. Note the bonnet release cable is still attached to the latch panel, so position it to one side.

7 Undo the retaining bolts and remove the two radiator support brackets, one at each side **(see illustrations)**.

8 Slacken the retaining clips and disconnect the air intake hoses/ducts from the intercooler/charge air cooler **(see illustrations)**.

9 Undo the two bolts (one at each side) and remove the intercooler/charge air cooler from the front of the radiator **(see illustrations)**.

Refitting

10 Refitting is a reversal of removal. Check the intake and outlet air hoses/ducts for signs of damage, and make sure that the clips are securely tightened.

17.7a Undo the retaining bolts…

17.7b …and remove both support brackets

17.8a Disconnect the right-hand side hose…

17.8b …and left-hand side hose from the intercooler

17.9a Undo the right-hand side…

17.9b …and left-hand side bolts…

17.9c …then withdraw and remove the intercooler

18.1a Front pipe section – 2.4 litre (90 model)

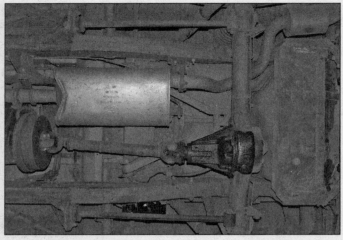

18.1b Intermediate silencer/pipe and rear silencer/tailpipe section – 2.4 litre (90 model)

18 Exhaust system – general information and component renewal

⚠️ **Warning: Inspection and repair of exhaust system components should be done only after the system has cooled completely. This applies particularly to the catalytic converter, which runs at very high temperatures.**

General information

1 The exhaust system consists of three main sections; a front pipe incorporating a catalytic converter (or Diesel Particle Filter – DPF), an intermediate pipe incorporating the silencers, and a rear silencer/tailpipe **(see illustrations)**.
2 The front pipe is fitted with a flexible section to allow for exhaust system movement and the system is suspended throughout its entire length by rubber mountings.
3 To remove a part of the system, first jack up the front or rear of the vehicle, and support it on axle stands (see *Jacking and vehicle support*). Alternatively, position the vehicle over an inspection pit, or on car ramps.
4 It is recommended that all nuts (such as flange joint nuts, clamp joint nuts, or converter-to-manifold nuts) are renewed on reassembly **(see illustrations)** – given that they may be in less-than-perfect condition as a result of corrosion, this would be a good idea, especially as it will make subsequent removal easier.

Component renewal

Note: *Refer to Chapter 4B Section 3 for details of catalytic converter and diesel particulate filter renewal.*

5 If any section of the exhaust is damaged or deteriorated, excessive noise and vibration will occur.
6 Carry out regular inspections of the exhaust system, to check security and condition. Look for any damaged or bent parts, open seams, holes, loose connections, excessive corrosion, or other defects which could allow exhaust fumes to enter the vehicle. Deteriorated sections of the exhaust system should be renewed.
7 If the exhaust system components are extremely corroded or rusted together, it may not be possible to separate them. In this case, simply cut off the old components with a hacksaw, and remove any remaining corroded pipe with a cold chisel. Be sure to wear safety glasses to protect your eyes, and wear gloves to protect your hands.
8 Here are some simple guidelines to follow when repairing the exhaust system:
a) Work from the back to the front when removing exhaust system components.
b) Apply penetrating fluid to the flange nuts before unscrewing them.
c) Use new gaskets and rubber mountings when installing exhaust system components.
d) Apply anti-seize compound to the threads of all exhaust system studs during reassembly.
e) Be sure to allow sufficient clearance between newly-installed parts and all points on the underbody, to avoid overheating the floorpan.

18.4a Front pipe to intermediate pipe/ silencer flange bolts

18.4b Intermediate pipe to rear silencer/tail pipe flange bolts

Chapter 4 Part B
Emission control systems

Contents

Degrees of difficulty

Easy, suitable for novice with little experience	Fairly easy, suitable for beginner with some experience	Fairly difficult, suitable for competent DIY mechanic	Difficult, suitable for experienced DIY mechanic	Very difficult, suitable for expert DIY or professional

Specifications

Torque wrench settings	Nm	lbf ft
Catalytic converter support bracket bolts	25	19
Catalytic converter-to-turbocharger nuts*	48	35
EGR pipe retaining nuts/bolts	10	7
EGR valve-to-EGR cooler....................................	23	17
Exhaust manifold-to-EGR cooler*	23	17

* Use new nuts/bolts

1 General Information

1 All models are designed to meet strict emission requirements. The engines are fitted with a crankcase emission control system and a catalytic converter (incorporating a diesel particulate filter on some models) to keep exhaust emissions down to a minimum. An exhaust gas recirculation (EGR) system is also fitted to further decrease exhaust emissions.

2 The emission control systems function as follows.

Crankcase emission control

3 To reduce the emission of unburned hydrocarbons from the crankcase into the atmosphere, the engine is sealed and the blow-by gases and oil vapour are drawn from inside the crankcase, through an oil separator, into the inlet tract to be burned by the engine during normal combustion.

4 Under all conditions the gases are forced out of the crankcase by the (relatively) higher crankcase pressure; if the engine is worn, the raised crankcase pressure (due to increased blow-by) will cause some of the flow to return under all manifold conditions.

5 The components of this system require no attention other than to check that the hose(s) are clear and undamaged at regular intervals.

Exhaust emission control

6 To minimise the level of exhaust pollutants released into the atmosphere, a catalytic converter is fitted in the exhaust system.

7 The catalytic converter consists of a canister containing a fine mesh impregnated with a catalyst material, over which the hot exhaust gases pass. The catalyst speeds up the oxidation of harmful carbon monoxide, unburned hydrocarbons and soot, effectively reducing the quantity of harmful products released into the atmosphere via the exhaust gases.

8 On some engines, the catalytic converter is combined with a diesel particulate filter. The diesel particulate filter contains a silicon carbide honeycomb block containing microscopic channels in which the exhaust gasses flow. As the gasses flow through the honeycomb channels, soot particles are deposited on the channel walls. To prevent clogging of the honeycomb channels, the soot particles are burned off at regular intervals during what is known as a 'regeneration phase'. Under the control of the engine management system ECM, the injection characteristics are altered to raise the temperature of the exhaust gasses to approximately 600°C. At this temperature, the soot particles are effectively burned off the honeycomb walls as the exhaust gasses pass through. A differential pressure sensor and temperature sensors are used to inform the ECM of the condition of the particulate filter, and the temperature of the exhaust gasses during the regeneration phase. When the ECM detects that soot build-up is reducing the efficiency of the particulate filter, it will instigate the regeneration process. This occurs at regular intervals under certain driving conditions and will normally not be detected by the driver.

Exhaust gas recirculation (EGR) system

9 This system is designed to recirculate small quantities of exhaust gas into the inlet tract, and therefore into the combustion process. This process reduces the level of unburnt hydrocarbons present in the exhaust gas before it reaches the catalytic converter. The system is controlled by the engine control module (ECM), using the information from its various sensors, via the EGR valve.

2 Exhaust Gas Recirculation (EGR) system – checking and component renewal

Checking

1 Checking of the system as a whole entails a close visual inspection of all hoses, pipes and connections for condition and security. Apart from this, any known or suspected faults should be attended to by your local dealer or suitably-equipped specialist.

EGR valve renewal

2 Disconnect the battery negative terminal (refer to *Disconnecting the battery*).

3 Drain the cooling system as described in Chapter 1 Section 47.

4 Undo the retaining bolts and remove the heater control valve and mounting bracket from the left-hand rear of the engine compartment **(see illustration)**, to make access easier to the EGR valve.

5 Disconnect the wiring connector from the EGR valve **(see illustration)**.

6 Release the retaining clips and disconnect the coolant hoses from the EGR valve.

7 On 2.2 litre engines, undo the two bolts securing the metal EGR pipe to the intake manifold **(see illustration)**.

8 On 2.4 litre engines, undo the two bolts

2.4 Remove the heater control valve and bracket

securing the metal EGR pipe to the EGR valve **(see illustration)**.

9 Undo the nuts/bolts securing the EGR valve to the EGR cooler. Withdraw the EGR valve from the cooler and collect the gasket(s) **(see illustration)**.

10 Refitting is a reversal of removal, bearing in mind the following points:

a) Thoroughly clean the mating faces of the EGR valve, pipe and cooler and use new gaskets.

b) Tighten the retaining bolts to the specified torque.

c) Top-up the cooling system as described in Weekly checks. If the coolant was drained, refill the cooling system as described in Chapter 1 Section 47.

2.5 Disconnect the wiring connector from the EGR valve

EGR cooler renewal

11 Disconnect the battery negative terminal (refer to *Disconnecting the battery*).

12 Drain the cooling system as described in Chapter 1 Section 47.

13 Release the retaining clips and disconnect the two coolant hoses from the EGR cooler, which is located at the rear of the cylinder head **(see illustration)**.

14 Firmly apply the handbrake, then jack up the front of the vehicle and support it securely on axle stands (see *Jacking and vehicle support*).

15 Undo the two nuts securing the EGR cooler to the exhaust manifold **(see illustration)**.

16 Undo the two bolts securing the EGR cooler to the EGR valve **(see illustration 2.9a)**.

17 Undo the bolt securing the EGR cooler to

2.7 Undo the two bolts (arrowed) securing the metal EGR pipe to the EGR valve

2.8 Undo the two bolts securing the EGR pipe to the valve

2.9a Undo the two bolts (arrowed) securing the EGR valve to the EGR cooler

2.9b Withdraw the EGR valve from the cooler and collect the valve-to-cooler gasket...

2.9c ...and the EGR pipe-to-valve gasket

2.13 Location of EGR cooler

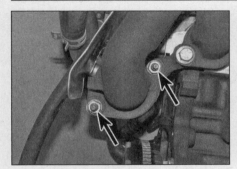

2.15 Undo the two nuts (arrowed) securing the EGR cooler to the exhaust manifold

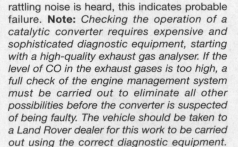

3.7 Removing the upper heat shield

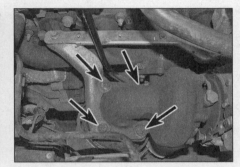

3.8 Undo the nuts (arrowed) securing the catalytic converter to the turbocharger

the cylinder head. Withdraw the EGR cooler and collect the two gaskets.

18 Refitting is a reversal of removal, bearing in mind the following points:

a) *Thoroughly clean the mating faces of the EGR valve, cooler and exhaust manifold and use new gaskets.*

b) *Tighten the retaining bolts to the specified torque.*

c) *Top-up the cooling system as described in Weekly checks. If the coolant was drained, refill the cooling system as described in Chapter 1 Section 47.*

---

3 Catalytic converter – general information, precautions, removal and refitting

General information

Note: *On some models, the catalytic converter also incorporates the diesel particulate filter.*

1 The catalytic converter reduces harmful exhaust emissions by chemically converting the more poisonous gases to ones which (in theory at least) are less harmful. The chemical reaction is known as an 'oxidising' reaction, or one where oxygen is 'added'.

2 Inside the converter is a honeycomb structure, made of ceramic material and coated with the precious metals palladium, platinum and rhodium (the 'catalyst' which promotes the chemical reaction). The chemical reaction generates heat, which itself promotes the reaction – therefore, once the vehicle has been driven several miles, the body of the converter will be very hot.

3 The ceramic structure contained within the converter is understandably fragile, and will not withstand rough treatment. Since the converter runs at a high temperature, driving through deep standing water (in flood conditions, for example) is to be avoided, since the thermal stresses imposed when plunging the hot converter into cold water may well cause the ceramic internals to fracture, resulting in a 'blocked' converter – a common cause of failure. A converter which has been damaged in this way can be checked by shaking it (do not strike it) – if a

rattling noise is heard, this indicates probable failure. **Note:** *Checking the operation of a catalytic converter requires expensive and sophisticated diagnostic equipment, starting with a high-quality exhaust gas analyser. If the level of CO in the exhaust gases is too high, a full check of the engine management system must be carried out to eliminate all other possibilities before the converter is suspected of being faulty. The vehicle should be taken to a Land Rover dealer for this work to be carried out using the correct diagnostic equipment. Do not waste time trying to test the system without such facilities.*

Precautions

4 The catalytic converter is a reliable and simple device which needs no maintenance in itself, but there are some facts of which an owner should be aware if the converter is to function properly for its full service life.

a) *DO NOT use fuel or engine oil additives – these may contain substances harmful to the catalytic converter.*

b) *DO NOT continue to use the vehicle if the engine burns oil to the extent of leaving a visible trail of blue smoke.*

c) *Remember that the catalytic converter operates at very high temperatures. DO NOT, therefore, park the vehicle in dry undergrowth, over long grass or piles of dead leaves after a long run.*

d) *Remember that the catalytic converter is FRAGILE – do not strike it with tools during servicing work.*

e) *The catalytic converter, used on a well-maintained and well-driven vehicle, should last for between 50,000 and 100,000 miles*

3.11 Front pipe securing nuts

– if the converter is no longer effective it must be renewed.

Removal and refitting

Note: *Do not over bend the front exhaust flexible pipe as it is removed or damage will occur. Support the flexible pipe with a support wrap or a splint.*

5 Disconnect the battery negative terminal (refer to *Disconnecting the battery*.

6 Remove the air outlet duct, with reference to Chapter 4A Section 4.

2.4 litre engine

7 Undo the retaining bolts and remove the heat shields from the top of the exhaust manifold/catalytic converter **(see illustration)**.

8 Undo the nuts securing the top of the catalytic converter to the turbocharger **(see illustration)**.

9 Firmly apply the handbrake, then jack up the front of the vehicle and support it securely on axle stands (see *Jacking and vehicle support*).

10 Where fitted, disconnect the oxygen sensor wiring connector.

11 Undo the retaining nuts securing the front pipe to the intermediate pipe **(see illustration)**. Support the exhaust system, before detaching the rubber mounting.

12 Undo the retaining bolts and remove the catalytic converter support bracket **(see illustration)**, then remove the catalytic converter from under the vehicle. Collect the flange gaskets.

2.2 litre engine

13 Trace the wiring back from the oxygen

3.12 Remove the lower support bracket

3.13 Disconnect the wiring connector

3.14 Remove the heat shield

sensor and disconnect the wiring connector **(see illustration)**.

14 Undo the retaining bolts and remove the heat shields from the top of the exhaust manifold/catalytic converter **(see illustration)**.

15 Firmly apply the handbrake, then jack up the front of the vehicle and support it securely on axle stands (see *Jacking and vehicle support*).

16 Remove the crossmember from under the transmission **(see illustration)**.

17 On models incorporating a diesel particulate filter, note their fitted positions, and disconnect the temperature sensors from the particulate filter. Trace the temperature sensor wiring back to its connectors on the upper right-hand side of the transmission housing **(see illustrations)**, and disconnect the connectors.

18 Also on models incorporating a diesel particulate filter, note their fitted positions, and disconnect the pressure pipes from the particulate filter.

19 Undo the retaining nuts securing the front pipe to the intermediate pipe **(see illustration)**. Support the exhaust system, before detaching the rubber mounting.

20 Undo the retaining bolts and remove the support bracket **(see illustration)**, from the lower part of the catalytic converter/particle filter.

21 Slacken the retaining clip, and remove the air intake hose from the lower part of the turbocharger.

22 Slacken the clamp retaining bolt, and disconnect the catalytic converter/particle filter from the turbocharger **(see illustration)**.

23 Slacken and remove the two engine mounting upper retaining nuts **(see illustration)**.

24 Before the catalytic converter/particle filter can be removed from under the vehicle, the engine will need to be lifted slightly to allow for enough room. Check around the engine to make sure nothing is damaged as the engine is raised slightly, then withdraw the catalytic converter/particle filter from under the vehicle.

Refitting

25 Refitting is a reversal of removal. Use new nuts, bolts and gaskets as necessary, and tighten all fasteners to the specified torque. **Note:** *Exhaust sealant paste should not be used on any part of the exhaust system upstream of the catalytic converter (between the engine and the converter) – even if the sealant does not contain additives harmful to the converter, pieces of it may break off and foul the element, causing local overheating.*

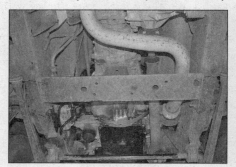

3.16 Remove the lower crossmember

3.17a Remove the temperature sensors...

3.17b ...and disconnect the wiring connectors

3.19 Front pipe securing nuts

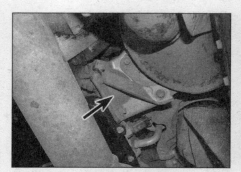

3.20 Remove the lower support bracket

3.22 Undo the clamp to the turbocharger

3.23 Remove engine mounting nuts – one side shown

Chapter 5
Engine electrical systems

Contents

Degrees of difficulty

Easy, suitable for novice with little experience 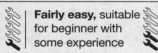	**Fairly easy,** suitable for beginner with some experience	**Fairly difficult,** suitable for competent DIY mechanic	**Difficult,** suitable for experienced DIY mechanic	**Very difficult,** suitable for expert DIY or professional

Specifications

General
Electrical system type . . . .   12 volt, negative-earth

Battery
Type . . . .   Lead-acid, low-maintenance or maintenance-free

Alternator
Type . . . .   Denso 85/150 Amps
Regulated voltage . . . .   13.6 to 14.4 volts at 3000 engine rpm

Starter motor
Make and type . . . .   Lucas or Paris-Rhone, or Bosch

Oil pressure sensor
Operating pressures . . . .   0.15 to 0.41 bar

Torque wrench settings

	Nm	lbf ft
Alternator mounting bolts	48	35
Alternator support bracket	25	18
Auxiliary drivebelt tensioner bolt	50	37
Glow plugs	13	10
Oil level sensor	27	19
Oil pressure sensor	15	11
Starter motor mounting bolts	35	26
Vacuum pump bolts	10	7
Vacuum pump oil feed pipe bolt	10	7

1 General information and precautions

1 The engine electrical system includes all charging, starting and preheating components, and the engine oil pressure sensor. Because of their engine-related functions, these components are covered separately from the body electrical devices such as the lights, instruments, etc (which are covered in Chapter 13).

2 The electrical system is of the 12 volt, negative-earth type.

3 The battery is of the low-maintenance or maintenance-free type, and is charged by the alternator, which is belt-driven from a crankshaft-mounted pulley.

4 The starter motor is of the pre-engaged reduction gear type, incorporating an integral solenoid. On starting, the solenoid moves the drive pinion into engagement with the flywheel ring gear before the starter motor is energised. Once the engine has started, a one-way clutch prevents the motor armature being driven by the engine until the pinion disengages from the flywheel. The motor is fitted with a reduction gear mechanism, in order to achieve the high torque necessary to turn the engine against the high compression pressures encountered in a diesel engine.

Precautions

5 Further details of the various systems are given in the relevant Sections of this Chapter. While some repair procedures are given, the usual course of action is to renew the component concerned.

6 It is necessary to take extra care when working on the electrical system, to avoid damage to semi-conductor devices (diodes and transistors), and to avoid the risk of personal injury. In addition to the precautions given in *Safety first!* at the beginning of this manual, observe the following when working on the system:

● Always remove rings, watches, etc, before working on the electrical system. Even with the battery disconnected, capacitive discharge could occur if a component's live terminal is earthed through a metal object. This could cause a shock or nasty burn.

● Do not reverse the battery connections. Components such as the alternator, preheating electronic control unit, or any other components having semi-conductor circuitry could be irreparably damaged.

● If the engine is being started using jump leads and a slave battery, connect the batteries positive-to-positive and negative-to-negative (see Jump starting). This also applies when connecting a battery charger.

● Never disconnect the battery terminals, the alternator, any electrical wiring or any test instruments, when the engine is running.

● Do not allow the engine to turn the

alternator when the alternator is not connected.

● Never 'test' for alternator output by 'flashing' the output lead to earth.

● Never use an ohmmeter of the type incorporating a hand-cranked generator for circuit or continuity testing.

● Always ensure that the battery negative lead is disconnected when working on the electrical system.

● Before using electric-arc welding equipment on the car, disconnect the battery, alternator and components such as the preheating electronic control unit, ABS electronic control unit, etc, to protect them from the risk of damage.

● The radio/cassette unit fitted as standard equipment by Land Rover may have a built-in security code, to deter thieves. If the power source to the unit is cut, the anti-theft system will activate. Even if the power source is immediately reconnected, the radio/cassette unit will not function until the correct security code has been entered. Therefore, if you do not know the correct security code for the radio/cassette unit, do not disconnect the battery negative terminal of the battery, nor remove the radio/cassette unit from the vehicle. Refer to the manufacturer's handbook supplied with the vehicle for details of how to enter the security code.

2 Electrical fault finding – general information

1 Refer to Chapter.

3 Battery – testing and charging

Note: *Refer to the precautions given in 'Safety first!' and in Section 1 of this Chapter before proceeding.*

Testing

Standard and low-maintenance battery

1 If the vehicle covers a small annual mileage, it is worthwhile checking the specific gravity of the electrolyte every three months to determine the state of charge of the battery. Use a hydrometer to make the check and compare the results with the following table. Note that the specific gravity readings assume an electrolyte temperature of 15°C; for every 10°C below 15°C subtract 0.007. For every 10°C above 15°C add 0.007.

	Above 25°C	Below 25°C
Fully-charged	1.210 to 1.230	1.270 to 1.290
70% charged	1.170 to 1.190	1.230 to 1.250
Discharged	1.050 to 1.070	1.110 to 1.130

2 If the battery condition is suspect, first check the specific gravity of electrolyte in each cell. A variation of 0.040 or more between any cells indicates loss of electrolyte or deterioration of the internal plates.

3 If the specific gravity variation is 0.040 or more, the battery should be renewed. If the cell variation is satisfactory but the battery is discharged, it should be charged as described later in this Section.

Maintenance-free battery

4 In cases where a 'sealed for life' maintenance-free battery is fitted, topping-up and testing of the electrolyte in each cell is not possible. The condition of the battery can therefore only be tested using a battery condition indicator or a voltmeter.

5 Certain models may be fitted with a maintenance-free battery, with a built-in charge condition indicator. The indicator is located in the top of the battery casing, and indicates the condition of the battery from its colour. If the indicator shows green, then the battery is in a good state of charge. If the indicator shows black, then the battery requires charging, as described later in this Section. If the indicator shows blue, then the electrolyte level in the battery is too low to allow further use, and the battery should be renewed.

Caution: Do not attempt to charge, load or jump start a battery when the indicator shows clear/yellow.

All battery types

6 If testing the battery using a voltmeter, connect the voltmeter across the battery. The test is only accurate if the battery has not been subjected to any kind of charge for the previous six hours. If this is not the case, switch on the headlights for 30 seconds, then wait four to five minutes before testing the battery after switching off the headlights. All other electrical circuits must be switched off, so check that the doors or tailgate are fully shut when making the test.

7 If the voltage reading is less than 12.2 volts, then the battery is discharged, whilst a reading of 12.2 to 12.4 volts indicates a partially discharged condition.

8 If the battery is to be charged, remove it from the vehicle (Section 4) and charge it as described later in this Section.

Charging

Note: *The following is intended as a guide only. Always refer to the manufacturer's recommendations (often printed on a label attached to the battery) before charging a battery.*

Standard and low-maintenance battery

9 Charge the battery at a rate of 3.5 to 4 amps and continue to charge the battery at this rate until no further rise in specific gravity is noted over a four hour period.

10 Alternatively, a trickle charger charging

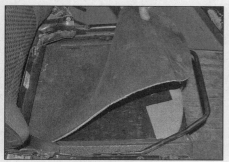

4.2 Lift up the rubber cover

4.3a Release the cover retaining clip…

4.3b …and slide the cover forwards

4.4 Disconnect the negative lead

4.5a Unclip the cover…

4.5b …and disconnect the positive lead clamp

at the rate of 1.5 amps can safely be used overnight.

11 Specially rapid 'boost' charges which are claimed to restore the power of the battery in 1 to 2 hours are not recommended, as they can cause serious damage to the battery plates through overheating.

12 While charging the battery, note that the temperature of the electrolyte should never exceed 38°C.

Maintenance-free battery

13 This battery type takes considerably longer to fully recharge than the standard type, the time taken being dependent on the extent of discharge, but it can take anything up to three days.

14 A constant voltage type charger is required to be set, when connected, to 13.9 to 14.9 volts with a charger current below 25 amps. Using this method, the battery should

be usable within three hours, giving a voltage reading of 12.5 volts, but this is for a partially-discharged battery and, as mentioned, full charging can take considerably longer.

15 If the battery is to be charged from a fully-discharged state (condition reading less than 12.2 volts), have it recharged by your Land Rover dealer or local automotive electrician, as the charge rate is higher and constant supervision during charging is necessary.

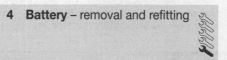

4   Battery – removal and refitting

Note: *Refer to the precautions given in 'Safety first!' and in Section 1 of this Chapter before proceeding.*

Note: *To prevent the alarm from sounding*

when the battery is disconnected, the negative lead needs to be disconnected from the battery within 17 seconds of the ignition being switched off and the key removed. It is a good idea to just slacken the negative lead clamp bolt (do not disconnect clamp), in preparation for disconnecting the negative lead, when the ignition is switch off.

Removal

1 The battery is located under the front passenger's seat.

2 Remove the passenger's seat cushion, and lift the rubber insulation material to expose the battery cover and clip **(see illustration)**.

3 Release the clip and slide the battery cover from over the battery compartment **(see illustrations)**.

4 In order to prevent the anti-theft alarm from sounding and the vehicle being immobilised, turn the ignition switch to position II, then to position 0, remove the ignition key and disconnect the battery negative lead within 17 seconds **(see illustration)**.

5 Remove the red plastic cover (where fitted), then slacken the nut and disconnect the battery positive lead clamp **(see illustrations)**.

6 Slacken the bolts and remove the two battery clamps **(see illustration)**.

7 Lift the battery out from it's position in the compartment from under the seat **(see illustration)**.

Refitting

8 Refitting is a reversal of removal, but always connect the positive terminal clamp

4.6 Remove the two battery clamps

4.7 Lift out the battery

4.8 Apply petroleum jelly to terminals

6.3 Remove the air outlet hose

first and the negative terminal clamp last. After connecting the battery terminals, it's a good idea to apply a layer of petroleum jelly to the terminals to prevent corrosion **(see illustration)**.

5 Charging system – testing

Note: *Refer to the warnings given in 'Safety first!' and in Section 1 of this Chapter before proceeding.*

1 If the ignition (no-charge) warning light fails to illuminate when the ignition is switched on, first check the security of the alternator wiring connections. If satisfactory, check that the warning light bulb has not blown, and that the bulbholder is secure in its location in the instrument panel. If the light still fails to illuminate, check the continuity of the warning light feed wire from the alternator to the bulbholder. If all is satisfactory, the alternator is at fault, and should be renewed, or taken to an auto-electrician for testing and repair.

2 If the ignition warning light illuminates when the engine is running, stop the engine and check that the drivebelt is correctly tensioned (Chapter 1) and that the alternator connections are secure. If all is so far satisfactory, check the alternator brushes and slip-rings (see Section 7). If the fault persists, the alternator should be renewed, or taken to an auto-electrician for testing and repair.

3 If the alternator output is suspect even though the warning light functions correctly, the regulated voltage may be checked as follows.

4 Connect a voltmeter across the battery terminals, and start the engine.

5 Increase the engine speed until the voltmeter reading remains steady; as a rough guide, the reading should be between 13.6 and 14.4 volts.

6 Switch on as many electrical accessories (headlights, heater blower, cigarette lighter, etc) as possible, and check that the alternator maintains the regulated voltage between 13.6 and 14.4 volts. It may be necessary to increase engine speed slightly.

7 If the regulated voltage is not as stated, the fault may be due to worn brushes, weak brush springs, a faulty voltage regulator, a faulty diode, a severed phase winding, or worn or damaged slip-rings. The brushes and slip-rings may be checked (see Section), but if the fault persists, the alternator should be renewed, or taken to an auto-electrician for testing and repair.

6 Alternator – removal and refitting

Note: *Refer to the precautions given in 'Safety first!' and in Section 1 of this Chapter before proceeding.*

Removal

1 Disconnect the battery negative lead (see Section 4).

2 Remove the auxiliary drivebelt as described in Chapter 1 Section 52.

3 Slacken the securing clips and remove the air cleaner outlet hose from the turbocharger **(see illustration)**, and move it to one side.

4 Undo the four mounting bolts that secure the alternator to the mounting bracket and support the weight of the alternator.

5 With the alternator supported and moved forwards, disconnect the wiring from the rear of the alternator **(see illustrations)**.

6 The alternator can then be withdrawn from the engine compartment.

Refitting

7 Refitting is a reversal of removal, but tension the drivebelt as described in Chapter 1.

7 Alternator brushes – inspection and renewal

Lucas A115 and A133 alternators

1 For improved access, remove the alternator as described in Section 6.

2 Disconnect the wiring plug, then remove the securing screw and withdraw the interference

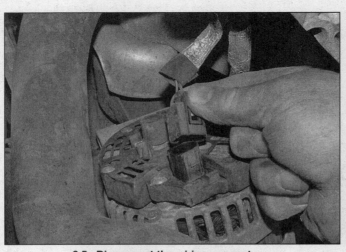

6.5a Disconnect the wiring connector...

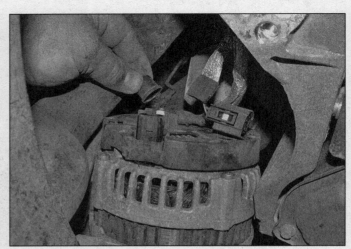

6.5b ...then unclip the rubber cover and undo cable terminal nut

suppression capacitor from the rear cover **(see illustration)**.

3 Extract the two securing screws, and remove the alternator rear cover.

4 Make a careful note of the fitted positions of the regulator wires, then disconnect the wires from the diode pack and the brush box.

5 Remove the regulator securing screws, and withdraw the regulator. Note that the regulator securing screw also holds one of the brush mounting plates in position.

6 Remove the two securing screws, and withdraw the brush box. Remove the securing screws, and lift the brushes from the brush box.

7 If the length of either brush is less than the minimum given in the Specifications, renew both brushes.

8 Wipe the slip-rings clean with a fuel-moistened cloth. If the rings are very dirty, use fine glass paper to clean them, then wipe with the cloth.

9 Refitting is a reversal of removal, but make sure that the brushes move freely in their holders.

10 Where applicable, refit the alternator as described in Section 6.

Lucas A127 alternator

11 For improved access, remove the alternator as described in Section 6.

12 If necessary, unscrew the suppressor securing nut from the through-bolt, then disconnect the wiring and withdraw the suppressor for access to the voltage regulator/brush box assembly **(see illustration)**.

13 Remove the three screws securing the voltage regulator/brush box assembly to the rear of the alternator.

14 Tip the outside edge of the assembly upwards, and withdraw it from its location. Disconnect the wiring plug, and withdraw the assembly from the alternator.

15 If the length of either brush is less than

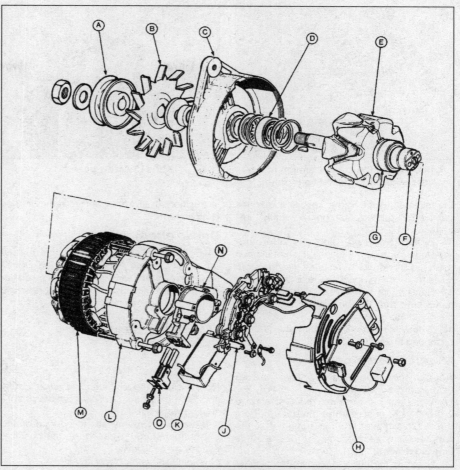

7.2 Exploded view of Lucas A115 and A133-type alternators

A Pulley	F Slip-ring	L Slip-ring end housing
B Fan	G Bearing	M Stator
C Drive end housing	H End cover	N Brush box
D Bearing	J Diode pack	O Brushes
E Rotor	K Regulator	

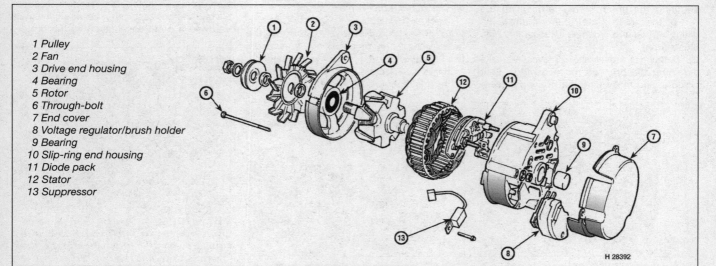

1 Pulley
2 Fan
3 Drive end housing
4 Bearing
5 Rotor
6 Through-bolt
7 End cover
8 Voltage regulator/brush holder
9 Bearing
10 Slip-ring end housing
11 Diode pack
12 Stator
13 Suppressor

H 28392

7.12 Exploded view of Lucas A127-type alternator

7.19 Unscrew the studs from the rear of the alternator – Marelli alternator

7.20a Unscrew the nut ...

7.20b ... and remove the wiring terminal – Marelli alternator

the minimum given in the Specifications, the complete regulator/brush box assembly must be renewed.

16 Before refitting, wipe the alternator slip-rings clean with a fuel-moistened cloth. If the rings are very dirty, use fine glasspaper to clean them, then wipe with the cloth.

17 Refitting is a reversal of removal, but make sure that the brushes move freely in their holders.

18 Where applicable, refit the alternator as described in Section 6.

Marelli alternator

Note: Check on the availability of new brushes before proceeding.

19 With the alternator removed as described in Section 6, unscrew the three studs from the rear of the alternator, noting that the suppressor is secured by one of the studs **(see illustration)**.

20 Unscrew the nut and recover the washer securing the wiring terminal to the rear of the alternator, then remove the terminal **(see illustrations)**. Note that the suppressor wiring is connected to the terminal.

21 Withdraw the alternator rear cover **(see illustration)**.

22 To remove a brush, remove the screw securing the brush wiring terminal to the top of the brush plate, then withdraw the wiring, spring and brush as an assembly **(see illustration)**.

23 Refitting is a reversal of removal, but make sure that the brushes move freely in their holders, and make sure that the suppressor

is positioned as noted before removal (see **Haynes hint**).

Denso alternator

24 At the time of writing, no information on repairs where available for the Denso alternator. Check with a Land Rover dealer or automotive electrical specialist concerning exchange/repaired units.

8 Starting system – testing

Note: Refer to the precautions given in 'Safety first!' and in Section 1 of this Chapter before starting work.

1 If the starter motor fails to operate during the normal starting procedure, the possible causes are as follows:
a) The engine immobiliser is faulty.
b) The battery is faulty.
c) The electrical connections between the switch, solenoid, battery and starter motor are somewhere failing to pass the necessary current from the battery through the starter to earth.
d) The solenoid is faulty.
e) The starter motor is mechanically or electrically defective.

2 To check the battery, switch on the headlights. If they dim after a few seconds, this indicates that the battery is discharged – recharge (see Section 5) or renew the battery. If the headlights glow brightly, operate the

starter switch while watching the headlights. If they dim, then this indicates that current is reaching the starter motor, therefore the fault must lie in the starter motor. If the lights continue to glow brightly (and no clicking sound can be heard from the starter motor solenoid), this indicates that there is a fault in the circuit or solenoid – see the following paragraphs. If the starter motor turns slowly when operated, but the battery is in good condition, then this indicates either that the starter motor is faulty, or there is considerable resistance somewhere in the circuit.

3 If a fault in the circuit is suspected, disconnect the battery leads (including the earth connection to the body), the starter/solenoid wiring and the engine/transmission earth strap. Thoroughly clean the connections, and reconnect the leads and wiring. Use a voltmeter or test light to check that full battery voltage is available at the battery positive lead connection to the solenoid. Smear petroleum jelly around the battery terminals to prevent corrosion – corroded connections are among the most frequent causes of electrical system faults.

4 If the battery and all connections are in good condition, check the circuit by disconnecting the ignition switch supply wire from the solenoid terminal. Connect a voltmeter or test lamp between the wire end and a good earth (such as the battery

7.21 Withdrawing the alternator rear cover – Marelli alternator

7.22 Removing an alternator brush – Marelli alternator

HAYNES HiNT

When fitting a brush, use a small screwdriver to push the brush into position in the brush holder as the wiring terminal is lined up with the securing screw.

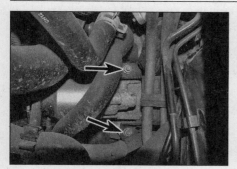

9.4 Undo the nuts and remove the wiring harness retainer

9.5a Slacken and remove the two retaining nuts...

9.5b ...and disconnect the wiring from the solenoid

negative terminal), and check that the wire is live when the ignition switch is turned to the 'start' position. If it is, then the circuit is sound – if not the circuit wiring can be checked as described in Section 2.

5 The solenoid contacts can be checked by connecting a voltmeter or test light between the battery positive feed connection on the starter side of the solenoid and earth. When the ignition switch is turned to the 'start' position, there should be a reading or lighted bulb, as applicable. If there is no reading or lighted bulb, the solenoid is faulty.

6 If the circuit and solenoid are proved sound, the fault must lie in the starter motor. In this event, it may be possible to have the starter motor overhauled by a specialist, but check on the cost of spares before proceeding, as it may prove more economical to obtain a new or exchange motor.

9 Starter motor – removal and refitting

Removal

1 Disconnect the battery negative terminal (refer to Section 4.

2 Firmly apply the handbrake, then jack up the front of the vehicle and support it securely on axle stands (see *Jacking and Vehicle support*).

3 Undo the retaining nut and remove the fuel

line support bracket from the top of the starter motor.

4 Undo the retaining nuts and remove the wiring harness retainer off the starter motor mounting bolts **(see illustration)**.

5 Unclip the plastic cover, then slacken and remove the two retaining nuts and disconnect the wiring from the starter motor solenoid **(see illustrations)**. Recover the washers under the nuts.

6 Unscrew the starter motor mounting bolts, then manoeuvre the starter motor downwards and out from under the vehicle **(see illustration)**.

Refitting

7 Refitting is a reversal of removal, tightening the mounting bolts to the specified torque. Ensure all wiring is correctly routed and the retaining nuts are securely tightened.

10 Starter motor – testing and overhaul

1 If the starter motor is thought to be suspect, it should be removed from the vehicle and taken to an auto electrician for testing. Most auto electricians will be able to supply and fit brushes at a reasonable cost. However, check on the cost of repairs before proceeding as it may prove more economical to obtain a new or exchange motor.

11 Ignition switch – removal and refitting

1 The ignition switch is integral with the steering column lock, and can be removed as described in Chapter 11 Section 19.

12 Oil pressure and oil level/temperature sensor – removal and refitting

Removal

Oil pressure sensor

Note: *If the oil pressure sensor fails, the low pressure warning light on the instrument panel will be permanently illuminated. The oil pressure sensor is earthed through the switch body to the engine control module (ECM).*

1 The oil pressure warning light sensor is located in the oil filter adapter plate at the left-hand side of the cylinder block **(see illustration)**.

2 Disconnect the wiring connector from the sensor**(see illustration)**.

3 Carefully unscrew the sensor, and withdraw it from the oil filter adapter plate. Be prepared for some oil spillage. Where applicable, recover the sealing ring.

9.6 Manoeuvre the starter motor downwards and out from under the vehicle

12.1 Oil pressure warning light sensor

12.2 Disconnect the wiring connector

Oil level/temperature sensor (2.2 litre engines only)

Note: *The oil level signal from the sensor is not used on this engine, as a normal mechanical dipstick is provided to check oil level. The temperature signal is used to prevent the oil from exceeding 140°C in extreme conditions, by sending information to the engine control module (ECM), which limits engine torque.*

4 The oil level/temperature sensor is located in the lower part of the cylinder block. at the right-hand side of the engine **(see illustration)**.

5 Disconnect the wiring connector **(see illustration)**, then unscrew the sensor from the cylinder block, recover the O-ring seal and discard, as a new one will be required for refitting. Be prepared for some oil spillage.

Refitting

6 Refitting is a reversal of removal, but clean the threads of the sensor before refitting, and where applicable, use a new sealing ring/washer.

13 Pre/post-heating system – general information

System description

1 There are four glow plugs, also known as heater plugs (one for each cylinder), fitted between the inlet valves in the cylinder head. These preheat the combustion chamber to aid the starting procedure and also provides additional heat to the combustion chamber, to reduce emissions and engine noise, whilst the engine warms up.

2 Cold-starting performance is automatically controlled by the engine control module (ECM). Under cold start conditions, the cylinder head temperature (CHT) sensor (2.4 litre engine) or engine coolant temperature (ECT) sensor (2.2 litre engine), informs the ECM of the engine temperature and this determines the pre/post-heat time.

3 On 2.2 litre engines, there is also a glow plug control module, which feeds each glow plug individually and reports diagnostic status back to the ECM.

4 During the preheat stage, the engine control module (ECM) receives a signal from the coolant temperature sensor, and this will determine the length of time for the preheat stage.

● On 2.4 litre engines, there is a maximum preheat time of 8 seconds, when the temperature is at -20°C or lower. There will be no preheat stage if the temperature is above 80°C.

● On 2.2 litre engines, there is a maximum preheat time of 2.1 seconds, when the temperature is at -20°C or lower. There will be no preheat stage if the temperature is above 20°C.

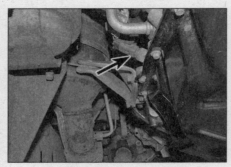

12.4 Oil level/temperature sensor

12.5 Disconnect the wiring connector

5 The glow plugs also provide a post-heating function, whereby the glow plugs remain switched on after the engine has started, this helps the engine to run more smoothly during idling and reduces exhaust emissions through more efficient combustion just after starting.

● On 2.4 litre engines, the post-heating function only operates at below 2500 rpm, and below temperatures of 50°C.

● On 2.2 litre engines, the post-heating function operates for a maximum time of 500 seconds, or until the temperature reaches 70°C.

Component locations

6 The pre/post-heating is controlled by the engine control module (ECM) which is located at the rear of the engine compartment on the bulkhead. Refer to Chapter 4A Section 9 for removal and refitting details.

7 The cylinder head temperature (CHT) sensor is screwed into the rear of the cylinder head, and the engine coolant temperature (ECT) sensor is fitted to the top hose. Refer to Chapter 3 Section 6 for removal and refitting details.

8 The glow plug control module (on 2.2 litre engines) is located next to the ECM on the bulkhead, at the rear of the engine compartment. Refer to Section 15 for further details.

14 Glow plugs – testing, removal and refitting

Testing

1 If the system malfunctions, testing is ultimately by substitution of known good units, but some preliminary checks may be made as follows.

2 Connect a voltmeter or 12 volt test lamp between the glow plug supply cable and earth (engine or vehicle metal). Make sure that the live connection is kept clear of the engine and bodywork.

3 Have an assistant switch on the ignition, and check that voltage is applied to the glow plugs. Note the time for which the warning light is lit, and the total time for which voltage

is applied before the system cuts out. Switch off the ignition.

4 If an ammeter of suitable range (0 to 50 amp) is available, connect it between the glow plug feed wire and the busbar (the wire that connects the four plugs together). During the pre-heating period, the ammeter should show a current draw of approximately 8 amps per working plug, ie, 32 amps if all four plugs are working. If one or more plugs appear not to be drawing current, remove the busbar and check each plug separately with a continuity tester or self-powered test light.

5 If there is no supply at all to the glow plugs, the relay or associated wiring may be at fault. Otherwise this points to a defective engine coolant/cylinder head temperature sensor (see Chapter 3 Section 6), or to a problem with the engine control module (ECM).

6 To locate a defective glow plug, disconnect the main feed wire and the interconnecting busbar from the top of the glow plugs. Be careful not to drop the nuts and washers.

7 Use a continuity tester, or a 12 volt test lamp connected to the battery positive terminal, to check for continuity between each glow plug terminal and earth. The resistance of a glow plug in good condition is very low (less than 1 ohm), so if the test lamp does not light or the continuity tester shows a high resistance, the glow plug is certainly defective.

8 If an ammeter is available, the current draw of each glow plug can be checked. After an initial surge of 15 to 20 amps, each plug should draw 10 amps. Any plug which draws much more or less than this is probably defective.

9 As a final check, the glow plugs can be removed and inspected as described below.

Removal

Caution: Caution: If the pre/post-heating system has just been energised, or if the engine has been running, the glow plugs will be very hot.

10 Disconnect the battery negative terminal (refer to Section 4).

11 Remove the inlet manifold as described in Chapter 4A Section 15.

12 Unscrew the nut and remove the washer securing each glow plug connector, then lift the wiring away from the plugs **(see**

14.12 Unscrew the retaining nut (two of four arrowed) from each glow plug

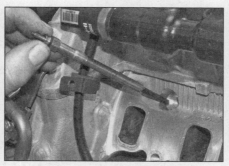

14.13 Remove the glow plug from the cylinder head

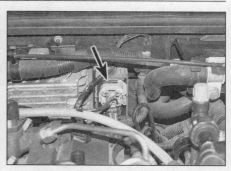

15.1 Location of control module

illustration). Note that the wiring need not be removed completely for access to the plugs.

13 Unscrew the glow plugs and remove them from the engine for inspection (see illustration).

14 Inspect the glow plug stems for signs of damage. A badly burned or charred stem may be an indication of a faulty fuel injector – consult a diesel specialist for advice if necessary. Otherwise, if one plug is found to be faulty and the engine has completed a high mileage, it is probably worth renewing all four plugs as a set.

Refitting

15 Refitting is a reversal of removal, noting the following points:

a) Tighten the glow plugs to the specified torque.

b) Make sure when remaking the glow plug wiring connections that the contact surfaces are clean.

c) Refit the inlet manifold as described in Chapter 4A Section 15.

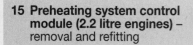

15 Preheating system control module (2.2 litre engines) – removal and refitting

Note: Refer to the precautions given in 'Safety first!' and in Section 1 of this Chapter before proceeding.

Removal

1 The control module is located at the rear of the engine compartment on the bulkhead (see illustration).

2 Disconnect the battery negative lead with reference to Section 4.

3 Disconnect the two wiring plug connectors from the control module (see illustration).

4 Unclip the control module from the mounting bracket on the bulkhead (see illustration), and withdraw the unit.

Refitting

5 Refitting is a reversal of removal.

15.3 Disconnect the wiring connector

16 Inertia switch (2.2 litre engines) – description, removal and refitting

Description

1 The inertia switch is located at the rear of the engine compartment on the bulkhead (see illustration), to the right-hand side of the engine control module (ECM). When the switch is activated the supply is cut to the engine fuel injection system and fuel tank pump. After the switch has been activated, it can be reset by pressing down on the rubber

16.1 Location of the inertia switch

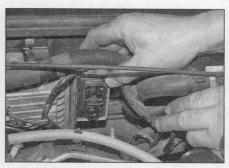

15.4 Unclip module from bracket

cap, which is positioned on top of the inertia switch.

Removal

Note: Refer to the precautions given in 'Safety first!' and in Section 1 of this Chapter before proceeding.

2 Disconnect the battery negative lead, with reference to Section 4.

3 Disconnect the wiring connector, and then undo the retaining screws and remove it from the bulkhead (see illustration).

Refitting

4 Refitting is a reversal of removal.

16.3 Disconnecting the wiring from the inertia switch

Notes

Chapter 6
Clutch

Contents

Degrees of difficulty

Easy, suitable for novice with little experience	**Fairly easy,** suitable for beginner with some experience	**Fairly difficult,** suitable for competent DIY mechanic	**Difficult,** suitable for experienced DIY mechanic	**Very difficult,** suitable for expert DIY or professional

Specifications

General
Clutch type	Single dry plate, diaphragm spring, hydraulically-operated
Adjustment	Automatic
Hydraulic fluid type	see *Lubricants and fluids*

Clutch pedal adjustment
Pedal height	140.0 mm
Master cylinder pushrod-to-piston freeplay	1.5 mm
Pedal free movement at pedal rubber	6.0 mm

Torque wrench settings
	Nm	lbf ft
Clutch cover bolts	29	21
Clutch master cylinder to pedal bracket	23	17
Clutch pedal bracket to body	23	17
Clutch pedal sensor	15	11
Clutch slave cylinder bolts	10	7
Hydraulic fluid pipe and hose unions	15	11

1 General Information

1 All models are fitted with a single dry plate clutch, which consists of five main components – friction disc, pressure plate, diaphragm spring, cover, and release bearing.
2 The friction disc is free to slide along the splines of the gearbox input shaft, and is held in position between the flywheel and the pressure plate by the pressure exerted on the pressure plate by the diaphragm spring. Friction lining material is riveted to both sides of the friction disc, and spring cushioning between the friction linings and the hub absorbs transmission shocks, and helps to ensure a smooth take-up of power as the clutch is engaged.
3 The diaphragm spring is mounted on pins, and is held in place in the cover by annular fulcrum rings.
4 The release bearing is located on a guide sleeve at the front of the gearbox. The bearing is free to slide on the sleeve, under the action of the release arm which pivots inside the clutch bellhousing.
5 The release mechanism is operated by the clutch pedal, using hydraulic pressure. The pedal acts on the hydraulic master cylinder pushrod, and a slave cylinder, mounted on the gearbox bellhousing, operates the clutch release lever via a pushrod.
6 When the clutch pedal is depressed, the release arm pushes the release bearing forwards, to bear against the centre of the diaphragm spring, thus pushing the centre of the diaphragm spring inwards. The diaphragm spring acts against the fulcrum rings in the cover; as the centre of the spring is pushed in, the outside of the spring is pushed out, so allowing the pressure plate to move backwards away from the friction disc.
7 When the clutch pedal is released, the diaphragm spring forces the pressure plate into contact with the friction linings on the friction disc, and simultaneously pushes the friction disc forwards on its splines, forcing it against the flywheel. The friction disc is now firmly sandwiched between the pressure plate and the flywheel, and drive is taken up.

8 The clutch is self-adjusting. As wear takes place on the friction disc over a period of time, the pressure plate automatically moves closer to the friction disc to compensate.

2 Clutch assembly – removal, inspection and refitting

⚠️ *Warning: Dust created by clutch wear and deposited on the clutch components may contain hazardous material, which could be a health issue. DO NOT blow it out with compressed air, nor inhale any of it. DO NOT use petrol (or petroleum-based solvents) to clean off the dust. Brake system cleaner or methylated spirit should be used to flush the dust into a suitable receptacle. After the clutch components are wiped clean with rags, dispose of the contaminated rags and cleaner in a sealed, marked container.*

Removal

1 Remove the transmission, as described in Chapter 7A. Note that if no other work is to be carried out on the gearbox, it may be simpler to remove the engine.
2 If the original clutch is to be refitted, make alignment marks between the clutch cover and the flywheel, so that the clutch can be refitted in its original position.
3 Progressively unscrew the bolts securing the clutch cover to the flywheel.
4 Withdraw the clutch cover from the flywheel. Be prepared to catch the clutch friction disc, which may drop out of the cover as it is withdrawn, and note which way round the friction disc is fitted **(see illustration)**.

Inspection

5 With the clutch assembly removed, clean off all traces of dust using a dry cloth. Take suitable precautions; as harmful dust should not be inhaled.
6 Examine the linings of the friction disc for wear or loose rivets, and for distortion, cracks, broken torsion springs (where applicable) and worn splines. The surface of the friction linings may be highly glazed, but, as long as the friction material pattern can be clearly

seen, this is satisfactory. If there is any sign of oil contamination, indicated by a continuous, or patchy, shiny black discolouration, the disc must be renewed. The source of the contamination must be traced and rectified before fitting new clutch components; typically, a leaking crankshaft rear oil seal or gearbox input shaft oil seal – or both – will be to blame (renewal procedures are given in the appropriate part of Chapter 2A or 2B and Chapter). The disc must also be renewed if the lining thickness has worn down to, or just above, the level of the rivet heads.
7 Check the machined faces of the flywheel and pressure plate. If either is grooved, or heavily scored, renewal is necessary. The pressure plate must also be renewed if any cracks are apparent, or if the diaphragm spring is damaged or its pressure suspect.
8 With the clutch removed, it is advisable to check the condition of the release bearing, as described in Section. It is considered good practice to renew the release bearing as a matter of course, whenever new clutch components are fitted, given the amount of work required to gain access to the clutch.

Refitting

9 It is important to ensure that no oil or grease gets onto the friction disc linings, or the pressure plate and flywheel faces. It is advisable to refit the clutch assembly with clean hands, and to wipe down the pressure plate and flywheel faces with a clean rag before assembly begins.
10 Apply a smear of clutch assembly grease to the splines of the friction disc hub, then offer the disc to the flywheel, with the greater projecting side of the hub facing the flywheel (most friction discs will have a Flywheel side or FW SIDE marking, which should face the flywheel) **(see illustration)**. Hold the friction disc against the flywheel while the cover/pressure plate assembly is offered into position.
11 Fit the clutch cover assembly, where applicable aligning the marks on the flywheel and clutch cover. Refit the securing bolts/nuts and washers, and tighten them finger-tight, so that the friction disc is gripped, but can still be moved. Note that the pressure plate assembly locates on dowels **(see illustration)**.
12 The friction disc must now be centralised,

2.4 Withdrawing the clutch cover and friction disc

2.10 FW SIDE mark on clutch friction disc

2.11 The pressure plate assembly locates on dowels (arrowed)

so that when the engine and gearbox are mated, the gearbox input shaft splines will pass through the splines in the friction disc hub.

13 Centralisation can be carried out by inserting a round bar or a long screwdriver through the hole in the centre of the friction disc, so that the end of the bar rests in the spigot bearing in the centre of the crankshaft. Where possible, use a blunt instrument, but if a screwdriver is used, wrap tape around the blade, to prevent damage to the bearing surface. Moving the bar sideways or up-and-down as necessary, move the friction disc in whichever direction is necessary to achieve centralisation. With the bar removed, view the friction disc hub in relation to the hole in the centre of the crankshaft and the circle created by the ends of the diaphragm spring fingers. When the hub appears exactly in the centre, all is correct. Alternatively, use a clutch plate alignment tool (see **Haynes hint**).

14 Tighten the cover retaining bolts/nuts gradually in a diagonal sequence, to the specified torque. Remove the alignment tool.

15 Refit the transmission or engine, as applicable, as described in Chapter 7A Section 5 or Chapter 2C Section 4 respectively.

3 Slave cylinder release bearing – removal, inspection and refitting

Note: *Refer to the warning in Section 5 concerning the dangers of hydraulic fluid before proceeding.*

If a suitable clutch alignment tool can be obtained, this will eliminate all the guesswork, and obviate the need for visual alignment.

Removal

1 The release bearing and slave cylinder are combined to form a release cylinder unit, which is located in the bellhousing of the transmission.

2 Remove the transmission as described in.

3 Extract the retaining clip and withdraw the hydraulic pipe from the release cylinder and bellhousing **(see illustrations)**.

4 Remove the three mounting bolts, and withdraw the release cylinder from the transmission **(see illustration)**.

Inspection

5 Check the release bearing for smoothness of operation, and renew it if there is any sign of harshness or roughness as the bearing is spun. Do not attempt to dismantle, clean or lubricate the bearing.

6 Repair kits are not available from Land Rover. If a fault develops, the complete release cylinder must be renewed.

Refitting

7 Refitting is a reversal of the removal procedure, noting the following points:

a) *Tighten the mounting bolts to the specified torque.*

b) *Refit the transmission as described in.*

4 Master cylinder – removal, overhaul and refitting

 Warning: Refer to the warning at the beginning of Section before proceeding.

Note: *Suitable sealant or a new gasket (as applicable) will be required to seal the pedal box to the bulkhead on refitting, and a new pedal box cover gasket will be required.*

Removal

1 Disconnect the battery negative lead, with reference to Chapter 5 Section 4.

2 To improve access, remove the bonnet as described in Chapter 12 Section 7.

3 Drain the clutch hydraulic system. Follow the procedure described in Section 5 for bleeding the hydraulic system, but do not top-up the fluid reservoir. Pump the clutch pedal until all the hydraulic fluid has been expelled from the bleed screw.

4 Working inside the driver's footwell, remove the brake light switches, as described in Chapter 10 Section 18.

5 Then release the fasteners and pull back the trim panel from above the pedals to access the clutch pedal bracket bolts, then unscrew the six bolts securing the clutch pedal box to the bulkhead.

6 Unclip the rubber from the pedal.

7 Working under the bonnet, undo the securing nut and move the coolant reservoir to one side to make access to the master cylinder easier.

8 Disconnect the wiring connector from the clutch pressure switch **(see illustration)**.

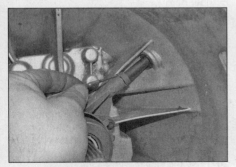

3.3a Extract the retaining clip…

3.3b …and withdraw the hydraulic pipe from the release cylinder and bellhousing

3.4 Remove the three mounting bolts, and withdraw the release cylinder from the transmission

4.8 Disconnect the wiring connector from the switch

4.9 Remove the cover plate

4.11 Withdrawing the clutch pedal box from the engine compartment

4.12 Unscrewing a clutch master cylinder securing nut

4.13 Unscrew the nut and washer (arrowed) from the end of the master cylinder pushrod

withdraw the pedal box/master cylinder assembly from the bulkhead, and manipulate the assembly from the engine compartment. The pedal box may be sealed to the bulkhead using sealant or a gasket – where applicable, recover the gasket. It will be necessary to turn the pedal box in order to allow the pedal to pass through the aperture in the bulkhead **(see illustration)**.

12 Unscrew the two nuts and bolts securing the master cylinder to the pedal box **(see illustration)**.

13 Unscrew the nut and recover the washer from the end of the master cylinder pushrod, then withdraw the master cylinder from the pedal box **(see illustration)**. Recover the mounting plate, and recover the remaining washer from the end of the pushrod.

Overhaul

Note: *Before dismantling the master cylinder, check on the availability of spares, and ensure that the appropriate overhaul kit is obtained. Suitable rubber grease will be required to lubricate the new seals refitting.*

14 With the master cylinder removed as described previously in this Section, thoroughly clean the exterior of the assembly, then proceed as follows.

15 Where applicable, prise the dust cover from the end of the cylinder then, if desired, unscrew the locknuts from the end of the pushrod.

16 Depress the pushrod into the cylinder, then using a suitable pair of circlip pliers, extract the pushrod retaining circlip from the cylinder bore.

17 Withdraw the pushrod, circlip and washer **(see illustration)**.

18 Withdraw the piston assembly and spring. If necessary, tap the cylinder body on a clean wooden surface to dislodge the components. Alternatively, apply low pressure air (such as from a tyre foot pump) to the fluid inlet to eject the components.

19 Using a small screwdriver, release the spring seat locking tab from the slot in the piston, then withdraw the piston **(see illustration)**.

20 Prise the seal from the piston.

21 Compress the spring, and manipulate the valve stem to align with the larger diameter of the keyhole slot in the spring seat.

22 Withdraw the spring and the spring seat **(see illustration)**.

23 Withdraw the valve spacer and the spring washer from the valve stem.

24 Prise the seal from the end of the valve.

25 Clean all the components thoroughly, using clean fresh hydraulic fluid, and dry them using a clean, lint-free cloth. Check that the fluid port is free from obstructions.

26 Examine the cylinder bore, which must be free from corrosion, scoring and ridges. Similarly, examine the piston. If either the cylinder bore or the piston show signs of damage or wear, the complete assembly must be renewed.

9 Undo the six retaining screws and remove the mounting bracket plate **(see illustration)**, from the clutch master cylinder mounting bracket.

10 Unscrew the union nut, and disconnect

the hydraulic fluid pipe from the master cylinder, pressure switch adaptor **(see illustration 4.8)**. Plug the open ends of the pipe and adaptor, to prevent dirt ingress.

11 Working in the engine compartment,

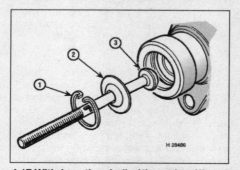

4.17 Withdraw the circlip (1), washer (2) and pushrod (3) from the master cylinder bore

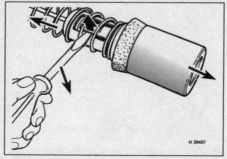

4.19 Release the spring seat locking tab (arrowed), then withdraw the piston

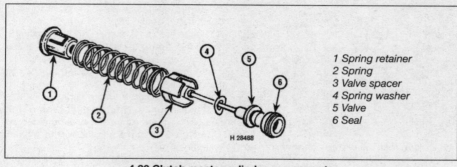

1 Spring retainer
2 Spring
3 Valve spacer
4 Spring washer
5 Valve
6 Seal

4.22 Clutch master cylinder components

27 Clean the fluid reservoir cap, and check that the vent hole in the cap is free from obstructions.

28 Smear the new seals with a little rubber grease, then lubricate the remaining components with clean hydraulic fluid.

29 Fit the valve seal, flat side first, onto the end of the valve.

30 Fit the spring washer, domed side first, over the valve stem.

31 Fit the valve spacer, legs first, over the valve stem.

32 Fit the spring over the valve stem, then fit the spring seat.

33 Compress the spring until the valve stem can be engaged with the keyhole slot in the spring seat. Manipulate the valve stem as necessary to lock it in position in the spring seat.

34 Fit the new seal to the piston, small diameter first.

35 Push the piston into the spring seat until the spring seat locking tab engages with the slot in the piston.

36 Slide the piston assembly, valve end first, into the cylinder.

37 Fit the pushrod, complete with the washer and circlip, to the cylinder, ensuring that the end of the pushrod engages with the piston. Push the assembly into position until the circlip engages in the slot in the cylinder bore.

38 Where applicable, refit the locknuts to the end of the pushrod, and refit the dust cover to the end of the cylinder.

39 Operate the pushrod several times to check for free movement of the piston.

Refitting

40 Where applicable, clean all traces of old sealant from the mating faces of the pedal box and the bulkhead.

41 Ensure that the adjuster nut, locknut and washer have been refitted to the end of the master cylinder pushrod.

42 Fit the master cylinder mounting plate to the pedal box, then manipulate the master cylinder into position, feeding the pushrod through the pedal trunnion. Loosely fit the washer and nut to the end of the pushrod.

43 Secure the master cylinder to the pedal box with the two nuts and bolts.

44 If the pedal box was originally sealed to the bulkhead with sealant, apply fresh sealant to the bulkhead mating face of the pedal box. Alternatively, place a new gasket in position.

45 Refit the pedal box, then refit and tighten the securing bolts.

46 Refit the rubber to the pedal.

47 Check and if necessary adjust the pedal height, as described in Section 6.

48 Where applicable, clean all traces of old gasket from the pedal box top cover, then refit the cover using a new gasket, and tighten the securing bolts.

49 Refit the footwell trim panel.

50 Reconnect the fluid pipe to the master cylinder.

51 Refill the reservoir with fluid of the recommended type (see *Lubricants and fluids*), then bleed the hydraulic system as described in Section.

52 Refit the bonnet as described in Chapter 12.

53 Reconnect the battery negative lead.

5 Clutch hydraulic system – bleeding

 Warning: Hydraulic fluid is poisonous. Wash off immediately and thoroughly in the case of skin contact, and seek immediate medical advice if any fluid is swallowed or gets into the eyes. Certain types of hydraulic fluid are inflammable, and may ignite when allowed into contact with hot components. When servicing any hydraulic system, it is safest to assume that the fluid IS inflammable, and to take precautions against the risk of fire as though it is petrol that is being handled. Hydraulic fluid is also an effective paint stripper, and will attack plastics. If any is spilt, it should be washed off immediately, using copious quantities of clean water. When topping-up or renewing the fluid, always use the recommended type, and ensure that it comes from a freshly-opened sealed container.

1 The clutch hydraulic system will not normally require bleeding, and this task should only be necessary when the system has been opened for repair work. However, as with the brake pedal, if the clutch pedal feels at all soggy or unresponsive in operation, this may indicate the need for bleeding.

2 The 'back-bleeding' method using a hand pump kit entails connecting the hand pump kit, containing fresh brake fluid, to the slave cylinder or release cylinder bleed screw. After syphoning some of the fluid out of the master cylinder reservoir, the bleed screw is opened, the pump is operated, and hydraulic fluid is delivered under pressure, backwards, to the reservoir.

3 In practice, this method would normally only be required if new hydraulic components have been fitted, or if the system has been completely drained of hydraulic fluid. If the system has only been disconnected to allow component removal and refitting procedures to be carried out, such as removal and refitting of the transmission (for example for clutch replacement) or engine removal and refitting, then it is quite likely that normal bleeding will be sufficient.

4 Our advice would therefore be as follows:

a) *If the hydraulic system has only been partially disconnected, and suitable precautions were taken to minimise fluid loss, try bleeding by the conventional method described in the relevant paragraphs below.*

5.9 Slave cylinder bleed screw (arrowed)

b) *If conventional bleeding fails to produce a firm pedal on completion, it will be necessary to 'back-bleed' the system using the Land Rover hand-pump kit or suitable alternative equipment as described in the relevant paragraphs below.*

5 During the bleeding procedure, add only clean, unused hydraulic fluid of the recommended type; never re-use fluid that has already been bled from the system. Ensure that sufficient fluid is available before starting work.

6 If there is any possibility of incorrect fluid being already in the system, the hydraulic circuit must be flushed completely with uncontaminated fluid of the specified type (see *Lubricants and fluids*).

7 If hydraulic fluid has been lost from the system, or air has entered because of a leak, ensure that the fault is cured before continuing further.

8 The bleeding procedure varies slightly according to engine/transmission type. Proceed as described in the relevant sub-Section below.

Conventional method

9 The system bleed screw is located at the top of the transmission bellhousing, or on the clutch slave cylinder fitted to the left-hand side of the transmission **(see illustration)**.

10 Firmly apply the handbrake, then jack up the front of the vehicle and support it securely on axle stands (see *Jacking and vehicle support*).

11 Obtain a clean jar, a suitable length of rubber or clear plastic tubing, which is a tight fit over the bleed screw on the clutch release cylinder, and a bottle of the specified hydraulic fluid (see *Lubricants and fluids*). The help of an assistant will also be required.

12 Remove the filler cap from the brake master cylinder reservoir, and if necessary top-up the fluid. Keep the reservoir topped-up during subsequent operations.

13 Remove the bleed screw dust cap.

14 Connect one end of the bleed tube to the bleed screw, and insert the other end of the tube in the jar containing sufficient clean hydraulic fluid to keep the end of the tube submerged.

6.4 Driving out the clutch pedal pivot shaft retaining pin

6.13 Slacken the master cylinder pushrod locknuts (arrowed)

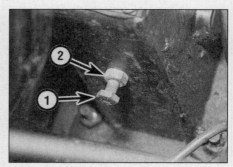

6.14 Clutch pedal adjustment screw (1) and locknut (2)

15 Open the bleed screw approximately a full turn.

16 Have your assistant depress the clutch pedal and then slowly release it. Continue this procedure until clean hydraulic fluid, free from air bubbles, emerges from the tube. Make sure that the brake master cylinder reservoir is checked frequently to ensure that the level does not drop too far, allowing air into the system. At the end of a downstroke, tighten the bleed screw.

17 Check the operation of the clutch pedal. After a few strokes, it should feel normal. Any sponginess would indicate air still present in the system.

18 On completion remove the bleed tube and refit the dust cap. Top-up the master cylinder reservoir if necessary and refit the cap. Fluid expelled from the hydraulic system should now be discarded as it will be contaminated with moisture, air and dirt, making it unsuitable for further use.

'Back-bleeding' method

19 If conventional bleeding does not work, it may be necessary to 'back-bleed' the system using the hand pump kit described previously.

20 Syphon some of the fluid out of the master cylinder reservoir until the level is at the MIN mark.

21 Remove the bleed screw dust cap and connect the hose from the hand pump to the bleed screw. Fill the hand pump reservoir with new hydraulic fluid, open the bleed screw as previously described, and pump the fluid backwards through the system and up to the reservoir until it reaches its MAX mark.

22 On completion, tighten the bleed screw.

23 Remove the hand pump hose and refit the bleed screw dust cap. Top-up the master cylinder reservoir if necessary and refit the cap.

24 Depress the clutch pedal five to ten times to dispel any residual air still remaining in the system.

6 Clutch pedal – removal, refitting and adjustment

Note: *A new pedal box cover gasket should be used on refitting. Where applicable, a new pedal pivot shaft retaining pin should be used on refitting.*

Removal

1 Remove the pedal box assembly, as described for the master cylinder removal procedure in Section 4.

2 Remove the securing screws, and lift the top cover from the pedal box. Recover the gasket.

3 Unscrew the nut from the end of the master cylinder pushrod, and recover the washer.

4 Working at the side of the pedal box, unscrew the pedal pivot pin securing screw, and recover the washer. Alternatively, drive out the pivot shaft retaining pin using a suitable punch, as applicable **(see illustration)**.

5 Slide the pivot pin from the pedal box, then withdraw the pedal, manipulating the pedal trunnion from the master cylinder pushrod. Note that the pedal return spring is located on the pedal pivot shaft, and the ends of the return spring locate in bushes in the pedal box. Take care not to allow the spring to fly out during dismantling, and ensure that the spring is correctly located on the pivot shaft on reassembly.

Refitting

6 If desired, the pedal pivot bushes in the pedal box can be renewed. Pull the old bushes from the pedal box, and press the new bushes into position.

7 Lightly grease the pedal pivot bushes.

8 Manipulate the pedal into position in the pedal box, engaging the pedal trunnion with the master cylinder pushrod.

9 Slide the pedal pivot pin into position in the pedal box, and through the pedal. Secure with the screw, ensuring that the washer is in place (or fit a new pivot shaft retaining pin, as applicable).

10 Refit the pedal box assembly, as described in Section 4.

11 If not already done, check the pedal adjustment as described in the following paragraphs.

Adjustment

Note: *A new pedal box cover gasket should be used on refitting.*

12 Working in the engine compartment, if not already done, remove the securing screws, and withdraw the cover from the clutch pedal box **(see illustration 4.9)**. Recover the gasket.

13 Slacken the master cylinder pushrod locknuts, to allow free movement of the pushrod through the pedal trunnion **(see illustration)**.

14 Slacken the adjustment screw locknut **(see illustration)**.

15 Measure the distance between the floor of the footwell (without a mat in place) to the lower edge of the clutch pedal rubber. The distance should be as specified (see Specifications).

16 If adjustment is necessary, turn the adjustment screw clockwise to reduce the pedal height, or anti-clockwise to increase the pedal height. When the height is correct, tighten the adjustment screw locknut.

17 The master cylinder pushrod must now be adjusted, to give the specified freeplay between the pushrod and the master cylinder piston. Adjust the position of the three locknuts on the pushrod as necessary to give the specified freeplay, then tighten the locknuts.

18 Check that the free movement of the pedal, measured at the pedal rubber, is as specified. If not, re-adjust the pushrod locknuts to give the specified free movement.

19 On completion of adjustment, refit the pedal box cover using a new gasket.

Chapter 7 Part A
Manual transmission

Contents

Degrees of difficulty

| Easy, suitable for novice with little experience | | Fairly easy, suitable for beginner with some experience | | Fairly difficult, suitable for competent DIY mechanic | | Difficult, suitable for experienced DIY mechanic | | Very difficult, suitable for expert DIY or professional | |

Specifications

General

Type .... 6 forward speeds and reverse. Synchromesh on all forward speeds and on reverse
Designation: MT82

Lubrication

Lubricant type .... See *Lubricants and fluids* on page 0•18
Lubricant capacity .... See Chapter 1

Torque wrench settings

	Nm	lbf ft
Front subframe mountings:		
Bolts	300	221
Nuts	175	129
Output shaft flange retaining bolt:		
Stage 1	210	155
Stage 2	Slacken the bolt completely	
Stage 3	180	133
Propeller shaft centre bearing retaining bolts*	22	16
Propeller shaft rubber coupling-to-output shaft flange*	175	129
Transmission (main gearbox) oil drain plug	50	37
Transmission (main gearbox) oil filler/level plug	35	26
Reversing light switch	20	15
Steering column intermediate shaft flexible coupling pinch bolt nut* ..	23	17
Transmission mounting-to-subframe bracket nut	48	35
Transmission mounting-to-transmission	80	59
Transmission-to-engine	40	30

* Use new nuts/bolts

1 General Information

1 Models covered by this manual are fitted with a 6-speed manual transmission. The transmission is mounted in-line, and to the rear of the engine. A propeller shaft transfers the drive to the rear axle.

2 The MT82 (6-speed) transmissions is of a constant-mesh type, with six forward speeds and one reverse. The input shaft and mainshaft are in-line, and rotate on ball and roller bearings in the front and rear transmission housings. Caged needle-roller bearings are used to support the mainshaft spigot, the countershaft gear assembly and the gears on the mainshaft.

3 The synchronisers are of baulk ring type, and operate in conjunction with tapered cones machined onto the gears. When engaging a gear, the synchroniser sleeve pushes the baulk ring against the tapered gear cone by means of synchroniser rings. The drag of the baulk ring causes the gear to rotate at the same speed as the synchroniser unit, and at this point, further movement of the sleeve locks the sleeve, baulk ring and gear dog teeth together.

4 Reverse gear is obtained by moving the reverse idler gear into mesh with the countershaft gear and the spur teeth of the 1st/2nd synchroniser.

5 Gear selection is by means of a floor-mounted gearchange lever, acting directly on the gearchange rail in the gearbox.

6 Because of the complexity, possible unavailability of parts and special tools necessary, internal repair procedures for the transmission are not recommended for the home mechanic. The bulk of the information in this Chapter is therefore devoted to removal and refitting procedures.

2 Gearchange levers – removal and refitting

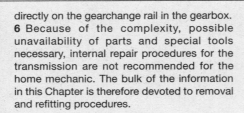

Removal

1 Lift out the rubber floor mats from the front footwells.

2 Remove the handbrake lever, as described in Chapter 10 Section 15.

3 Remove the floor covering from over the transmission tunnel (**see illustration**).

4 Unclip the rubber gaiter from around the gear levers (**see illustration**).

5 Release the two lower retaining clips and withdraw the gearchange lever (**see illustrations**). If required the high/low range gear knob can be removed by pulling it upwards from the gear lever, this is a very tight fit and may release suddenly, take care not to cause any personal injury.

6 Withdraw the foam insulator from around the gear levers (**see illustration**).

7 Release the retaining clip and remove the plastic cover from the top of the transmission housing (**see illustration**).

Refitting

8 Refitting is a reversal of removal.

3 Front (input shaft) oil seal – renewal

1 Remove the transmission from the vehicle as described in Section.

2 Thoroughly clean the transmission assembly, paying particular attention to the area inside the clutch housing.

3 Remove the clutch slave cylinder release bearing, as described in Chapter 6 Section 3.

4 Carefully punch or drill two small holes opposite each other in the oil seal. Screw a self-tapping screw into each and pull on the screws with pliers to extract the seal.

5 Clean the seal housing and polish off any burrs or raised edges which may have caused the seal to fail in the first place.

6 Lubricate the lip of the new oil seal with a smear of multi-purpose grease, then ease the seal into position on the end of the input shaft. Press the seal a little way into the housing by hand, making sure that it is square to its seating then, using suitable tubing, carefully drive the oil seal fully into the housing. Take great care not to damage the seal lips during fitting and ensure that the seal lips face inwards.

7 Refit the clutch slave cylinder release bearing, as described in Chapter 6 Section 3, then refit the transmission as described in Section.

2.3 Remove the floor covering

2.4 Remove rubber gaiter

2.5a Release the retaining clips...

2.5b ...and remove the gear lever

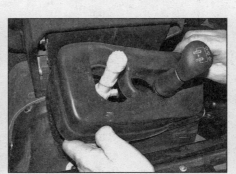

2.6 Remove the insulation

2.7 Unclip the plastic cover

4.1 Location of reversing light switch

4.3 Remove the transmission cover panel

4.4 Disconnect the wiring connector

4   Reversing light switch – removal and refitting

Removal

1 The reversing light circuit is controlled by a plunger-type switch screwed into the upper left-hand side of the transmission casing (see illustration).

2 Remove the gearchange levers, as described in Section 2.

3 Undo the retaining screws and remove the cover panel from the transmission tunnel (see illustration).

4 Disconnect the wiring connector from the reversing light switch (see illustration).

5 Unscrew the reversing light switch and remove it from the transmission. Discard the O-ring seal, as a new one will be required for refitting.

Refitting

6 Refitting is a reversal of the removal procedure, ensuring that the switch is tightened to the torque specified. Fit a new O-ring seal to the switch.

5   Transmission – removal and refitting

Note: *Although the following procedure is not difficult, the transmission assembly (the main gearbox is removed complete with the transfer gearbox) is heavy, and awkward to handle. Read through the procedure to familiarise yourself with the steps before proceeding. The help of an assistant will prove invaluable during this operation.*

Removal

1 Disconnect the battery negative lead as described in Chapter 5 Section 4.

2 Jack up the vehicle, and support securely on axle stands placed under the axle tubes (see *Jacking and vehicle support*). Note that the vehicle must be raised to give enough clearance for the transmission assembly to be removed from under the vehicle.

3 Remove the gearchange levers, as described in Section 2.

4 Disconnect the wiring connector from the reversing light switch, with reference to Section 4.

5 Remove the catalytic converter/particle filter, as described in Chapter 4A Section 18.

6 From inside the vehicle, disconnect the high-low selector rod ball joint from the transfer box (see illustration).

7 Undo the securing nut and disconnect the differential lock control operating rod (see illustration).

8 Undo the retaining screws and remove the gear lever and high-low lever from the top of the transmission (see illustration).

9 Remove the centre front seat cushion/compartment (see Chapter 12 Section 23), then remove the securing screws and withdraw the central floor cover panel (see illustration).

10 Remove the cooling fan upper shroud, to allow for engine movement, as the transmission is removed (see illustration).

5.6 Disconnect the selector rod

5.7 Undo the operating rod securing nut

5.8 Undo the gear lever securing screws and remove levers

5.10 Remove the upper shroud

5.9 Remove the central floor cover panel

5.12 Disconnect the speedo wiring connector

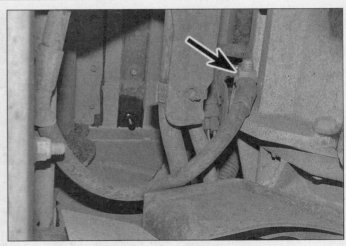

5.14 Disconnect the earth cable

11 Working under the vehicle, remove the propeller shafts, as described in Chapter 8 Section 2 (it is only strictly necessary to disconnect the propeller shaft from the transfer gearbox, but it is recommended that the shaft is removed completely, to provide additional working space).

12 Disconnect the wiring connector from the electronic speedo drive at the rear of the transfer housing **(see illustration)**.

13 Remove the parking brake drum from the rear of the transfer box, with reference to Chapter 10 Section 14.

14 Undo the retaining nut and disconnect the earth cable from the left-hand side of the transfer box **(see illustration)**.

15 Undo the retaining bolt and disconnect the earth cable from the right-hand side of the transfer box **(see illustration)**.

16 Disconnect the wiring connectors, and release them from the mounting bracket on the top of the transmission **(see illustration)**.

17 Undo the breather banjo bolt from the top of the transfer box **(see illustration)**, discard the sealing washers, as new ones will be required for refitting.

18 Working your way around the transmission, release the wiring loom from the retaining clips on the transmission housing.

19 Undo the retaining nut and disconnect the clutch slave cylinder hose mounting bracket from the transmission housing **(see illustration)**. Clamp the clutch hose using a pipe clamp, and then disconnect the clutch fluid pipe from the slave cylinder. Discard the O-ring seal as a new one will be required for refitting.

20 If work is to be carried out on the main gearbox and/or transfer gearbox, drain the oil from the main gearbox and/or the transfer gearbox, with reference to Chapter 1 Section 40, 431, if necessary.

21 The main gearbox/transfer gearbox assembly must now be supported. This is most easily and safely accomplished using an engine crane as follows:

a) *Working through the hole in the transmission tunnel, unscrew one of the top securing bolts from the power take-off cover at the rear of the transfer gearbox. Make up a lifting bracket, and bolt it to the transfer gearbox using the previously-removed bolt* **(see illustration)**.

b) *Pass a lifting strap or chain around the main gearbox casing. Pass the ends of*

5.15 Disconnect the earth cable

5.16 Disconnect the wiring connectors

5.17 Undo the breather banjo bolt

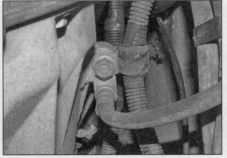

5.19 Disconnect the clutch hose bracket from the transmission

5.21a Lifting bracket in place on top power take-off cover bolt

5.23a Right-hand side transmission mounting

5.23b Left-hand side transmission mounting

the strap/chain up through the hole in the transmission tunnel.

c) *Attach a second lifting strap/chain to the lifting bracket on the transfer gearbox, and again pass the end of the strap/chain up through the transmission tunnel.*

d) *Open one of the front doors, and secure the door in the fully open position.*

e) *Pass the engine lifting crane in through the front door aperture, and position the lifting hook over the transmission tunnel aperture. Attach the previously-fitted lifting straps to the crane, allowing enough length to lower the transmission. Take care not to damage the interior trim when positioning the lifting gear.*

f) *Raise the crane sufficiently to just take the weight of the transmission assembly.*

22 Ensure that the transmission assembly is adequately supported before proceeding.

23 Working under the vehicle, unscrew the nuts securing the transmission mounting rubbers to the mounting brackets and bolts securing the transmission mounting brackets to the chassis, then withdraw the two transmission mountings **(see illustrations)**.

24 Lower the transmission assembly slightly, using the engine crane, to gain access to the upper engine flywheel housing-to-gearbox bellhousing nuts.

25 Progressively unscrew the lower flywheel housing-to-gearbox bellhousing nuts. Note that the transmission assembly may move backwards from the engine once the nuts are removed – be prepared for this, and do not allow the assembly to swing uncontrolled.

26 Slide the transmission assembly back from the engine (approx. 30mm), taking care not to strain the gearbox input shaft.

27 Before the transmission can be lowered and removed from the vehicle, it will be necessary to remove the gear selector housing from the top of the transmission.

28 Position a trolley jack and a large block of wood under the transmission assembly (the

wood should be suitably shaped to support the transmission when it is lowered). Lower the engine crane, to position the transmission assembly on the trolley jack and support block.

29 Disconnect the lifting straps/chains from the transmission assembly and the engine crane, then carefully slide the transmission assembly out from under the vehicle, using the trolley jack. Take care when moving the transmission, and do not attempt to lift the assembly without suitable lifting tackle – the assembly is very heavy.

30 If desired, the transfer gearbox can be separated from the main gearbox as described in Part B of this Chapter.

Refitting

31 Where applicable, refit the transfer gearbox to the main gearbox, as described in Part B of this Chapter. Ensure that the Low range is selected in the transfer gearbox.

32 Position the transmission assembly under the vehicle using the trolley jack and support block, then fit the lifting straps/chains to the transmission (as during removal). Pass the lifting straps/chains up through the transmission tunnel, and connect them to the engine crane.

33 Using the crane, lift the transmission assembly into position, and refit the gear selector housing to the top of the transmission, then slide the bellhousing onto the flywheel housing studs/engine block dowels. Ensure that the wiring harness and connectors, and the breather pipes, are not trapped as the transmission is moved into position. Note that it will be necessary to tilt the rear of the engine down to align the engine and gearbox (the engine can easily be tilted on its mountings, if an assistant pushes the assembly from above). Push the gearbox bellhousing onto the studs/dowels sufficiently to refit the nuts to the studs.

34 Manipulate the engine and gearbox as necessary, to align the gearbox input shaft

splines with the splines in the clutch friction disc hub (it may be necessary to turn the crankshaft using a spanner or socket on the pulley bolt). Once the input shaft is engaged with the clutch, progressively tighten the engine-to-gearbox nuts/bolts, to draw the gearbox bellhousing flush against the flywheel housing/engine block.

35 Using the crane, raise the transmission assembly sufficiently to enable the transmission mounting brackets to be fitted, then fit the brackets, and tighten all the fixings.

36 The remainder of the refitting procedure is a reversal of removal, bearing in mind the following points:

a) *Ensure that all wiring is routed correctly, and that all plugs are reconnected to their correct locations.*

b) *Reconnect the handbrake cable to the linkage, and check the cable adjustment, as described in Chapter 10 Section 16.*

c) *Refit the propeller shafts with reference to Chapter 8 Section 2.*

d) *Refit the catalytic converter/particulate filter with reference to Chapter 4A Section 18.*

e) *Where applicable, on completion, refill the main gearbox and transfer gearbox with oil of the correct type, as described in Chapter 1 Section 40 and 43.*

6 Transmission mounting –
checking and renewal

1 This procedure is covered in Chapter 2A Section 17 or Chapter 2B Section 17.

7 Transmission overhaul –
general information

1 Overhauling a manual transmission unit is a difficult and involved job for the DIY home mechanic. In addition to dismantling and reassembling many small parts, clearances must be precisely measured and, if necessary, changed by selecting shims and spacers. Internal transmission components are also often difficult to obtain, and in many instances, extremely expensive. Because of this, if the transmission develops a fault or becomes noisy, the best course of action is to have the unit overhauled by a specialist repairer, or to obtain an exchange reconditioned unit.

2 Nevertheless, it is not impossible for the more experienced mechanic to overhaul the transmission, provided the special tools are available, and the job is done in a deliberate step-by-step manner, so that nothing is overlooked.

3 The tools necessary for an overhaul include internal and external circlip pliers, bearing pullers, a slide hammer, a set of pin punches, a dial test indicator, and possibly a hydraulic press. In addition, a large, sturdy workbench and a vice will be required.

4 During dismantling of the transmission, make careful notes of how each component is fitted, to make reassembly easier and more accurate.

5 Before dismantling the transmission, it will help if you have some idea what area is malfunctioning. Certain problems can be closely related to specific areas in the transmission, which can make component examination and replacement easier. Refer to the Fault finding Section of this manual for more information.

8 Transmission oil – draining and refilling

1 This procedure is covered in Chapter 1 Section 40.

Chapter 7 Part B
Transfer gearbox

Contents

Degrees of difficulty

Easy, suitable for novice with little experience	**Fairly easy,** suitable for beginner with some experience	**Fairly difficult,** suitable for competent DIY mechanic	**Difficult,** suitable for experienced DIY mechanic	**Very difficult,** suitable for expert DIY or professional

Specifications

General

Transfer gearbox type.	LT230QRS
Ratios:	
High	1.211: 1
Low	3.269: 1

Torque wrench settings	Nm	lbf ft
Rear output flange nut*	140	103
Transfer gearbox-to-main gearbox bolts and nuts.	45	33

* Do not re-use

1 General Information

1 The transfer gearbox is mounted in-line with the main gearbox. The transfer gearbox is a two-speed ratio-reducing gearbox, and provides drive to the front and rear axles via the propeller shafts.

2 Permanent four-wheel-drive is provided, and the unit incorporates a differential assembly, to allow for any difference in the rotational speed of the front and rear wheels (and a resulting difference in speed between the front and rear propeller shafts). This centre differential (the axles also incorporate differentials to allow for the difference in rotational speed between left- and right-hand wheels on the same axle) can be locked by mechanical means to provide increased traction in particularly slippery conditions.

3 Selection of the High/Low ranges, and of the differential lock, is made using a selector lever mounted behind the main gear lever.

4 A shiftlock/neutral switch is fitted to some models, and is used as a safety device to ensure that the handbrake is effective when parking. The shiftlock/neutral switch prevents accidental disengagement of the transfer gears when the ignition is switched off. Additionally, an audible alarm is provided, which alerts the driver to move the gear selector lever to the High or Low position when parking.

2 Transfer gearbox – removal and refitting

General

1 The transfer gearbox is most easily removed complete with the main gearbox as an assembly. This procedure is described in Part A of this Chapter.

Removal

2 To separate the transfer gearbox from the main gearbox, proceed as follows.
3 Position the transmission assembly securely on a bench or a suitable stand, or rest the assembly on wooden blocks on the workshop floor.
4 Unscrew the four bolts and two nuts securing the transfer housing to the transmission extension housing. With the bolts/nuts removed, withdraw the transfer box from the end of the transmission extension housing.
5 If required, undo the ten retaining bolts and remove the extension housing from the transmission.

Refitting

6 Refitting is a reversal of removal, bearing in mind the following points:
a) *Thoroughly clean the mating faces of the transfer gearbox and the main gearbox.*
b) *Ensure that the upper locating dowel is fitted to the gearbox casing before mating the transfer gearbox and main gearbox together.*
c) *Refit the complete transmission assembly as described in Chapter 7A.*

3 Transfer gearbox overhaul – general information

1 Overhauling a transfer gearbox is a difficult and involved job for the DIY home mechanic. In addition to dismantling and reassembling many small parts, clearances must be precisely measured and, if necessary, changed by selecting shims and spacers. Gearbox internal components are also often difficult to obtain, and in many instances, extremely expensive. Because of this, if the gearbox develops a fault or becomes noisy, the best course of action is to have the unit overhauled by a specialist repairer, or to obtain an exchange reconditioned unit.
2 Nevertheless, it is not impossible for the more experienced mechanic to overhaul a gearbox, provided the special tools are available and the job is done in a deliberate step-by-step manner so that nothing is overlooked.
3 The tools necessary for an overhaul include internal and external circlip pliers, bearing pullers, a slide-hammer, a set of pin punches, a dial test indicator, and possibly a hydraulic press. In addition, a large, sturdy workbench and a vice will be required. Certain Land Rover special tools will be required for work on the differential assembly.
4 During dismantling of the gearbox, make careful notes of how each component is fitted, to make reassembly easier and more accurate.
5 Before dismantling the gearbox, it will help if you have some idea of which area is malfunctioning. Certain problems can be closely related to specific areas in the gearbox, which can make component examination and renewal easier. Refer to the Fault finding Section at the end of this manual for more information.

4 Transfer gearbox rear oil seal – renewal

1 Remove the handbrake drum as described in Chapter 10.
2 Prevent the output flange from rotating using a lever bar, then undo the retaining nut. Discard the nut, steel and felt washers – new ones must be fitted.
3 Use a three-legged puller to remove the output flange.
4 Note its fitted depth, then use a flat-bladed screwdriver to carefully prise out the oil seal.
5 Ensure the seal recess is clean and dry, then use a large tubular spacer to drive the new seal home. The seal must be fitted dry.
6 Refit the drive flange, then the new felt and steel washer.
7 Using the same method as during removal, restrain the drive flange, and tighten the new nut to the specified torque.
8 Refit the brake drum as described in Chapter, then top-up the transfer gearbox oil level as described in Chapter.

5 Transfer gearbox oil – draining and refilling

1 This procedure is covered in Chapter 1 Section 43.

Chapter 8
Propeller shafts

Contents

Degrees of difficulty

Easy, suitable for novice with little experience	**Fairly easy,** suitable for beginner with some experience	**Fairly difficult,** suitable for competent DIY mechanic	**Difficult,** suitable for experienced DIY mechanic	**Very difficult,** suitable for expert DIY or professional

Specifications

General
Propeller shaft type . . . . Tubular, splined joint
End joints . . . . Hookes non-constant velocity joints, with needle-roller bearings

Torque wrench setting	**Nm**	**lbf ft**
Propeller shaft securing nuts and bolts	47	35

1 General Information

1 The drive is transmitted from the transfer gearbox to the front and rear axle differentials by two tubular propeller shafts.
2 The propeller shafts are fitted with non-constant velocity universal joints at each end, which run in needle-roller bearings. The universal joints cater for the varying angle between the axle and the transmission, caused by suspension movement.
3 To allow for the fore-and-aft movement between the axles and transmission, a sliding, splined joint is incorporated in each propeller shaft. On certain models, a rubber gaiter is fitted to protect the front propeller shaft sliding joint.
4 Grease nipples are fitted to the universal joints, and the universal joints and sliding joints should periodically be lubricated in

accordance with the maintenance schedule given in Chapter 1 Section 30.

2 Propeller shaft – removal and refitting

Front propeller shaft

Removal

1 Jack up the vehicle, and support securely on axle stands positioned under the axles, as described in at the rear of this manual. Undo the fasteners and lower the engine undershield.
2 If the original propeller shaft is to be refitted, make alignment marks between the front propeller shaft flange and the differential flange.
3 Counterhold the bolts, and unscrew the nuts securing the front of the propeller shaft to the differential flange.

4 Again, if the original propeller shaft is to be refitted, make alignment marks between the rear propeller shaft flange and the transfer gearbox flange**(see illustration)**.
5 Unscrew the nuts (again, where applicable, counterhold the bolts) securing the rear of the

2.4 Making alignment marks between the rear propeller shaft flange and the transfer gearbox flange

2.10 Make alignment marks between the propeller shaft flange and the handbrake drum

2.13 Counterhold the bolts, and unscrew the nuts securing the propeller shaft to the rear differential flange

2.14 Withdraw the front of the propeller shaft from the studs on the brake drum

propeller shaft to the transfer gearbox flange.

6 Remove the bolts from the front shaft flange, then compress the propeller shaft sliding joint until the rear of the shaft can be withdrawn from the bolts or studs (as applicable) on the transfer gearbox flange.

7 Withdraw the propeller shaft from under the vehicle.

Refitting

8 Refitting is a reversal of removal, bearing in mind the following points:

a) *Ensure that the propeller shaft is refitted with the sliding joint towards the front of the vehicle (nearest the front axle).*

b) *If the original propeller shaft is being refitted, align the marks made on the differential flange, transfer gearbox flange, and the propeller shaft flanges before removal.*

c) *Tighten the securing nuts and bolts to the specified torque.*

Rear propeller shaft

Removal

9 Proceed as described in paragraph 1.

10 If the original propeller shaft is to be

refitted, make alignment marks between the front propeller shaft flange and the handbrake drum at the transfer gearbox **(see illustration)**.

11 Unscrew the nuts securing the front of the propeller shaft to the handbrake drum.

12 Again, if the original propeller shaft is to be refitted, make alignment marks between the rear propeller shaft flange and the rear differential flange.

13 Counterhold the bolts, and unscrew the nuts securing the rear of the propeller shaft to the rear differential flange **(see illustration)**.

14 Withdraw the flange bolts, then compress the propeller shaft sliding joint until the front of the propeller shaft can be withdrawn from the studs on the brake drum **(see illustration)**.

15 Withdraw the propeller shaft from under the vehicle.

Refitting

16 Refitting is a reversal of removal, bearing in mind the following points:

a) *Ensure that the propeller shaft is refitted with the sliding joint towards the front of the vehicle (nearest the transfer gearbox).*

b) *If the original propeller shaft is being refitted,*

align the marks made on the handbrake drum, rear differential flange, and the propeller shaft flanges before removal.

c) *Tighten the securing nuts and bolts to the specified torque.*

3 Propeller shaft – inspection and overhaul

Inspection

1 Wear in the universal joint needle-roller bearings is characterised by vibration in the transmission, 'clonks' on taking up the drive, and in extreme cases unpleasant metallic noises as the bearings break up (lack of lubrication).

2 To test the universal joints for wear with the propeller shaft in place, apply the handbrake, and chock the wheels.

3 Working under the vehicle, apply leverage between the yokes using a large screwdriver or a flat metal bar. Wear is indicated by movement between the shaft yoke and the coupling flange yoke. Check all the universal joints in this way.

4 To check the splined sleeve on the front of both shafts, attempt to push the shafts from side-to-side, and look for any excessive movement between the sleeve and the shaft. A further check can be made by gripping the shaft and sleeve, and turning them in opposite directions, again looking for excessive movement. As a rough guide, if any movement can be seen, the splines are worn, and the shaft assembly should be renewed.

5 If a universal joint is worn, a new joint must be obtained and fitted as described later in this Section.

6 If the sliding joint is excessively worn, the complete shaft assembly must be renewed.

Overhaul

Dismantling

7 With the propeller shaft removed as described in Section 2, proceed as follows.

8 Where applicable, release the clips securing the rubber gaiter over the sliding joint, and slide the gaiter towards the rear of the shaft **(see illustration)**.

3.8 Propeller shaft components

A *Yoke*
B *Grease nipple for universal joint*
C *Spider*
D *Dust cap*
E *Splined shaft*
F *Splined sleeve*
G *Grease nipple for splined joint*

H *Washer*
J *Seal*
K *Needle-roller bearing assembly*
L *Bearing retaining circlip*
M *Gaiter clips (early models only)*
N *Sliding joint gaiter (early models only)*

H 28459

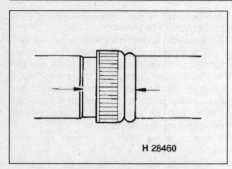

3.9 Alignment marks on two halves of propeller shaft

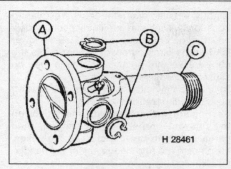

3.14 Propeller shaft universal joint

A Coupling flange   B Circlips   C Shaft

3.15 Tapping the uppermost bearing cup

9 Check that alignment marks are visible on the two halves of the shaft (normally two stamped arrows) **(see illustration)**. If no marks can be found, scribe a line along the two halves of the shaft, to ensure that the two halves are reassembled in exactly the same position. This is vital, to ensure that the correct universal joint alignment and shaft balance is maintained.

10 Unscrew the dust cap, and withdraw the front section of the shaft from the splined end of the rear section.

11 Working on one of the universal joints, note the position of the grease nipple on the spider, in relation to the adjacent shaft yoke and coupling flange yoke (make alignment marks on the yokes). This is vital to ensure correct reassembly, and to ensure that the shaft balance is maintained.

12 Clean away all traces of dirt and grease from the circlips located on the ends of the joint spiders, and from the grease nipple.

13 Unscrew the grease nipple.

14 Using a suitable pair of circlip pliers, remove the four joint circlips **(see illustration)**. If a circlip proves difficult to remove, as a last resort, place a drift on the bearing cup, in the centre of the circlip, and tap the top of the bearing cup to ease the pressure on the circlip.

15 Support the end of the shaft in a vice, with the yoke in a vertical plane. Using a hammer and a suitable drift, tap the uppermost bearing cup until the bottom bearing cup protrudes from the yoke **(see illustration)**.

16 Remove the shaft from the vice, then securely grip the protruding bearing cup in the vice jaws. Turn the shaft from side-to-side, at the same time lifting the shaft until the bearing cup comes free.

17 Refit the shaft to the vice, with the exposed spider uppermost. Tap the spider with the hammer and drift until the lower bearing cup protrudes, then remove the cup as described previously.

18 The coupling flange and the spider can now be removed from the shaft, and the remaining two bearing cups can be removed as described previously.

19 Where applicable, repeat the operations described in paragraphs 11 to 18 to remove the remaining joint from the shaft.

Inspection

20 With the universal joint dismantled, carefully examine the needle-rollers, bearing cups and spider for wear, scoring and pitting of the surface finish. If any wear is detected, the joint must be renewed **(see illustration)**.

21 Where applicable, unscrew the sliding joint grease nipple, and thoroughly clean the nipple and its hole.

22 Where applicable, examine the condition of the sliding joint rubber gaiter, and renew if necessary.

23 Temporarily fit the front section of the shaft to the rear section, ensuring that the alignment marks are correctly positioned. Grip the front section of the shaft in a vice, and check for wear in the sliding joint splines, as described in paragraph 4.

Reassembly

24 If a new joint is being fitted, remove the bearing cups from the new spider. Check that all the needle-rollers are present, and correctly positioned in the bearing cups.

25 Ensure that the bearing cups are one-third full of fresh grease (multi-purpose lithium-based grease – see *Lubricants and fluids* at the front of this manual).

26 Fit the new spider, complete with seals, into the coupling flange yoke. Make sure that the grease nipple hole is aligned with the mark on the yoke made during dismantling, and note that the grease nipple hole must face away from the coupling flange.

27 Partially insert one of the bearing cups into the yoke, and enter the spider trunnion into the bearing cup, taking care not to dislodge the needle-rollers **(see illustration)**.

28 Similarly, insert a bearing cup into the opposite yoke.

3.20 Universal joint bearing components

3.27 Press the cups into place using a vice and socket

3.31 Fit new circlips to retain the bearing cups

29 Using the vice, carefully press both bearing cups into place, ensuring that the spider trunnions do not dislodge any of the needle-rollers.

30 Using a suitable tube or socket of a slightly smaller diameter than the bearing cups, press each cup into its respective yoke, until the top of the cup just reaches the lower land of the circlip groove. Do not press the cups below this point, as damage may be caused to the cups and seals.

31 Fit the new circlips to retain the bearing cups **(see illustration)**.

32 Engage the spider with the yokes on the relevant propeller shaft section, then partially fit both bearing cups to the yokes, taking care not to dislodge any of the needle-rollers.

33 Press the bearing cups into position, and fit the new circlips, as described in paragraphs 29 to 31.

34 Screw the grease nipple into position in the joint spider.

35 Where applicable, repeat the operations described in paragraphs 24 to 34 to fit the remaining joint to the shaft.

36 Where applicable, screw the sliding joint grease nipple into position.

37 Smear the sliding joint splines on the end of the rear section of the shaft with grease, then slide the rear section of the shaft into the front section, ensuring that the marks made during dismantling are aligned. **Note:** *Do not pack grease into the open end of the shaft front section, as this may prevent the shaft from being pushed fully home.*

38 Screw the sliding joint dust cap into position.

39 Where applicable, slide the rubber gaiter over the sliding joint, and secure in position with the two clips. If screw-type clips are used, fit the clips with the screws 180° apart, to help maintain the balance of the shaft.

40 Refit the propeller shaft, as described in Section 2, then lubricate the joints using a grease gun applied to the grease nipples (see Chapter 1 Section 30).

Chapter 9
Front and rear axles

Contents

Degrees of difficulty

Easy, suitable for novice with little experience 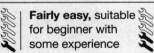	**Fairly easy,** suitable for beginner with some experience	**Fairly difficult,** suitable for competent DIY mechanic	**Difficult,** suitable for experienced DIY mechanic	**Very difficult,** suitable for expert DIY or professional

Specifications

Type

Front	Spiral bevel, with enclosed CV joints and fully-floating halfshafts
Rear	Spiral bevel, with fully-floating halfshafts
Differential ratio (front and rear)	3.54: 1

Torque wrench settings

	Nm	lbf ft
Driving member retaining bolts	65	48
Halfshaft flange retaining bolts	65	48
Hub locknut (staked nut)*	210	155
Rear axle upper link balljoint nut	176	130
Roadwheel nuts:		
Steel wheels	108	80
Alloy wheels	130	96
Heavy duty wheel	170	125
Stub axle bolts	65	48
Swivel pin assembly-to-axle bolts	72	53
Swivel pin housing oil seal retaining plate bolts	10	7
Swivel pin retaining bolts		
Upper pin bolts	65	48
Lower pin bolts	25	18

* Do not re-use

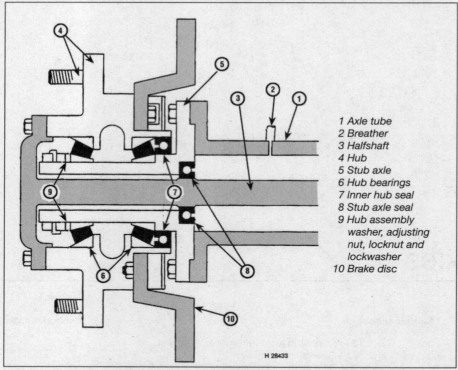

1 Axle tube
2 Breather
3 Halfshaft
4 Hub
5 Stub axle
6 Hub bearings
7 Inner hub seal
8 Stub axle seal
9 Hub assembly washer, adjusting nut, locknut and lockwasher
10 Brake disc

H 28433

1.1 Cross-sectional view of rear axle hub and associated components

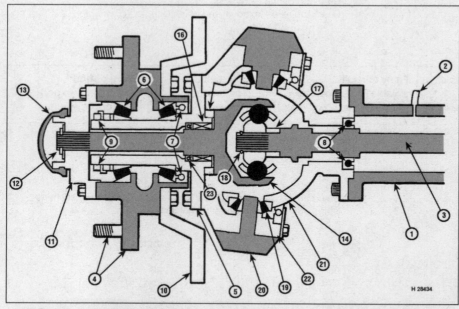

H 28434

1.2 Cross-sectional view of front axle hub and associated components – later model (early model similar)

1 Axle tube	9 Hub assembly washer, adjusting nut, locknut and lockwasher	16 Needle roller bearing
2 Breather		17 Spacer
3 Inner halfshaft section		18 Circlip
4 Hub	10 Brake disc	19 Swivel pin bearing
5 Stub axle	11 Driving member	20 Swivel pin
6 Hub bearings	12 Shim and circlip	21 Swivel ball
7 Inner hub seal	13 Hub cap	22 Swivel pin housing
8 Circlip	14 Outer halfshaft section	23 Seal

1 General Information

1 Both the front and rear axles are of a similar design, comprising a one-piece steel casing, which houses the differential assembly and two driveshafts (halfshafts). The rear shafts are of solid steel construction, the inner ends of which are splined into the differential assembly, while the outer ends are attached to the hubs **(see illustration)**.

2 To enable the front wheels to turn from lock-to-lock while being driven, the front halfshafts incorporate a CV joint on their outer ends. The CV joint runs inside an oil-filled swivel pin housing, the swivel pins being located in tapered roller bearings **(see illustration)**.

3 Refer to Chapter for details of axle attachment and suspension details.

2 Front axle halfshaft – removal, inspection and refitting

Removal

1 Apply the handbrake, then jack up the front of the vehicle and support it on axle stands positioned underneath the chassis. Remove the relevant front roadwheel.

2 Remove the stub axle as described in Section 5.

3 Pull the halfshaft assembly out from the axle **(see illustration)**.

4 Clamp the inner section of the shaft in a vice with soft jaws then, using a soft-faced mallet, tap the constant velocity joint off the end of the inner shaft.

5 Remove the circlip from the end of the inner shaft, and slide off the spacer. Discard the circlip – a new one must be used on refitting.

Inspection

6 Thoroughly clean all components using paraffin, or a suitable solvent, and dry thoroughly. Carry out a visual inspection as follows.

7 Inspect the halfshaft inner sections for

2.3 Removing the halfshaft assembly

3.3 Slide the brake caliper assembly off the disc

signs of wear or damage, paying particular attention to its splines. Check the bush for signs of wear or damage, and renew worn components as necessary. Note that the constant velocity joint circlip must be renewed whenever it is disturbed.

8 Move the constant velocity joint inner member from side-to-side, to expose each ball in turn at the top of its track. Examine the balls for cracks, flat spots or signs of surface pitting.

9 Inspect the ball tracks on the inner and outer members. If the tracks have widened, the balls will no longer be a tight fit. At the same time, check the ball cage windows for wear or cracking between the windows.

10 If the constant velocity joint assembly shows signs of wear or damage, it must be renewed.

Refitting

11 Slide the spacer onto the inner shaft, then fit a new circlip, making sure that it is correctly located in the shaft groove.

12 Locate the constant velocity joint on inner shaft splines, and tap it onto the driveshaft until the circlip engages in its groove. Make sure that the joint is securely retained by the circlip.

13 Insert the halfshaft inner section into the axle, aligning its splines with those of the differential sunwheel.

14 Check the halfshaft inner section is correctly located, then refit the stub axle as described in Section.

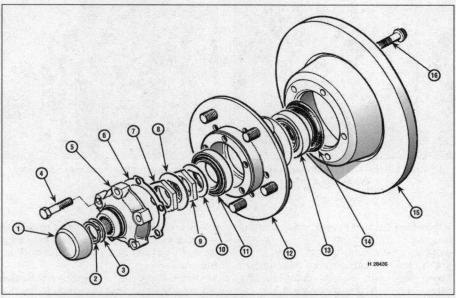

3.4 Exploded view of the front hub assembly and associated components

1 Dust cap	7 Locknut (models up to 1999 model year only)	10 Spacer
2 Circlip		11 Outer bearing and race
3 Shim	8 Lockwasher (models up to 1999 model year only)	12 Hub
4 Bolt		13 Inner bearing and race
5 Driving member	9 Adjusting nut (models up to 1999 model year only)	14 Seal
6 Gasket		15 Brake disc
		16 Bolt

3 Front hub assembly – removal and refitting

Note: *The following information applies only to the standard hub assembly. For information on freewheeling hubs, refer to your Land Rover dealer.*

Removal

1 Apply the handbrake, then jack up the front of the vehicle and support it on axle stands positioned underneath the chassis. Remove the relevant front road-wheel.

2 Clamp the flexible brake hose, then undo the union nut and disconnect the brake pipe from the caliper.

3 Slacken and remove the two retaining bolts securing the brake caliper in position. Slide the caliper assembly off the disc **(see illustration)**.

4 Lever off the dust cap from the centre of the hub assembly **(see illustration)**.

5 Using circlip pliers, remove the circlip from the end of the halfshaft, then slide off the thrustwasher(s) **(see illustrations)**.

6 Slacken and remove the five retaining bolts, then slide the driving member off the end of the halfshaft **(see illustration)**. Remove the member gasket and discard it, a new gasket must be used on refitting.

7 Knock back the staking, then undo the hub nut – 52 mm socket required **(see**

3.5a Remove the circlip from the end of the halfshaft …

3.5b … and recover the thrustwasher(s)

3.6 Removing the hub driving member

3.7 Knock back the staking and unscrew the hub nut

3.9 Removing the front hub assembly

3.11 Fit the inner and outer bearings to the hub

illustration). Discard the nut, a new one must be fitted.

8 Remove the washer.

9 Slide the hub assembly off the stub axle, taking care not to allow the outer bearing to fall out of position (see illustration).

Refitting

10 Prior to refitting, remove all traces of locking compound from the hub assembly threads, ideally by running a tap of the correct size and pitch down them.

11 Fit the inner and outer bearing cups to the hub, then pack the inner bearing with grease and fit it to the hub (see illustration).

12 Fit the new seal so that it bears against the shoulder in the hub. This should correspond to a fitted depth of 4 mm (see illustration).

13 Pack the outer bearing with grease, then fit spacer and outer bearing to the hub assembly (see illustrations).

14 Fit the hub assembly, taking care not to damage the seal lips on the stub axle threads.

15 Fit the washer and new hub nut, then tighten it to 30 Nm only at this stage.

16 Rotate the hub, pushing and pulling it at the same time to settle the bearings, then tighten the nut to the full specified torque.

17 Attach a dial test indicator to the hub assembly, positioning it so that its pointer

is in contact with the face of the nut (see illustration). Move the hub assembly in-and-out, and measure the hub endfloat. Compare the measurement obtained with that shown in the table to determine the correct spacer size (see illustration). If no endfloat is present, proceed to paragraph 23.

18 With the correct sized spacer obtained, undo the nut, remove the washer, and fit the new spacer.

19 Remove the DTI gauge.

20 Fit the washer, tighten the nut, and use a punch to 'stake' the nut (see illustrations).

21 Ensure that the hub and driving member mating surfaces are clean and dry, and fit a new gasket (see illustration).

3.12 The new seal should have a fitted depth of approximately 4 mm

3.13b ... followed by the outer bearing

3.13a Fit the spacer ...

3.17a Measure the hub endfloat

End float (mm)	Colour code	Spacer size (mm)
0.000	Purple	15.5
0.025	Yellow	15.4
0.050	Yellow	15.4
0.075	Yellow	15.4
0.100	Red	15.3
0.125	Red	15.3
0.150	Red	15.3
0.175	Blue	15.2
0.200	Blue	15.2
0.225	Blue	15.2
0.250	Blue	15.2
0.275	Green	15.1
0.300	Green	15.1
0.325	Green	15.1
0.350	Green	15.1
0.375	Black	15.0
0.400	Black	15.0
0.425	Black	15.0
0.450	Black	15.0
0.475	White	14.9
0.500	White	14.9
0.525	White	14.9
0.550	White	14.9

H46036

3.17b Front hub spacer selection table

3.20a Fit the washer …

3.20b … then stake the nut to the stub axle

3.21 Ensure that the mating surfaces are clean and dry, and fit a new driving member gasket to the hub

22 Slide the driving member into position.

23 Clean the threads of each driving member retaining bolt, and apply a drop of fresh locking compound to each one. Install the bolts, and tighten them to the specified torque setting **(see illustration)**.

24 Slide the thrustwasher(s) onto the halfshaft, and secure it in position with the circlip. Ensure that the circlip is correctly located in the halfshaft groove.

25 Once the halfshaft endfloat is correctly set (where applicable), unscrew the bolt (where applicable) and refit the dust cap to the hub assembly **(see illustration)**.

26 Slide the brake caliper assembly back into position, ensuring that its pads pass either side of the disc. Refit the caliper retaining bolts, tighten them to the specified torque setting (see Chapter 10).

27 Reconnect the metal brake pipe to the caliper, remove the hose clamp, then bleed the relevant caliper as described in Chapter 10.

28 Refit the roadwheel, then lower the vehicle to the ground and tighten the wheel nuts to the specified torque setting.

4 Front hub bearing – renewal

Note: *A press may be required to dismantle and rebuild the assembly, if the bearing outer races are a tight fit in the hub. If such a tool is not available, a large bench vice and suitable spacers (such as very large sockets) will serve as an adequate substitute.*

1 Remove the hub assembly as described in Section 3.

2 Remove the brake disc as described in Chapter 10.

3 Note its fitted depth, then using a large flat-bladed screwdriver, lever out the inner oil seal from the hub assembly**(see illustration)**.

4 Remove the outer and inner bearing inner races from the hub assembly.

5 Support the hub securely on blocks or in a vice, then using a hammer and suitable punch, carefully tap the inner and outer bearing outer races out from the hub assembly.

3.23 Prior to installation, apply locking compound to the driving member retaining bolt threads

6 Thoroughly clean the hub bore, removing all traces of dirt and grease, and polish away any burrs or raised edges which might hinder reassembly. Check both for cracks or any other signs of wear or damage, and renew them if necessary. Examine the stub axle for signs of wear or damage and renew, if necessary (see Section 5). Renew both bearings and oil seal(s) as a matter of course.

7 On reassembly, apply a light film of oil to the inner bearing outer race and hub bore, to aid installation.

8 Securely support the hub, and locate the inner bearing outer race in the hub. Press the race fully into position, ensuring that it enters the hub squarely, using a suitable tubular spacer which bears only on the bearing outer race.

4.3 Lever the oil seal out from the hub using a large flat-bladed screwdriver

3.25 Refit the dust cap to the hub

9 Pack the bearing inner race with a multi-purpose lithium-based grease. Work the grease well into the bearing race, apply a smear to the outer race surface, then fit the inner race to the hub assembly **(see illustration)**.

10 Install the new inner oil seal, making sure that its sealing lip is facing inwards. Press the seal into position, ensuring that it enters the hub squarely, to the same depth as noted on removal.

11 Turn the hub over, and fit the outer bearing as described in paragraphs 7 to 9.

12 Refit the brake disc as described in Chapter 10.

13 Install the hub assembly as described in Section 3.

4.9 Pack the hub bearings with a suitable multi-purpose lithium-based grease

5.6 Inspect the bearing, oil seal and thrust ring fitted to the rear of the stub axle for signs of wear or damage

5.11 Fit a new gasket (arrowed), then slide the stub axle into position

5.12 Refit the mudshield ...

5 Front stub axle – removal and refitting

Removal

1 Remove the hub assembly as described in Section 3.
2 If not already done, drain the swivel pin housing oil as described in Chapter 1.
3 Make alignment marks between the stub axle and housing, then slacken and remove the six retaining bolts and washers.
4 Lift off the mudshield (where fitted), then remove the stub axle from the swivel pin housing and recover the gasket. Discard the gasket – a new one must be used on refitting.
5 Inspect the stub axle for signs of wear or damage, and renew if necessary.
6 Check the needle-roller bearing and oil seal arrangement fitted to the inside of the stub axle, and the thrust ring fitted to the rear of the axle flange, for signs of wear or damage **(see illustration)**. If renewal is necessary, the task should be entrusted to a Land Rover dealer.

Refitting

7 Prior to refitting, remove all traces of locking compound from the swivel housing threads, ideally by running a tap of the correct size and pitch down them.

5.13a ... then apply locking compound to the threads of the stub axle retaining bolts ...

8 Ensure that the halfshaft is correctly engaged with the differential splines.
9 Make sure that the stub axle and swivel pin housing mating surfaces are clean and dry, then fit a new gasket to the swivel housing.
10 Apply a smear of oil to the stub axle bush/bearing and seal (as applicable).
11 Slide the stub axle into position, aligning the marks made prior to removal **(see illustration)**.
12 Refit the mudshield to the stub axle (where applicable) **(see illustration)**.
13 Clean the threads of the retaining bolts, and apply a drop of fresh locking compound to them. Install the bolts and washers, and tighten them to the specified torque setting **(see illustrations)**.

5.13b ... and tighten them to the specified torque

14 Refit the hub assembly as described in Section.

6 Front axle swivel pin housing assembly – removal, overhaul and refitting

Removal

1 Remove the halfshaft as described in Section 2.
2 Withdraw the split-pin, then unscrew the nut securing the track rod to the swivel pin housing. Using a universal balljoint separator, free the track rod from the hub.
3 Where necessary, also free the drag link from the swivel pin housing as described in paragraph 2.
4 Slacken and remove the bolts and washers securing the swivel housing assembly to the axle, and remove it from the vehicle **(see illustrations)**. Recover the gasket and discard it – a new one must be used on refitting.

Overhaul

5 Remove all traces of grease and dirt from the outside of the swivel housing assembly **(see illustration)**.
6 Undo the retaining bolts and washers, and remove the retaining plate and oil seal from

6.4a Slacken and remove the swivel pin housing retaining bolts ...

6.4b ... then lift off the housing assembly and recover the gasket (arrowed)

1 Mudshield bracket
2 Lower swivel pin
3 Gasket
4 Swivel pin housing
5 Gasket
6 Upper swivel pin and
  brake hose bracket
7 Swivel pin bearing and
  race
8 Shim
9 Swivel ball
10 Oil seal
11 Oil seal
12 Retaining plate and gasket

H 28437

6.5 Exploded view of the swivel pin housing components

the rear of the swivel housing, noting which way around the seal is fitted **(see illustration)**.
7 Undo the brake disc mudshield retaining bracket bolt and nut, and remove the shield **(see illustration)**.
8 Bend back the locking tabs (where

necessary), then slacken and remove the two bolts securing the lower swivel pin to the housing. Remove the brake disc mudshield bracket **(see illustration)**.
9 Ease the lower swivel pin out of position, and recover the gasket.

10 Undo the retaining bolts and washers, ease the upper swivel pin from the housing, and recover its shims.
11 Free the swivel ball from the housing, and recover the swivel pin bearings. Support the swivel ball, and tap the bearing races out of position with a hammer and suitable punch **(see illustrations)**.
12 Check all components, paying particular attention to the contact surfaces of the swivel ball and swivel pins. Check that each bearing rotates smoothly, without any sign of roughness – renew worn components as necessary. Renew the oil seals and gaskets as a matter of course.
13 Obtain the necessary components from your Land Rover dealer. Prior to reassembly, remove all traces of locking compound from the swivel housing threads, ideally by running a tap of the correct size and pitch down them **(see illustration)**.
14 Remove the oil seal from the rear of the swivel ball, noting which way around it is fitted. Fit the new oil seal to the rear of the swivel ball, making sure that its sealing lip is facing away from the ball. Press the seal squarely into the housing, until it is flush with the housing face.
15 Fit the new swivel pin bearing races to the swivel ball, tapping them squarely into

6.6 Remove the retaining plate from the rear of the swivel housing, and recover the oil seal

6.7 Removing the brake disc mudshield

6.8 Remove the lower swivel pin retaining bolts, and recover the mudshield bracket, noting which way around it is fitted

6.11a Separate the swivel ball and housing, and recover the bearings

6.11b Tap the bearing outer races out of position using a hammer and suitable punch

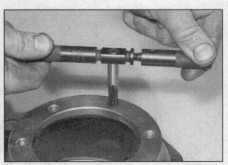

6.13 Prior to reassembly, remove all traces of old locking compound from the housing threads

6.15 Install the new bearing outer races using a suitable tubular drift which bears only on the hard outer edge of the race

6.16 Lubricate the bearings with the specified oil, and seat them in their races

6.19 Insert the lower swivel pin and gasket ...

position with a suitable tubular drift which bears only on the outer edge of the race **(see illustration)**.

16 Lubricate the bearings with the specified oil (see Chapter 1), and seat them in the races **(see illustration)**.

17 Reassemble the swivel ball with the housing, making sure that the bearings remain correctly seated.

18 Apply a smear of suitable sealant to either

6.20 ... then fit the upper swivel pin and shim assembly

side of the lower swivel pin gasket, and fit the gasket to the pin.

19 Install the lower swivel pin with its lug outermost, then fit the mudshield bracket and refit the retaining bolts, tightening them loosely only at this stage **(see illustration)**.

20 Fit the upper swivel pin and shim(s) to the top of the swivel housing, and install the retaining bolts, tightening them loosely only at this stage **(see illustration)**.

21 With both pins in position, remove the lower pin retaining bolts, and clean their threads. Apply a drop of fresh locking compound to the bolt threads, then refit them and tighten them to the specified torque setting **(see illustration)**. Secure the bolts in position by bending down the locking tabs (where fitted).

22 Tighten the top swivel pin bolts to the specified torque setting.

23 It is now necessary to check the swivel pin bearing preload setting. Secure retain the swivel ball axle flange, and attach a spring balance to the swivel housing track rod balljoint hole. Use the spring balance to move the swivel housing back-and-

forth, whilst noting the force necessary to do this **(see illustration)**. If the bearing preload is correct, a weight (force) of approximately 3.6 to 4.5 kg (36 to 45 N) will be required to turn the housing. The preload is adjusted by varying the thickness of the shim(s) fitted beneath the upper swivel pin. If the preload is too high (more force then specified required to turn housing), thicker shim(s) will be needed; if the preload is too low (less force than specified required to turn the housing), thinner shim(s) will be required. Remove the upper swivel pin, measure the thickness of the shims fitted, and obtain the relevant new shims from your Land Rover dealer. Refit the swivel pin and shim(s), and tighten the retaining bolts to the specified torque. Repeat the above procedure as necessary until the preload is correctly set.

24 Once the swivel housing bearing preload is correctly adjusted, apply a smear of lithium-based grease to the lip of the swivel housing oil seal. Apply a smear of oil to the outer edge seal to aid installation then, making sure that its sealing lip is facing inwards, fit the seal to the swivel housing. Ensure that

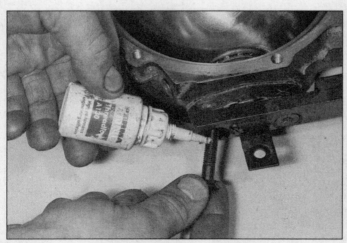

6.21 Apply locking compound to the lower swivel pin retaining bolts, and tighten them to the specified torque setting

6.23 Checking swivel pin bearing preload (see text)

6.24 Fit a new oil seal to the rear of the swivel pin housing, making sure that it is fitted the correct way around

6.28 Ensure that the axle mating surface is clean and dry, and fit a new swivel pin housing gasket

8.3 Removing a rear axle halfshaft

it enters the housing squarely **(see illustration)**.

25 Ensure that the housing and retaining plate mating surfaces are clean and dry, and refit the plate to the housing. Refit the plate retaining bolts, tightening them to the specified torque setting.

26 Refit the mudshield to the housing, and securely tighten its retaining nut and bolt.

Refitting

27 Ensure that the swivel ball and axle mating surfaces are clean and dry, and remove all traces of locking compound from the axle threads, ideally by running a tap of the correct size and pitch down them.

28 Fit a new gasket, and locate the swivel pin housing assembly on the axle **(see illustration)**.

29 Apply a drop of locking compound to the thread of each retaining bolt, then refit the bolts and washers, tightening them evenly and progressively to the specified torque setting.

30 Engage the track rod balljoint with the swivel pin housing, and refit its retaining nut. Tighten the nut to the specified torque setting (see Chapter 11), and secure it in position with a new split-pin.

31 Where necessary, reconnect the drag link to the swivel pin housing.

32 Refit the halfshaft as described in Section 2.

33 On completion, check and if necessary adjust the steering lock stops as described in Chapter.

7 Front axle –
removal and refitting

⚠️ *Warning: This procedure requires at least two people, ideally three, to be carried out safely.*

Removal

1 Apply the handbrake, then jack up the front of the vehicle and support it on axle stands positioned underneath the chassis. Remove both front roadwheels.

2 Undo the (upper swivel pin) bolts securing the brake hose retaining bracket to the swivel housing. Position the bracket clear of the housing, then refit the bolts to prevent oil leakage. Repeat the procedure on the opposite side.

3 Slacken and remove the two retaining bolts securing the brake caliper in position. Slide the caliper assembly off the disc and, using a piece of wire or string, tie the caliper to the front suspension coil spring, to avoid placing any strain on the hydraulic brake hose. Repeat the procedure on the opposite side.

4 Disconnect the propeller shaft from the front differential as described in Chapter 8.

5 Position a hydraulic jack beneath the front axle assembly, then raise the jack until it is supporting the axle weight.

6 Carry out the following procedures as described in Chapter 11 :
a) *Remove both radius arms.*
b) *Remove the Panhard rod.*
c) *Remove the track rod.*
d) *Disconnect the drag link from the swivel pin housing.*
e) *Disconnect the anti-roll bar connecting links from the axle (where fitted).*
f) *Remove the nuts securing the shock absorbers to the axle.*

7 With an assistant supporting either end of the axle, carefully lower the axle away from the vehicle, making sure that all the relevant components have been disconnected.

8 Remove the axle from underneath the vehicle, and recover the front coil springs.

Refitting

9 On refitting, position the axle assembly on the jack.

10 With the aid of two assistants, carefully raise the axle assembly into position, whilst aligning the front coil springs with their upper and lower spring seats.

11 With the axle raised and both coil springs correctly seated, carry out the following procedures as described in Chapter 11 :
a) *Refit the nuts securing the shock absorbers to the axle.*
b) *Connect the anti-roll bar connecting links to the axle (where applicable).*
c) *Connect the drag link from the swivel pin housing.*

d) *Refit the track rod.*
e) *Refit the Panhard rod.*
f) *Refit both radius arms.*

12 Slide the brake caliper assembly back into position, ensuring that its pads pass either side of the disc. Refit the caliper retaining bolts, and tighten them to the specified torque setting (see Chapter 10). Repeat the procedure on the opposite side.

13 Clean the upper swivel pin retaining bolts, and apply a drop of locking compound to each one's threads. Position the brake hose bracket on top of the swivel pin, then refit the retaining bolts and tighten them to the specified torque setting. Repeat the procedure on the opposite side.

14 Reconnect the propeller shaft to the axle as described in Chapter 8.

15 Refit the front roadwheels, then lower the vehicle to the ground and tighten the wheel nuts to the specified torque setting.

16 Rock the vehicle to settle all disturbed suspension components in position, then go around and tighten all the relevant suspension fasteners which need to be tightened with the vehicle resting on its wheels.

8 Rear axle halfshaft –
removal, inspection and
refitting

Removal

1 Chock the front wheels, then jack up the rear of the vehicle and support it on axle stands positioned underneath the chassis (see). Remove the relevant rear roadwheel.

2 Drain the differential housing oil as described in Chapter 1, or be prepared for some oil spillage as the shaft is removed.

3 On 90 models, slacken and remove the five bolts and washers securing the halfshaft to the centre of the hub, and withdraw the shaft from the centre of the hub assembly **(see illustration)**. Recover the gasket from the halfshaft flange, and discard it.

4 On 110 and 130 models, with a two-piece halfshaft assembly, remove the dust cap from the end of the shaft, remove the circlip, and separate the shaft from the hub.

8.7a Fit a new gasket to the hub assembly ...

8.7b ... then refit the halfshaft, and tighten its retaining bolts to the specified torque

Inspection

5 Inspect the halfshaft splines and hub flange for signs of wear or damage, and renew if necessary.

Refitting

6 On 110 and 130 models, engage the halfshaft with the hub driving member, and secure it in position with the circlip. Ensure that the circlip is correctly seated in the shaft groove, and then refit the dust cap.

7 On 90 models, ensure that the halfshaft and hub mating surfaces are clean and dry, and fit a new gasket, then slide the halfshaft carefully into position, and refit its retaining bolts and washers, tightening them to the specified torque setting **(see illustrations)**

8 Refit the roadwheel, then lower the vehicle to the ground and tighten the wheel nuts to the specified torque.

9 If necessary, top-up/refill the differential housing with oil as described in Chapter 1.

---

9 Rear hub assembly –
removal and refitting

Note: *The following information applies only to the standard hub assembly. For information on freewheeling hubs, refer to your Land Rover dealer.*

Removal

1 Remove the halfshaft as described in Section 8 **(see illustration)**.

2 Release the retaining clips securing the rear brake pipe to the axle. Slacken and remove the two retaining bolts securing the brake caliper in position. Slide the caliper assembly off the disc and, using a piece of wire or string, tie the caliper to the suspension coil spring, to avoid placing any strain on the hydraulic brake pipe **(see illustrations)**. **Note:** *Do not bend the pipe any more than is absolutely necessary.*

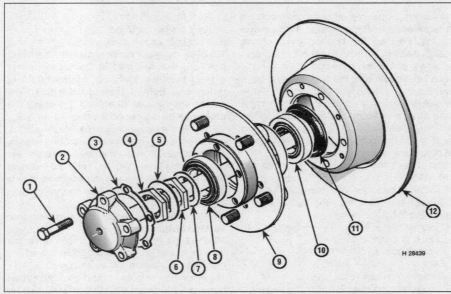

9.1 Exploded view of the rear hub and associated components – 90 model shown

1 Retaining bolt	5 Lockwasher	9 Hub
2 Halfshaft	6 Adjusting nut	10 Inner bearing and race
3 Gasket	7 Spacer	11 Seal
4 Locknut	8 Outer bearing and race	12 Brake disc

9.2a Slide the brake caliper assembly off the disc ...

9.2b ... and tie it to the coil spring, to prevent the brake pipe being strained

9.10 Measure the endfloat with a DTI gauge

11.3 Rear stub axle retaining bolts (arrowed)

3 Knock back the staking, then undo the hub nut **(see illustration 3.7)**. Discard the nut, a new one must be fitted.
4 Remove the washer.
5 Slide the hub assembly off the stub axle, complete with bearings.

Refitting

6 Apply a smear of lithium-based grease to the lips of the hub oil seal(s).
7 Fit the hub assembly, taking care not to damage the seal lips on the stub axle threads. It's essential that spacer is fitted between the inner bearings, to establish the correct spacer to eliminate endfloat.
8 Fit a new washer and hub nut, then tighten it to 30 Nm only at this stage.
9 Rotate the hub, pushing and pulling it at the same time to settle the bearings, then tighten the nut to the full specified torque.
10 Attach a dial test indicator to the hub assembly, positioning it so that its pointer is in contact with the end of the stub axle **(see illustration)**. Move the hub assembly in-and-out, and measure the hub endfloat. Compare the measurement obtained with that shown in the table to determine the correct spacer size **(see illustration 3.17b)**. If no endfloat is present, proceed to paragraph 12.
11 With the correct sized spacer obtained, undo the nut, remove the washer, and fit the new spacer.
12 Remove the DTI gauge.
13 Fit the washer, tighten the nut, and use a punch to 'stake' the nut **(see illustration 3.20b)**.
14 Slide the brake caliper assembly back into position, ensuring that its pads pass either side of the disc. Refit the caliper retaining bolts, and tighten them to the specified torque setting (see Chapter 10). Secure the brake pipe back in position with all the necessary retaining clips.
15 Refit the halfshaft as described in Section.

10 Rear hub bearing – renewal

Note: *A press may be required to dismantle and rebuild the assembly, if the bearing outer races are a tight fit in the hub. If such a tool is not available, a large bench vice and suitable spacers (such as large sockets) will serve as an adequate substitute.*

1 Remove the hub assembly as described in Section 9.
2 Remove the brake disc as described in Chapter 10.
3 Note the correct fitted depth of the seal(s) in the hub. Using a large flat-bladed screwdriver, lever the outer and/or inner oil seal(s) out from the hub assembly (as applicable).
4 Remove the outer and inner bearing inner races from the hub assembly. **Note:** *Remove the spacer from between the two bearing races.*
5 Support the hub securely on blocks or in a vice. Using a hammer and suitable punch, carefully tap the inner and outer bearing outer races out from the hub assembly.
6 Thoroughly clean the hub bore, removing all traces of dirt and grease, and polish away any burrs or raised edges which might hinder reassembly. Check both for cracks or any other signs of wear or damage, and renew them if necessary. Examine the stub axle for signs of wear or damage, and renew if necessary (see Section 11). Renew both bearings and oil seal(s) as a matter of course.
7 On reassembly, apply a light film of oil to the inner bearing outer race and hub bore, to aid installation.
8 Securely support the hub, and locate the inner bearing outer race in the hub. Press the race fully into position, ensuring that it enters the hub squarely, using a suitable tubular spacer which bears only on the bearing outer race.

9 Pack the bearing inner race with a multi-purpose lithium-based grease. Work the grease well into the bearing race, apply a smear to the outer race surface, then fit the inner race to the hub assembly.
10 Install the new inner oil seal, making sure that its sealing lip is facing inwards. Press the seal into position, ensuring that it enters the hub squarely, until it is positioned at the same depth as the original was noted prior to removal.
11 Turn the hub over, and fit the outer bearing (and, where necessary, oil seal) as described in paragraphs 7 to 10. **Note:** *Fit spacer before fitting the outer, inner bearing race.*
12 Refit the brake disc as described in Chapter 10.
13 Install the hub assembly as described in Section 9.

11 Rear stub axle – removal and refitting

Note: *New stub axle retaining bolt nuts will be required on refitting.*

Removal

1 Remove the rear hub assembly as described in Section 9.
2 If not already done, drain the differential housing oil as described in Chapter 1.
3 Make alignment marks between the stub axle and axle, then slacken and remove the six retaining bolts and nuts **(see illustration)**.
4 Lift off the mudshield, then remove the stub axle from the axle and recover the gasket. Discard the gasket – a new one must be used on refitting.
5 Inspect the stub axle for signs of wear or damage, and renew if necessary.
6 Check the oil seal fitted to the rear of the stub axle for signs of wear or damage. If renewal is necessary, lever out the old seal, noting which way around it is fitted. Apply

a smear of grease to the new seal lip, to aid installation. Fit the new seal to the axle, making sure that its sealing lip is facing away from the stub axle. Press it into position using a suitable tubular spacer which bears only on the outer edge of the seal. Ensure that the seal squarely enters the stub axle, and is positioned flush with the axle end.

Refitting

7 Make sure that the stub axle and axle mating surfaces are clean and dry, then fit a new gasket to the axle.

8 Slide the stub axle into position, aligning the marks made prior to removal, and refit the mudshield to the stub axle.

9 Fit the retaining bolts and new nuts, and tighten them to the specified torque setting.

10 Refit the hub assembly as described in Section 9.

12 Rear axle – removal and refitting

⚠️ **Warning: This procedure requires at least two people, ideally three, to be carried out safely.**

Removal

1 Chock the front wheels, then jack up the rear of the vehicle and support it on axle stands positioned underneath the chassis. Remove both rear roadwheels.

2 Unscrew the master cylinder fluid reservoir cap, then tighten the cap down onto a piece of polythene, to minimise fluid loss. Trace the brake pipes back from the wheel cylinders/calipers to their union piece situated on top of the axle. Slacken the union nut(s) and disconnect the pipe(s). Remove the retaining clips, and release the pipes from the axle/vehicle body.

 HAYNES HiNT *Plug the hydraulic pipe end(s) to minimise fluid loss and to prevent the entry of dirt into the hydraulic system.*

3 Disconnect the propeller shaft from the rear differential as described in Chapter 8.

4 Position a hydraulic jack beneath the rear axle assembly, then raise the jack until it is supporting the axle weight.

5 Carry out the following procedures as described in Chapter 11 :

a) *Disconnect the lower links from the axle.*

b) *Disconnect the shock absorbers from the axle.*

c) *Disconnect the anti-roll bar connecting links from the axle (where applicable).*

6 Withdraw the split-pin, then slacken and remove the nut securing the upper link balljoint to the top of the axle **(see illustration)**.

7 With an assistant supporting either end of the axle, carefully lower the axle away from the vehicle, making sure that all the relevant components have been disconnected.

8 Remove the axle from underneath the vehicle, and recover the spring seats from the tops of the front coil springs.

Refitting

9 On refitting, position the axle assembly on the jack, and refit the spring seats to the coil springs.

10 With the aid of two assistants, carefully raise the axle assembly into position, whilst aligning the front coil springs with their upper seats and the upper link balljoint with the axle.

11 With the axle raised and both coil springs correctly seated, refit the balljoint retaining nut, and tighten it to the specified torque setting. Secure the nut in position with a new split-pin.

12 Carry out the following procedures as described in Chapter 11 :

a) *Connect the anti-roll bar connecting links to the axle (where applicable).*

b) *Connect the shock absorbers to the axle.*

c) *Connect the lower links to the axle.*

13 Reconnect the propeller shaft to the differential as described in Chapter 8.

14 Referring to Chapter 10, reconnect the brake pipe(s) to the axle, tightening them to the specified torque setting, then bleed the complete hydraulic braking system.

15 Refit the roadwheels, then lower the vehicle to the ground and tighten the wheel nuts to the specified torque setting.

16 Rock the vehicle to settle all disturbed suspension components in position, then tighten the lower link pivot bolts to the specified torque (See Chapter).

12.6 Withdraw the split-pin, then slacken and remove the nut securing the upper link balljoint to the rear axle

13 Axle differential overhaul – general information

1 Overhauling a differential unit is a difficult and involved job for the DIY home mechanic. In addition to dismantling and reassembling many small parts, clearances must be precisely measured and, if necessary, changed by selecting shims and spacers. Components are also often difficult to obtain, and in many instances, extremely expensive. Because of this, if the differential develops a fault or becomes noisy, the best course of action is to have the unit overhauled by a specialist repairer, or to obtain an exchange reconditioned unit.

2 Nevertheless, it is not impossible for the more experienced mechanic to overhaul the differential, provided the special tools are available and the job is done in a deliberate step-by-step manner so that nothing is overlooked.

3 The tools necessary for an overhaul include internal and external circlip pliers, bearing pullers, a slide hammer, a set of pin punches, a dial test indicator, and possibly a hydraulic press. In addition, a large, sturdy workbench and a vice will be required.

4 During dismantling, make careful notes of how each component is fitted, to make reassembly easier and accurate.

5 Before dismantling, it will help if you have some idea what area is malfunctioning. Refer to Fault finding at the end of this manual for more information.

Chapter 10
Braking system

Contents

Degrees of difficulty

| Easy, suitable for novice with little experience | 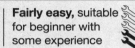 | Fairly easy, suitable for beginner with some experience | | Fairly difficult, suitable for competent DIY mechanic | | Difficult, suitable for experienced DIY mechanic | | Very difficult, suitable for expert DIY or professional | |

Specifications

Front brakes

Type	Disc, with opposed-piston caliper
Disc diameter	298 mm
Disc thickness:	
Non-ventilated disc	14.1 mm
Ventilated disc	24.0 mm
Maximum wear (per side)	1.0 mm
Maximum disc run-out	0.15 mm
Brake pad friction material minimum thickness	3.0 mm

Rear brakes

Type	Disc, with opposed-piston caliper
Disc diameter	290 mm
Disc thickness:	
90 models.	12.5 mm
110/130 models	14.1 mm
Maximum wear (per side):	
90 models.	0.38 mm
110/130 models	1.0 mm
Maximum disc run-out	0.15 mm
Brake pad friction material minimum thickness	3.0 mm

Parking brake (handbrake)

Type	Drum brake on rear of transfer box output shaft, cable operated
Drum internal diameter	254.0 mm
Drum width	70.0 mm

Master cylinder/Servo (booster)

Type	Tandem – 254.0 mm diameter
Manufacturer	Lucas
Servo (booster) type	LSC 80

Torque wrench settings

	Nm	lbf ft
Brake caliper mounting bolts (front and rear)	82	61
Brake disc bolts (front and rear)	72	53
Brake pipe union nut	15	11
Handbrake backplate bolts	25	18
Handbrake lever mounting bolts	22	16
Master cylinder mounting nuts	26	19
Roadwheel nuts:		
Steel wheels	108	80
Alloy wheels	130	96
Heavy duty wheel	170	125
Vacuum servo unit mounting nuts	14	10
Vacuum pump to coolant pump (2.4 litre engine)	23	17
Vacuum pump to cylinder head (2.2 litre engine)	23	17

1 General Information

1 The braking system is of the servo-assisted, dual-circuit hydraulic type, operating from a tandem master cylinder. The primary circuit operates the rear brake cylinders/calipers (as applicable), and the secondary circuit operates the front brake calipers. Under normal circumstances, both circuits operate in unison. However, in the event of hydraulic failure in one circuit, braking force will still be available for at least two wheels.

2 As with all diesel engines, since there is insufficient vacuum in the inlet manifold to operate the braking system servo unit, a vacuum pump is fitted to the engine to provide the required vacuum. On 2.2 litre engines the vacuum pump is fitted to the rear of the cylinder head and driven by the camshaft. On 2.4 litre engines, the vacuum pump is located on top of the coolant pump and driven by the auxiliary belt.

3 The disc brakes are actuated by opposed-piston type calipers, which ensure that equal pressure is applied to each disc pad.

4 The handbrake is in the form of a drum brake assembly mounted onto the rear of the transfer box. When the handbrake is applied, it locks the rear axle by preventing propeller shaft rotation.

Note: *When servicing any part of the system, work carefully and methodically; also observe scrupulous cleanliness when overhauling any part of the hydraulic system. Always renew components (in axle sets, where applicable) if in doubt about their condition, and use only genuine Land Rover parts, or at least those of known good quality. Note the warnings given in 'Safety first!' and at relevant points in this Chapter concerning the dangers of asbestos dust and hydraulic fluid.*

2 Hydraulic system – bleeding

Note: *Hydraulic fluid is poisonous; wash off immediately and thoroughly in the case of skin contact, and seek immediate medical advice if any fluid is swallowed or gets into the eyes. Certain types of hydraulic fluid are inflammable, and may ignite when allowed into contact with hot components; when servicing any hydraulic system, it is safest to assume that the fluid IS inflammable, and to take precautions against the risk of fire as though it is petrol that is being handled. Finally, it is hygroscopic (it absorbs moisture from the air) – old fluid may be contaminated, and unfit for further use. When topping-up or renewing the fluid, always use the recommended type, and ensure that it comes from a freshly-opened sealed container.*

Caution: Hydraulic fluid is also an effective paint stripper, and will attack plastics; if any is spilt, it should be washed off immediately, using copious quantities of fresh water.

General

1 The correct operation of any hydraulic system is only possible after removing all air from the components and circuit; this is achieved by bleeding the system.

2 During the bleeding procedure, add only clean, unused hydraulic fluid of the recommended type; never re-use fluid that has already been bled from the system. Ensure that sufficient fluid is available before starting work.

3 If there is any possibility of incorrect fluid being already in the system, the brake components and circuit must be flushed completely with uncontaminated, correct fluid, and new seals should be fitted to the various components.

4 If hydraulic fluid has been lost from the system, or air has entered because of a leak, ensure that the fault is cured before proceeding further.

5 Park the vehicle on level ground, switch off the engine and select first or reverse gear, then chock the wheels and release the handbrake.

6 Check that all pipes and hoses are secure, unions tight, and bleed screws closed. Clean any dirt from around the bleed screws.

7 Unscrew the master cylinder reservoir cap, and top the master cylinder reservoir up to the MAX level line; refit the cap loosely. Remember to maintain the fluid level at least above the MIN level line throughout the procedure, or there is a risk of further air entering the system.

8 There is a number of one-man, do-it-yourself brake bleeding kits currently available from motor accessory shops. It is recommended that one of these kits is used whenever possible, as they greatly simplify the bleeding operation, and also reduce the risk of expelled air and fluid being drawn back into the system. If such a kit is not available, the basic (two-man) method must be used, which is described in detail below.

9 If a kit is to be used, prepare the vehicle as described previously, and follow the kit manufacturer's instructions, as the procedure may vary slightly according to the type being used; generally, they are as outlined below in the relevant sub-Section.

10 Whichever method is used, the same sequence must be followed (paragraphs 11 and 12) to ensure the removal of all air from the system.

Bleeding sequence

11 If the system has been only partially disconnected, and suitable precautions were taken to minimise fluid loss, it should be necessary only to bleed that part of the system (ie, the primary or secondary circuit).

12 If the complete system is to be bled, then it should be done working in the following sequence:

a) *Left-hand rear brake.*
b) *Right-hand rear brake.*
c) *Right-hand front brake.*
d) *Left-hand front brake.*

Bleeding

Basic (two-man) method

13 Collect a clean glass jar, a suitable length of plastic or rubber tubing which is a tight fit over the bleed screw, and a ring spanner to fit the screw. The help of an assistant will also be required.

14 Remove the dust cap from the first screw in the sequence. Fit the spanner and tube to the screw, place the other end of the tube in the jar, and pour in sufficient fluid to cover the end of the tube.

15 Ensure that the master cylinder reservoir

fluid level is maintained at least above the MIN level line throughout the procedure.

16 Have the assistant fully depress the brake pedal several times to build-up pressure, then maintain it on the final stroke.

17 While pedal pressure is maintained, unscrew the bleed screw (approximately one turn), and allow the compressed fluid and air to flow into the jar. The assistant should maintain pedal pressure, following it down to the floor if necessary, and should not release it until instructed to do so. When the flow stops, tighten the bleed screw again, then the pedal can be released slowly. Recheck the reservoir fluid level.

18 Repeat the steps given in paragraphs 16 and 17 until the fluid emerging from the bleed screw is free from air bubbles. If the master cylinder has been drained and refilled, and air is being bled from the first screw in the sequence, allow approximately five seconds between cycles for the master cylinder passages to refill.

19 When no more air bubbles appear, tighten the bleed screw securely, remove the tube and spanner, and refit the dust cap. Do not overtighten the bleed screw.

20 Repeat the procedure on the remaining screws in the sequence, until all air is removed from the system and the brake pedal feels firm again.

Using a one-way valve kit

21 As their name implies, these kits consist of a length of tubing with a one-way valve fitted, to prevent expelled air and fluid being drawn back into the system; some kits include a translucent container, which can be positioned so that the air bubbles can be more easily seen flowing from the end of the tube **(see illustration)**.

22 The kit is connected to the bleed screw, which is then opened. The user returns to the driver's seat, depresses the brake pedal with a smooth, steady stroke, and slowly releases it; this is repeated until the expelled fluid is clear of air bubbles.

23 These kits simplify work so much that it is easy to forget the master cylinder reservoir fluid level; ensure that this is maintained at least above the MIN level line at all times.

Using a pressure-bleeding kit

Note: *Ensure that the pressure in the reservoir does not exceed 4.5 bars (60 psi approx).*

24 These kits are usually operated by the reservoir of pressurised air contained in the spare tyre, although note that it will probably be necessary to reduce the pressure to a lower limit than normal; refer to the instructions supplied with the kit.

25 By connecting a pressurised, fluid-filled container to the master cylinder reservoir, bleeding can be carried out simply by opening each screw in turn (in the specified sequence), and allowing the fluid to flow out until no more air bubbles can be seen in the expelled fluid.

26 This method has the advantage that the large reservoir of fluid provides an additional

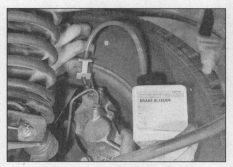

2.21 Bleeding a rear brake caliper using a one-way valve kit

safeguard against air being drawn into the system during bleeding.

27 Pressure bleeding is particularly effective when bleeding 'difficult' systems, or when bleeding the complete system at the time of routine fluid renewal.

All methods

28 When bleeding is complete, and firm pedal feel is restored, wash off any spilt fluid, tighten the bleed screws securely, and refit their dust caps.

29 Check the hydraulic fluid level, and top-up if necessary (*Weekly checks*).

30 Discard any hydraulic fluid that has been bled from the system; it will not be fit for re-use.

31 Check the feel of the brake pedal. If it feels at all spongy, air must still be present in the system, and further bleeding is required. Failure to bleed satisfactorily after a reasonable repetition of the bleeding procedure may be due to worn master cylinder seals.

3 Hydraulic pipes and hoses – renewal

Note: *Before starting work, refer to the note at the beginning of Section 2 concerning the dangers of hydraulic fluid.*

1 If any pipe or hose is to be renewed, to minimise fluid loss, remove the master cylinder reservoir cap, then tighten it down onto a piece of polythene to obtain an airtight seal. Alternatively, flexible hoses can be sealed, if required, using a proprietary brake hose clamp, while metal brake pipe unions can be plugged (if care is taken not to allow dirt into the system) or capped immediately they are disconnected. Place a wad of rag under any union that is to be disconnected, to catch any spilt fluid.

2 If a flexible hose is to be disconnected, unscrew the brake pipe union nut before removing the spring clip which secures the hose to its mounting bracket (where fitted).

3 To unscrew the union nuts, it is preferable to obtain a proper brake pipe spanner of the correct size; these are available from most large motor accessory shops **(see**

3.3 Using a brake pipe spanner to slacken a union nut

illustration). Failing this, a close-fitting open-ended spanner will be required, though if the nuts are tight or corroded, their flats may be rounded-off if the spanner slips. In such a case, a self-locking wrench is often the only way to unscrew a stubborn union, but it follows that the pipe and the damaged nuts must be renewed on reassembly. Always clean a union and surrounding area before disconnecting it.

> **HAYNES HiNT**
> *If disconnecting a component with more than one union, make a careful note of the connections before disturbing any of them.*

4 If a brake pipe is to be renewed, it can be obtained, cut to length and with the union nuts and end flares in place, from Land Rover dealers. All that is then necessary is to bend it to shape, following the line of the original, before fitting it to the car. Alternatively, most motor accessory shops can make up brake pipes from kits, but this requires very careful measurement of the original, to ensure that the replacement is of the correct length. The safest answer is usually to take the original to the shop as a pattern.

5 On refitting, do not overtighten the union nuts. It is not necessary to exercise brute force to obtain a sound joint.

6 Ensure that the pipes and hoses are correctly routed with no kinks, and that they are secured in the clips or brackets provided. After fitting, remove the polythene from the reservoir (or the hose clamps/plugs, if used) and bleed the hydraulic system as described in Section. Wash off any spilt fluid, and check carefully for fluid leaks.

4 Front brake pads – renewal

⚠ **Warning: Renew BOTH sets of front brake pads at the same time – NEVER renew the pads on only one wheel, as uneven braking may result. Note that the dust created by wear**

4.2a Remove the split-pins...

4.2b ...and spring clip (where fitted)...

4.2c ... then withdraw the pad retaining pins and recover the anti-rattle springs

4.3a Withdraw the outer brake pad...

4.3b ...and inner brake pad from the caliper

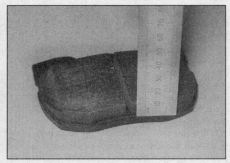

4.5 Measuring brake pad friction material thickness

of the pads may contain asbestos, which is a health hazard. Never blow it out with compressed air, and don't inhale any of it. An approved filtering mask should be worn when working on the brakes. DO NOT use petroleum-based solvents to clean brake parts – use brake cleaner or methylated spirit only.

1 Apply the handbrake, then jack up the front of the vehicle and support it on axle stands. Remove both front roadwheels.

2 Using a pair of pliers, remove the split-pins from the inner end of each pad retaining pin, then carefully withdraw the pad retaining pins, recovering the anti-rattle springs as they are released **(see illustrations)**.

3 Withdraw the pads from caliper **(see illustrations)**, noting the location of any brake pad shims fitted.

4 Brush the dirt and dust from the caliper, but take care not to inhale it. Carefully remove any rust from the edge of the brake disc.

5 First measure the thickness of each brake pad's friction material **(see illustration)**. If either pad is worn at any point to the specified minimum thickness or less, all four pads must be renewed. Also, the pads should be renewed if any are fouled with oil or grease; there is no satisfactory way of degreasing friction material, once contaminated. If any of the brake pads are worn unevenly or fouled with oil or grease, trace and recjpgy the cause before reassembly. The pad retaining pins and anti-rattle springs should be also renewed if

the pads are to be renewed. New brake pads, pins and springs are available from Land Rover dealers.

6 If the brake pads are still serviceable, carefully clean them using a clean, fine wire brush or similar, paying particular attention to the sides and back of the metal backing. Clean out the grooves in the friction material, and pick out any large embedded particles of dirt or debris. Carefully clean the pad locations in the caliper body/mounting bracket.

7 Prior to fitting the pads, brush the dust and dirt from the caliper pistons, but do not inhale it, as it is a health hazard. Inspect the dust seal around the piston for damage, and the piston for evidence of fluid leaks, corrosion or damage. If attention to any of these components is necessary, refer to Section 8.

8 If new brake pads are to be fitted, the caliper pistons must be pushed back into the caliper, to make room for them. Either use a G-clamp or similar tool, or use suitable pieces of wood as levers. Provided that the master cylinder reservoir has not been overfilled with hydraulic fluid, there should be no spillage, but keep a careful watch on the fluid level while retracting the piston. If the fluid level rises above the MAX level line at any time, the surplus should be syphoned off, or ejected via a plastic tube connected to the bleed screw (see Section 2). **Note:** *Do not syphon the fluid by mouth, as it is poisonous; use a syringe or an old poultry baster.*

9 Apply a thin smear of high-temperature brake grease or anti-seize compound to the sides of each pad's metal backing, and to those surfaces of the caliper body which bear on the pads. Do not allow the lubricant to foul the friction material.

10 Locate the pads in the caliper, ensuring that the friction material of each pad is against the brake disc. **Note:** *The friction material on new pads may have a chamfered edge. The pads must be fitted with this chamfer on the leading edge, ie, this edge is the first part of the pad that the disc encounters in the normal direction of rotation* **(see illustration)**.

11 Fit the anti-rattle springs between the pads, then insert the pad retaining pins. Make sure each pin passes through its anti-rattle

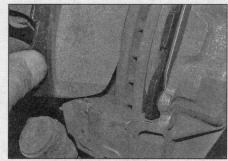

4.10 New pads may have a chamfered edge which must be fitted at the leading edge

4.11a Fit the outer pad...

4.11b ...and the inner pad...

4.11c ...making sure the chamfer on the pads is correct

4.11d Fit the pins and anti-rattle springs...

spring and both pads. Secure each retaining pin in position with a new split-pin **(see illustrations)**.

12 Depress the brake pedal repeatedly, until the pads are pressed into firm contact with the brake disc and normal (non-assisted) pedal pressure is restored.

13 Repeat the above procedure on the remaining front brake caliper.

14 Refit the roadwheels, then lower the vehicle to the ground and tighten the roadwheel nuts to the specified torque setting.

15 Check the hydraulic fluid level as described in *Weekly checks*.

4.11e ...and the spring clips (where fitted)

4.11f Fit new split pins...

4.11g ...and check they are all fitted correctly

5 Rear brake pads – renewal

⚠️ **Warning: Renew BOTH sets of rear brake pads at the same time – NEVER renew the pads on only one wheel, as uneven braking may result. Note that the dust created by wear of the pads may contain hazardous materials. Never blow it out with compressed air, and don't inhale any of it. An approved filtering mask should be worn when working on the brakes. DO NOT use petroleum-based solvents to clean brake parts – use brake cleaner or methylated spirit only.**

1 There are two types of brake pads fitted to the rear of this vehicle, depending on model. Pad renewal can be carried out by following the accompanying photos **(see illustrations)**. Note that on some models, shims will be fitted to the rear of the brake pad(s) (as applicable).

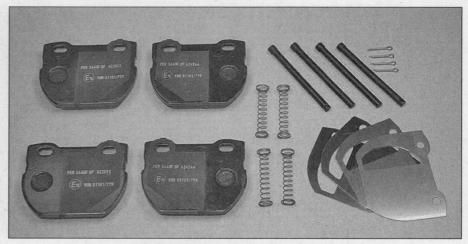

5.1a Typical brake pad kit – Type B shown

Where this is so, note their correct fitted locations on removal, and ensure that they are correctly positioned on refitting **(see illustration)**.

Type A – 90 models

5.1b Close the ends of the split pins...

5.1c ...and withdraw the retaining split-pins...

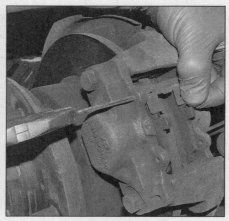

5.1d ...then the anti-rattle springs

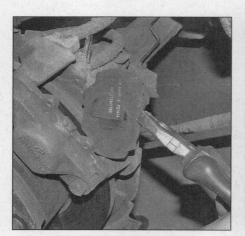

5.1e Withdraw the outer...

5.1f ...and inner brake pads

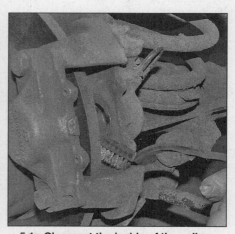

5.1g Clean out the inside of the caliper where the pads sit

5.1h Pressing back the pistons to accept new pads – check fluid level in reservoir

5.1i Fit new inner...

5.1j ...and outer brake pads

5.1k Make sure the chamfer on the pads are at the leading edge

5.1l Fit the new split pins...

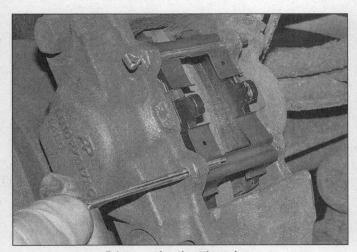

5.1m ...and anti-rattle springs

5.1n Secure the split pins by opening up the ends and make sure all is secure

Type B – 110/130 models

2 This type of caliper fitted on the rear of 110/130 models, is similar to the front brakes. Pad renewal can be carried out by following the accompanying photos **(see illustrations)**.

5.2a Remove the split pins...

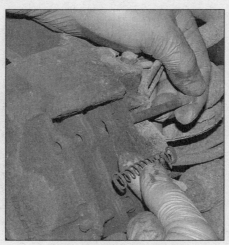

5.2b ...withdraw the retaining pins...

5.2c ...and remove the anti-rattle spring

5.2d Remove the brake pads...

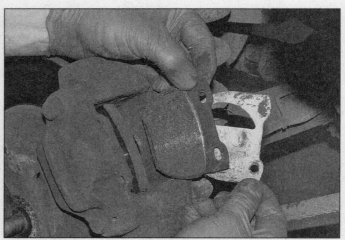

5.2e ...and shims (where fitted) – note there fitted position

5.2f Pressing back the pistons to accept new pads – check fluid level in reservoir

5.2g Clean out the inside of the caliper, where the pads sit

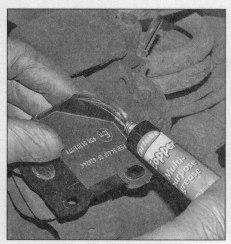

5.2h Apply a small amount of high temperature grease to the metal outer edge of the pad

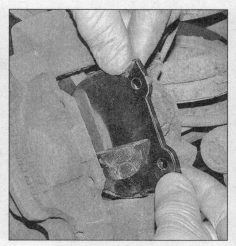

5.2i Fit the new brake pads...

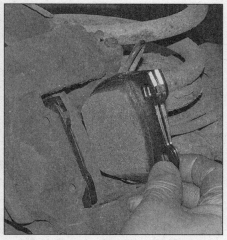

5.2j ...and shims (where fitted) in the position noted on removal

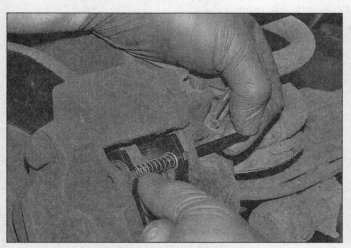

5.2k Fit the new retaining pins...

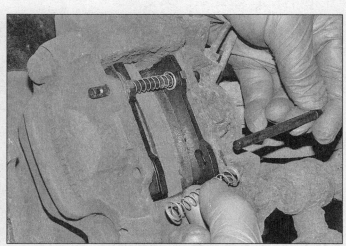

5.2l ...and anti-rattle springs

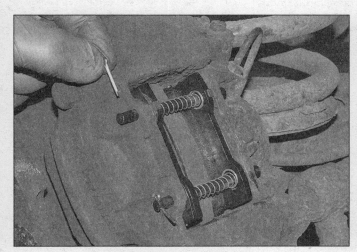

5.2m Fit new split pins...

5.2n ...to secure the retaining pins and check

6.3 Measuring brake disc thickness using a micrometer

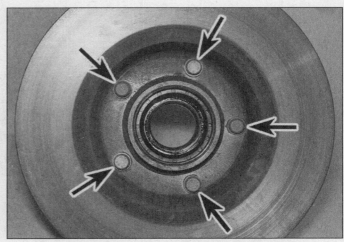

6.8 Front brake disc retaining bolts (arrowed)

6 Front brake disc – inspection, removal and refitting

Note: *Before starting work, refer to the note at the beginning of Section 4 concerning the dangers of asbestos dust.*

Inspection

Note: *If either disc requires renewal, BOTH should be renewed at the same time, to ensure even and consistent braking.*

1 Firmly apply the handbrake, then jack up the front of the car and support it on axle stands. Remove the appropriate front roadwheel.

2 Slowly rotate the brake disc so that the full area of both sides can be checked; remove the brake pads if better access is required to the inner surface. Light scoring is normal in the area swept by the brake pads, but if heavy scoring is found, the disc must be renewed.

3 It is normal to find a lip of rust and brake dust around the disc's perimeter; this can be scraped off if required. If, however, a lip has formed due to excessive wear of the brake pad swept area, the disc's thickness must be measured using a micrometer **(see illustration)**. Take measurements at several places around the disc, at the inside and outside of the pad swept area. If any disc is found to be excessively worn, it may be possible to have it refinished, otherwise it will have to be renewed.

4 If the disc is thought to be warped, it can be checked for run-out as follows. Use a dial gauge mounted on any convenient fixed point, while the disc is slowly rotated, or use feeler blades to measure (at several points all around the disc) the clearance between the disc and a fixed point such as the brake caliper. If the measurements obtained indicate a run-out at the specified maximum or beyond, the disc is excessively warped and must be renewed; however, it is worth checking first that the axle hub bearing is in good condition (Chapter 9).

5 Check the disc for cracks, especially around the wheel studs, and for any other wear or damage.

Removal

6 Remove the front hub assembly as described in Chapter 9.

7 Using chalk or paint, make alignment marks between the disc and hub.

8 Slacken and remove the bolts securing the brake disc to the hub assembly, and separate the two components **(see illustration)**.

Refitting

9 Refitting is the reverse of the removal procedure, noting the following points:
a) *Ensure that the mating surfaces of the disc and hub are clean and flat.*
b) *If a new disc has been fitted, use a suitable solvent to wipe any preservative coating from the disc before refitting the caliper.*
c) *Remove all traces of old locking compound from the brake disc holes in the hub assembly, ideally by running a tap of the correct size and pitch through them.*
d) *Fit the disc to the hub, aligning (if applicable) the marks made prior to removal.*
e) *Apply a suitable locking compound to the threads of the disc retaining bolts, then fit the bolts and tighten them to the specified torque setting.*
f) *Refit the roadwheel, lower the vehicle to the ground and tighten the roadwheel nuts to the specified torque. On completion, repeatedly depress the brake pedal until normal (non-assisted) pedal pressure returns.*

7 Rear brake disc – inspection, removal and refitting

Note: *Before starting work, refer to the note at the beginning of Section 5 concerning the dangers of asbestos dust.*

Inspection

1 Refer to Section 6.

Removal

2 Remove the rear hub assembly as described in Chapter 9. Using chalk or paint, make alignment marks between the disc and hub.

3 Slacken and remove the bolts securing the disc to the hub assembly, and separate the two.

Refitting

4 Refitting is the reverse of the removal procedure, noting the following points:
a) *Ensure that the mating surfaces of the disc and hub are clean and flat.*
b) *If a new disc has been fitted, use a suitable solvent to wipe any preservative coating from the disc before refitting the caliper.*
c) *Remove all traces of old locking compound from the brake disc holes in the hub assembly, ideally by running a tap of the correct size and pitch through them.*
d) *Fit the disc to the hub, aligning (if applicable) the marks made prior to removal.*
e) *Apply a suitable locking compound to the threads of the disc retaining bolts, then fit the bolts and tighten them to the specified torque setting.*
f) *Refit the roadwheel, lower the vehicle to the ground and tighten the roadwheel nuts to the specified torque. On completion, repeatedly depress the brake pedal until normal (non-assisted) pedal pressure returns.*

8 Front brake caliper – removal, overhaul and refitting

Note: *Before starting work, refer to the note at the beginning of Section 2 concerning the dangers of hydraulic fluid, and to the warning at the beginning of Section 4 concerning the dangers of asbestos dust.*

Removal

1 Apply the handbrake, then jack up the front of the vehicle and support it on axle stands. Remove the appropriate roadwheel.

2 Remove the brake pads as described in Section 4.

3 To minimise fluid loss, remove the master cylinder reservoir cap, then tighten it down onto a piece of polythene to obtain an airtight seal. Alternatively, use a brake hose clamp, a G-clamp or a similar tool to clamp the flexible hose at the nearest convenient point to the caliper.

4 Clean the area around the caliper brake hose union nut. Undo the union nut, and disconnect the brake pipe from the caliper. Plug the hose end and caliper hole, to minimise fluid loss and to prevent the ingress of dirt into the hydraulic system.

5 Slacken and remove the two retaining bolts, and remove the caliper assembly from the vehicle.

Overhaul

Note: *Prior to dismantling the caliper, check the availability of spares from your Land Rover dealer; on some models, it may prove difficult to obtain caliper components.*

6 With the caliper on the bench, wipe away all traces of dust and dirt, but avoid inhaling the dust, as it is a health hazard **(see illustration)**.

7 Push both the pistons on one side of the caliper fully into the caliper bore and retain them in position with a suitable G-clamp.

8 Withdraw both the partially-ejected pistons from the opposite side of the caliper body. The pistons can be withdrawn by hand, if loose. If one or both of the pistons are not loose enough to be withdrawn by hand, they can be pushed out by applying compressed air to the (relevant) brake hose union hole. Only low pressure should be required, such as is generated by a foot pump. **Note:** *Ensure that both pistons are expelled from the caliper at the same time.*

9 Extract both pistons from the caliper. Mark identification marks between the caliper and bore, to ensure that each piston is refitted to its original bore.

10 Using a small screwdriver, carefully remove the wiper seal retainer from the caliper, taking great care not to mark the bore. Repeating the procedure, remove the wiper seal and piston (fluid) seal in the same way.

11 Thoroughly clean all components, using only methylated spirit, isopropyl alcohol or clean hydraulic fluid as a cleaning medium. Never use mineral-based solvents such as petrol or paraffin, as they will attack the hydraulic system's rubber components. Dry the components immediately, using compressed air or a clean, lint-free cloth. Use compressed air to blow clear the fluid passages.

 Warning: Wear eye protection when using compressed air.

12 Check all components, and renew any that are worn or damaged. Check particularly

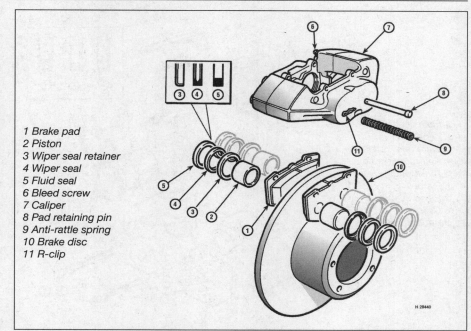

1 Brake pad
2 Piston
3 Wiper seal retainer
4 Wiper seal
5 Fluid seal
6 Bleed screw
7 Caliper
8 Pad retaining pin
9 Anti-rattle spring
10 Brake disc
11 R-clip

8.6 Exploded view of the front brake caliper and associated components. Inset shows cross-section of each seal – later models shown (early models similar)

the cylinder bores and pistons; these should be renewed if they are scratched, worn or corroded in any way.

13 If the assembly is fit for further use, obtain the necessary components from your Land Rover dealer or specialist. Renew the caliper seals and retainers as a matter of course; these should never be re-used.

14 On reassembly, ensure that all components are absolutely clean and dry.

15 Soak the pistons and the new piston (fluid) seals in clean hydraulic fluid. Smear clean fluid on the cylinder bore surface.

16 Fit the new piston (fluid) seals, using fingers only (no tools) to manipulate them into the cylinder bore grooves.

17 Ensure that the piston (fluid) seals are correctly located, then fit the new wiper seals in the same way.

18 Make sure that each wiper seal is correctly seated, then install the new wiper seal retainers in the caliper body, ensuring that both are fitted the correct way around.

19 Fit each piston using a twisting motion, ensuring that they enter the caliper bore squarely. If the original pistons are being re-used, use the marks made on removal to ensure that they are refitted to the correct bores.

20 Remove the G-clamp from the caliper, and repeat the operations described in paragraphs 7 to 19 on the remaining two pistons in the caliper.

Refitting

21 Refit the caliper assembly to the vehicle, apply a little thread locking compound and tighten its retaining bolts to the specified torque setting.

22 Refit the brake pipe to the caliper,

tightening the union nut to the specified torque setting.

23 Refit the brake pads as described in Section 4.

24 Remove the brake hose clamp or polythene, where fitted, and bleed the hydraulic system as described in Section 2. Note that, providing the precautions described were taken to minimise brake fluid loss, it should only be necessary to bleed the relevant front brake.

25 Refit the roadwheel, then lower the vehicle to the ground and tighten the roadwheel nuts to the specified torque.

9 Rear brake caliper – removal, overhaul and refitting

Note: *Before starting work, refer to the note at the beginning of Section 2 concerning the dangers of hydraulic fluid, and to the warning at the beginning of Section 5 concerning the dangers of asbestos dust.*

Removal

1 Chock the front wheels, then jack up the rear of the vehicle and support on axle stands. Remove the relevant rear wheel.

2 Remove the brake pads as described in Section 5.

3 To minimise fluid loss, remove the master cylinder reservoir cap, then tighten it down onto a piece of polythene to obtain an airtight seal. Alternatively, use a brake hose clamp, a G-clamp or a similar tool to clamp the flexible hose at the nearest convenient point to the brake caliper.

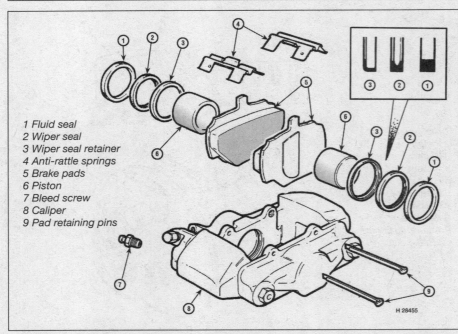

1 Fluid seal
2 Wiper seal
3 Wiper seal retainer
4 Anti-rattle springs
5 Brake pads
6 Piston
7 Bleed screw
8 Caliper
9 Pad retaining pins

9.6 Exploded view of the rear brake caliper and associated components. Inset shows cross-section of each seal

10.1 Remove the wiring connectors and filler cap

4 Wipe away all traces of dirt around the brake pipe union on the caliper, then undo the union nut and disconnect the brake pipe from the caliper. Plug the hose end and caliper hole, to minimise fluid loss and to prevent the ingress of dirt into the hydraulic system.

5 Slacken the two bolts securing the caliper assembly in position. Lift the caliper assembly away from the disc, and remove it from the vehicle.

Overhaul

Note: *Prior to dismantling the caliper, check the availability of spares from your Land Rover dealer or specialist; on some models, it may prove difficult to obtain caliper components.*

6 With the caliper on the bench, wipe away all traces of dust and dirt, but avoid inhaling the dust, as it is a health hazard **(see illustration)**.

Note: *Illustration is of brake caliper fitted to the rear of the Land Rover 90 model, the rear caliper fitted to the 110/130 models is similar to the front caliper **(see illustration 8.6)**, only it has two pistons (one each side) and not four (two each side).*

7 Push the piston on one side of the caliper fully into the caliper bore, and retain it in position with a suitable G-clamp.

8 Withdraw the partially ejected piston from the opposite side of the caliper body. The piston can be withdrawn by hand, if loose, or can be pushed out by applying compressed air to the brake hose union hole. Only low pressure should be required, such as is generated by a foot pump.

9 Using a small screwdriver, carefully remove the wiper seal retainer from the caliper, taking great care not to mark the bore. Repeating the

procedure, remove the wiper seal and piston (fluid) seal in the same way.

10 Thoroughly clean all components, using only methylated spirit, isopropyl alcohol or clean hydraulic fluid as a cleaning medium. Never use mineral-based solvents such as petrol or paraffin, as they will attack the hydraulic system's rubber components. Dry the components immediately, using compressed air or a clean, lint-free cloth. Use compressed air to blow clear the fluid passages.

> ⚠ **Warning: Wear eye protection when using compressed air.**

11 Check all components, and renew any that are worn or damaged. Check particularly the cylinder bore and piston; these should be renewed if they are scratched, worn or corroded in any way.

12 If the assembly is fit for further use, obtain the necessary components from your Land Rover dealer or specialist. Renew the caliper seals and retainers as a matter of course; these should never be re-used.

13 On reassembly, ensure that all components are absolutely clean and dry.

14 Soak the piston and new piston (fluid) seal in clean hydraulic fluid. Smear clean fluid on the cylinder bore surface.

15 Fit the new piston (fluid) seal, using fingers only (no tools) to manipulate it into the cylinder bore groove.

16 Ensure that the piston (fluid) seal is correctly located, then fit the new wiper seal in the same way.

17 Make sure that the wiper seal is correctly seated, then install the new wiper seal retainer in the caliper body, ensuring that it is fitted the correct way around.

18 Fit the piston using a twisting motion, ensuring that it enters the caliper bore squarely.

19 Remove the G-clamp from the caliper, and repeat the operations described in paragraphs 7 to 18 on the remaining caliper piston.

Refitting

20 Refit the caliper assembly to the vehicle, and tighten its retaining bolts to the specified torque setting.

21 Refit the brake pipe to the caliper, and tighten its union nut to the specified torque setting.

22 Refit the brake pads as described in Section 5.

23 Remove the brake hose clamp or polythene, as applicable, and bleed the hydraulic system as described in Section 2. Providing the precautions described were taken to minimise brake fluid loss, it should only be necessary to bleed the relevant rear brake.

24 Refit the roadwheel, then lower the vehicle to the ground and tighten the roadwheel nuts to the specified torque.

---

10 Master cylinder – removal, overhaul and refitting

Note: *Before starting work, refer to the warning at the beginning of Section 2 concerning the dangers of hydraulic fluid.*

Removal

1 Disconnect the wiring connector from the brake fluid level sender unit **(see illustration)**. Remove the master cylinder reservoir cap, and syphon the hydraulic fluid from the reservoir. **Note:** *Do not syphon the fluid by mouth, as it is poisonous; use a syringe or an old anti-freeze tester. Alternatively, open any convenient bleed screw in the system, and gently pump the brake pedal to expel the fluid through a plastic tube connected to the screw (see Section 2).*

2 Wipe clean the area around the brake pipe unions on the side of the master cylinder, and place absorbent rags beneath the pipe unions to catch any surplus fluid. Make a note of the correct fitted positions of the unions, then unscrew the union nuts and carefully withdraw the pipes **(see illustration)**. Wash off any spilt fluid immediately with cold water. Plug or tape over the pipe ends and master cylinder orifices, to minimise the loss of brake fluid and to prevent the entry of dirt into the system.

3 Slacken and remove the two nuts and washers securing the master cylinder to the vacuum servo unit **(see illustration)**. Withdraw the master cylinder assembly from the engine compartment, and recover the O-ring from the rear of the cylinder.

Overhaul

Note: *Prior to dismantling the master cylinder, check the availability of spares from your Land Rover dealer or specialist.*

4 Carefully ease the reservoir out from the master cylinder body, and recover the two mounting seals from the master cylinder ports, noting each seal's correct fitted location **(see illustration)**.

5 Carefully grip the master cylinder body in a vice with soft jaws. Using a suitable pair of grips, ease the rear housing cover out from the cylinder. The housing should come away complete with the vacuum seal.

6 Carefully remove the retaining ring from the master cylinder, along with its O-ring.

7 Ease the guide ring out from the rear of the master cylinder. **Note:** *The guide is not supplied with the repair kit, and will have to be re-used, so take care not to damage it.*

8 Withdraw the primary piston assembly from the cylinder.

9 Noting the order of removal and the direction of fitting of each component, tap the body on a clean wooden surface, and

10.2 Undo the brake pipe union nuts

10.3 Undo the master cylinder securing nuts

withdraw the secondary piston assembly, springs and swirl tube from the master cylinder. Note which way around the swirl tube is fitted.

10 Thoroughly clean all components, using only methylated spirit, isopropyl alcohol or clean hydraulic fluid as a cleaning medium. Never use mineral-based solvents such as petrol or paraffin, as they will attack the hydraulic system's rubber components. Dry the components immediately, using compressed air or a clean, lint-free cloth.

11 Check all components, and renew any that are worn or damaged. Check particularly the cylinder bores and pistons; the complete assembly should be renewed if these are scratched, worn or corroded. If there is any doubt about the condition of the assembly or of any of its components, renew it. Check that the body's fluid passages are clear.

12 If the assembly is fit for further use, obtain a repair kit from your Land Rover dealer or

specialist. The kit consists of the primary piston assembly, all seals and springs, as well as a rear housing. Renew all seals disturbed on dismantling, and the rear housing, as a matter of course; these should never be re-used.

13 Prior to reassembly, soak the piston assemblies and all new seals in clean hydraulic fluid. Smear clean fluid into the cylinder bore.

14 Using a small flat-bladed screwdriver, remove the seal retainer from the inner end of the secondary piston, and slide off the inner piston seal and washer. Remove the outer seal, taking great care not to mark the piston. Carefully manipulate the new outer seal into position on the piston, making sure that it is the correct way around. Fit the washer and inner seal, again making sure that it is the correct way around, and secure it in position with the seal retainer **(see illustration)**.

15 Fit the new swirl tube to the master cylinder bore, ensuring that it is fitted the correct way around.

16 Locate both springs on the end of the secondary piston assembly, and insert the assembly into the master cylinder body. Insert the piston assembly using a twisting motion, ensuring that the piston seals do not become trapped as they enter the cylinder.

17 Fit the new primary piston assembly as described above.

18 With both piston assemblies in position, refit the guide ring to the end of the cylinder bore.

19 Fit the smaller O-ring to the groove on the master cylinder body.

20 Fit the new vacuum seal to the new rear housing, making sure that its sealing lip is

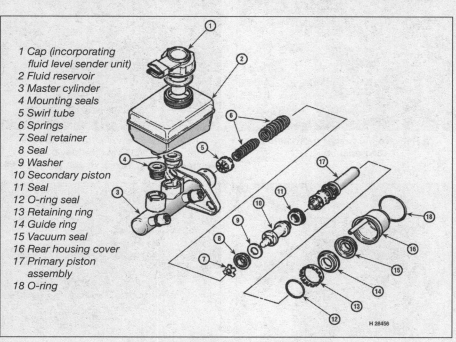

1 Cap (incorporating fluid level sender unit)
2 Fluid reservoir
3 Master cylinder
4 Mounting seals
5 Swirl tube
6 Springs
7 Seal retainer
8 Seal
9 Washer
10 Secondary piston
11 Seal
12 O-ring seal
13 Retaining ring
14 Guide ring
15 Vacuum seal
16 Rear housing cover
17 Primary piston assembly
18 O-ring

10.4 Exploded view of the master cylinder

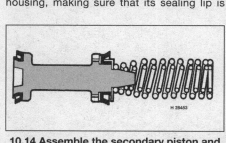
10.14 Assemble the secondary piston and associated components as shown, noting that the inner and outer seals are different

11.5a Slacken and remove the six retaining bolts (one hidden behind pedal) …

11.5b … then manoeuvre the pedal box assembly out through the engine compartment

correctly positioned (facing the towards the primary piston).

21 Fit the new retaining ring to the rear of the master cylinder body, so that its teeth are in contact with the cylinder body.

22 Carefully ease the rear housing assembly into position on the master cylinder, and press it fully into the cylinder body. Fit the larger O-ring to the outside of the housing.

Refitting

23 Inspect the master cylinder O-ring for signs of damage or deterioration and, if necessary, renew it.

24 Remove all traces of dirt from the master cylinder and servo unit mating surfaces, then fit the master cylinder, ensuring that the servo unit pushrod enters the master cylinder bore

centrally. Refit the master cylinder washers and mounting nuts, and tighten them to the specified torque.

25 Wipe clean the brake pipe unions, then refit them to the master cylinder ports and tighten them to the specified torque setting.

26 Refill the master cylinder reservoir with new fluid, and bleed the complete hydraulic system as described in Section.

11 Brake pedal – removal and refitting

Removal

1 Disconnect the battery negative terminal, as described in Chapter 5.

2 Slacken and remove the retaining nuts and washers securing the master cylinder to the servo unit (see illustration 10.3). Disengage the master cylinder from the servo, and position it clear, taking great care not to place any excess strain on the brake pipes. Recover the O-ring from the rear of the master cylinder.

3 Remove the brake pedal switches, as described in Section 18.

4 From within the vehicle, undo the retaining screws and remove the trim panel from around the pedals, to reveal the pedal box retaining bolts.

5 Unscrew the six retaining bolts, then return to the engine compartment and lift out the pedal box assembly. Recover the rubber seal fitted between the box and bulkhead (see illustrations).

6 With the assembly on the bench, carefully unhook the return springs from the base of the brake pedal (see illustration).

7 Prise out the rubber sealing grommets, then remove the split-pin and washer, and withdraw the clevis pin securing the pedal to the servo unit pushrod (see illustrations).

8 Using a hammer and punch, tap out the roll-pin securing the pedal pivot shaft in position, then slide out the shaft and remove the pedal (see illustrations).

9 Inspect the pedal pivot bushes and shaft for signs of wear, and renew if necessary (see illustration).

Refitting

10 Press the pivot bushes into the pedal bore.

11.6 Unhook the pedal return springs using a pair of pliers

11.7a Remove the rubber grommets from the pedal box …

11.7b … then remove the split-pin and washer, and withdraw the clevis pin and washer securing the servo unit to the pedal

11.8a Tap out the roll-pin …

11.8b … then withdraw the pivot shaft and remove the pedal from its mounting box

11.9 Inspect the pedal pivot bushes for signs of wear or damage, and renew if necessary

11 Apply a smear of multi-purpose grease to the bushes, and fit the return springs to the pedal mounting box **(see illustration)**.

12 Manoeuvre the pedal assembly into position, ensuring that it is correctly engaged with the servo pushrod, and insert the pivot shaft. Secure the pivot shaft in position with the roll-pin.

13 Align the pedal hole with the pushrod end, and insert the clevis pin. Refit the washer, and secure the pin in position with a new split-pin **(see illustration)**. Refit the sealing grommets to the box.

14 Refit the seal to the bulkhead, then manoeuvre the pedal box assembly into position.

15 Refit the pedal box retaining bolts, tighten them securely, then refit the pedal trim panel.

16 Return to the engine compartment, and reconnect the wiring connectors to the stop-light switch.

17 Ensure that the seal is in position, and refit the master cylinder to the servo unit. Fit the washers and retaining nuts, tightening them to the specified torque.

18 Reconnect the battery, and check the operation of the brake pedal and stop-light switch.

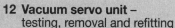

12 Vacuum servo unit –
testing, removal and refitting

Testing

1 To test the operation of the servo unit, with the engine switched off, depress the footbrake several times to exhaust the vacuum. Keeping the pedal depressed, start the engine. As the engine starts, there should be a noticeable 'give' in the brake pedal as the vacuum builds-up. Allow the engine to run for at least two minutes, then switch it off. If the brake pedal is now depressed it should feel normal, but further applications should result in the pedal feeling firmer, with the pedal stroke decreasing with each application.

2 If the servo does not operate as described, first inspect the servo unit check valve as described in Section 13.

3 If the servo unit still fails to operate satisfactorily, the fault lies within the unit itself. On early models, it is possible to overhaul the unit but this is a task which should be entrusted to a Land Rover dealer. On later models, repairs to the unit are not possible, and if faulty the servo unit must be renewed.

Removal

4 Disconnect the battery negative terminal, as described in Chapter 5.

5 Slacken and remove the retaining nuts and washers securing the master cylinder to the servo unit **(see illustration 10.3)**. Disengage the master cylinder from the servo, and position it clear, taking great care not to place any excess strain on the brake pipes. Recover the O-ring from the rear of the master cylinder.

11.11 Prior to refitting, ensure that the return springs are correctly engaged with the holes in the mounting box

6 Carefully prise the end of the vacuum hose from the rubber grommet in the servo unit **(see illustration)**.

7 Prise out the rubber sealing grommets from the brake pedal mounting box.

8 Working through the mounting box aperture, remove the split-pin and washer, and withdraw the clevis pin securing the pedal to the servo unit pushrod, with reference to Section 11.

9 Slacken and remove the four nuts and washers securing the servo unit to the pedal mounting bracket, and lift the servo unit out of position.

10 Recover the rubber seal which is fitted between the servo unit and bracket. Examine the seal for signs of damage or deterioration, and renew if necessary.

Refitting

11 Apply a smear of grease to the pushrod fork, fit the rubber seal to the rear of the servo unit, and manoeuvre the assembly into position.

12 Ensure that the servo unit pushrod is correctly engaged with the brake pedal, then refit the washers and mounting nuts, and tighten them to the specified torque setting.

13 Align the pedal hole with the pushrod end, and insert the clevis pin. Refit the washer, and secure the pin in position with a new split-pin. Refit the sealing grommets to the box.

14 Reconnect the vacuum hose to the servo unit check valve.

12.6 Release the vacuum hose from the servo unit

11.13 Align the servo unit pushrod with the pedal, then refit the clevis pin and washers, and secure in position with a new split-pin

15 Ensure that the seal is in position, then refit the master cylinder, tightening its retaining nuts to the specified torque.

13 Vacuum servo unit check valve – removal, testing and refitting

Removal

Note: *The vacuum servo check valve is part of the molded plastic vacuum hose and cannot be replaced separately.*

1 The check valve is located in the vacuum hose between the servo unit and the vacuum pump **(see illustration)**.

2 Withdraw one end of the vacuum hose from the servo unit **(see illustration 12.6)**, then follow the vacuum hose and disconnect the other end from the vacuum pump. **Note:** *On 2.2 litre engines the vacuum pump is bolted to the rear of the cylinder head driven by the camshaft. On 2.4 litre engines, the vacuum pump is bolted to the coolant pump on the left-hand side front of the engine driven by the auxiliary belt.*

Testing

3 Examine the check valve for signs of damage, and renew if necessary. The valve may be tested by blowing through it in both directions. Air should flow through the valve in one direction only – when blown through

13.1 Check valve in vacuum hose – 2.2 litre engine shown

from the servo unit end of the valve. Renew the valve if this is not the case.

4 Examine the rubber sealing grommet in the servo unit and molded plastic vacuum hose for signs of damage or deterioration, and renew as necessary.

Refitting

5 Fit the sealing grommet into position in the servo unit, if removed.

6 Reconnect the vacuum hose to the servo unit and vacuum pump, where necessary, securely tighten its retaining nut/clip.

7 On completion, start the engine, and check the connections for signs of air leaks.

14 Handbrake shoes – renewal

1 Chock the front wheels, then jack up the rear of the vehicle and support on axle stands.

2 Working as described in Chapter 8, disconnect the propeller shaft from the rear of the transfer box, and position the shaft clear of the handbrake assembly.

3 Apply the handbrake, then slacken and remove the handbrake drum retaining screw(s) **(see illustration)**.

4 Release the handbrake, and remove the brake drum from the rear of the transfer box. It may be difficult to remove the drum, due to the brake shoes binding on the inner circumference of the drum. If the brake shoes are binding, first check that the handbrake is fully released then, referring to Chapter 1 for further information, fully slacken

the handbrake cable adjuster nut to obtain maximum freeplay in the cable, and rotate the adjuster bolt anti-clockwise so that the shoes are retracted clear of the drum. The brake drum should then slide easily off the transfer box.

5 With the drum removed, inspect the shoes for signs of wear or damage. If the friction material of either shoe has worn down to, or close to, the rivets, the shoes must be renewed. The shoes should also be renewed if any are fouled with oil; there is no satisfactory way of degreasing friction material, once contaminated. If there are traces of oil on the shoes, the transfer box output shaft seal should be renewed before new handbrake shoes are fitted (see Chapter 7B). Proceed as described under the relevant sub-heading.

6 Note the correct fitted locations of all components then, using a suitable pair of pliers, unhook the return springs and remove them from the brake shoes **(see illustration)**.

7 Using a pair of pliers, remove the left-hand shoe retainer spring cup by depressing and turning it through 90º. With the cup removed, lift off the spring and withdraw the retainer pin from the rear of the backplate.

8 Remove the left-hand shoe, and recover the strut which is fitted between the shoe upper ends, noting which way around it is fitted.

9 Remove the right-hand shoe spring cup, spring and retainer pin as described in paragraph 16, then detach the shoe from the handbrake cable and remove it from the vehicle.

10 If the new handbrake shoes are supplied without the operating lever already fitted to

14.3 Removing the handbrake drum retaining screw

the right-hand shoe, it will be necessary to transfer the old one over from the original shoe. Remove the spring clip, then withdraw the pivot pin and recover the spring washers, noting their correct fitted positions. Inspect the pivot pin and spring clip for signs of wear or damage, and renew if necessary. Apply a smear of high melting-point grease to the pin, then fit the operating lever to the new shoe, and insert the pin and spring washers, securing them in position with the spring clip.

11 Whilst the shoes are removed, rotate the adjuster bolt, and check that both the adjuster plungers are free to move easily. If necessary, withdraw both the plungers from the adjuster, and unscrew the adjuster bolt and tapered nut. Remove all traces of corrosion from them, and apply a smear of high-temperature grease to both the plungers and adjuster bolt threads. Screw the adjuster bolt and tapered nut into position, and refit the plungers. If this does not cure the problem, renew the adjuster assembly components.

12 With the adjuster assembly operating correctly, apply a smear of high melting-point grease to the contact areas of the new shoes and backplate. Take care to ensure that the grease does not contaminate the friction material.

13 Engage the right-hand shoe with the handbrake cable, and locate the shoe on the backplate. Install the shoe retainer pin and spring, and secure it in position with the spring cup.

14 Refit the strut to the upper end of the right-hand shoe, making sure that it is the correct way up.

15 Hook the lower return spring onto the right-hand shoe, then engage the left-hand shoe with the return spring. Locate the left-hand shoe on the backplate, engaging it with the adjuster plunger slot and strut, and secure it in position with its retainer pin, spring and spring cup.

16 Check that all components are correctly positioned, then refit the upper return spring.

17 Refit the brake drum to the transfer box, tightening its retaining screws securely.

18 Adjust the handbrake as described in Chapter then, if all is well, reconnect the propeller shaft to the transfer box as described in Chapter.

1 Pin
2 Washer
3 'C' clip
4 Brake shoe
5 Cable lever
6 Hold down spring
7 Dished washer
8 Brake drum
9 Screw
10 Brake cable
11 Adjuster slide
12 Adjuster nut
13 Spring
14 Adjuster slide
15 Adjuster bolt
16 Dished washer
17 Hold down spring
18 Brake shoe
19 Hold down pin
20 Hold down pin
21 Abutment plate
22 Back plate
23 Spring

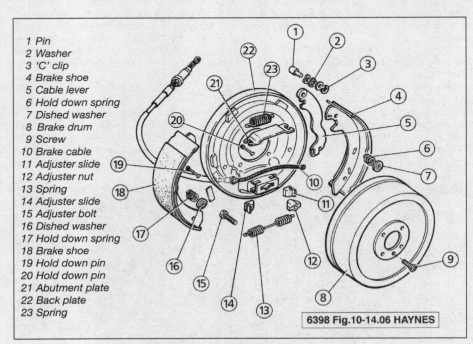

6398 Fig.10-14.06 HAYNES

14.6 Handbrake shoe and drum components

15 Handbrake lever – removal and refitting

Removal

1 Remove the three fasteners securing the handbrake lever gaiter in position, and slide the gaiter off the lever **(see illustration)**.
2 Disconnect the wiring connector from the warning light switch **(see illustration)**.
3 Remove the split-pin and washer **(see illustration)**, and withdraw the clevis pin securing the handbrake cable to the lever.
4 Slacken and remove the handbrake lever retaining bolts, and then as the lever assembly is removed from the floor panel, pass the wiring and cable through the mounting bracket **(see illustration)**.

Refitting

5 Refit the handbrake lever, making sure that it is correctly engaged with the cable. Refit the retaining bolts, and tighten to the specified torque.
6 Apply a smear of multi-purpose grease to the clevis pin, then align the cable with the lever, and insert the pin. Refit the washer, and secure the pin in position with a new split-pin.
7 Re-connect the wiring connector to the handbrake light switch.
8 Refit the gaiter over the lever, and secure it in position with its fasteners.
9 Adjust the handbrake cable as described in Chapter 1.

16 Handbrake cable – removal and refitting

Removal

1 Chock the front wheels, then jack up the rear of the vehicle and support on axle stands.
2 Remove the handbrake lever, as described in Section 15.
3 From underneath the vehicle, free the cable from the handbrake lever mounting plate, then work back along the cable, freeing it from any relevant retaining clips and ties whilst noting its correct routing.
4 Referring to Section 14, remove the upper and lower return springs, then remove the spring cup, spring and retainer pin, and remove the right-hand handbrake shoe. Note that the left-hand shoe and strut can be left in position on the backplate.
5 Free the handbrake cable from the rear of the backplate, and withdraw it from underneath the vehicle.

Refitting

6 Apply a smear of high melting-point grease to the cable lower end fitting, then insert the cable through the rear of the backplate.

15.1 Remove the gaiter from the handbrake lever

15.2 Disconnect the wiring connector

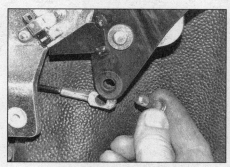

15.3 Remove the clevis pin

15.4 Withdraw the cable and wiring through bracket

7 Refit the right-hand brake shoe as described in Section 14, and refit the brake drum.
8 Work along the cable, routing it correctly and securing it in position with all the relevant clips and ties. Feed it up through the handbrake lever mounting plate, and secure it in position.
9 From inside the vehicle, apply a smear of grease to the clevis pin, then align the cable with the lever, and insert the pin. Refit the washer, and secure the pin in position with a new split-pin.
10 Re-connect the wiring connector to the handbrake warning light switch.
11 Refit the gaiter over the lever, and secure it in position with its fasteners.
12 Adjust the handbrake cable as described in Chapter 1.

17 Rear brake pressure-regulating valve – testing, removal and refitting

Testing

1 On most models (except models fitted with ABS), a pressure-regulating valve is incorporated in the hydraulic braking circuit, to regulate the pressure applied to the rear brakes, and reduce the risk of the rear wheels locking under heavy braking. The valve is situated on either the left- or right-hand side of the engine compartment, mounted onto the wing valance.
2 Depending on specification, the valve may

incorporate a switch, connected to a warning light in the instrument panel. This warning light should illuminate temporarily as the starter is actuated, and then go out. If the light illuminates at any time when the vehicle is being used, a fault in the valve/braking system is present. The vehicle should be taken immediately to a Land Rover dealer.
3 Specialist equipment is required to check the performance of the valve, and therefore if the valve is thought to be faulty, the vehicle should be taken to a suitably-equipped Land Rover dealer for testing. Repairs are not possible and, if faulty, the valve must be renewed.

Removal

Note: *Before starting work, refer to the note at the beginning of Section 2 concerning the dangers of hydraulic fluid.*

4 Disconnect the sender unit wiring connector, and unscrew the master cylinder reservoir filler cap. Place a piece of polythene over the filler neck, and securely refit the cap (taking care not to damage the sender unit). This will minimise brake fluid loss during subsequent operations. As an added precaution, place absorbent rags beneath the pressure-regulating valve brake pipe unions.
5 Wipe clean the area around the brake pipe unions on the pressure-regulating valve, then make a note of how the pipes are arranged, to use as a reference on refitting. Unscrew the union nuts, and carefully withdraw the pipes. Wash off any spilt fluid immediately with cold water.

HAYNES HiNT *Plug or tape over the pipe ends and valve orifices, to minimise the loss of brake fluid and to prevent the entry of dirt into the system.*

6 Slacken the retaining bolt(s), and remove the valve from the engine compartment. Note that on some models, there is a spacer fitted behind the valve – take care not to lose this as the retaining bolt is withdrawn.

Refitting

7 Refit the pressure-regulating valve, positioning the spacer (where fitted) between the valve and body, and securely tighten its mounting bolt.

8 Wipe the brake pipe unions clean and refit them to the valve, using the notes made prior to removal to ensure that they are correctly positioned. Tighten the union nuts to the specified torque.

9 Remove the polythene from the master cylinder reservoir filler neck, and bleed the complete hydraulic system as described in Section.

18 Brake pedal switches – general information, removal and refitting

General information

1 There are two switches fitted on a bracket above the brake pedal, the one on the left is the brake diagnostic switch, and the one on the right is the stop-light switch **(see illustration)**. The switches are plunger type switches, and they supply information to the ECM, as to the position of the brake pedal. The ECM compares the information from both switches, to ensure that the correct pedal position is determined.

● Brake diagnostic switch (left) – when the brake pedal is not being operated the contacts are closed connecting an earth to the ECM, when the brake pedal is operated the contacts are open and disconnect the earth to the ECM.

● Brake stop-light switch (right) – when the brake pedal is not being operated the contacts are open, when the brake pedal is operated the contacts are closed and connects a positive feed from the central junction box (CJB) to the ECM.

2 In the event of a switch failure, the engine will idle at a higher rpm when the brake pedal is not operated and the vehicle will go into a restricted limp-home mode.

Removal

3 Unclip the plastic cover from over the brake pedal switches **(see illustration)**.

4 Disconnect the wiring connector(s) from the brake pedal switches **(see illustrations)**.

5 Turn the brake diagnostic switch anti-clockwise to remove it from the mounting bracket, and turn the brake stop-light switch clockwise to remove it from the mounting bracket **(see illustrations)**.

Refitting

6 Refitting is a reversal of removal, making sure that the brake pedal is in the rest position (DO NOT press the brake pedal downwards when fitting the switches).

● Brake diagnostic switch (left) – turn the switch clockwise to lock it into position in the mounting bracket, and then refit the wiring connector.

● Brake stop-light switch (right) – turn the switch anti-clockwise to lock it into position in the mounting bracket, and then refit the wiring connector.

7 When completed, refit the plastic cover over the pedal switches.

19 Vacuum pump – removal and refitting

Note: *On 2.2 litre engines the vacuum pump is bolted to the rear of the cylinder head driven by the camshaft. On 2.4 litre engines, the vacuum pump is bolted to the coolant pump on the left-hand side front of the engine driven by the auxiliary belt.*

1 Disconnect the battery negative terminal (refer to Chapter 5 Section 4).

2.2 litre engines

Removal

2 Disconnect the quick-release fitting and

18.1 Brake pedal switches

18.3 Remove the plastic cover

18.4a Disconnect wiring from brake diagnostic switch...

18.4b ...and brake stop-light switch

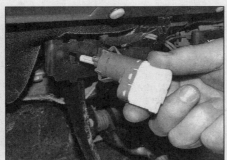

18.5a Remove the diagnostic switch...

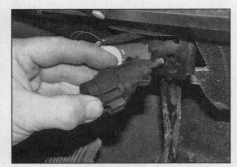

18.5b ...and the stop-light switch

19.2 Disconnect the vacuum hose

19.10 Undo the vacuum hose union

detach the vacuum hose from the side of the vacuum pump **(see illustration)**.

3 Unscrew the two mounting bolts, withdraw the vacuum pump from the end of the cylinder head and recover the seal. Note that a new seal will be required for refitting.

4 Thoroughly clean the mating surfaces of the vacuum pump and cylinder head.

Refitting

5 Locate a new seal on the vacuum pump. Refit the pump to the cylinder head, making sure that the drive dog engages correctly with the end of the camshaft. Insert the mounting bolts and tighten them to the specified torque.

6 Reconnect the vacuum hose to the vacuum pump.

7 On completion, reconnect the battery negative terminal.

2.4 litre engines

Removal

8 Remove the auxiliary drivebelt as described in Chapter 1 Section 52.

9 Move the wiring harness to one side for access to the vacuum pump..

10 Unscrew the union nut and disconnect the vacuum hose from the vacuum pump **(see illustration)**.

11 Unscrew the three mounting bolts, withdraw the vacuum pump from the top of the coolant pump and recover the gasket **(see illustrations)**. Note that a new gasket will be required for refitting.

Refitting

12 Locate a new gasket on the coolant pump, then refit the vacuum pump to the coolant pump. Insert the mounting bolts and tighten them to the specified torque.

13 Refit the vacuum hose to the vacuum pump and tighten the union nut securely.

14 Reposition the wiring harness, then refit the auxiliary drivebelt as described in Chapter 1 Section 52.

15 On completion, reconnect the battery negative terminal.

20 Anti-lock braking and stability control – general information

1 ABS is available on all models, the system comprises a hydraulic block (modulator) which contains the hydraulic solenoid valves and the electrically-driven return pump, the four roadwheel sensors (one fitted to each wheel), and the electronic control unit (ECU). The purpose of the system is to prevent the wheel(s) locking during heavy braking. This is achieved by automatic release of the brake on the relevant wheel, followed by re-application of the brake.

2 The solenoids are controlled by the ECU, which itself receives signals from the four wheel sensors (one fitted on each hub), which monitor the speed of rotation of each wheel. By comparing these signals, the ECU can determine the speed at which the vehicle is travelling. It can then use this speed to determine when a wheel is decelerating at an abnormal rate, compared to the speed of the vehicle, and therefore predicts when a wheel is about to lock. During normal operation, the system functions in the same way as a non-ABS braking system.

3 If the ECU senses that a wheel is about to lock, it operates the relevant solenoid valve in the hydraulic unit, which then isolates the brake caliper on the wheel which is about to lock from the master cylinder, effectively sealing-in the hydraulic pressure.

4 If the speed of rotation of the wheel continues to decrease at an abnormal rate, the ECU switches on the electrically-driven return pump operates, and pumps the hydraulic fluid back into the master cylinder, releasing pressure on the brake caliper so that the brake is released. Once the speed of rotation of the wheel returns to an acceptable rate, the pump stops; the solenoid valve opens, allowing the hydraulic master cylinder pressure to return to the caliper, which then re-applies the brake. This cycle can be carried out at up to 10 times a second.

5 The action of the solenoid valves and return pump creates pulses in the hydraulic circuit. When the ABS system is functioning, these pulses can be felt through the brake pedal.

6 The operation of the ABS system is entirely dependent on electrical signals. To prevent the system responding to any inaccurate signals, a built-in safety circuit monitors all signals received by the ECU. If an inaccurate signal or low battery voltage is detected, the ABS system is automatically shut down, and the warning light on the instrument panel is illuminated, to inform the driver that the ABS system is not operational. Normal braking should still be available, however.

7 There is a yaw rate/longitudinal acceleration sensor fitted on models with ABS. **Note:** *The Yaw rate information is not used by the ABS module, but the longitudinal acceleration part of the sensor provides the ABS module with information.*

8 If a fault does develop in the ABS system, the vehicle must be taken to a Land Rover dealer or specialist for fault diagnosis and repair.

19.11a Unscrew the vacuum pump mounting bolts (arrowed)...

19.11b ...withdraw the vacuum pump from the top of the coolant pump...

19.11c ...and recover the gasket

21.2 Disconnect the two pipes on the side of the hydraulic unit

21.3 Disconnect the four pipes on the top of the hydraulic unit

21.4 Disconnect the wiring harness plug from the ECU on the side of the hydraulic unit

21 Anti-lock braking and stability control components – removal and refitting

Note: *Faults on the ABS system can only be diagnosed using Land Rover diagnostic equipment or compatible alternative equipment.*
Note: *Before starting work, refer to the note at the beginning of Section 2 concerning the dangers of hydraulic fluid.*

Hydraulic unit and ECU

Removal

1 Disconnect the battery negative terminal (refer to Chapter 5 Section 4).
2 Remove the master cylinder reservoir cap, and syphon the hydraulic fluid from the reservoir, then slacken the pipe unions and remove the two brake pipes from the master cylinder to the right-hand side of the hydraulic unit **(see illustration)**. Note and record the fitted position of the brake pipes. As a precaution, place absorbent rags beneath the brake pipe unions when unscrewing them.

Suitably plug or cap the disconnected unions to prevent dirt entry and fluid loss.
Caution: Do not syphon the fluid by mouth, as it is poisonous. Use a syringe or an old hydrometer.
3 Note and record the fitted position of the brake pipes on the top of the hydraulic unit, then unscrew the union nuts and release the pipes **(see illustration)**. As a precaution, place absorbent rags beneath the brake pipe unions when unscrewing them. Suitably plug or cap the disconnected unions to prevent dirt entry and fluid loss.
4 Pull out the locking bar and disconnect the wiring harness plug from the ECU on the side of the hydraulic unit **(see illustration)**.
5 Release the wiring harness from the clip on the side of the hydraulic unit mounting bracket.
6 Undo the two bolts securing the hydraulic unit to the bracket on the side of the brake servo mounting bracket, then manipulate the hydraulic unit out from its location in the engine compartment.

Refitting

7 Refitting is the reverse of the removal procedure, noting the following points:

a) Refit the brake pipes to their respective locations, and tighten the union nuts securely.
b) Ensure that the wiring is correctly routed, and that the ECU wiring harness plug is firmly pressed into position and locked.
c) On completion, bleed the complete hydraulic system as described in Section 2.

Front wheel speed sensors

Removal

8 Firmly apply the handbrake, then jack up the front of the vehicle and support it securely on axle stands (see Chapter 14 Section 5). Remove the roadwheel. **Note:** *Access to the sensor an be made with the wheel still fitted, if required.*
9 Open the bonnet and disconnect the ABS sensor wiring connector(s) on the inner wing panel **(see illustrations)**.
10 Working back along the sensor wiring, release it from the suspension strut and from the support bracket and clips under the wheel arch.
11 Carefully prise the sensor from the top

21.9a Sensor wiring connector – front left-hand side

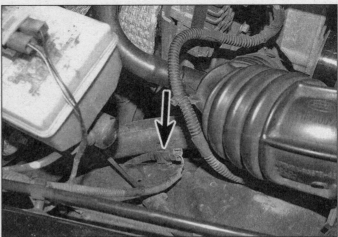

21.9b Sensor wiring connector – front right-hand side

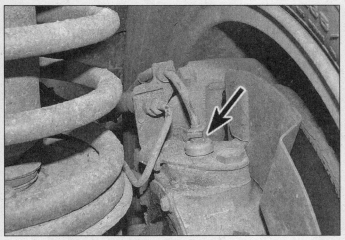

21.11 Front wheel speed sensor

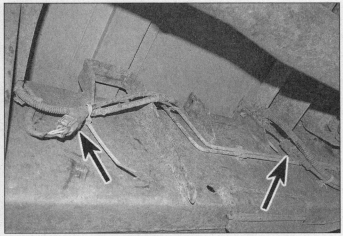

21.14 Sensor wiring connections along the inside of the chassis

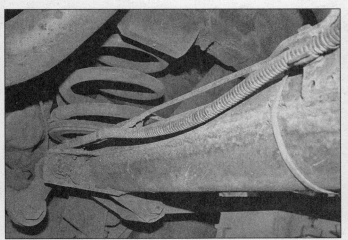

21.15 Unclip the wiring from along the rear axle

21.16 Rear wheel sensor

of the hub assembly, and remove it **(see illustration).**

Refitting

12 Refitting is the reverse of the removal procedure. Apply a small amount of anti-seize grease around the side of the sensor, before fitting.

Rear wheel speed sensors

Removal

13 Chock the front wheels then jack up the rear of the vehicle and securely support it on axle stands (see Chapter 14 Section 5).
14 Working under the rear of the vehicle,

disconnect the ABS sensor wiring connector(s) on the inside of the chassis frame **(see illustration).**
15 Working back along the sensor wiring, release it from the chassis and support brackets/clips along the rear axle **(see illustration).**
16 Carefully prise the sensor from the rear of the hub assembly, and remove it **(see illustration).**

Refitting

17 Refitting is the reverse of the removal procedure. Apply a small amount of anti-seize grease around the side of the sensor, before fitting.

Yaw rate/longitudinal acceleration sensor

Removal

18 Remove the left-hand front speaker from under the facia panel.
19 Reaching inside the aperture, disconnect the wiring connector from the sensor, which is bolted to the crossmember behind the facia panel.
20 Undo the two retaining bolts and remove the sensor.

Refitting

21 Refitting is the reverse of the removal procedure.

Notes

Chapter 11
Suspension and steering

Contents

Degrees of difficulty

Easy, suitable for novice with little experience	Fairly easy, suitable for beginner with some experience	Fairly difficult, suitable for competent DIY mechanic	Difficult, suitable for experienced DIY mechanic	Very difficult, suitable for expert DIY or professional

Specifications

Front suspension
Type . . . . Axle with coil springs and shock absorbers. Axle movement controlled by radius arms and Panhard rod, with an anti-roll bar fitted to some models

Rear suspension
Type . . . . Axle with coil springs and shock absorbers. Axle movement controlled by upper and lower links, with an anti-roll bar being fitted on some models

Steering
Type . . . . Steering box (power-assisted on some models) with drag link and track rod arrangement. Steering damper fitted to drag link

Front wheel alignment and steering angles
Note: *All measurements should be taken with the vehicle unladen, with approximately five gallons of fuel in the tank.*

Camber angle (front & rear) . . . . -10' ± 45'
Castor angle. . . . . 3° 15' ± 45'
Swivel pin inclination (with vehicle on level ground and at EEC
  kerb weight) . . . . 7°
Toe setting:
  Front wheel alignment . . . . -10' ± 10' toe-out
  Rear wheel alignment. . . . . +5' ± 15' toe-in

Roadwheels

Type . . . . Pressed-steel or alloy
Sizes:
    Steel (UK & Western Europe) . . . . 6F x 16
    Steel (other markets – except Japan) . . . . 5.5F x 16
    Steel (Japan) . . . . 6.5J x 16
    Alloy . . . . 7J x 16

Tyres

Size:
    90 models. . . . . 205/80 R 16, 265/75 R 16 or 7.50 R16 (depending on model)
    110 models (except Japan) 7.50 R16
    110 models (Japan) 7.50 R16C
    130 models. 7.50R16
Pressures . . . . See *Weekly checks*

Torque wrench settings	Nm	lbf ft
Front suspension		
Anti-roll bar:		
Connecting link balljoint nuts	40	30
Mounting clamp bolts	30	22
Pivot bolt nuts	68	50
Panhard rod	230	170
Radius arm:		
Pivot bolts	197	145
Retaining nut	176	130
Rear suspension		
Anti-roll bar:		
Connecting link balljoint nuts	40	30
Mounting clamp bolts	24	18
Pivot bolt nuts	68	50
Lower link:		
Front nut	176	130
Pivot bolt	176	130
Shock absorber:		
Mounting bracket nuts and bolts	64	47
Upper mounting nut	82	61
Lower mounting nut	75	55
Upper link:		
Mounting bracket bolts	47	35
Balljoint bracket bolts	176	130
Pivot bolt	176	130
Upper link balljoint nut	176	130
Steering		
Drag link:		
Balljoint/end fitting nuts	40	30
Clamp bolts	14	10
Drop arm retaining nut	176	130
Power steering pump:		
Feed pipe union nut	25	18
Mounting bolts	23	17
Steering box:		
Mounting bolts	81	60
Tie-bar bolts/nuts	81	60
Steering pipe union nuts:		
14 mm thread	15	11
16 mm thread	20	15
Steering wheel nut	43	32
Track rod:		
Balljoint nuts	40	30
Clamp bolts	14	10
Universal joint clamp bolts	25	18
Roadwheels		
Roadwheel nuts:		
Steel wheels	108	80
Alloy wheels	130	96
Heavy duty wheel	170	125

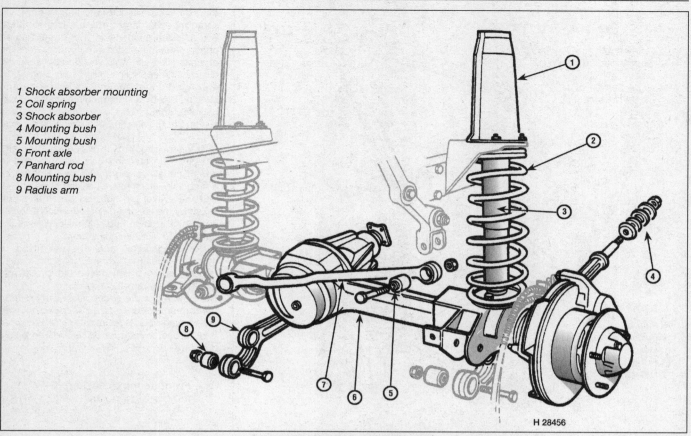

1 Shock absorber mounting
2 Coil spring
3 Shock absorber
4 Mounting bush
5 Mounting bush
6 Front axle
7 Panhard rod
8 Mounting bush
9 Radius arm

H 28456

1.2a Front suspension components

1   General Information

1 The front and rear suspension are of live beam axle type, with coil springs and shock absorbers.

2 On the front suspension, axle movement is controlled by two radius arms and a Panhard rod. On some models, an anti-roll bar is also fitted. The anti roll bar is rubber-mounted onto the vehicle body, and is connected to the axle at each end by a balljointed connecting link **(see illustrations)**.

3 On the rear suspension, axle movement is controlled by the upper and lower links. The upper link is connected to the top of

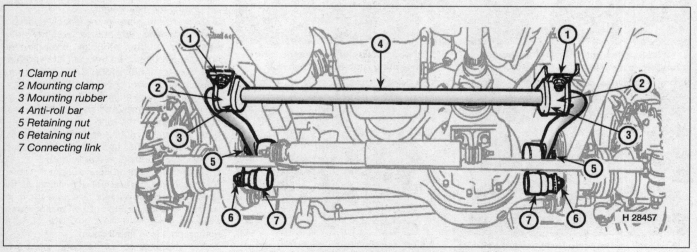

1 Clamp nut
2 Mounting clamp
3 Mounting rubber
4 Anti-roll bar
5 Retaining nut
6 Retaining nut
7 Connecting link

H 28457

1.2b Front suspension anti-roll bar components

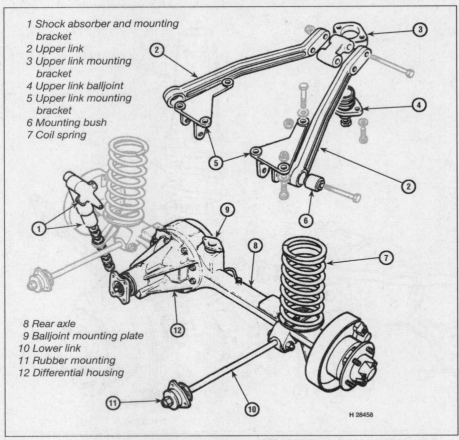

1 Shock absorber and mounting bracket
2 Upper link
3 Upper link mounting bracket
4 Upper link balljoint
5 Upper link mounting bracket
6 Mounting bush
7 Coil spring

8 Rear axle
9 Balljoint mounting plate
10 Lower link
11 Rubber mounting
12 Differential housing

H 28458

1.3 Rear suspension components

the axle via a balljoint (see illustration). On some models, an anti-roll bar is also fitted. Self-levelling suspension was offered as an option on some models. The system consists of a gas-filled unit which is fitted between the chassis and upper link balljoint bracket.
4 The steering column is linked to the steering box by an intermediate shaft and two universal joints. The lower universal joint is secured to the steering box pinion by a clamp bolt.
5 The steering box is mounted onto the chassis. The steering box is connected to one of the swivel pin housing assemblies by a drag link, which has a balljoint at each end, and the swivel pin housing assemblies are linked by means of a track rod which also has a balljoint at each end. All balljoint ends are threaded to facilitate adjustment.
6 Power-assisted steering was fitted to some models. The hydraulic steering system is powered by a belt-driven pump which is driven off the crankshaft pulley.
Note: *Many of the suspension and steering components are secured in position with self-locking nuts. Whenever a self-locking nut is disturbed, it must be discarded and a new nut fitted.*

2 Front shock absorber – removal, testing and refitting

Note: *New shock absorber mounting nuts will be required on refitting (see Note in Section 1).*

Removal

1 Apply the handbrake, then jack up the front of the vehicle and support it on axle stands positioned underneath the chassis. Remove both front roadwheels.
2 Position a hydraulic jack beneath the front axle assembly, then raise the jack until it is supporting the axle weight.
3 Slacken and remove the shock absorber lower mounting nut, and recover the outer washer and rubber mounting arrangement, noting each component's correct fitted position (see illustrations). **Note:** *The washers are different, and must not be interchanged.*
4 From within the engine compartment, undo the retaining screws and remove the access cover from inside the wing.
5 Undo the four nuts and washers securing the shock absorber upper mounting bracket to the vehicle body (see illustration).
6 Lift the shock absorber and upper mounting assembly upwards and out of position. As the shock absorber is removed, recover the inner washer and mounting rubber arrangement from its lower end – refer to the Note in paragraph 3 (see illustration).
7 With the assembly on a bench, unscrew the upper mounting nut, and lift off the outer washer and mounting rubber arrangement

2.3a Slacken and remove the shock absorber lower mounting nut (arrowed) ...

2.3b ... and slide off the washer and mounting rubber arrangement

2.5 Slacken and remove the four shock absorber mounting nuts and washers

2.6 Lift out the shock absorber, and recover the second washer and mounting rubber arrangement from the its lower end

2.7 Shock absorber upper mounting nut

– refer to the Note in paragraph 3 **(see illustration)**.

8 Separate the shock absorber and mounting, and recover the inner washer and mounting rubber arrangement from the upper end of the shock absorber – refer to the Note in paragraph 3.

Testing

9 Examine the shock absorber for signs of fluid leakage or damage. Test the operation of the strut, while holding it in an upright position, by moving the piston through a full stroke, and then through short strokes of 50 to 100 mm. In both cases, the resistance felt should be smooth and continuous. If the resistance is jerky, or uneven, or if there is any visible sign of wear or damage to the strut, renewal is necessary. Renew the complete unit if any damage or excessive wear is evident.

10 Inspect the mounting rubber for signs of damage or deterioration, and renew if necessary.

Refitting

11 Refitting is a reversal of the removal procedure, noting the following points:

a) Ensure that all washer and rubber mounting arrangement components are positioned correctly. The flat (seating) washer should be fitted so that its flat face abuts the upper mounting bracket/axle (as applicable), and the slightly-cupped washer should be fitted with its concave side towards the rubber mounting **(see illustration)**.

b) Fit new shock absorber mounting nuts, and tighten them to the securely.

3 Front coil spring – removal and refitting

Note: A suitable tool to hold the coil spring in compression must be obtained. Adjustable coil spring compressors are readily available, and are essential for this operation.

Removal

1 Remove the relevant shock absorber assembly as described in Section 2. Note that it is not necessary to separate the shock

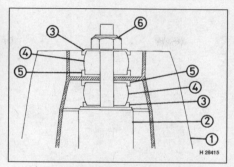

2.11 On refitting, ensure that the shock absorber mounting rubbers and washers are correctly positioned (upper mounting shown)

1 Shock absorber mounting
2 Shock absorber
3 Cupped washer
4 Mounting rubber
5 Flat (seating) washer
6 Mounting nut

absorber from the upper mounting bracket.

2 Fit the spring compressors to the coil spring, and compress the spring slightly to relieve the spring tension from its seats.

3 Carefully lower the axle, until it is possible to withdraw the coil spring. Whilst lowering the axle, keep a careful watch on the brake pipes and hoses, to ensure that no excess strain is being placed on them.

4 Remove the coil spring, noting which way around it is fitted, and recover the upper spring seat **(see illustrations)**.

5 Slacken and remove the retaining bolts and

3.4a Remove the front suspension coil spring …

3.5 Lower spring seat is secured to the axle by two bolts (arrowed)

washers, and remove the lower spring seat from the axle **(see illustration)**.

6 Inspect the spring closely for signs of damage, such as cracking, and check the spring seats for signs of wear or damage. Renew worn components as necessary.

Refitting

7 Refit the lower spring seat to the axle, and securely tighten its retaining bolt.

8 Fit the upper spring seat to the body, and secure it in position by temporarily fitting one of the strut nuts.

9 Install the coil spring, then carefully raise the axle into position, making sure that the upper spring seat studs remain correctly aligned with the body holes.

10 Refit the shock absorber as described in Section, then carefully remove the spring compressors.

4 Front suspension Panhard rod – removal, inspection and refitting

Note: New pivot bolt nuts will be required on refitting (see Note in Section 1).

Removal

1 To improve access, jack up the front of the vehicle and support it on axle stands positioned underneath the chassis.

2 Slacken and remove the nuts and pivot bolts securing the Panhard rod to the chassis and axle, and remove the rod from underneath the vehicle **(see illustration)**.

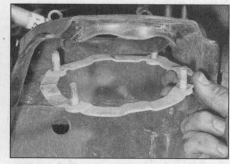

3.4b … and recover the upper spring seat

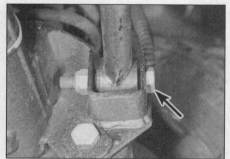

4.2 Panhard rod-to-axle pivot bolt (arrowed)

3 If necessary, slacken and remove the retaining nuts and bolts, and remove the Panhard rod mounting bracket from the chassis.

Inspection

4 Inspect the rod bar and mounting bracket for signs of damage, paying particular attention to the areas around the mounting bushes. Check the pivot bolt shanks for signs of wear, and renew if necessary.

5 Examine the Panhard rod mounting bushes for signs of wear and damage. If renewal is necessary, a hydraulic press and suitable spacers will be required, to press the bush out of position and install the new one. Press the old bush out, and install the new bush using a suitable tubular spacer which bears only on the hard outer edge of the bush, not the bush rubber.

Refitting

6 Where removed, refit the mounting bracket to the chassis, and insert its retaining bolts and nuts, tightening them to the specified torque setting.

7 Offer up the Panhard rod, and insert both pivot bolts. Fit the new nuts to the pivot bolts, tightening them loosely only.

8 Lower the vehicle to the ground. With the vehicle resting on its wheels, tighten both pivot bolt nuts to the specified torque setting.

<table>
<tr><td>**5**</td><td>**Front suspension radius arm** – removal, inspection and refitting</td></tr>
</table>

Note: *New radius arm upper and lower pivot bolt nuts will be required on refitting (see Note in Section 1).*

Removal

1 Apply the handbrake, then jack up the front of the vehicle and support it on axle stands positioned underneath the chassis. Remove the relevant front roadwheel.

2 Position a hydraulic jack beneath the front axle assembly, then raise the jack until it is supporting the axle weight.

3 Unscrew the nut securing the radius arm to the chassis, and remove the washer and outer mounting bush **(see illustrations)**.

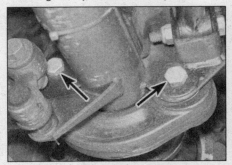

5.5 Unscrew the radius arm to axle bolts (arrowed) and remove the arm from underneath the vehicle

5.3a Slacken and remove the nut and washer securing the radius arm to the chassis …

4 Remove the split-pin, then slacken and remove the nut and washer securing the steering gear track rod balljoint to the swivel pin housing. Release the balljoint tapered shank using a universal balljoint separator.

5 Slacken and remove the nuts and bolts securing the radius arm to the axle, and remove the arm from underneath the vehicle **(see illustration)**.

6 With the arm removed, slide off the inner mounting bush and washer from its upper end.

Inspection

7 Inspect the arm for signs of damage, paying particular attention to the threaded end of the arm, and the areas around the mounting bushes. Check the pivot bolt shanks for signs of wear, and renew if necessary.

8 Inspect the upper mounting bushes for signs of damage or deterioration, and renew if necessary.

9 Examine the radius arm lower mounting bushes for signs of wear and damage. If renewal is necessary, a hydraulic press and suitable spacers will be required, to press the bush out of position and install the new one. Press the old bush out, and install the new bush using a suitable tubular spacer which bears only on the hard outer edge of the bush, not the bush rubber.

Refitting

10 Fitted the washer and inner mounting bush to the threaded end of the radius arm.

11 Manoeuvre the arm assembly into

6.5 Front anti-roll bar mounting clamp. Note which way the mounting rubber split is facing

5.3b … then slide off the outer mounting bush

position, and insert the pivot bolts. Fit the new nuts to the pivot bolts, tightening them loosely only at this stage.

12 Reconnect the track rod balljoint to the swivel pin housing assembly, tightening its retaining nut to the specified torque setting. Secure the nut in position with a new split-pin.

13 Slide the outer mounting bush and washer onto the threaded end of the arm, and fit the new retaining nut, tightening it to the specified torque setting.

14 Refit the wheel, then lower the vehicle to the ground and tighten the wheel nuts to the specified torque.

15 With the vehicle resting on its wheels, tighten both radius arm pivot bolt nuts to the specified torque setting.

<table>
<tr><td>**6**</td><td>**Front anti-roll bar** – removal and refitting</td></tr>
</table>

Note: *New anti-roll bar mounting clamp and connecting link nuts will be required on refitting (see Note in Section 1).*

Removal

1 Apply the handbrake, then jack up the front of the vehicle and support it on axle stands positioned underneath the chassis.

2 Position a hydraulic jack beneath the front axle assembly, then raise the jack until it is supporting the axle weight.

3 Prior to removal, mark the position of each mounting clamp rubber on the anti-roll bar.

4 Slacken and remove the nuts, and withdraw the bolts and washers securing each end of the anti-roll bar to the connecting links.

5 Unscrew the nuts and washers securing the mounting clamps to the vehicle body. Remove bolts and mounting clamps, and lower the anti-roll bar out from underneath the vehicle **(see illustration)**.

6 Remove the mounting rubbers from the anti-roll bar, and inspect them for signs of damage. Renew both rubbers if they are damaged or show signs of deterioration.

Refitting

7 Fit the mounting rubbers to the anti-roll bar, positioning them so that their splits will

7.4a Release the balljoint shank with a balljoint separator ...

7.4b ... and remove the connecting link from underneath the vehicle

7.7 Offer up the connecting link, and insert its pivot bolt and washer

be facing towards the axle once the bar is installed.

8 Align both rubbers with the marks made prior to removal, and manoeuvre the anti-roll bar into position.

9 Ensure that the flat side of each rubber is against the vehicle body, then refit the mounting clamps. Insert the bolts and fit the washers and new nuts, tightening them loosely only at this stage.

10 Align the anti-roll bar ends with the connecting links, and insert the pivot bolts and washers. Fit the new retaining nuts to the bolts, and tighten them loosely only.

11 Lower the vehicle to the ground. With the vehicle resting on its wheels, tighten the mounting clamp and pivot bolt nuts to the specified torque.

7 Front anti-roll bar connecting link – removal, inspection and refitting

Note: *New connecting link pivot bolt nuts will be required on refitting (see Note in Section 1).*

Removal

1 Apply the handbrake, then jack up the front of the vehicle and support it on axle stands positioned underneath the chassis. Remove the relevant front roadwheel.

2 Position a hydraulic jack beneath the front axle assembly, then raise the jack until it is supporting the axle weight.

3 Slacken and remove the nut, then withdraw the pivot bolt and washer securing the connecting link to the anti-roll bar.

4 Remove the split-pin, and undo the nut and washer securing the connecting link balljoint to the axle assembly. Release the balljoint tapered shank using a universal balljoint separator, and remove the connecting link from the vehicle **(see illustrations)**.

Inspection

5 Check that the link balljoint moves freely, without any sign of roughness. Also check that the balljoint gaiter shows no sign of deterioration, and is free from cracks and splits. If any sign of wear or damage is found, the complete link must be renewed.

6 Examine the upper mounting bushes for signs of wear and damage, and renew if necessary. A hydraulic press and suitable spacers may be required, to press the bushes out of position and install the new ones.

Refitting

7 Fit the connecting link assembly, and insert its pivot bolt and washer **(see illustration)**.

8 Locate the balljoint shank in the axle, and refit its washer and nut. Tighten the nut to the specified torque setting, and secure it in position with a new split-pin **(see illustrations)**.

9 Fit a new nut to the pivot bolt, tighten it to the specified torque setting, then lower the vehicle to ground.

8 Suspension bump stop – inspection, removal and refitting

Inspection

1 The bump stops are mounted onto the chassis, directly above the axle assembly **(see illustration)**. Inspect each bump stop rubber for signs of damage or deterioration, and renew if necessary.

Removal

2 Slacken and remove the nuts, washers and bolts securing the bump stop in position, and remove it from the chassis.

Refitting

3 Fit the bolts to the slots in the chassis, then offer up the bump stop, ensuring it is correctly located in the chassis slot. Refit the washers and nuts to the retaining bolts, and tighten them securely.

9 Rear shock absorber – removal, testing and refitting

Removal

1 Chock the front wheels, then jack up the rear of the vehicle and support it on axle stands positioned underneath the rear axle

7.8a Locate the balljoint in the axle, and refit its retaining nut and washer

7.8b Tighten the nut to the specified torque, and secure it in position with a new split-pin

8.1 Bump stops are mounted onto the vehicle underbody (arrowed), directly above each end of the axle

9.2 Slacken and remove the shock absorber upper mounting nut and washer ...

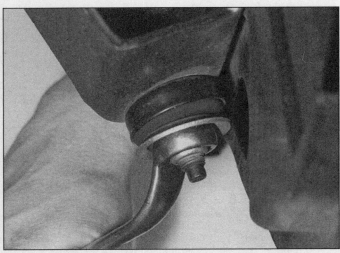

9.3 ... then unscrew the lower mounting nut, and recover the washers and mounting rubber

(see *Jacking and vehicle support*). Remove the relevant rear roadwheel.

2 Slacken and remove the nut and outer washer from the shock absorber upper mounting **(see illustration)**.

3 Unscrew the nut from the lower mounting, and slide off the outer mounting rubber and its washers, noting their correct fitted positions **(see illustration)**. Free the shock absorber from the axle, and recover the second mounting rubber and washer arrangement from its lower end.

4 Remove the shock absorber from the vehicle, and recover the inner washer from its upper mounting.

5 If necessary, slacken and remove the retaining nuts and bolts, and remove the upper mounting bracket from the chassis.

Testing

6 Examine the shock absorber for signs of fluid leakage or damage. Test the operation of the strut, while holding it in an upright position, by moving the piston through a full stroke, and then through short strokes of 50 to 100 mm. In both cases, the resistance felt should be smooth and continuous. If the resistance is jerky, or uneven, or if there is any visible sign of wear or damage to the strut, renewal is necessary. Renew the complete unit if any damage or excessive wear is evident.

7 Inspect the upper mounting bush and the lower mounting rubbers for signs of damage or deterioration, and renew as necessary.

Refitting

8 Where removed, refit the upper mounting bracket to the chassis, and insert its retaining bolts and nuts, tightening them securely.

9 Fit the inner washer, then locate the shock absorber on the upper mounting bracket.

10 Fit the first mounting rubber and washer arrangement to the lower end of the shock absorber, positioning a washer on each side of the rubber. Engage the shock absorber with the axle, then fit the second rubber mounting

and washer arrangement, followed by the retaining nut.

11 Refit the outer washer and upper retaining nut, then tighten both retaining nuts to the specified torque setting.

10 Rear coil spring – removal and refitting

Note: *A suitable tool to hold the coil spring in compression must be obtained. Adjustable coil spring compressors are readily available, and are essential for this operation. Any attempt to dismantle the strut without such a tool is likely to result in damage or personal injury.*

Removal

1 Chock the front wheels, then jack up the rear of the vehicle and support it on axle stands positioned underneath the chassis. Remove the relevant rear roadwheel.

2 Position a hydraulic jack beneath the rear axle assembly, then raise the jack until it is supporting the axle weight.

3 Slacken and remove the nut and outer washer from the shock absorber upper mounting, and disengage the shock absorber from its mounting bracket.

4 Fit the spring compressor, and compress the coil spring.

5 Carefully lower the axle, until the upper end of the spring is released from its seat. Whilst lowering the axle, keep a careful watch on the brake pipes and hoses, to ensure that no strain is being placed on them.

6 Recover the upper spring seat, slacken and remove the retaining bolts and washers, then remove the retaining plate securing the spring to the axle. Withdraw the coil spring, and lift off the lower spring seat from the axle.

7 Inspect the spring closely for signs of damage, such as cracking, and check the

spring seats for signs of wear or damage. Renew worn components as necessary.

Refitting

8 If a new spring is being installed, slowly release the old spring, then transfer the spring compressor from the old spring to the new one.

9 Refit the lower spring seat to the axle, then manoeuvre the coil spring into position.

10 Ensure that the spring is correctly seated, then refit the retaining plate to the axle, and securely tighten its retaining bolts.

11 Fit the upper spring seat to the top of the coil spring.

12 Align the upper spring seat with the chassis, then carefully raise the axle assembly with the jack.

13 Locate the shock absorber on its upper mounting, then refit the outer washer and retaining nut, tightening it to the specified torque setting.

14 Carefully release the spring compressor, ensuring that the spring remains correctly seated.

15 Remove the jack from underneath the axle, and lower the vehicle to the ground.

11 Rear suspension lower link – removal, inspection and refitting

Note: *New a new lower link pivot bolt nut and front mounting nut will be required on refitting (see Note in Section 1). If the rubber mounting is to be removed, new mounting bolt nuts will also be required.*

Removal

1 Chock the front wheels, then jack up the rear of the vehicle and support it on axle stands positioned underneath the rear axle. Remove the relevant rear roadwheel.

2 Slacken and remove the nut, then withdraw

11.2 Remove the pivot bolt securing the lower link to the axle ...

11.3a ... then unscrew the front retaining nut and washer ...

11.3b ... and manoeuvre the lower link out from underneath the vehicle

11.4 The lower link mounting is secured to the chassis by three bolts

11.12a With the vehicle standing on its wheels, tighten the lower link pivot bolt ...

11.12b ... and front retaining nut to the specified torque

the pivot bolt securing the lower link to the axle **(see illustration)**.

3 Slacken and remove the lower link front retaining nut and washer, then manoeuvre the link out from underneath the vehicle **(see illustrations)**.

4 If necessary, undo the three nuts and bolts securing the rubber mounting in position, and remove it from the chassis **(see illustration)**.

Inspection

5 Inspect the link for signs of damage, paying particular attention to its threaded end, and the area around its mounting bush. Check the pivot bolt shanks for signs of wear, and renew if necessary.

6 Examine the lower link mounting bush for signs of wear and damage. If renewal is necessary, a hydraulic press and suitable spacers will be required, to press the bush out of position and install the new one. Press the old bush out, and install the new bush using a suitable tubular spacer which bears only on the hard outer edge of the bush, not the bush rubber.

7 Inspect the rubber mounting for signs of damage or deterioration, and renew if necessary.

Refitting

8 Where necessary, fit the rubber mounting to the chassis, and insert its mounting bolts. Fit new nuts to the bolts, and tighten them securely.

9 Manoeuvre the link into position, and insert the pivot bolt.

10 Refit the washer to the threaded end of the link, then fit the new nuts to both the link and pivot bolt. Tighten each nut loosely only at this stage.

11 Refit the roadwheel, then lower the vehicle to the ground and tighten the wheel nuts to the specified torque.

12 With the vehicle resting on its wheels, tighten both the lower link front nut and pivot bolt nut to the specified torque setting **(see illustrations)**.

12 Rear suspension lower link mounting – renewal

1 To renew the rubber mounting, the lower link must be removed. Refer to Section for removal and refitting details.

13 Rear suspension upper link – removal, inspection and refitting

Note: *New upper link pivot bolt and mounting bracket retaining bolt nuts will be required on refitting (see Note in Section 1).*

Removal

1 Chock the front wheels, then jack up the rear of the vehicle and support it on axle stands positioned underneath the chassis.

2 Position a hydraulic jack beneath the rear axle assembly, then raise the jack until it is supporting the axle weight.

3 Slacken and remove the nuts and bolts securing the upper link mounting bracket to the chassis.

4 Slacken and remove the nuts securing the upper links to the balljoint bracket on the top of the axle **(see illustration)**. Withdraw both retaining bolts, and remove the relevant upper link and mounting bracket assembly from underneath the vehicle.

5 If necessary, undo the nut, withdraw the pivot bolt, and separate the link from its mounting bracket.

Inspection

6 Inspect the link for signs of damage, paying particular attention to the area around its mounting bush. Check the pivot bolt shanks for signs of wear, and renew if necessary.

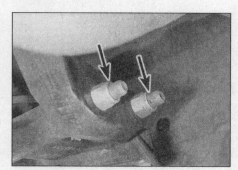

13.4 Upper link-to-balljoint bracket retaining bolts (arrowed)

15.4 Rear anti-roll bar mounting clamp assembly

15.5 Unbolt the connecting link from the anti-roll bar

7 Examine the upper link mounting bush for signs of wear and damage. If renewal is necessary, a hydraulic press and suitable spacers will be required, to press the bush out of position and install the new one. Press the old bush out, and install the new bush using a suitable tubular spacer which bears only on the hard outer edge of the bush, not the bush rubber.

8 Inspect the mounting bracket for signs of damage, and renew if necessary.

Refitting

9 Reassemble the upper link and mounting bracket, and insert the pivot bolts. Fit a new nut to the bolt, tightening it loosely only at this stage.

10 Manoeuvre the link and bracket assembly into position, and insert the bolts securing them to the balljoint bracket and second upper link. Fit the new nuts to the bolts, and tighten them to the specified torque setting.

11 Insert the mounting bracket-to-chassis bolts, then fit the new nuts and tighten them to the specified torque setting.

12 Lower the vehicle to the ground and, with the vehicle resting on its wheels, tighten the upper pivot bolt nut to the specified torque setting.

14 Rear suspension upper link balljoint – removal and refitting

Removal

1 Remove both rear suspension upper links as described in Section 13.

2 Withdraw the split-pin, then slacken and remove the nut securing the balljoint to the top of the rear axle.

3 Remove the balljoint and upper link bracket assembly from the top of the axle, then slacken and remove the two retaining

bolts and washers, and separate the two components.

4 Check that the lower arm balljoint moves freely, without any sign of roughness. Also check that the balljoint gaiter shows no sign of deterioration, and is free from cracks and splits. If necessary, renew the balljoint.

Refitting

5 Refit the upper link bracket to the balljoint, and securely tighten its retaining bolts.

6 Locate the balljoint shank in its bracket on top of the axle, and refit its retaining nut. Tighten the balljoint nut to the specified torque setting, and secure it in position with a new split-pin.

7 Refit the rear suspension upper links as described in Section 13.

15 Rear anti-roll bar – removal and refitting

Note: *New anti-roll bar mounting clamp and connecting link nuts will be required on refitting (see Note in Section 1).*

Removal

1 Chock the front wheels, then jack up the rear of the vehicle and support it on axle stands positioned underneath the chassis.

2 Position a hydraulic jack beneath the axle assembly, then raise the jack until it is supporting the axle weight.

3 Prior to removal, mark the position of each mounting clamp rubber on the anti-roll bar.

4 Unscrew the nuts/bolts and washers securing the mounting clamps to the vehicle body**(see illustration)**.

5 Slacken and remove the nuts, and withdraw the bolts and washers securing each end of the anti-roll bar to the connecting links **(see illustration)**. If they are loose, remove the mounting rubbers from the connecting link.

Remove the anti-roll bar out from underneath the vehicle

6 Remove the mounting rubbers from the anti-roll bar, and inspect them for signs of damage. Renew both rubbers if they are damaged or show signs of deterioration.

Refitting

7 Fit the mounting rubbers to the anti-roll bar, aligning them with the marks made prior to removal.

8 Manoeuvre the anti-roll bar into position, ensuring that the flat side of each mounting rubber is against the vehicle body, then refit the mounting clamps. Insert the bolts and fit the washers and new nuts, tightening them loosely only at this stage.

9 Ensure that the mounting rubbers are in position, and align the anti-roll bar ends with the connecting links. Insert the pivot bolts and washers, then fit the new retaining nuts and tighten them loosely.

10 Lower the vehicle to the ground and, with it resting on its wheels, tighten the mounting clamp and pivot bolt nuts to the specified torque.

16 Rear anti-roll bar connecting link – removal, inspection and refitting

Note: *New connecting link pivot bolt nuts will be required on refitting (see Note in Section 1).*

Removal

1 Chock the front wheels, then jack up the rear of the vehicle and support it on axle stands positioned underneath the chassis.

2 Position a hydraulic jack beneath the axle assembly, then raise the jack until it is supporting the axle weight.

3 Slacken and remove the nut, then withdraw the pivot bolt and washer securing the

16.3a Slacken and remove the nut …

16.3b … then withdraw the pivot bolt and washer securing the anti-roll bar to the connecting link

16.3c If they are loose, remove the mounting rubbers from the connecting link

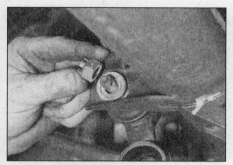

16.4a Slacken and remove the nut and washer …

16.4b … then use a universal balljoint separator …

16.4c … to free the connecting link from the axle

connecting link to the anti-roll bar. If they are loose, remove the mounting rubbers from the connecting link **(see illustrations)**.

4 Remove the split-pin, and undo the nut and washer securing the connecting link balljoint to the axle assembly. Release the balljoint tapered shank using a universal balljoint separator, and remove the connecting link from the vehicle **(see illustrations)**.

Inspection

5 Check that the link balljoint moves freely, without any sign of roughness. Also check that the balljoint gaiter shows no sign of deterioration, and is free from cracks and splits. If any sign of wear or damage is found, the complete link must be renewed.

6 Examine the link mounting bushes for signs of wear and damage. If renewal is necessary, a hydraulic press and suitable spacers may be required, to press the bushes out of position and install the new ones.

Refitting

7 Locate the balljoint shank in the axle, and refit its washer and nut. Tighten the nut to the specified torque setting, and secure it in position with a new split-pin **(see illustration)**.

8 Ensure that the mounting rubbers are correctly fitted, and insert the pivot bolt and washer.

9 Fit a new nut to the pivot bolt, tighten it to the specified torque setting, then lower the vehicle to ground.

---

17 Rear suspension self-levelling unit – removal, inspection and refitting

Note: *New upper bracket retaining nuts will be required on refitting (see Note in Section 1).*

Removal

1 Chock the front wheels, then jack up the rear of the vehicle and support it on axle stands positioned underneath the chassis (see *Jacking and vehicle support*).

2 Slacken and remove the two bolts and nuts securing the reservoir support bracket in position.

3 Slacken and remove the four nuts and bolts securing the self-levelling unit upper mounting bracket to the chassis.

4 Release the circlip, and free the gaiter from the lower balljoint.

5 Using a suitable open-ended spanner, unscrew the self-levelling unit lower balljoint from the upper link balljoint bracket, and manoeuvre the assembly out from underneath the vehicle. **Note:** *Do not attempt to separate the reservoir from the unit.*

Inspection

6 Inspect the self-levelling unit balljoint gaiters for signs of damage or deterioration. Check that both the upper and lower balljoints pivot smoothly, without any sign of roughness or free play. Renew damaged components as necessary.

16.7 Tighten the balljoint nut to the specified torque setting, and secure it in position with a new split-pin

7 If renewal is necessary, unscrew the relevant balljoint from the self-levelling unit, and remove the gaiter. The upper balljoint can also be unscrewed from its mounting bracket, if required. Fit the new gaiter, and clean the threads of the balljoints and levelling unit. Apply a few drops of locking compound to the balljoint shank threads, and screw them into the levelling unit, tightening them securely. Ensure that the upper balljoint gaiter is correctly seated, and secure it in position with its circlips.

Refitting

8 Manoeuvre the assembly into position, and screw the lower balljoint into the upper link balljoint bracket.

18.2 Remove the trim cover from the centre of the steering wheel

18.3 Remove the centre trim from the steering wheel...

18.4 Slacken and remove the steering wheel retaining nut, recover the washer, and remove the wheel

9 Securely tighten the balljoint, then align the upper bracket with the chassis, and insert its retaining bolts. Fit the new nuts to the bolts, and tighten them securely.

10 Ensure that the lower balljoint is securely tightened, and seat the lower gaiter in its grooves. Secure the gaiter in position with its circlips.

11 Refit the reservoir support bracket retaining bolts, tighten them securely, then lower the vehicle to the ground.

18 Steering wheel – removal and refitting

Removal

1 Set the front wheels in the straight-ahead position, and release the steering lock by inserting the ignition key.

2 On some models, unclip and remove the trim cover from the centre of the steering wheel (see illustration).

3 On other models, carefully prise the badge out from the centre of the wheel, to reveal the retaining nut (see illustration).

4 Slacken and remove the steering wheel retaining nut and washer (see illustration).

5 Make alignment marks between the steering wheel and steering column shaft,

then pull the wheel off the column. If the wheel is a tight fit on the column splines, it will be necessary to draw the wheel off using a suitable puller which screws into the threaded holes in the wheel. A suitable home-made puller can be fabricated from a strip of steel and two suitable size bolts (see illustration).

Refitting

6 Prior to refitting, inspect the indicator cancelling cam (which is fitted to the base of the wheel) for signs of damage, and renew if necessary.

7 Ensure that the indicator switch is in the central (off) position, and locate the wheel on the column splines, aligning the marks made on removal. As the wheel is fitted, make sure that the cancelling cam lugs engage correctly with the cancelling ring slots.

8 Refit the washer and retaining nut, and tighten it to the specified torque setting.

9 Refit the trim cover or clip the badge back to the centre of the steering wheel.

19 Ignition switch/steering column lock – removal and refitting

Note: *If the lock assembly is to be removed, new shear-bolts will be required on refitting.*

Removal

1 Remove the instrument panel as described in Chapter 13.

2 Undo the retaining screws from the steering column shrouds, then unclip the shrouds and remove them from the steering column.

3 If necessary, remove the steering wheel as described in Section 18 to improve access.

Lock assembly

4 Noting their correct fitted locations, disconnect the wiring connectors from the rear of the lock assembly (see illustration).

5 Using a hammer and suitable chisel, tap the head of each shear-bolt around anti-clockwise until each bolt is loose enough to be unscrewed by hand (see illustration). If this proves difficult, it will be necessary to carefully drill the head off each bolt, taking great care not to damage the lock clamp.

6 Unscrew both shear-bolts and remove the retaining clamp, collecting the washers which are fitted between the clamp and lock assembly. Remove the lock assembly from the steering column.

Ignition switch wiring block

7 Noting their correct fitted locations, disconnect the wiring connectors from the rear of the lock assembly.

8 Slacken and remove the wiring block retaining screw(s), and withdraw the wiring

18.5 ... if it is a tight fit, a suitable puller will be required to draw the wheel off the column splines

19.4 Disconnect the wiring connectors from the rear of the lock assembly, noting each one's correct fitted location

19.5 Undo the two shear bolts

19.8 Remove the wiring block

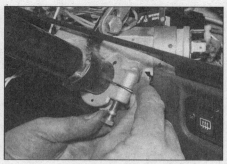

19.10 On refitting, fit the washer between the lock and clamp, and screw in the new shear-bolts

20 Steering column – removal, inspection and refitting

Note: *A new universal joint clamp bolt nut will be required on refitting (see Note in Section 1).*

Removal

1 Remove the steering wheel as described in Section 18.

2 Remove the steering column lock assembly as described in Section 19.

3 Remove the facia panel as described in Chapter 12 Section 24. It may be possible to partly remove the facia to access the steering column, although Land Rover recommends that the facia be completely removed.

4 Undo the two retaining screws and remove the trim from across the lower part of the instrument panel **(see illustration)**.

5 Pull back the rubber gaiters from around the three switch stalks, and release them from the steering column shrouds **(see illustration)**.

6 Remove the rubber grommet from the lower right-hand side of the lower shroud **(see illustration)**.

7 Undo the six retaining screws, then unclip the steering column upper and lower shrouds and remove them from the vehicle **(see illustrations)**.

8 Trace the wiring back from the combination switches, and disconnect their wiring

---

block from the end of the switch assembly **(see illustration)**.

Refitting

Lock assembly

9 Refit the lock assembly retaining clamp, making sure that its lug is correctly located in the steering column hole.

10 Manoeuvre the lock assembly onto the column, positioning the washers between the lock and retaining clamp. Fit the new shear-bolts, tightening them loosely at this stage **(see illustration)**.

11 Reconnect the switch wiring, ensuring it is correctly routed. Reconnect the battery, then check the operation of the ignition switch and steering column lock. If all is well, tighten each lock assembly bolt until its head shears off.

12 Manoeuvre the steering column shrouds

into position, and clip them securely together. Refit the shroud retaining screws, and tighten them securely.

13 Refit the instrument panel as described in Chapter 13.

Ignition switch wiring block

14 Fit the wiring block to the rear of the column lock, making sure that it is correctly seated, and secure it in position with its retaining screw(s).

15 Reconnect the switch wiring, ensuring that it is correctly routed. Reconnect the battery, then check the operation of the ignition switch.

16 Manoeuvre the steering column shrouds into position, and clip them securely together. Refit the shroud retaining screws, and tighten them securely.

17 Refit the instrument panel as described in Chapter 13.

20.4 Remove the trim panel

20.5 Release the gaiters from the switch stalks

20.6 Remove the rubber grommet

20.7a Undo the six retaining screws...

20.7b ... and remove the upper shroud...

20.7c ...then the lower shroud

20.8a Disconnect the wiring connectors ...

20.8b ... then slacken the clamp bolt, and slide the combination switch assembly off the column

20.9 Slacken and remove bolt (arrowed) securing the upper end of the column to its tie-bar

20.10 Undo the nuts and move the central junction box to one side

20.15 Remove the clamp bolt securing the column to the universal joint ...

20.16 ... then slacken and remove the column lower mounting bolts (arrowed) and nuts

connectors. Slacken the switch assembly clamp bolt, then slide the switch assembly off the top of the steering column **(see illustrations)**.

9 Slacken and remove the nut and bolt securing the upper end of the steering column to its tie-bar **(see illustration)**.

10 Slacken the four retaining nuts and remove the central junction box (CJB) from the bulkhead over the lower part of the steering column **(see illustration)**.

11 From within the engine compartment, slacken and remove the two nuts and washers securing the braking system master cylinder to the servo unit (refer to Chapter 10 Section 10). Carefully disengage the master cylinder;

position it clear of the servo unit, taking great care not to place any excess strain on the brake pipes. Recover the seal from the rear of the master cylinder.

12 Carefully release the brake vacuum hose/check valve from the grommet in the servo unit.

13 From inside of the vehicle, undo the six brake pedal mounting box retaining bolts. Return to the engine compartment, and disconnect the wiring connectors from the stop-light switch. Manoeuvre the pedal box upwards and out of position, and recover the seal fitted between the box and bulkhead (refer to Chapter 10 Section 11).

14 Using paint or a similar, make alignment

marks between the steering column and universal joint.

15 Slacken and remove the nut and clamp bolt securing the universal joint to the steering column **(see illustration)**.

16 Unscrew the two bolts and nuts securing the column lower mounting to its mounting bracket **(see illustration)**.

17 Slacken and remove the bolts securing the top half of the column upper mounting clamp in position. Undo the two clamp bolts and remove both halves of the clamp, complete with its rubber seal **(see illustrations)**.

18 Undo the two bolts securing the upper mounting bracket in position, then manoeuvre the column and bracket assembly out from

20.17a Slacken and remove the four bolts (arrowed) ...

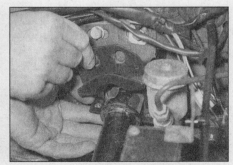

20.17b ... then remove both halves of the column upper mounting clamp ...

20.17c ... and recover the rubber seal from the steering column

the vehicle **(see illustration)**. Recover the bracket seal from the bulkhead.

Inspection

19 Examine the steering column and mountings for signs of damage and deformation, and check the steering shaft for signs of freeplay in the column bushes. If there are signs of damage or play, the column must be renewed since, at the time of writing, it appears no spare parts are available for the column. Refer to your Land Rover dealer or specialist for the latest information.
20 Examine the upper mounting bracket and clamp rubber seals, and renew them if they show signs of damage or deterioration.

Refitting

21 Ensure that the mounting bracket seal is in position, and manoeuvre the column assembly into position.
22 Align the marks made prior to removal, and engage the steering column shaft with the universal joint splines **(see illustration)**.
23 Fit the upper mounting bracket retaining bolts, tightening them lightly only.
24 Fit the rubber seal to the column, then refit the upper mounting clamp, tightening its bolts by hand only.
25 Refit the column lower mounting bolts and nuts, and tighten them by hand.
26 From inside the vehicle, refit the bolt securing the upper end of the column to the tie-bar, and tighten it securely.
27 Working in the engine compartment, tighten the upper mounting bracket bolts, followed by the mounting clamp bolts, and then the lower bracket retaining bolts. Ensure that all bolts are securely tightened.
28 The remainder of refitting is a direct reversal of the removal procedure, ensuring that all bolts are tightened securely.

21 Steering column intermediate shaft – removal, inspection and refitting

Note: *New clamp bolt nuts will be required on refitting (see Note in Section 1).*

Removal

1 Set the front wheels in the straight-ahead position.
2 Using paint or a similar, make alignment marks between the intermediate shaft and the upper and lower universal joints.
3 Slacken and remove the nuts and clamp bolts securing the intermediate shaft to the universal joints.
4 Disengage the shaft from both universal joints, and remove it from the vehicle.

Inspection

5 Inspect the intermediate shaft collapsible joint for signs of wear or damage and, if necessary, renew the shaft assembly.

20.18 Manoeuvre the column assembly out of position

Refitting

6 Aligning the marks made on removal, engage the shaft with the upper and lower universal joints.
7 Make sure that the shaft is correctly seated, then insert both its clamp bolts. Fit a new nut to each clamp bolt, and tighten them both securely.

22 Steering column universal joint – removal, inspection and refitting

Note: *New clamp bolt nuts will be required on refitting (see Note in Section 1).*

Removal

1 Set the front wheels in the straight-ahead position.
2 Using paint or a similar, make alignment marks between the universal joint and intermediate shaft, and the steering column/steering box pinion (as applicable).
3 Slacken and remove the nuts and clamp bolts securing the universal joint in position, then disengage it from the splines and remove it from the vehicle.

Inspection

4 Inspect the universal joint for signs of roughness in its bearings, and for ease of movement. If it is damaged in any way, the joint must be renewed.

23.2 Location of steering lock stop

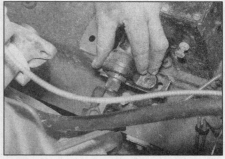

20.22 On refitting, engage the steering column with the universal joint prior to refitting its mounting bolts

Refitting

5 Aligning the marks made on removal, engage the universal joint with the intermediate shaft splines and steering column/steering box pinion (as applicable).
6 Make sure that the joint is correctly seated, then insert both its clamp bolts. Fit a new nut to each clamp bolt, and tighten them both securely.

23 Steering – adjustment

1 If at any time it is noted that the steering action has become stiff or sloppy, the vehicle should be taken to a Land Rover dealer or specialist for the steering components to be checked. Adjustments of the steering components and steering box are possible, but specialist knowledge and equipment are needed. Therefore, this task must be entrusted to a Land Rover dealer.
2 The only adjustment which can easily be carried out by the home mechanic is steering lock stop adjustment **(see illustration)**. Once the wheel alignment is known to be correct (see Section 33), turn the steering onto full lock, and measure the clearance between the front tyre wall and the radius arm. this should be no less than 20 mm. Carry out this procedure on both left and right-hand locks.
3 Alternatively measure the bolt protrusion **(see illustration)**. If adjustment is necessary, slacken the stop bolt locknut, and rotate

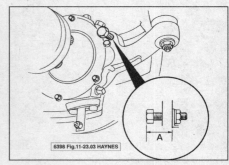

23.3 Measure stop bolt (A) protrusion

the bolt as required. Once the clearance is correctly set, securely tighten the locknut. Turn the steering onto full right-hand lock, and then repeat the adjustment on the right-hand side. Refer to the chart below for the correct setting, depending on size and tyre fitted.

Alloy wheels	
BF Goodrich (Mud terrain) – tyre size 265	59.7 mm
Goodyear GT+4 – tyre size 235	55.7 mm
Michelin M+S 4X4 – tyre size 235	52.2 mm
Steel wheels	
Avon, Goodyear and Michelin – tyre size 7.50	56.0 mm
Goodyear and Michelin – tyre size 205	55.2 mm

24 Steering box – removal, inspection and refitting

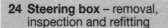

Note: *New tie-bar mounting bolt nuts, and a new clamp bolt nut, will be required on refitting (see Note in Section 1).*

Removal

1 Apply the handbrake, then jack up the front of the vehicle and support it on axle stands positioned underneath the chassis (see).
2 Position the front wheels in the straight-ahead position.
3 Using brake hose clamps, clamp both the supply and return hoses near the power steering fluid reservoir, to minimise fluid loss. Clean the area around the steering box hose unions, then make identification marks between on each pipe to ensure that they are correctly positioned on reassembly. Unscrew the feed and return pipe union nuts from the steering box; be prepared for fluid spillage, and position a suitable container beneath the pipes whilst unscrewing the union nuts. Once both pipes have been disconnected, plug the pipe ends and steering box orifices, to prevent excessive fluid leakage and to keep dirt out of the hydraulic system.
4 On all models, withdraw the split-pin, then

24.5 Using a balljoint separator to release the drag link balljoint from the steering box drop arm

unscrew the nut securing the drag link to the steering box drop arm.
5 Using a universal balljoint separator, free the drag link from the drop arm **(see illustration)**.
6 Using paint or a similar, make an alignment mark between the universal joint and steering box pinion.
7 Slacken and remove the clamp bolt securing the universal joint to the steering box pinion **(see illustration)**.
8 Loosen the nut securing the steering box tie-bar to its mounting. Slacken and remove the remove the nuts, washers and bolts securing the tie-bar to the steering box, and position the tie-bar clear of the box **(see illustration)**.
9 Unscrew the mounting bolts, and remove the steering box assembly from the vehicle chassis.

Inspection

10 Inspect the steering box assembly for signs of wear or damage. If overhaul of the steering box assembly is necessary, the task must be entrusted to a Land Rover dealer.

Refitting

11 Manoeuvre the steering box into position, and engage it with the universal joint splines, aligning the marks made prior to removal.
12 Position the steering box assembly on the chassis, making sure that it is locating lug is correctly engaged, then fit the mounting bolts and tighten them to the specified torque setting.
13 Insert the clamp bolt securing the universal joint to the steering box. Fit a new

24.7 Undo the clamp bolt on the universal joint

nut to the clamp bolt, and tighten the bolt to the specified torque.
14 Align the tie-bar with the box, and insert the retaining bolts and washers. Fit new nuts to the bolts, tighten them to the specified torque setting, then tighten the tie-bar-to-mounting nut to the specified torque setting.
15 Connect the drag link to the drop arm, and refit its retaining nut. Tighten the nut to the specified torque setting, and secure it in position with a new split-pin **(see illustrations)**.
16 Wipe clean the feed and return pipe unions, and refit them to their respective unions on the steering box. Tighten the union nuts to the specified torque setting, and ensure that the pipes are securely retained by all the necessary retaining clips. Remove the clamp from the steering hoses.
17 Lower the vehicle to the ground. On power-assisted steering models, bleed the hydraulic system as described in Section.

25 Steering box drop arm – removal and refitting

Note: *A new retaining nut lockwasher will be required on refitting.*

Removal

1 Apply the handbrake, then jack up the front of the vehicle and support it on axle stands positioned underneath the chassis (see *Jacking and vehicle support*).

24.8 Steering box tie-bar retaining nut locations (arrowed)

24.15a Refit the balljoint retaining nut …

24.15b … then tighten it to the specified torque, and secure it in position with a new split-pin

25.5a Unscrew the drop arm retaining nut ...

25.5b ... and recover the lockwasher

25.7 Using a two legged-puller to draw the drop arm off the steering box

2 Position the front wheels in the straight-ahead position.

3 Withdraw the split-pin, then unscrew the nut securing the drag link to the steering box drop arm.

4 Using a universal balljoint separator, free the drag link from the drop arm.

5 Bend down the lockwasher tab, then slacken and remove the drop arm retaining nut and lockwasher (see illustrations).

6 Make alignment marks between the drop arm and steering box shaft.

7 A suitable legged puller will now be required to draw the arm off the box shaft. Locate the legs of the puller behind the arm, and carefully draw it off the steering box shaft (see illustration).

8 Once the arm is loose, remove the puller, then lower the drop arm away from the steering box.

9 Check that the link balljoint moves freely, without any sign of roughness. Also check that the balljoint gaiter shows no sign of deterioration, and is free from cracks and splits. If any sign of wear or damage is found, the drop arm assembly should be renewed (or overhauled). Overhaul of the balljoint components requires the use of several special service tools, and should be entrusted to a Land Rover dealer or specialist.

Refitting

10 Align the marks made prior to removal, and locate the drop arm on the steering box shaft splines.

25.11 Tighten the drop arm retaining nut to the specified torque, and secure it in position by bending down the lockwasher against one of its flats (arrowed)

11 Fit the new lockwasher to the shaft, and refit the retaining nut. Tighten the nut to the specified torque setting, then secure it in position by bending down the tab of the lockwasher so that it contacts one of the nut flats (see illustration).

12 Connect the drag link to the drop arm, and refit its retaining nut. Tighten the nut to the specified torque setting, and secure it in position with a new split-pin.

13 Lower the vehicle to the ground, and reconnect the battery.

26 Power steering pump – removal and refitting

Removal

1 Remove the auxiliary drivebelt as described in Chapter 1 Section 52

2 Using brake hose clamp, clamp the supply hose from the fluid reservoir to the power steering pump, this will minimise fluid loss during subsequent operations.

3 Slacken the retaining clip, and disconnect the fluid supply hose from the pump and also slacken the high pressure pipe union nut (see illustration), and disconnect it from the lower part of the pump; be prepared for some fluid spillage as the pipe and hose are disconnected. Plug the hose/pipe end and pump unions, to minimise fluid loss and to prevent the entry of dirt into the system.

4 Slacken and remove the power steering

26.3 Fluid supply hose and high-pressure pipe

pump mounting bolts, and remove the pump from the engine (see illustration).

5 Overhaul of the pump is not possible; if the pump is worn or damaged, it must be renewed.

Refitting

6 Manoeuvre the pump into position, then refit its mounting bolts and tighten them to the specified torque.

7 Reconnect the high-pressure pipe to the pump, and tighten its union nut to the specified torque.

8 Reconnect the supply hose, and securely tighten its retaining clip.

9 Refit and tension the auxiliary drivebelt as described in Chapter 1.

10 Bleed the hydraulic system as described in Section.

27 Power steering system – bleeding

1 With the engine stopped, top-up the fluid reservoir to the maximum mark with the specified type of fluid.

2 Have an assistant start the engine, whilst you keep watch on the fluid level. Be prepared to add more fluid as the engine starts, since the fluid level is likely to drop quickly.

3 Once the fluid level has stabilised, warm the engine up to normal operating temperature. Ensure that the front wheels are in the straight-ahead position, then turn the engine off.

26.4 Power steering pump mounting bolts

27.6 Bleed screw in top of steering box

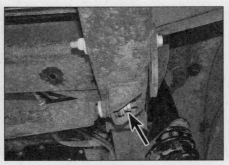

28.1 Undo the retaining nut from the mounting bracket end of the damper

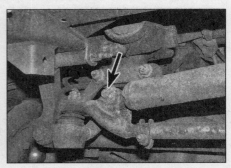

28.2 Remove bolt from other end of damper

4 Check that the power steering fluid level is still up to the maximum mark, topping-up if necessary.

5 Start the engine and allow it idle. During the following procedure, the engine must remain at idle speed, and the steering must not be turned.

6 Slowly slacken the bleed screw, which is situated on the top of the power steering box assembly (see illustration). Ensuring that the fluid level in the reservoir remains at the maximum level, allow fluid to seep from the screw until a steady flow of fluid which is free from air bubbles is seen to be emerging. Once this is so, securely tighten the bleed screw, and mop-up all traces of fluid from the top of the steering box.

7 Turn the steering onto full left-hand lock, holding it there for a few seconds, and then onto full right-hand lock; check all steering hose/pipe unions for signs of leakage. Note: Do not hold the steering at full lock for more than 10 seconds at a time, otherwise the hydraulic system may become damaged.

8 Once all air is removed from the system, stop the engine, and check the fluid level as described in Chapter.

28 Steering damper – removal and refitting

Note: A new pivot bolt nut will be required on refitting (see Note in Section 1).

Removal

1 Slacken and unscrew the locknut and retaining nut securing the damper to its mounting bracket (see illustration). Slide off the outer washer, rubber mounting and mounting seat arrangement, noting each component's correct fitted location. Free the damper from the bracket, and recover the inner washer rubber mounting and mounting seat arrangement from the damper.

2 Slacken and remove the nut and washer, then withdraw the pivot bolt securing the damper to the drag link (see illustration).

3 Remove the steering damper from underneath the vehicle.

4 Inspect the damper assembly for signs of

wear or damage, and renew if necessary. Inspect the rubber mountings for signs of damage and deterioration, and renew if necessary.

Refitting

5 Refitting is the reverse of removal, ensuring that the mounting rubber components are correctly positioned. Fit a new nut to the pivot bolt, and tighten it securely. Tighten the retaining nut, and secure it in position by securely tightening the locknut.

29 Drag link – removal and refitting

Note: A new steering damper pivot bolt nut will be required on refitting (see Note in Section 1).

Removal

1 Apply the handbrake, then jack up the front of the vehicle and support it on axle stands positioned underneath the chassis (see).

2 Position the front wheels in the straight-ahead position.

3 Slacken and remove the nut and washer, then withdraw the pivot bolt securing the steering damper to the drag link (see illustration 28.2).

4 Withdraw the split-pin, then unscrew the nut securing the drag link to the steering box drop arm. Using a universal balljoint separator, free the drag link from the drop arm (see illustration).

29.4 Remove the split pin and lock nut

5 Repeat paragraph 4, and free the drag link from the swivel pin housing assembly (see illustration). Remove the drag link from underneath the vehicle. If necessary, remove the roadwheel to improve access to the balljoint nut.

6 Check that the link balljoint moves freely, without any sign of roughness. Also check that the balljoint gaiter shows no sign of deterioration, and is free from cracks and splits. If any sign of wear or damage is found, the balljoint must be renewed (see Section 30). If the drag link itself is damaged it must be renewed; do not attempt to straighten it.

Refitting

7 Offer up the drag link, and engage it with the swivel pin housing and steering box drop arm. Refit the retaining nuts, and tighten them to the specified torque setting. Secure each nut in position with a new split-pin.

8 Engage the steering damper with the drag link, and insert its pivot bolt. Fit a new nut to the pivot bolt, and tighten it to the specified torque setting.

9 Refit the roadwheel (where removed), then lower the vehicle to the ground and reconnect the battery negative terminal. Where necessary, tighten the roadwheel nuts to the specified torque setting.

10 Road test the vehicle, and check that the steering wheel is centralised when the vehicle is driven straight-ahead. If the steering wheel is more than 5° out of position, adjustment should be made by removing the wheel and

29.5 Remove split pin and lock nut

repositioning it on the column splines. If the wheel is less than 5° out of alignment, adjustment can be made by altering the drag link length as follows.

11 Apply the handbrake, then raise the front of the vehicle, and detach the outer balljoint from the swivel pin housing assembly as described above. Slacken the balljoint clamp bolt, and adjust the drag link length by screwing the balljoint in or out (as applicable). On right-hand drive models, if the steering wheel was found to be slightly right of centre, shorten the drag link length; if it was found to be slightly left of centre, extend the drag link length. On left-hand drive models, if the steering wheel was found to be slightly right of centre, extend the drag link length; if it was found to be slightly left of centre, shorten the drag link length. Once the drag link length is correct, refit the balljoint to the swivel pin housing, and tighten its retaining nut to the specified torque setting. Secure the nut in position with a new split-pin, then tighten the drag link clamp bolt to the specified torque. Refit the roadwheel, then lower the vehicle to the ground and tighten the wheel nuts to the specified torque. Road test the vehicle and, if necessary, repeat the adjustment procedure.

30 Drag link balljoint/end fitting – removal and refitting

Removal

1 Remove the drag link as described in Section 29.
2 Using a straight-edge and a scriber, or similar, mark the relationship of the balljoint/end fitting to the drag link. Also note the correct fitted relationship between the end fitting and balljoint.
3 Slacken the clamp bolt **(see illustration)**, then counting the exact number of turns

necessary to do so, unscrew the balljoint/end fitting from the drag link end.
4 Carefully clean the balljoint/end fitting and the drag link threads. Renew the balljoint if its movement is sloppy or if it is too stiff, if it is excessively worn, or if it is damaged in any way; carefully check the stud taper and threads. If the balljoint gaiter is damaged, the complete balljoint assembly must be renewed; it is not possible to obtain the gaiter separately.

Refitting

5 Screw the balljoint/end fitting into the drag link by the exact number of turns noted on removal, and tighten the clamp bolt(s) to the specified torque. This should line up the balljoint in relation to the end fitting, and should set the track rod to its original length.
6 Check that the balljoint and end fitting are correctly positioned in relation to each other, then tighten the drag link clamp bolt to the specified torque setting.
7 Refit the drag link as described in Section, and check that the steering wheel is centralised.

31 Track rod – removal and refitting

Removal

1 Apply the handbrake, then jack up the front of the vehicle and support it on axle stands positioned underneath the chassis (see).
2 Position the front wheels in the straight-ahead position. The track rod is positioned at the rear of the front axle, connecting the right and left-hand side front wheels.
3 Withdraw the split-pin, then unscrew the nut securing the track rod to the left-hand swivel pin housing **(see illustration)**. Using a universal balljoint separator, free the track rod from the swivel pin housing.

4 Repeat paragraph 3, and free the track rod from the right-hand swivel pin housing assembly. Remove the track rod from underneath the vehicle.
5 Check that the track rod balljoints move freely, without any sign of roughness. Also check that the balljoint gaiters show no sign of deterioration, and are free from cracks and splits. If any sign of wear or damage is found, the balljoint(s) must be renewed (see Section 32). If the track rod itself is damaged, it must be renewed; do not attempt to straighten it.

Refitting

6 Offer up the track rod, and engage it with the swivel pin housings. Refit the retaining nuts, and tighten them to the specified torque setting. Secure each nut in position with a new split-pin.
7 Check the front wheel alignment as described in Section.

32 Track rod balljoint – removal and refitting

Removal

1 Remove the track rod as described in Section 31.
2 Using a straight-edge and a scriber, or similar, mark the relationship of the balljoint to the track rod.
3 Slacken the clamp bolt(s) then counting the exact number of turns necessary to do so, unscrew the balljoint from the track rod end.
4 Carefully clean the balljoint and the track rod threads. Renew the balljoint if its movement is sloppy or if it is too stiff, if it is excessively worn, or if it is damaged in any way; carefully check the stud taper and threads. If the balljoint gaiter is damaged,

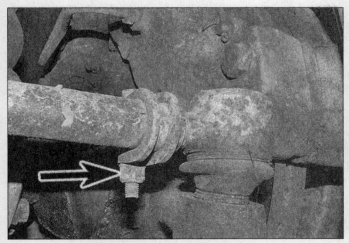

30.3 Clamp on the end of drag link

31.3 Remove the split pin and lock nut

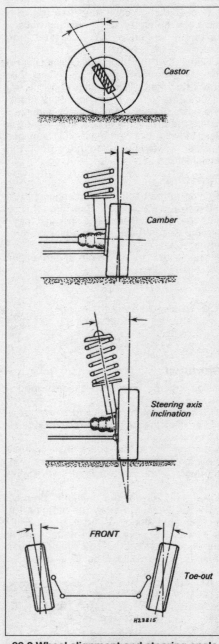

33.2 Wheel alignment and steering angle measurements

the complete balljoint assembly must be renewed; it is not possible to obtain the gaiter separately.

Refitting

5 Screw the balljoint into the track rod by the exact number of turns noted on removal, and tighten the clamp bolt(s) to the specified torque. This should set the track rod to its original length.

6 Ensure that both balljoints are correctly aligned, then tighten the clamp bolt(s) to the specified torque setting.

7 Refit the track rod as described in Section 31.

8 Prior to using the vehicle, check the front wheel alignment as described in Section.

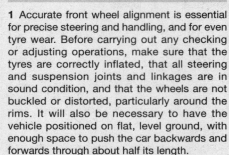

33 Wheel alignment and steering angles – general information

1 Accurate front wheel alignment is essential for precise steering and handling, and for even tyre wear. Before carrying out any checking or adjusting operations, make sure that the tyres are correctly inflated, that all steering and suspension joints and linkages are in sound condition, and that the wheels are not buckled or distorted, particularly around the rims. It will also be necessary to have the vehicle positioned on flat, level ground, with enough space to push the car backwards and forwards through about half its length.

2 Front wheel alignment consists of four factors **(see illustration)**:

3 Camber is the angle at which the roadwheels are set from the vertical, when viewed from the front or rear of the vehicle. 'Positive' camber is the angle (in degrees) that the wheels are tilted outwards at the top from the vertical.

4 Castor is the angle between the steering axis and a vertical line when viewed from each side of the vehicle. 'Positive' castor is indicated when the steering axis is inclined towards the rear of the vehicle at its upper end.

5 Steering axis inclination is the angle, when viewed from the front or rear of the vehicle, between the vertical and an imaginary line drawn between the upper and lower front suspension strut mountings.

6 Toe setting is the amount by which the distance between the front inside edges of the roadwheels differs from that between the rear inside edges, when measured at hub height. If the distance between the front edges is less than at the rear, the wheels are said to 'toe-in'. If it is greater than at the rear, the wheels are said to 'toe-out'.

7 Camber, castor and steering axis inclination are set during manufacture, and are not adjustable. Unless the vehicle has suffered accident damage, or there is gross wear in the suspension mountings or joints, it can be assumed that these settings are correct. If for any reason it is believed that they are not correct, the task of checking them should be left to a Land Rover dealer, who will have the necessary special equipment needed to measure the small angles involved.

8 It is, however, within the scope of the home mechanic to check and adjust the front wheel toe setting. To do this, a tracking gauge must first be obtained. Two types of gauge are available, and can be obtained from motor accessory shops. The first type measures the distance between the front and rear inside edges of the roadwheels, as previously described, with the vehicle stationary. The second type, known as a `scuff plate', measures the actual position of the contact surface of the tyre, in relation to the road surface, with the vehicle in motion. This is achieved by pushing or driving the front tyre over a plate, which then moves slightly according to the scuff of the tyre, and shows this movement on a scale. Both types have their advantages and disadvantages, but either can give satisfactory results if used correctly and carefully.

9 Many tyre specialists will also check toe settings free, or for a nominal charge.

10 Make sure that the steering is in the straight-ahead position when making measurements. If adjustment is necessary, apply the handbrake then jack up the front of the vehicle and support it securely on axle stands. Slacken the track rod balljoint clamp bolts then rotate the track rod to alter the length of the rod (as necessary); shortening the track rod will reduce toe-in/increase toe-out.

11 When the setting is correct, tighten both the clamp bolts to the specified torque setting.

12 Recheck the toe setting and, if necessary, repeat the adjustment procedure.

Chapter 12
Bodywork and fittings

Contents

Degrees of difficulty

Easy, suitable for novice with little experience	**Fairly easy,** suitable for beginner with some experience	**Fairly difficult,** suitable for competent DIY mechanic	**Difficult,** suitable for experienced DIY mechanic	**Very difficult,** suitable for expert DIY or professional

Specifications

Torque wrench setting	Nm	lbf ft
Seat belt mounting nuts and bolts	31	23
Seat mounting bolts	23	17

1 General Information

1 The bodyshell and associated panels consist of a mixture of both pressed-steel and aluminium alloy sections. Most components are welded together, but some use is made of structural adhesives; the front wings are bolted on.
2 Extensive use is made of plastic materials, mainly on the interior but also in exterior components. Plastic components such as wheel arch liners are fitted to the underside of the vehicle, to improve the body's resistance to corrosion.

2 Maintenance – bodywork and underframe

1 The general condition of a vehicle's bodywork is the one thing that significantly affects its value. Maintenance is easy, but needs to be regular. Neglect, particularly after minor damage, can lead quickly to further deterioration and costly repair bills. It is important also to keep watch on those parts of the vehicle not immediately visible, for instance the underside, inside all the wheel arches, and the lower part of the engine compartment.
2 The basic maintenance routine for the bodywork is washing – preferably with a lot of water, from a hose. This will remove all the loose solids which may have stuck to the vehicle. It is important to flush these off in such a way as to prevent grit from scratching the finish. The wheel arches and underframe need washing in the same way, to remove any accumulated mud, which will retain moisture and tend to encourage rust. Paradoxically enough, the best time to clean the underframe and wheel arches is in wet weather, when the mud is thoroughly wet and soft. In very wet weather, the underframe is usually cleaned of large accumulations automatically, and this is a good time for inspection.
3 Periodically, except on vehicles with a wax-based underbody protective coating,

it is a good idea to have the whole of the underframe of the vehicle steam-cleaned, engine compartment included, so that a thorough inspection can be carried out to see what minor repairs and renovations are necessary. Steam-cleaning is available at many garages, and is necessary for the removal of the accumulation of oily grime, which sometimes is allowed to become thick in certain areas. If steam-cleaning facilities are not available, there are some excellent grease solvents available which can be brush-applied; the dirt can then be simply hosed off. Note that these methods should not be used on vehicles with wax-based underbody protective coating, or the coating will be removed. Such vehicles should be inspected annually, preferably just prior to Winter, when the underbody should be washed down, and any damage to the wax coating repaired. Ideally, a completely fresh coat should be applied. It would also be worth considering the use of such wax-based protection for injection into door panels, sills, box sections, etc, as an additional safeguard against rust damage, where such protection is not provided by the vehicle manufacturer.

4 After washing paintwork, wipe off with a chamois leather to give an unspotted clear finish. A coat of clear protective wax polish will give added protection against chemical pollutants in the air. If the paintwork sheen has dulled or oxidised, use a cleaner/polisher combination to restore the brilliance of the shine. This requires a little effort, but such dulling is usually caused because regular washing has been neglected. Care needs to be taken with metallic paintwork, as special non-abrasive cleaner/polisher is required to avoid damage to the finish. Always check that the door and ventilator opening drain holes and pipes are completely clear, so that water can be drained out. Brightwork should be treated in the same way as paintwork. Windscreens and windows can be kept clear of the smeary film which often appears, by the use of proprietary glass cleaner. Never use any form of wax or other body or chromium polish on glass.

3 Maintenance – upholstery and carpets

1 Mats and carpets should be brushed or vacuum-cleaned regularly, to keep them free of grit. If they are badly stained, remove them from the vehicle for scrubbing or sponging, and make quite sure they are dry before refitting. Seats and interior trim panels can be kept clean by wiping with a damp cloth. If they do become stained (which can be more apparent on light-coloured upholstery), use a little liquid detergent and a soft nail brush to scour the grime out of the grain of the material. Do not forget to keep the headlining clean in the same way as the upholstery.

When using liquid cleaners inside the vehicle, do not over-wet the surfaces being cleaned. Excessive damp could get into the seams and padded interior, causing stains, offensive odours or even rot.

 HAYNES HINT *If the inside of the vehicle gets wet accidentally, it is worthwhile taking some trouble to dry it out properly, particularly where carpets are involved. Do not leave oil or electric heaters inside the vehicle for this purpose.*

4 Minor body damage – repair

Minor scratches

1 If the scratch is very superficial, and does not penetrate to the metal of the bodywork, repair is very simple. Lightly rub the area of the scratch with a paintwork renovator, or a very fine cutting paste, to remove loose paint from the scratch and to clear the surrounding bodywork of wax polish. Rinse the area with clean water.

2 Apply touch-up paint to the scratch using a thin paintbrush; continue to apply thin layers of paint until the surface of the paint in the scratch is level with the surrounding paintwork. Allow the new paint at least two weeks to harden, then blend it into the surrounding paintwork by rubbing the paintwork in the scratch area with a paintwork renovator or a very fine cutting pastepaste. Finally, apply wax polish.

3 Where the scratch has penetrated right through to the metal of the bodywork, a different repair technique is required. Remove any loose paint, etc from the bottom of the scratch with a penknife. Using a rubber or nylon applicator, fill the scratch with bodystopper paste. Before the stopper-paste in the scratch hardens, wrap a piece of smooth cotton rag around the top of a finger. Dip the finger in cellulose thinners, and then quickly sweep it across the surface of the stopper-p aste in the scratch; this will ensure that the surface of the stopper-paste is lightly hollowed. The scratch can now be painted over as described earlier in this Section.

Dents

4 The alloy body panels on the Land Rover are easier to work on than steel, and minor dents or creases can be beaten out fairly easily. However, if the damaged area is quite large, prolonged hammering will cause the metal to harden; to avoid the possibility of cracking, it must be softened or 'annealed'. This can be done easily with a gas blowlamp, but great care is required to avoid actually melting the metal. The blowlamp must always be kept moving in a circular pattern, whilst

being held a respectable distance from the metal.

5 One method of checking when the alloy is hot enough is to rub down the surface to be annealed, and then apply a thin film of oil over it. The blowlamp should be played over the rear side of the oiled surface, until the oil evaporates and the surface is dry. Turn off the blowlamp, and allow the metal to cool naturally; the treated areas will now be softened, and it will be possible to work it with a hammer or mallet. After panel-beating, the damaged section should be rubbed down and painted as described later in this Section.

6 When deep denting of the vehicle's bodywork has taken place, the first task is to pull the dent out until the affected bodywork almost attains its original shape. There is little point in trying to restore the original shape completely, as the metal in the damaged area will have stretched on impact, and cannot be reshaped to its original contour. It is better to bring the level of the dent up to a point which is about 3 mm below the level of the surrounding bodywork. In cases where the dent is very shallow anyway, it is not worth trying to pull it out at all.

7 If the underside of the dent is accessible, it can be hammered out gently from behind using the method described earlier.

8 Should the dent be in a section of the bodywork which has a double skin, or some other factor making it inaccessible from behind, a different technique is called for. Drill several small holes through the metal inside the dent area, particularly in the deeper sections. Then screw long self-tapping screws into the holes just sufficiently for them to gain a good purchase in the metal. Now the dent can be pulled out by pulling on the protruding heads of the screws with a pair of pliers.

9 The next stage of the repair is the removal of the paint from the damaged area, and from an inch or so of the surrounding 'sound' bodywork.

Note: *On no account should coarse abrasives be used on aluminium panels in order to remove paint. The use of a wire brush or abrasive on a power drill for example, will cause deep scoring of the metal and in extreme cases, penetrate the thickness of the relatively soft aluminium alloy.*

10 Removal of paint is best achieved by applying paint remover to the area, allowing it to act on the paintwork for the specified time, and then removing the softened paint with a wood or nylon scraper. This method may have to be repeated in order to remove all traces of paint. A good method of removing small stubborn traces of paint is to rub the area with a nylon scouring pad soaked in thinners or paint remover. **Note:** *If it is necessary to use this method, always wear rubber gloves to protect the hands from burns from the paint remover. It is also advisable to wear eye protection, as any paint remover that gets into the eyes will cause severe inflammation, or worse.*

11 Finally, remove all traces of paint and remover by washing the area with plenty of clean fresh water.

12 To complete the preparations for filling, score the surface of the bare metal with a screwdriver or the tang of a file, or alternatively, drill small holes in the affected area. This will provide a really good 'key' for the filler paste.

13 To complete the repair, see the Section on filling and respraying.

Holes or gashes

14 Remove all the paint from the affected area, and from an inch or so of the surrounding ' sound' bodywork, using the method described in the previous Section. With the paint removed, you will be able to gauge the severity of the damage, and therefore decide whether to replace the whole panel (if this is possible) or to repair the affected area. It is often quicker and more satisfactory to fit a new panel than to attempt to repair large areas of damage.

15 Remove all fittings from the affected area, except those which will act as a guide to the original shape of the damaged bodywork (eg, headlight shells, etc). Then, using tin snips or a hacksaw blade, remove all loose metal and other metal badly affected by damage. Hammer the edges of the hole inwards, in order to create a slight depression for the filler paste.

16 Before filling can take place, it will be necessary to block the hole in some way. This can be achieved by the use of zinc gauze or aluminium tape.

17 Zinc gauze is probably the best material to use for a large hole. Cut a piece to the approximate size and shape of the hole to be filled, then position it in the hole so that its edges are below the level of the surrounding bodywork. It can be retained in position by several blobs of filler paste around its periphery.

18 Aluminium tape should be used for small or very narrow holes. Pull a piece off the roll and trim it to the approximate size and shape required, then pull off the backing paper (if used) and stick the tape over the hole; it can be overlapped if the thickness of one piece is insufficient. Burnish down the edges of the tape with the handle of a screwdriver or similar, to ensure that the tape is securely attached to the metal underneath.

Filling and respraying

19 Before using this Section, see the Section on dent, deep scratch, hole and gash repairs.

20 Many types of bodyfiller are available, but generally speaking, those proprietary kits which contain a tin of filler paste and a tube of resin hardener are best for this type of repair. A wide, flexible plastic or nylon applicator will be found invaluable for imparting a smooth and well-contoured finish to the surface of the filler.

21 Mix up a little filler on a clean piece of card or board. Use the hardener sparingly (follow the maker's instructions on the packet) otherwise the filler will set rapidly.

22 Using the applicator, apply the filler paste to the prepared area; draw the applicator across the surface of the filler to achieve the correct contour, and to level the filler surfaces. As soon as a contour that approximates the correct one is achieved, stop working the paste; if you carry on too long, the paste will become sticky and begin to 'pick-up' on the applicator. Continue to add thin layers of filler paste at twenty-minute intervals until the level of the filler is just 'proud' of the surrounding bodywork.

23 Once the filler has hardened, excess can be removed using a metal plane or file. From then on, progressively finer grades of abrasive paper should be used, starting with a 40-grade production paper, and finishing with a 400-grade wet-or-dry paper. Always wrap the abrasive paper around a flat rubber, cork, or wooden block, otherwise the surface of the filler will not be completely flat. During the smoothing of the filler surface, the wet-or-dry paper should be periodically rinsed in water. This will ensure that a very fine smooth finish is imparted to the filler at the final stage.

24 At this stage, the 'dent' should be surrounded by a ring of bare metal, which in turn should be encircled by the finely 'feathered' edge of the good paintwork. Rinse and repair with clean water, until all the dust produced by the rubbing-down operation is gone.

25 Spray the whole area with a light coat of grey primer, this will show up any imperfections in the surface of the filler. If at all possible, it is recommended that an etch-primer is used on untreated alloy surfaces, otherwise the primer may not be keyed sufficiently, and may subsequently flake off. Repair imperfections with fresh filler paste or bodystopper and once more, smooth the surface with abrasive paper. Repeat the spray-and-repair procedures until you are satisfied that the surface of the filler, and the feathered edge of the paintwork, is perfect. Clean the repair area with clean water, and allow it to dry fully.

HAYNES HINT *If bodystopper is used, it can be mixed with cellulose thinners, to form a really thin paste which is ideal for filling small holes.*

26 The repair area is now ready for spraying. Paint spraying must be carried out in a warm, dry, windless and dust-free atmosphere. This condition can be created artificially if you have access to a large indoor working area, but if you are forced to work in the open, you will have to pick your day very carefully. If you are working indoors, dousing the floor in the work area with water will 'lay' the dust which would otherwise be in the atmosphere. If the repair is confined to one body panel, mask off the surrounding panels; this will help to minimise the effects of a slight mis-match in paint colours. Bodywork fittings will also need to be masked off. Use genuine masking tape and several thickness of newspaper for the masking operation.

27 Before commencing to spray, agitate the aerosol can thoroughly, then spray a test area (an old tin, or similar) until the technique is mastered. Cover the repair area with a thick coat of primer; the thickness should be built up using several thin layers of paint, rather than one thick one. Using 400-grade wet-or-dry paper, rub down the surface of the primer until it is really smooth. Whilst doing this, the work area should be thoroughly doused with water, and the wet-or-dry paper periodically rinsed in water. Allow to dry before spraying on more paint.

28 Spray on the top coat, again building up the thickness by using several thin layers of paint. Start spraying at the top of the repair area and then, using a side-to-side motion, work downwards until the whole repair area and about 50 mm of the surrounding original paintwork is covered. Remove all masking material 10 to 15 minutes after spraying on the final coat of paint.

29 Allow the new paint at least two weeks to harden, then, using a paintwork renovator or a very fine cutting paste, blend the edges of the paint into the existing paintwork. Finally, apply wax polish.

Plastic components

30 With the use of more and more plastic body components by the vehicle manufacturers (eg bumpers. spoilers, and in some cases major body panels), rectification of more serious damage to such items has become a matter of either entrusting repair work to a specialist in this field, or renewing complete components. Repair of such damage by the DIY owner is not really feasible, owing to the cost of the equipment and materials required for effecting such repairs. The basic technique involves making a groove along the line of the crack in the plastic, using a rotary burr in a power drill. The damaged part is then welded back together, using a hot-air gun to heat up and fuse a plastic filler rod into the groove. Any excess plastic is then removed, and the area rubbed down to a smooth finish. It is important that a filler rod of the correct plastic is used, as body components can be made of a variety of different types (eg, polycarbonate, ABS, polypropylene).

31 Damage of a less serious nature (abrasions, minor cracks etc) can be repaired by the DIY owner using a two-part epoxy filler repair material. Once mixed in equal proportions, or applied directly from the tube, this is used in similar fashion to the bodywork filler used on metal panels. The filler is usually cured in twenty to thirty minutes, ready for sanding and painting.

6.1 On air conditioned models, undo the 6 screws (3 left-hand ones arrowed) and remove the radiator grille

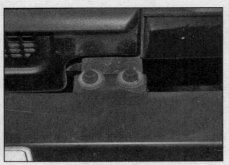

6.2 Undo the four bolts (two at each side)

32 If the owner is renewing a complete component himself, or if he has repaired it with epoxy filler, he will be left with the problem of finding a suitable paint for finishing which is compatible with the type of plastic used. At one time, the use of a universal paint was not possible, owing to the complex range of plastics encountered in body component applications. Standard paints, generally speaking, will not bond to plastic or rubber satisfactorily. However, it is now possible to obtain a plastic body parts finishing kit which consists of a pre-primer treatment, a primer and coloured top coat. Full instructions are normally supplied with a kit, but basically, the method of use is to first apply the pre-primer to the component concerned, and allow it to dry for up to 30 minutes. Then the primer is applied, and left to dry for about an hour before finally applying the special-coloured top coat. The result is a correctly-coloured component, where the paint will flex with the plastic or rubber, a property that standard paint does not normally possess.

5 Major body damage – repair

1 Where serious damage has occurred, or large areas need renewal due to neglect, it means that complete new panels will need welding-in, and this is best left to professionals. If the damage is due to impact, it will also be necessary to check completely the alignment of the bodyshell, and this can only be carried out accurately by a Land Rover dealer, using special jigs. If the body is left misaligned, it is primarily dangerous, as the car will not handle properly; secondly, uneven stresses will be imposed on the steering, suspension and possibly transmission, causing abnormal wear, or complete failure, particularly to such items as the tyres.

6 Front bumper – removal and refitting

Removal

1 On models with air conditioning, undo the 6 screws and remove the radiator grille **(see illustration)**.
2 Slacken and remove the four mounting bolts from the top of the bumper, and recover the nut retaining plates from under the bumper **(see illustration)**. Where applicable remove the plastic caps from over he heads of the bolts.
3 Remove the bumper from the vehicle.

Refitting

4 Refitting is the reverse of removal, ensuring that the mounting bolts are securely tightened.

7 Bonnet – removal, refitting and adjustment

Removal

1 Where necessary, remove the spare wheel from the bonnet.
2 With the aid of an assistant, lift the bonnet to the upright position, then lift the bonnet to remove it from the vehicle. Recover the bush from each bonnet hinge pivot, and store them with the bonnet for safe-keeping **(see illustration)**.
3 Inspect the bonnet hinges for signs of wear or damage; the hinges are bolted in position, and can easily be renewed.

Refitting and adjustment

4 Refitting is the reverse of removal, ensuring that the bushes are in position on the bonnet pivots.
5 Close the bonnet, and check for alignment with the adjacent panels. If necessary, slacken the bonnet bolts and realign the bonnet to suit. The bonnet height is adjusted by rotating the striker on the front edge of the bonnet. Once the bonnet is correctly aligned, securely tighten the bolts.
6 Once the bonnet is correctly aligned, check that the bonnet fastens and releases in a satisfactory manner. If necessary, adjust the release cable described in Section.

8 Bonnet release cable – removal and refitting

Removal

1 Remove the bonnet lock assembly as described in Section 9.
2 Work back along the cable, releasing it from all the relevant retaining clips and ties, whilst noting its correct routing. Release the rubber sealing grommets from the body, and slide them off the end of the cable. Tie a piece of string to the cable end – this can then be used to draw the cable back into position. **Note:** The cable may be in two parts and there will be a connector that joins the two pieces together on the inner wing panel **(see illustration)**.
3 From inside the vehicle, pull back the bonnet release handle and unclip the outer cable from the mounting bracket and the inner cable from the release handle. If required, undo the two retaining nuts and remove the bonnet release handle from the bulkhead **(see illustrations)**.
4 Withdraw the cable from inside the vehicle. Once the cable end appears, untie the string and leave it in position in the vehicle – the string can then be used to draw the new cable back into position.

7.2 Recover the bush from the bonnet hinge pivot

8.2 Cable joiner on inner wing panel

8.3a Release the cable from the release handle

8.3b Release handle retaining nuts

Refitting

5 Tie the string to the end of the cable, and use the string to draw the bonnet release cable through from inside the vehicle into the engine compartment. Once the cable is through, untie the string, and slide on both the rubber sealing grommets. Re-connect the cable to the release handle and (if removed) refit the release handle to the bulkhead and tighten the retaining nuts.

6 Ensure that the cable is correctly routed and retained by all the relevant clips and ties, then seat the cable grommets in the vehicle body.

7 Refit the bonnet lock assembly as described in Section.

9 Bonnet lock – removal and refitting

Removal

1 Undo the retaining screws, and remove the radiator grille from the front of the vehicle.

2 Open the bonnet, then slacken the clamp securing bolt and disconnect the bonnet release cable from the lock mechanism, through the hole in the upper crossmember **(see illustration)**.

3 Using a suitable marker pen, draw around the outline of the bonnet lock top plate and adjusting plates. These marks can then be used as a guide on refitting **(see illustration)**.

4 Undo the two retaining bolts, and lift the top plate away from the bonnet crossmember.

5 Free the lock assembly and mounting plate from the underside of the bonnet crossmember, and detach the lock assembly from its return spring.

Refitting

6 Refitting is the reverse of the removal procedure, using the alignment marks made prior to removal. Prior to refitting the radiator grille, check the operation of the release mechanism.

Adjustment of the cable can be made by either slackening the clamp and adjusting the inner cable or, alternatively, by releasing the outer cable retaining clip and repositioning the clip on the cable (as applicable).

10 Door – removal, refitting and adjustment

Front door removal

1 Remove the split-pin and washer, then

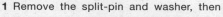

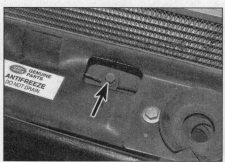

9.2 Slacken the cable clamp bolt

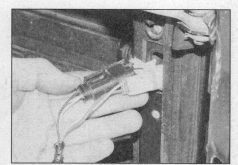

10.1 Remove the split-pin, and withdraw the clevis pin from the check link

withdraw the clevis pin securing the check link to the door **(see illustration)**.

2 On vehicles with electric front windows and/or central locking, pull the rubber loom covering from the A-pillar and disconnect the door loom wiring plugs **(see illustration)**.

3 Have an assistant support the weight of the door, then slacken and remove the bolts securing each hinge to the pillar. Remove the door from the vehicle, and recover the nylon spacers which are fitted between the hinge and pillar.

4 Examine the hinges for signs of wear or damage. If renewal is necessary, mark the

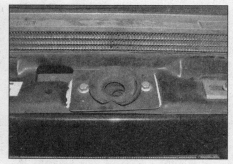

9.3 Make markings at each side of the lock plate

10.2 On models with electric front windows, pull the gaiter from the A-pillar and disconnect the door wiring loom plugs

10.5 Unclip the rubber wiring grommet from the pillar

10.6 Undo the check link securing nut

10.7 Undo the bolts securing the door hinges to the body pillar

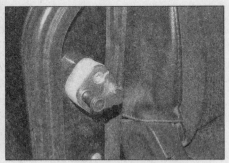

10.18 Adjust door striker plate

outline of the original hinge on the door, then slacken and remove the retaining bolts and remove the hinge. Recover the special retaining nuts, and remove the hinge seal. Fit the seal and new hinge, and refit the retaining bolts. Align the hinge with the marks made prior to removal, and securely tighten the retaining bolts.

Rear door removal

5 On vehicles with electric front windows and/or central locking, pull the rubber loom covering from the A-pillar and disconnect the door loom wiring plugs **(see illustration)**.
6 Unscrew the retaining nut, then free the check link from its pivot **(see illustration)**, recovering the washer which is fitted on each side of the link.

7 Have an assistant support the weight of the door, then slacken and remove the bolts securing the door hinges to the body pillar. Remove the door **(see illustration)**.
8 Examine the hinges for signs of damage. If necessary, they can be renewed as described in paragraph 4.

Front door refitting

9 Ensure that the nylon spacers are in position on the rear of the hinge then, with the aid of an assistant, offer up the door.
10 Refit the hinge retaining bolts, tighten them loosely at this stage.
11 Apply a smear of grease to the clevis pin, then align the check link with its bracket, and insert the pin. Refit the washer, and

secure the pin in position with a new split-pin.
12 Connect the wiring and refit the rubber grommet to the door pillar.
13 Close the door, and check that it is correctly aligned with the surrounding body panels. Adjust the door position on the hinges, then securely tighten the four hinge retaining bolts.

Rear door refitting

14 Position the door, and refit the hinge-to-body bolts, tighten them loosely at this stage.
15 Refit the check link and tighten the retaining nut.
16 Connect the wiring and refit the rubber grommet to the door pillar.
17 Close the door and check that it aligns correctly with the surrounding body panels. Securely tighten the hinge-to-body bolts.

Adjustment

18 Some vertical adjustment of the doors can be achieved by slackening the hinge retaining bolts and re-positioning the hinge/door. To adjust door closing, slacken the retaining screws and adjust the striker plate **(see illustration)**.

11 Door inner trim panel –
removal and refitting

Removal

1 Unclip the access covers from the armrest/grab handle, then undo the two retaining screws and remove it from the door **(see illustration)**.
2 Lift the inner door lock handle, and carefully prise the trim cap out from the handle surround. Undo the retaining screw, and remove the handle surround from the door panel **(see illustrations)**.
3 On models with manual windows, carefully

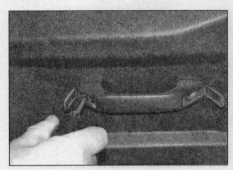

11.1 Open up the access cover, and undo the two armrest handle retaining screws

11.2a Undo the retaining screw ...

11.2b ... and unclip the handle surround from the trim panel

11.3a Remove the trim cap, then undo the retaining screw and remove the regulator handle from the door

11.3b Using a special tool...

11.3c ...to release the securing clip

prise the trim cap out from the centre of the regulator handle, then slacken and remove the retaining screw and washer **(see illustrations)**. On some models, no centre screw is fitted to the regulator handle. On these vehicles, use a special tool to slide up behind the handle to release the spring clip. **Note:** *A length of rag behind the handle, and using a sawing motion to release the clip, can also work. Remove the handle from the regulator, and recover the handle surround.*

4 Release the retaining clip and slide up the inner lock button surround, and remove it from the trim panel **(see illustration)**.

5 Push in the centre pins and prise out the expanding rivets/studs, from the corners of the trim panel **(see illustrations)**.

6 Release the door trim panel studs by carefully levering between the panel and door with a trim tool. Work around the outside of the panel, and when all the studs are released, slide the panel upwards and away from the door **(see illustrations)**.

Refitting

7 Refitting is a reverse of the removal procedure. Prior to refitting, examine the panel retaining clips for signs of damage, and renew any broken clips.

11.4 Unclip the lock button surround from the trim panel

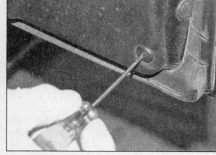

11.5a Press in the centre pin...

11.5b ...prise out the plastic rivet...

11.5c ...and remove it from the trim panel

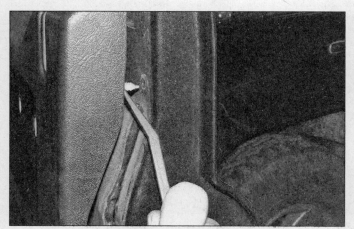

11.6a Release the securing clips...

11.6b ...and remove the trim panel

12 Door reinforcement panel – removal and refitting

Removal

1 Remove the inner trim panel as described in Section 11.

2 Peel the polythene weathershield away from the door **(see illustrations)**, to gain access to the door lock components, then proceed as described under the relevant sub-heading. A sharp blade co cut the sealant around the edge of the weathershield, taking care not to cause any personal injury.

3 Release the locking clip and disconnect the central locking motor linkage rod from the lock assembly **(see illustrations)**.

4 Release the retaining clip, and remove the inner release handle link rod from the lock assembly **(see illustration 13.3)**.

5 Operate the window regulator, and lower the window glass, until the retaining bolts on the lower part of the window frame can be accessed **(see illustrations)**.

6 Slacken the window glass retaining bolts and disengage the window glass from the regulator assembly. Slide the window up to the top of the door frame, then securely tape the window glass to its frame, to prevent the window dropping when the reinforcement panel is removed **(see illustrations)**.

12.2a Using a blade…

12.2b …to remove the weathershield

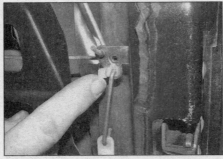

12.3a Release the locking clip…

12.3b …and disconnect the linkage rod

7 Disconnect the wiring connectors from the central locking motor and window regulator, then unclip the wiring loom from along the reinforcement panel and move it to one side **(see illustrations)**.

8 Slacken and remove the bolts securing the

12.5a Slacken the window glass securing bolts – front window

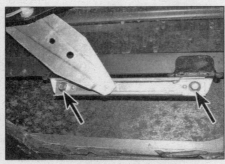

12.5b Slacken the window glass securing bolts – rear window

12.6a Disengage glass from regulator…

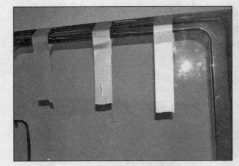

12.6b …and secure it to the window frame

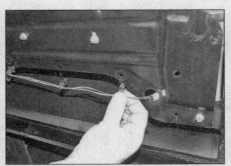

12.7a Disconnect the wiring connectors…

12.7b …and remove the wiring loom from the panel

12.8a Undo the retaining bolts (rear door shown)...

reinforcement panel and remove it from the door frame **(see illustrations)**.

9 If required undo the retaining bolts and remove the window regulator assembly from the rear of the reinforcement panel.

Refitting

10 Refitting is the reverse of the removal sequence. Make sure the window regulator and door locking operates correctly before refitting the door trim panel.

13 Door handle and lock components – removal and refitting

Removal

1 Remove the inner trim panel as described in Section 11.

2 Peel the polythene weathershield away from the door **(see illustrations 12.2a and 12.2b)**, to gain access to the door lock components, then proceed as described under the relevant sub-heading. A sharp blade co cut the sealant around the edge of the weathershield, taking care not to cause any personal injury.

Front door interior handle

3 Release the retaining clip, and release the handle link rod from the lock assembly **(see illustration)**.

4 Slacken and remove the retaining screws, and remove the handle and link rod assembly from the door **(see illustration)**.

13.6d ...and detach the link rod from the handle meachanism

12.8b ...and remove the reinforcement panel (front door shown)

Front door exterior handle

5 Remove the reinforcement panel, as described in Section 12.

6 Release the retaining clips, and disconnect

13.4 Undo the retaining screws, and remove the interior handle from the door

13.6b ...and detach the link rod from the lock cylinder

13.7a Undo the two retaining screws (arrowed) ...

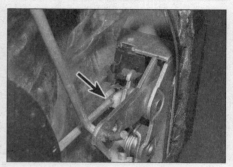

13.3 Release the linkage rod

the handle and lock cylinder link rods from the lock assembly **(see illustrations)**.

7 Slacken and remove the two retaining screws, and remove the exterior handle from the door **(see illustrations)**.

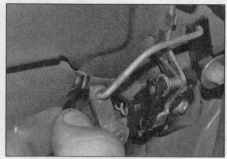

13.6a Release the retaining clip...

13.6c Release the retaining clip...

13.7b ... and remove the exterior handle from the door

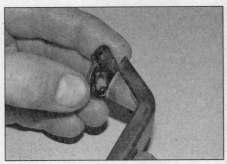

13.8a Check the seals...

13.8b ...on the door handle

13.10a Remove the securing clip...

13.10b ...and remove the operating arm

13.11a Remove the lock cylinder...

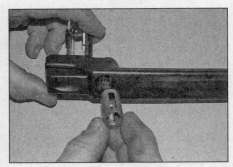

13.11b ...and the retaining sleeve

8 Recover the rubber seals fitted to the rear of the handle **(see illustrations)**.

Front lock cylinder

9 Remove the exterior handle as described above.

10 Insert the key into the lock cylinder, then release the securing clip on the rear of the lock cylinder and withdraw the operating arm **(see illustrations)**. Note the fitted position of the arm for refitting.

11 With the key still inserted, withdraw the lock cylinder, followed by the retaining sleeve from the handle **(see illustrations)**, noting there fitted position for refitting..

Front door lock

12 Remove the exterior handle as described above.

13 Slacken and remove the screw(s) securing the lower end of the window glass rear guide rail to the door **(see illustration)**.

14 Undo the three retaining screws (Torx screws), then carefully, taking great care not to damage it, ease the guide rail away from the door and manoeuvre the lock assembly out of position **(see illustrations)**.

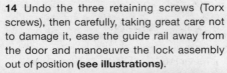

13.13 Undo the screw(s) securing the glass rear guide rail

Front door interior lock button

15 Release the retaining clip, and detach the lock button link rod from the lock assembly.

16 Undo the two retaining screws, and remove the lock button from the door **(see illustrations)**.

13.14a Undo the three retaining screws ...

13.14b ... and manoeuvre the lock assembly out from behind the window guide rail

13.16a Undo the two screws...

13.16b ...and remove the lock button...

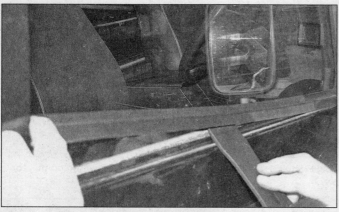

14.4 Remove the outer seal

14.5 Undo the screw from the front window guide

Rear interior door handle

17 Release the retaining clip, and release the handle link rod from the lock assembly.
18 Slacken and remove the retaining screws, and remove the handle and link rod assembly from the door.

Rear exterior door handle

19 Release the retaining clip, and detach the link rod from the handle.
20 Undo the two retaining screws, and remove the handle from the door. Recover the rubber seals fitted to the rear of the handle.

Rear door lock

21 Release the retaining clips, and detach the link rods from the lock assembly.
22 Release the retaining clip, and detach the link rod from the rear of the exterior door handle.
23 Undo the three retaining screws, and remove the lock assembly from the door.

Rear door interior lock button

24 Release the retaining clip, and detach the lock button link rod from the lock assembly.
25 Undo the two retaining screws, and remove the lock button from the door.

Refitting

26 Refitting is the reverse of the removal sequence, noting the following points:
a) *If a lock cylinder has been removed, on refitting, ensure that the spring and link rod bracket are correctly positioned, and*

are securely held by the screw. Check the operation of the lock cylinder before refitting the handle to the door.
b) *Ensure that all link rods are securely held in position by their retaining clips.*
c) *Apply grease to all lock and link rod pivot points.*
d) *On the front door, if the reinforcement panel has been removed, check the window regulator movement, before refitting the trim panel.*
e) *Before installing the relevant trim panel, thoroughly check the operation of all the door lock handles.*

14 Door window glass and regulator – removal and refitting

Removal

1 Remove the door inner trim panel as described in Section 11.
2 Peel the polythene weathershield away from the door to gain access to the door lock components **(see illustrations 12.2a and 12.2b)**. Proceed as described under the relevant sub-heading.

Front door window glass

3 Remove the reinforcement panel, as described in Section 12.
4 Carefully prise the window glass outer

sealing strip from the top edge of the door **(see illustration)**.
5 Undo the single screw securing the front window guide channel to the door frame **(see illustration)**.
6 Undo the two retaining screws from the rear window guide channel **(see illustration)**.
7 Remove the tape from the window glass, then carefully lower the glass down into the door. Free the glass from its guides, and manoeuvre it out from the door **(see illustrations)**.

Rear door window glass

8 Remove the reinforcement panel, as described in Section 12.
9 Undo the two nuts and remove the door check link torsion bar and plate **(see illustration)**, then undo the nut and detach the check link.

14.6 Undo the screws from the rear window guide – lower one shown

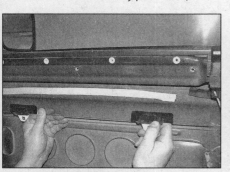

14.7a Slide the glass down inside the door…

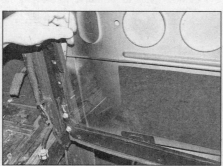

14.7b …and manoeuvre it out from bottom of the door

14.9 Remove the check link torsion bar and plate

14.11a Undo the front …

14.11b … and rear window guide rail screws

14.15 Disconnect the wiring connector from the regulator

14.16 Undo the guide retaining bolts

14.17 Undo the four window regulator bolts

14.20 The regulator assembly is secured by 4 bolts

10 Prise up and remove the inner and outer door waist rubber seals.

11 Undo the screw securing the front window guide rail, and the screw securing the rear window guide rail **(see illustrations)**.

12 Remove the tape from the window glass, then carefully lower the glass down into the door. Free the glass from its guides, and manoeuvre it out from the door.

Front door window regulator

13 Operate the window regulator, and lower the window glass, until the retaining bolts on the lower part of the window frame can be accessed **(see illustration 12.5a)**.

14 Slacken the window glass retaining bolts and disengage the window glass from the regulator assembly. Slide the window up to the top of the door frame, then securely tape the window glass to its frame, to prevent window dropping when the reinforcement

panel is removed **(see illustrations 12.6a and 12.6b)**.

15 Disconnect the wiring plug connector from the window regulator **(see illustration)**.

16 Slacken and remove the two bolts securing the window regulator guide to the door **(see illustration)**.

17 Undo the four retaining bolts, and remove the window regulator assembly from the door reinforcement panel **(see illustration)**.

Rear door window regulator

18 Operate the window regulator, and lower the window glass, until the retaining bolts on the lower part of the window frame can be accessed **(see illustration 12.5a)**.

19 Slacken the window glass retaining bolts and disengage the window glass from the regulator assembly. Slide the window up to the top of the door frame, then securely tape the window glass to its frame, to prevent the

window dropping when the reinforcement panel is removed **(see illustrations 12.6a and 12.6b)**.

20 Undo the 4 bolts retaining bolts and manoeuvre the regulator downwards from the door **(see illustration)**.

Refitting

21 Refitting is the reverse of the removal procedure, noting the following points:

a) *Check that the glass moves easily, and seats squarely in the frame, then securely tighten the regulator retaining bolts.*

b) *Refit the weathershield, making sure it is securely stuck to the door, then refit the trim panel as described in Section 11.*

15 Tailgate – removal and refitting

Removal

1 Disconnect the battery negative terminal and (see Chapter 5 Section 4), where necessary, remove the spare wheel from the tailgate.

2 Trace the wiring back from the tailgate harness to its wiring connectors, and prise out the rubber grommet, pull out the loom and disconnect the wiring plugs **(see illustration)**. On some models, it may be necessary to undo the retaining screws and remove the trim panel from inside the vehicle to gain access to the wiring connectors.

3 Undo the retaining bolt and disconnect the tailgate check link to the body **(see illustration)**.

15.2 Prise out the grommet and disconnect the wiring connectors

15.3 Undo the check link securing bolt

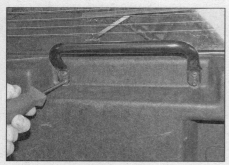

16.1a Undo the retaining screws...

16.1b ...and remove the grab handle

16.2a Prise out the plastic panel...

16.2b ...and remove it from the handle recess

16.3a Prise the tailgate trim...

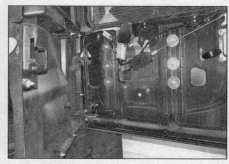

16.3b ...away from the tailgate

4 Remove the trim caps (where fitted) from the rear of the tailgate hinge bolts, to reveal the screws.

5 Using a suitable marker pen, make alignment marks between the tailgate and hinges.

6 Have an assistant support the tailgate, then slacken and retaining screws securing the hinges to the body, and remove the tailgate assembly from the vehicle.

7 Examine the tailgate hinges for signs of wear or damage. If renewal is necessary, first mark the outline of the hinge on the tailgate, then undo the retaining bolts and remove the hinge. Fit the new hinges, and align them with the marks made prior to removal before securely tighten their retaining screws.

Refitting

8 Refitting is the reverse of removal. Locate the tailgate hinges to the body, and refit the retaining screws, tightening them by hand only. Align the marks made prior to removal, then

securely tighten the hinge retaining screws. Reconnect the wiring connectors and check link, then close the tailgate and check for alignment with the surrounding body panels. Slight adjustments can be made by loosening the hinge bolts and re-positioning the tailgate.

16 Tailgate lock assembly – removal and refitting

Removal

1 Open the tailgate and undo the Torx retaining screws, and remove the grab handle **(see illustrations)**.

2 Prise out the small plastic panel from the tailgate latch handle recess **(see illustrations)**.

3 Using a flat-bladed tool, carefully release the 9 clips securing the panel to the tailgate **(see illustrations)**.

4 Undo the 4 retaining nuts and partially withdrawn the lock assembly from the tailgate **(see illustration)**. Recover the gasket.

5 Disconnect the central locking link rod, and remove the lock assembly **(see illustration)**.

6 To remove the lock cylinder, fit the key, then insert a small punch in through the hole in the lock assembly to depress the cylinder plunger **(see illustration)**. The cylinder can then be withdrawn from the lock assembly.

Refitting

7 Refitting is the reverse of the removal procedure, noting the following:

a) Ensure that the lock gasket is in good condition – don't forget to fit it between the lock and tailgate.

b) If required, the position of the striker plate can be adjusted by slackening the retaining bolts.

16.4 Tailgate lock retaining nuts (arrowed)

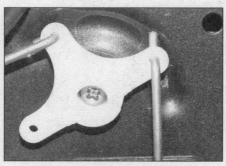

16.5 Central locking link rod (arrowed)

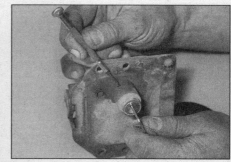

16.6 To remove the lock cylinder, insert the key, then depress the cylinder plunger with a suitable punch or screwdriver

17 Exterior mirror – removal and refitting

Removal

1 Undo the retaining screw, and remove the balljoint clamp from the base of the mirror. Lift the mirror assembly off its mounting bracket (see illustrations).

2 To remove the mounting bracket, first remove the front door as described in Section 10. Undo the retaining screws, and remove the mirror mounting bracket from the door hinge.

Refitting

3 Refitting is the reverse of removal. Position the mirror correctly, then securely tighten its balljoint clamp screw.

18 Windscreen, tailgate and fixed windows – general information

1 These areas of glass are secured by the tight fit of the weatherstrip in the body aperture, and are bonded in position with a special adhesive. The removal and refitting of these areas of fixed glass is difficult, messy and time-consuming task which is beyond the scope of the home mechanic. It is difficult, unless one has plenty of practice, to obtain a secure, waterproof fit. Furthermore, the task carries a high risk of breakage; this applies especially to the laminated glass windscreen.

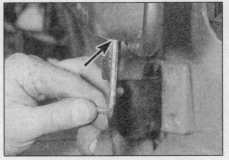

17.1a Undo the retaining screw (arrowed) ...

In view of this, owners are strongly advised to have this sort of work carried out by one of the many specialist windscreen fitters.

19 Body exterior fittings – removal and refitting

Wheel arch liners and body under panels

1 The various plastic covers fitted to the underside of the vehicle are secured in position by a mixture of screws, nuts and retaining clips, and removal will be fairly obvious on inspection. Work methodically around the panel, removing its retaining screws and releasing its retaining clips until the panel is free and can be removed from

17.1b ... then free the balljoint clamp and remove the mirror from its mounting bracket

the underside of the vehicle. Most clips used on the vehicle, with the exception of some of the trim fasteners, are simply prised out of position. These special clips are released by pressing out their centre pins and then removing the outer section of the clip; new clips will be required on refitting if the centre pins are not recovered.

2 On refitting, renew any retaining clips that may have been broken on removal, and ensure that the panel is securely retained by all the relevant clips, nuts and screws.

Body trim strips and badges

3 Most of the various body trim strips and badges are held in position with a special adhesive tape. Removal requires the trim/badge to be heated, to soften the adhesive, and then cut away from the surface. Due to the high risk of damage to the vehicle's paintwork during this operation, it is recommended that this task should be entrusted to a Land Rover dealer.

Front grille

4 Undo the eight retaining screws and remove the grille panel from the front of the vehicle (see illustrations).

5 On models with air conditioning, undo the four retaining screws along the upper edge of the grille surround and the two (one at each side) at the lower part of the grille surround (see illustrations). Release the plastic securing clips to remove the grille from the metal surround.

19.4a Undo the retaining screws...

19.4b ...and remove the grille

19.5a Undo the four upper retaining screws...

19.5b ...and the lower side retaining screws

19.5c Release the plastic securing clips to remove grille

19.7 Remove the wheel arch

19.8 Undo the damper retaining nut

19.9a Undo the retaining nuts...

Front wing

6 Jack up the front of the vehicle and remove the front wheel.

7 Release the fasteners and remove the wheel arch from the wing panel **(see illustration)**.

8 Remove damper cover from the the inner wing panel and remove the damper retaining nut **(see illustration)**.

9 From under the wheel arch, undo the four retaining nuts and remove the damper turret from under the wing panel **(see illustrations)**.

10 Working your way around the inner wing panel undo the fasteners from under the front wheel arch.

11 Remove the front grille, as described previously in this section.

12 Undo the four retaining screws along the upper edge of the grille surround and the two bolts (one at each side) inside the lower part of the grille surround, then withdraw it from the front of the vehicle **(see illustrations)**.

13 Undo the retaining bolts and remove the two stay brackets from in front of the radiator/intercooler **(see illustration)**.

14 Undo the six fasteners and remove the cooling fan upper shroud **(see illustration)**.

15 Working at each side of the crossmember/latch panel, undo the four retaining nuts (two at each side), and then remove the studs **(see illustrations)**. With the studs removed, the crossmember/latch panel can now be removed and moved to one side. Note the bonnet release cable is still attached to the latch panel, so position it to one side.

19.9b ...and remove the damper turret

19.12a Undo the four upper retaining screws...

19.12b ...and the inner securing bolts

19.13 Remove the stay brackets

19.14 Remove the upper shroud

19.15a Remove the securing nuts...

19.15b ...and remove the studs

19.16 Remove the mounting bracket

19.17 Remove the mounting bracket

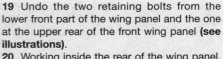

19 Undo the two retaining bolts from the lower front part of the wing panel and the one at the upper rear of the front wing panel **(see illustrations)**.
20 Working inside the rear of the wing panel, slacken the three retaining bolts, and then with the aid of an assistant, lift the front wing from the vehicle, making sure that everything is disconnected from the wing as it is removed. Note the three bolts do not have to be completely removed **(see illustration)**, as the holes in the front wing are elongated.
21 Refitting is the reversal of the removal.

20 Seats – removal and refitting

Note: *Due to the large amount of seating options available, it is not possible to give detailed instructions on how to remove each individual type of seat. Using the text as a guide; removal details will be self-evident on inspection.*

Removal

Front seats

1 Unclip/lift up the seat cushion, and remove it from the vehicle **(see illustration)**. Where applicable, disconnect the seat heating wiring plugs.
2 Slide the seat fully rearwards, then slacken and remove the front bolts securing the seat to the floor **(see illustrations)**. Note the position of the spacers between the seat rails

19.18a Disconnect the wiring block connector (left-hand side shown)

19.18b Disconnect the washer pipes (left-hand side shown)

16 On the left-hand front wing, undo the retaining bolts and remove the PAS reservoir mounting bracket from the wing panel **(see illustration)**.
17 Undo the retaining bolts and remove the

mounting bracket from between the radiator and the wing panel **(see illustration)**.
18 Working inside the inner wing, disconnect any wiring connectors or cables that are still attached to the wing panel **(see illustrations)**.

19.19a Undo the two bolts at the front...

19.19b ...and the one at the upper rear

19.20 Three bolts at the rear of the front wing

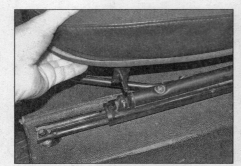

20.1 Lift the seat cushion to release from the locating clips

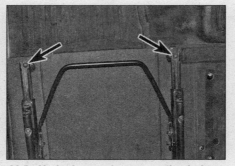

20.2a Undo the two front mounting bolts...

20.2b ...noting the position of the spacers and bracket

20.3a Undo the two rear bolts...

20.3b ...noting the position of the spacers

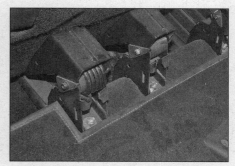

20.4 Undo the seat hinge retaining nuts

and the floor panel, the inner bolt also has an 'L' shaped bracket fitted.

3 Slide the seat fully forwards, undo the rear bolts securing the seat to the floor, then remove the seat from the vehicle **(see illustrations)**. Note the position of the spacers between the seat rails and the body,

Rear seat

4 Release the lever and fold the seat forwards, then slacken and remove the nuts securing the seat mounting brackets and/ or hinges to the floor **(see illustration)**, and remove the assembly from the vehicle.

Luggage compartment seats

5 On models with individual seats, slacken and remove the retaining bolts securing the seat hinges to the vehicle. Undo the seat back mounting bolts, and remove the seat from the vehicle.

6 On models with bench-type seats, unclip the seat cushion, and remove it from the vehicle. Slacken and remove the bolts securing the seat assembly in position, and remove it from the vehicle.

Refitting

7 Refitting is a reverse of the relevant removal procedure.

21 Seat belt components – removal and refitting

Front seat side belt removal

1 Unclip the trim cover from the seat belt upper mounting point, then unscrew the retaining bolt and free the belt from its

mounting **(see illustration)**. Recover the flanged spacer and washers which are fitted to the rear of the belt anchorage, noting their correct fitted locations.

2 On two door models, undo the inertia reel bracket retaining bolts, and remove from inside the vehicle **(see illustration)**.

3 On four door models, lower anchorage bolts, then unclip the cover and undo the inertia reel securing bolt, and remove from inside the vehicle **(see illustrations)**.

Front seat belt stalks and centre belt removal

4 Prise off the trim cap (where fitted), then slacken and remove the mounting bolt(s). Remove the stalk/belt **(see illustration)**, and recover the washers and spacer, noting their correct fitted location.

21.1 Remove the trim cover from the upper mounting to reveal the mounting bolt

21.2 Inertia reel retaining bolts

21.3a Undo the anchorage plate bolts...

21.3b ...unclip the cover...

21.3c ...and undo the inertia reel mounting bolt

21.4 Seat belt stalk retaining bolts...

21.6 Rear seat belt upper anchor bolt

21.7a Prise out the clip ...

21.7b ... and prise away the C-pillar trim panel

Rear seat side belt removal

5 Unclip the trim cover from the seat belt upper mounting point, then unscrew the retaining bolt, and free the belt from its mounting. Recover the flanged spacer and washers which are fitted to the rear of the belt anchorage, noting their correct fitted locations.
6 Prise out the seat belt guide, then unclip the upper seat belt anchor bolt cap and undo the bolt **(see illustration)**.
7 Carefully prise away the C-pillar trim panel

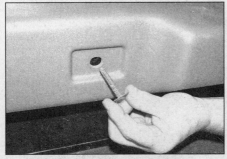

22.3a Release the securing clips...

sufficiently to access the inertia reel securing bolt **(see illustrations)**.
8 Unclip the cover and undo the seat belt lower retaining bolt.
9 Pull the seat belt through the pillar trim panel, then undo the bolts and remove the inertia reel securing bolt.

Rear seat belt buckles and centre belt removal

10 Free the seat belt/buckle (as applicable) from the rear seat, then prise off the trim cap (where fitted) and unbolt its mounting from the floor.

Refitting

11 Refitting is a reversal of the removal procedure, ensuring that all the mounting bolts are tightened to the specified torque, where given.

22 Interior trim –
removal and refitting

1 The interior trim panels are secured

using either screws or various types of trim fasteners, usually studs or clips.
2 Check that there are no other panels overlapping the one to be removed; usually there is a sequence to be followed that will become obvious on close inspection.
3 Remove all obvious fasteners, such as screws. If the panel will not come free, it is held by hidden clips or fasteners. These are usually situated around the edge of the panel, and can be prised up to release them **(see illustrations)**. Note, however, that they can break quite easily, so have new ones available. The best way of releasing such clips (in the absence of a proper forked type of tool) is to use a large flat-bladed screwdriver. Note in many cases that an adjacent sealing strip must be prised back to release a panel.
4 When removing a panel, never use excessive force, or the panel may be damaged; always check carefully that all fasteners have been removed or released before attempting to withdraw a panel.
5 Refitting is the reverse of the removal procedure; secure the fasteners by pressing them firmly into place, and ensure that all disturbed components are correctly secured, to prevent rattles.

22.3b ...from the trim panels...

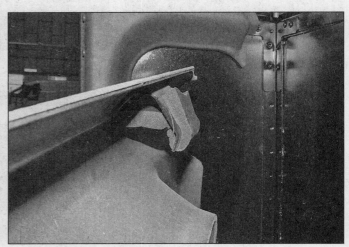

22.3c ...and lift up to release any retaining hooks on the rear of the panel

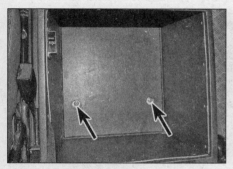

23.1 Undo the retaining screws (arrowed)

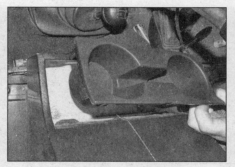

23.2a Lift out the cupholders ...

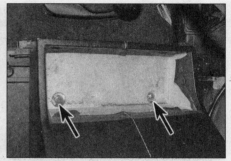

23.2b ... and undo the two screws (arrowed)

23 Storage box – removal and refitting

Storage box removal

1 Open the storage box lid, prise up the plastic caps (where fitted) and remove the two retaining screws **(see illustration)**.
2 Prise up the front flap/remove the cupholders, and remove the two bolts at the front of the storage box **(see illustrations)**.
3 Remove the box.

Refitting

4 Refitting is the reverse of removal.

24 Facia panel assembly – removal and refitting

 HAYNES HiNT *Label each wiring connector as it is disconnected from its relevant component. The labels will prove useful on refitting, when routing the wiring and feeding the wiring through the facia apertures.*

Note: *On models with air conditioning, if it is intended to remove the heater housing*

24.9a Undo the retaining screws...

24.9b ...and remove the centre instrument panel

assembly, have the refrigerant circuit discharged by a suitable equipped specialist, as the evaporator assembly must be removed.

Removal

1 Disconnect the battery negative terminal, as described in Chapter 5.
2 Remove the storage box from between the front seats, as described in Section 23.
3 Remove the gearchange levers, as described in Chapter 7A Section 2.
4 Remove the steering wheel as described in Chapter 11.
5 Remove the instrument panel, as described in Chapter 13 Section 9.
6 Remove the shrouds from around the steering column, with reference to Chapter 11 Section 20.

7 Remove the steering column switches, as described in Chapter 13 Section 4.
8 Remove the radio/CD player, as described in Chapter 13 Section 17.
9 Undo the two retaining screws from the instrument panel console in the centre of the facia, then withdraw it and disconnect the wiring connectors, noting there fitted position **(see illustrations)**.
10 Working on the passenger side, undo the two retaining screws and remove the grab handle from the facia **(see illustration)**.
11 Unclip the demister vent covers from the ends of the facia panel **(see illustration)**.
12 Unclip the speaker covers from the top of the facia panel **(see illustration)**. Where fitted, remove the speaker and disconnect the wiring connector.
13 Remove the speakers from the lower part

24.10 Remove the grab handle

24.11 Remove the vent trim

24.12 Unclip the speaker from the facia

24.13 Remove the speakers

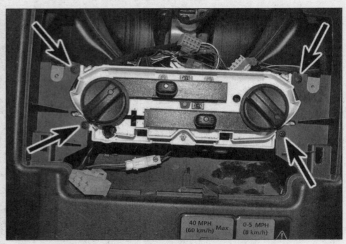

24.14a Undo the retaining screws...

24.14b ...and disconnect the cables and wiring

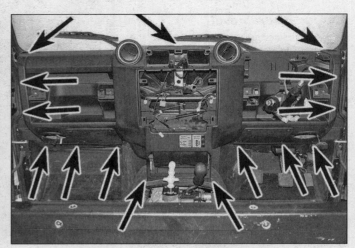

24.15 Undo the facia retaining screws

of the facia **(see illustration)**, disconnecting the wiring connectors, as they are removed.

14 Undo the retaining screws and remove the heater control panel, disconnect the operating cables and wiring connector, as the control panel is removed **(see illustrations)**. Note the position of the cables for refitting.

15 Working your way around the facia, undo the fifteen retaining screws securing the facia panel to the bulkhead **(see illustration)**. With the aid of an assistant withdraw the facia panel from the bulkhead and out from the passenger compartment.

Refitting

16 Refitting is a reversal of the removal procedure, noting the following points:

a) *Make sure that the facia is correctly located, then refit all its retaining screws and tighten them securely.*

b) *On completion, reconnect the battery and check that all the electrical components and switches function correctly.*

Chapter 13
Body electrical systems

Contents

Degrees of difficulty

Easy, suitable for novice with little experience	**Fairly easy,** suitable for beginner with some experience	**Fairly difficult,** suitable for competent DIY mechanic	**Difficult,** suitable for experienced DIY mechanic	**Very difficult,** suitable for expert DIY or professional 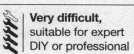

Specifications

System type . . . . 12 volt, negative-earth

Bulbs	**Wattage**
Direction indicator side repeater	4
Direction indicator	21
Headlight:	
Sealed-beam unit.	75/50
Quartz halogen light unit	60/55
High-level stop-light.	21
Instrument panel lights:	
Ignition/no-charge warning light.	2
All other warning/illumination lights	1.2
Interior lights.	10
Number plate light	4
Rear foglight.	21
Reversing light	21
Sidelight	5
Stop/tail light	21/5

1 General information and precautions

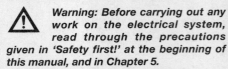

Warning: Before carrying out any work on the electrical system, read through the precautions given in 'Safety first!' at the beginning of this manual, and in Chapter 5.

1 The electrical system is of the 12 volt negative-earth type. Power for the lights and all electrical accessories is supplied by a lead-acid type battery, which is charged by the engine-driven alternator.

2 This Chapter covers repair and service procedures for the various electrical components not associated with engine. Information on the battery, alternator and starter motor can be found in Chapter 5.

3 It should be noted that, prior to working on any component in the electrical system, the battery negative terminal should first be disconnected, to prevent the possibility of electrical short-circuits and/or fires.

2 Electrical fault finding – general information

Note: *Refer to the precautions given in 'Safety first!' and in Section 1 of this Chapter before starting work. The following tests relate to testing of the main electrical circuits, and should not be used to test delicate electronic circuits, particularly where an electronic control module is used.*

General

1 A typical electrical circuit consists of an electrical component, any switches, relays, motors, fuses, fusible links or circuit breakers related to that component, and the wiring and connectors which link the component to both the battery and the chassis. To help to pinpoint a problem in an electrical circuit, wiring diagrams are included at the end of this Chapter.

2 Before attempting to diagnose an electrical fault, first study the appropriate wiring diagram, to obtain a complete understanding of the components included in the particular circuit concerned. The possible sources of a fault can be narrowed down by noting if other components related to the circuit are operating properly. If several components or circuits fail at one time, the problem is likely to be related to a shared fuse or earth connection.

3 Electrical problems usually stem from simple causes, such as loose or corroded connections, a faulty earth connection, a blown fuse, a melted fusible link, or a faulty relay (refer to Section 3 for details of testing relays). Visually inspect the condition of all fuses, wires and connections in a problem circuit before testing the components. Use the wiring diagrams to determine which terminal connections will need to be checked in order to pinpoint the trouble spot.

4 The basic tools required for electrical fault finding include a circuit tester or voltmeter (a 12 volt bulb with a set of test leads can also be used for certain tests); a self-powered test light (sometimes known as a continuity tester); an ohmmeter (to measure resistance); a battery and set of test leads; and a jumper wire, preferably with a circuit breaker or fuse incorporated, which can be used to bypass suspect wires or electrical components. Before attempting to locate a problem with test instruments, use the wiring diagrams to determine where to make the connections.

5 To find the source of an intermittent wiring fault (usually due to a poor or dirty connection, or damaged wiring insulation), a 'wiggle' test can be performed on the wiring. This involves wiggling the wiring by hand to see if the fault occurs as the wiring is moved. It should be possible to narrow down the source of the fault to a particular section of wiring. This method of testing can be used in conjunction with any of the tests described in the following sub-Sections.

6 Apart from problems due to poor connections, two basic types of fault can occur in an electrical circuit – open-circuit, or short-circuit.

7 Open-circuit faults are caused by a break somewhere in the circuit, which prevents current from flowing. An open-circuit fault will prevent a component from working, but will not cause the relevant circuit fuse to blow.

8 Short-circuit faults are caused by a 'short' somewhere in the circuit, which allows the current flowing in the circuit to 'escape' along an alternative route, usually to earth. Short-circuit faults are normally caused by a breakdown in wiring insulation, which allows a feed wire to touch either another wire, or an earthed component such as the bodyshell. A short-circuit fault will normally cause the relevant circuit fuse to blow.

Finding an open-circuit

9 To check for an open-circuit, connect one lead of a circuit tester or voltmeter to either the negative battery terminal or a known good earth.

10 Connect the other lead to a connector in the circuit being tested, preferably nearest to the battery or fuse.

11 Switch on the circuit, bearing in mind that some circuits are live only when the ignition switch is moved to a particular position.

12 If voltage is present (indicated either by the tester bulb lighting or a voltmeter reading, as applicable), this means that the section of the circuit between the relevant connector and the battery is problem-free.

13 Continue to check the remainder of the circuit in the same fashion.

14 When a point is reached at which no voltage is present, the problem must lie between that point and the previous test point with voltage. Most problems can be traced to a broken, corroded or loose connection.

Finding a short-circuit

15 To check for a short-circuit, first disconnect the load(s) from the circuit (loads are the components which draw current from a circuit, such as bulbs, motors, heating elements, etc).

16 Remove the relevant fuse from the circuit, and connect a circuit tester or voltmeter to the fuse connections.

17 Switch on the circuit, bearing in mind that some circuits are live only when the ignition switch is moved to a particular position.

18 If voltage is present (indicated either by the tester bulb lighting or a voltmeter reading, as applicable), this means that there is a short-circuit.

19 If no voltage is present, but the fuse still blows with the load(s) connected, this indicates an internal fault in the load(s).

Finding an earth fault

20 The battery negative terminal is connected to 'earth' – the metal of the engine/transmission and the car body – and most systems are wired so that they only receive a positive feed, the current returning via the metal of the car body. This means that the component mounting and the body form part of that circuit. Loose or corroded mountings can therefore cause a range of electrical faults, ranging from total failure of a circuit, to a puzzling partial fault. In particular, lights may shine dimly (especially when another circuit sharing the same earth point is in operation), motors (eg, wiper motors or the radiator cooling fan motor) may run slowly, and the operation of one circuit may have an apparently-unrelated effect on another. Note that on many vehicles, earth straps are used between certain components, such as the engine/transmission and the body, usually where there is no metal-to-metal contact between components due to flexible rubber mountings, etc.

21 To check whether a component is properly earthed, disconnect the battery and connect one lead of an ohmmeter to a known good earth point. Connect the other lead to the wire or earth connection being tested. The resistance reading should be zero; if not, check the connection as follows.

22 If an earth connection is thought to be faulty, dismantle the connection and clean back to bare metal both the bodyshell and the wire terminal or the component earth connection mating surface. Be careful to remove all traces of dirt and corrosion, then use a knife to trim away any paint, so that a clean metal-to-metal joint is made. On reassembly, tighten the joint fasteners securely; if a wire terminal is being refitted, use serrated washers between the terminal and the bodyshell to ensure a clean and secure connection. When the connection is remade, prevent the onset of corrosion in the future by applying a coat of petroleum jelly or silicone-based grease. Alternatively, spray on (at regular intervals) a proprietary ignition sealer, or a water-dispersant lubricant.

3 Fuses and relays – general information

Fuses

1 The fuses are located behind the small panel in the fascia, below the steering column, and in a compartment under the driver's seat.

2 To gain access to the fusebox, turn the fasteners through 90° and remove the panel situated below the steering column **(see illustrations)**.

3 Remove the seat cushion, release the securing clip and remove the cover from the compartment below the driver's seat, depending on model there will be a variation in size of fuesbox fitted **(see illustrations)**.

4 A label identifying each fuse should be attached to the cover panel **(see illustrations)**.

5 To remove a fuse, first switch off the circuit concerned (or the ignition), then pull the fuse out of its terminals. The wire within the fuse is clearly visible; if the fuse is blown, it will be broken or melted.

6 Always renew a fuse with one of an identical rating; never use one with a different rating from the original, nor substitute anything else. Never renew a fuse more than once without tracing the source of the trouble. The rating is stamped on top of the fuse; they are also colour-coded for easy recognition **(see illustration)**.

7 If a new fuse blows immediately, find the cause before renewing it again; a short to earth as a result of faulty insulation is most likely cause. Where more than one circuit is protected, try to isolate the defect by switching on each circuit in turn (if possible) until it blows again. Always carry a supply of spare fuses/fusible links of each relevant rating on the vehicle – a spare of each fuse rating should be clipped into the base of the fusebox.

Relays

8 The majority of relays are mounted in the fuseboxes, as described previously.

9 If a circuit or system controlled by a relay develops a fault and the relay is suspect, operate the system; if the relay is functioning, it should be possible to hear it click as it is energised. If this is the case, the fault lies with the components or wiring of the system. If the relay is not being energised, then either the relay is not receiving a main supply or a switching voltage, or the relay itself is faulty. Testing is by the substitution of a known good unit, but be careful; while some relays are identical in appearance and in operation, others look similar but perform different functions.

10 To renew a relay, first ensure that the ignition switch is off. The relay can then simply be pulled out from the socket, and the new relay pressed in.

3.2a Release the fasteners and open the cover…

3.2b … to gain access to the fusebox

3.3a Release the clip…

3.3b …and slide the panel forwards to access…

3.3c …the additional fusebox…

3.3d …depending on equipment level of model

3.4a A fuse identification sticker is attached…

3.4b …to the rear of the fusebox cover

3.6 Renew fuse with the same rating

4.4a Disconnect the wiring connectors...

4.4b ...slacken the clamp screw...

4.4c ...and withdraw the switch assembly

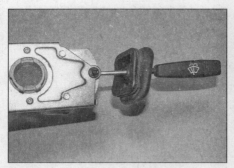

4.5 Undo the two screws and release the retaining clip

4.6 Switch is part of the switch clamp unit

4.9 Push the switch from the facia

4 Switches – removal and refitting

Note: *Disconnect the battery negative lead before removing any switch, and reconnect the lead after refitting the switch (see Chapter 5).*

Ignition switch/ steering column lock

1 Refer to Chapter 11 Section 19.

Steering column switches

2 Remove the steering wheel, as described in Chapter 11 Section 18.

3 Undo the steering column shroud retaining screws, unclip the shroud halves, and remove both the upper and lower shrouds from the steering column.

4 To remove the complete switch assembly from the top of the steering column, disconnect the wiring connectors, slacken the clamp retaining screw and withdraw the switch assembly **(see illustrations)**.

5 To remove the right-hand windscreen wiper washer switch, undo the two retaining screws and release the retaining clip, then remove the switch from the switch assembly **(see illustration)**.

6 The left-hand indicator/horn/main beam-high-low-flash switch, is part of the main switch body and cannot be renewed separately **(see illustration)**. Remove switch assembly, as described previously.

7 Refitting is a reversal of the relevant removal procedure.

Facia switches

8 Remove the radio/CD player as described in Section 17.

9 Reach through the radio/cassette player aperture, and push the switch from the facia **(see illustration)**. Disconnect the switch wiring plug as it is withdrawn.

10 Refitting is a reversal of removal.

Heater control panel/switch

11 Remove the radio/CD player as described in Section 17.

12 Undo the two retaining screws and remove the facia centre instrument panel **(see illustrations)**. Disconnect the wiring

4.12a Undo the retaining screws...

4.12b ...and remove the instrument panel

4.13a Undo the four screws...

4.13b ...and remove the control panel

4.14a Disconnect the wiring connectors...

connectors from the rear of the panel, as it is removed, noting there fitted position.

13 Undo the four retaining screws and withdraw the heater control panel from the facia **(see illustrations)**.

14 Disconnect the wiring connectors, from the rear of the control panel **(see illustrations)**.

15 Release the retaining clips from the outer cables, then detach the inner control cables from the switch/control lever assembly **(see illustrations)**. Note the fitted position of the control cables for refitting, as they have coloured tape around them for identification.

16 Refitting is the reverse of removal. Prior to refitting the instrument panel, check the operation of the ventilation control lever; if necessary, adjust the cable by releasing the retaining clip and repositioning the outer cable.

Headlight-levelling switch

17 Remove the radio/CD player as described in Section 17.

18 Remove the centre instrument panel from the facia, as described previously in this section **(see illustrations 4.12a and 4.12b)**.

19 Pull the knob from the switch, then undo the nut and remove the switch **(see illustration)**.

20 Refitting is a reversal of removal.

Handbrake warning switch

21 Release the three fasteners and remove the gaiter from the handbrake lever **(see illustration)**.

22 Disconnect the wiring connector from the warning light switch **(see illustration)**.

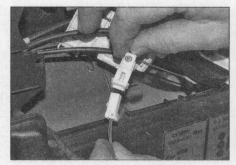

4.14b ...from the rear of the control panel

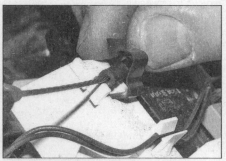

4.15a Release the outer cable...

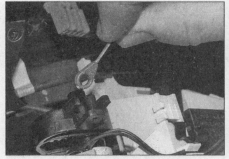

4.15b ...and disconnect the inner cable...

4.15c ...noting the cables are colour coded

4.19 Remove the switch knob and undo the retaining nut

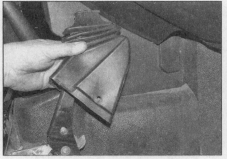

4.21 Remove the handbrake gaiter

4.22 Disconnect the wiring connector

5.3a Peel off the rubber boot ...

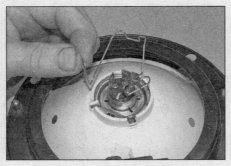

5.3b ... release the retaining clip...

5.3c ...and withdraw the bulb

23 Undo the two retaining screws and remove the switch from the lever.

24 Refitting is a reversal of removal, tightening the handbrake lever bolts securely.

5 Bulbs (exterior lights) – renewal

General

1 Whenever a bulb is renewed, note the following points:

a) Remember that if the light has just been in use, the bulb may be extremely hot.

b) Always check the bulb contacts and holder, ensuring that there is clean metal-to-metal contact between the bulb and its live(s) and earth. Clean off any corrosion or dirt before fitting a new bulb.

c) Wherever bayonet-type bulbs are fitted ensure that the live contact(s) bear firmly against the bulb contact.

d) Always ensure that the new bulb is of the correct rating, and that it is completely clean before fitting it; this applies particularly to halogen headlight bulbs (see below).

Headlight

2 Remove the headlight assembly, as described in Section 7.

3 Peel off the rubber boot, then release the retaining clip and remove the bulb **(see illustrations)**.

4 Refitting is a reversal of removal.

Direction indicator, sidelight and rear lights

5 Undo the two retaining screws and withdraw the light unit **(see illustrations)**.

6 Twist the bulbholder anti-clockwise to free it from the rear of the lens unit, then push the bulb in slightly and twist it anti-clockwise to remove it from the bulbholder **(see illustrations)**.

7 Fit the new bulb, then refit the bulbholder to the rear of the lens unit. Refit the light unit, and secure it in position with the retaining screws. Do not overtighten the screws, as the lens is easily cracked.

Direction indicator side repeater

8 Carefully push the lens firmly forward, and withdraw the rear end of the unit from the

5.5a Undo the screws – front indicator shown

5.5b Undo the screws – reversing light shown

5.6a Remove the bulb holder...

5.6b ...then remove the bulb – front indicator shown

5.6c Remove the bulb holder...

5.6d ...then remove the bulb – reversing light shown

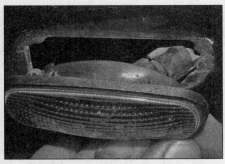

5.8 Push the repeater lens forward, and pull the rear end from the wing

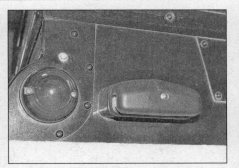

5.11 Undo the retaining screw, and remove the cover from the rear number plate light unit

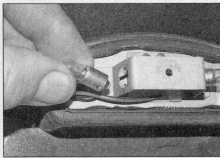

5.12 Twist the relevant bulb anti-clockwise, and remove it from the light unit

5.14 Remove the brake light cover

5.15 Twist the bulb holder to remove

5.16 Remove the bulb

wing **(see illustration)**. Turn the bulbholder anti-clockwise to release it, and remove it from the lens unit.

9 The bulb is of the capless (push-fit) type, and can be removed by simply pulling it out of the bulbholder.

10 Refitting is a reverse of the removal procedure.

Rear number plate light

11 Undo the retaining screw, and remove the light unit cover **(see illustration)**. Recover the seal, renewing it if it is damaged.

12 Push the bulb in slightly, and then twist the relevant bulb (two bulbs fitted) anti-clockwise, and withdraw it from the light unit **(see illustration)**.

13 Fit the new bulb, then refit the cover and seal, and secure them in position with the retaining screw.

High-level brake light

14 Undo the 2 retaining screws and remove the cover from the rear of the light unit, at the top of the rear door **(see illustration)**.

15 Rotate the bulbholder anti-clockwise and pull it from the light unit **(see illustration)**.

16 Push the bulb in slightly, and then twist the bulb anti-clockwise, and withdraw it from the bulbholder **(see illustration)**.

17 Refitting is a reversal of removal.

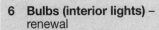

6 Bulbs (interior lights) – renewal

General

1 Refer to Section 5, paragraph 1.

Courtesy light

2 Carefully unclip the lens from the light unit, using a small flat-bladed screwdriver **(see illustrations)**.

3 Unclip the bulb from its contacts and remove it from the vehicle **(see illustration)**.

4 Fit the new bulb, ensuring that it is securely held by its contacts, then refit the lens.

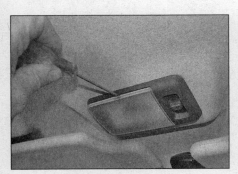

6.2a Using small screwdriver...

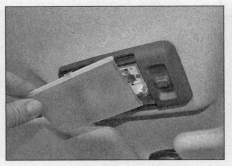

6.2b ...unclip the lens from the light unit

6.3 Remove the bulb from the contacts

6.6 Unclip the bulbholder

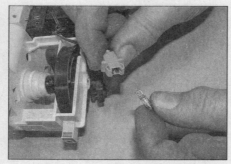

6.7 Remove the bulb from the holder

Heater control panel illumination

5 Remove the heater control panel as described in Section 4.
6 Unclip the bulbholder from the rear of the control panel **(see illustration)**.

7 The bulbs are of the capless (push-fit) type, and can be removed by simply pulling them out of the bulbholder **(see illustration)**.
8 Refit the bulbholder with a new bulb, and refit the control panel.

7.2a Undo the two screws...

7.2b ...and remove the trim panel

7.3a Remove the four screws...

7.3b ...disconnect the headlight wiring connector...

7.3c ...and the headlight leveling motor (where fitted)

7.6 Undo the screws and remove the light unit

Warning lights

9 Warning lights are illuminated by non-renewable LEDs (Light Emitting Diodes), so if the light inside the switch/gauge is not working the complete unit will need to be replaced.

7   Exterior light units – removal and refitting

Headlight

1 Undo the retaining screws and remove the sidelight and direction indicator light units, as described later in this section.
2 Undo the two screws and remove the headlight surround panel **(see illustrations)**.
3 Undo the four retaining screws and remove the headlight assembly, then disconnect the wiring plug(s) as the unit is removed **(see illustrations)**.
4 If necessary, release the headlight aim screws and the spring, and separate the headlight rim seating from the shell.
5 Refitting is the reverse of removal. On completion, check the headlight beam alignment using the information given in Section 8.

Direction indicator, sidelight and rear lights

6 Undo the retaining screws and withdraw the light unit **(see illustration)**.
7 Disconnect the wiring connector, and remove the light unit from the vehicle **(see illustration)**. Inspect the light unit seal for signs of damage or deterioration, and renew if necessary.
8 On refitting, reconnect the wiring connector, and secure the light unit in position with the retaining screws. Do not overtighten the screws, as the lens is easily cracked.

Direction indicator side repeater

9 Firmly push the lens forward, and carefully pull the rear end of the light unit out and withdraw the unit from the wing **(see illustration 5.8)**, disconnecting its wiring connectors as they become accessible. Examine the light unit seal, renewing it if it shows signs of damage or deterioration.

7.7 Disconnect the wiring connector

10 On refitting, ensure that the seal is in position, and reconnect the wiring connectors. Clip the light unit into position in the wing.

Rear foglight and reversing light

11 Undo the retaining screws and remove the light unit from the rear of the vehicle (**see illustrations 5.6c and 5.6d**).
12 Refitting is the reverse of removal, ensuring that the wiring is connected.

Rear number plate light

13 Working from inside the vehicle, undo the retaining nuts/screws and remove the metal cover from behind the number plate light unit (**see illustration**),
14 Undo the retaining nuts, disconnect the wiring connector, and then the light unit can be removed from the rear of the vehicle (**see illustration**). Inspect the seal, renewing it if it is damaged.
15 Refitting is the reverse of removal.

8 Headlight beam alignment – general information

1 Accurate adjustment of the headlight beam is only possible using optical beam-setting equipment, and this work should therefore be carried out by a Land Rover dealer or suitably-equipped workshop.
2 For reference, the headlights can be adjusted using the screws located in the headlight rim (**see illustration**).

9 Instrument panel – removal and refitting

Removal

1 Disconnect the battery negative terminal, as described in Chapter 5.
2 Undo the two retaining screws and unclip the upper part of the facia trim from above the instrument panel (**see illustrations**).
3 Undo the two retaining screws and unclip the facia trim from lower part of the instrument panel (**see illustration**).
4 Undo the two lower retaining screws, then

tilt the instrument panel back at the top until access can be gained to the wiring connector on the rear of the unit. Disconnect the wiring connector, and withdraw the instrument panel from the facia (**see illustrations**).

Refitting

5 Reconnect the panel wiring connector, and seat the instrument panel in position.
6 Securely tighten the retaining screws, refit the trim panels and reconnect the battery.

7.13 Remove the metal cover

7.14 Undo the two nuts and disconnect the wiring connector

8.2 Headlamp vertical (1) and horizontal adjustment screws (2)

9.2a Undo the two retaining screws...

9.2b ...and remove the upper trim panel

9.3 Remove the lower trim (steering wheel removed for clarity)

9.4a Undo the two retaining screws...

9.4b ... then withdraw the instrument panel from the facia...

9.4c ...and disconnect the wiring connector

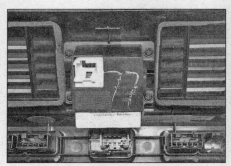

10.2 Undo the clock retaining screws...

11.3 Release the securing clips and remove the centre from the plastic surround

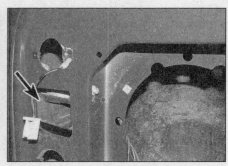

12.3a Horn fitted to right-hand side...

10 Clock – removal and refitting

Removal

1 Undo the two retaining screws and remove the instrument panel from the centre of the facia **(see illustrations 4.12a and 4.12b)**.
2 Turn the instrument panel over and undo the four retaining screws **(see illustration)**, then the clock can be removed from the rear of the panel.

Refitting

3 Refitting is the reverse of removal.

12.3b ...and the left-hand side

11 Cigarette lighter – removal and refitting

Removal

1 Disconnect the battery negative terminal as described in Chapter 5 Section 4.
2 Undo the two retaining screws and remove the instrument panel from the centre of the facia **(see illustrations 4.12a and 4.12b)**.
3 Release the clips and slide the centre of the lighter unit from the plastic surround, then remove the lighter body from the instrument panel **(see illustration)**.

Refitting

4 Refitting is the reverse of removal.

12 Horn – removal and refitting

Removal

Note: *Depending on model, the horn could be fitted to the right or left-hand side of the vehicle or both.*
1 Remove the headlight unit as described in Section 7.
2 Reach behind and disconnect the wiring connector from the horn.

3 Slacken and remove the retaining nut/bolt, then remove the horn from the vehicle **(see illustrations)**.

Refitting

4 Refitting is the reverse of removal.

13 Wiper arm – removal and refitting

Removal

1 Operate the wiper motor, then switch it off so that the wiper arm returns to the at rest ('parked') position.
2 Stick a piece of masking tape to the glass along the edge of the wiper blade, to use as an alignment aid on refitting. If the tailgate wiper arm is being removed, remove the spare wheel.
3 Lift up the spindle cover, and undo the spindle nut **(see illustration)**. Lift the blade from the glass and pull the wiper arm from the spindle.
4 To remove the tailgate wiper arm, lift up the wiper arm spindle nut cover, then slacken and remove the spindle nut. Lift the blade off the glass, and pull the wiper arm off its spindle **(see illustrations)**. On models where the spare wheel is mounted

13.3 Lift up the cover and undo the spindle nut

13.4a Lift up the trim cap, then undo the retaining nut...

13.4b ...and remove the tailgate wiper arm

13.5 Using a puller to remove the wiper arm

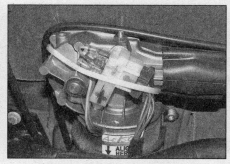

14.5 Disconnect the wiring connector

14.6 Undo the wiper motor clamp retaining screws

onto the tailgate, it will be necessary to remove the wheel to gain access to the wiper arm.

5 If the wiper arm is tight, a puller can be used to remove the wiper arm of the spindle **(see illustration)**.

Refitting

6 Ensure that the wiper arm and spindle splines are clean and dry.

7 Refit the arm, aligning the blade with the tape fitted on removal and tighten the spindle nut.

8 On the tailgate wiper arm, refit and securely tighten the spindle nut, and clip the nut cover back in position. Where necessary, refit the spare wheel to the tailgate.

14 Windscreen wiper motor and cable – removal and refitting

Removal

1 Disconnect the battery negative terminal as described in Chapter 5.

2 Remove both windscreen wiper arms as described in Section 13. Then undo the retaining nuts and washers from the base of the wiper spindles on the windscreen lower panel.

3 Remove the facia panel as described in Chapter 12 Section 24.

4 Release the fasteners and remove the heater ducts from around the wiper motor and linkage.

5 Release the cable tie (where fitted) and disconnect the wiring connector from the wiper motor **(see illustration)**.

6 Undo the 2 retaining screws from the clamp around the wiper motor and remove it from the bulkhead **(see illustration)**.

7 If required, pull back the rubber cover and undo the retaining nut and disconnect the wiper linkage operating cable from the wiper motor **(see illustration)**.

8 Working along the bulkhead, undo the retaining nuts and remove the two wheel box

wiper spindles and cable from the vehicle **(see illustrations)**.

Refitting

9 Ensure the mounting pad is correctly positioned, then refit the motor and secure it in place with the retaining strap. Securely tighten the strap screws.

10 Tighten the drive tube nut securely, and reposition the nut cover.

11 The remainder of refitting is a reversal of removal.

12 Refit the windscreen wiper arms, then reconnect the battery and check the operation of the motor.

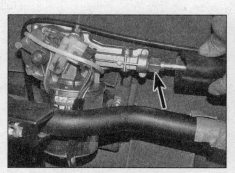

14.7 Wiper operating cable securing nut

15 Tailgate wiper motor – removal and refitting

Removal

1 Remove the spare wheel (where necessary).

2 Remove the wiper arm as described in Section 13.

3 Unscrew the large nut from the wiper spindle, and recover the washer and rubber seal **(see illustration)**.

4 Remove the tailgate trim panel as described in Chapter 12 Section 15.

14.8a Undo the retaining nuts...

14.8b ...and remove the cable operated wheel boxes

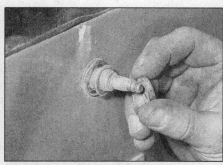

15.3 Unscrew the nut, and remove the washer and rubber seal from the tailgate wiper motor spindle

15.5 Disconnect the wiring connectors

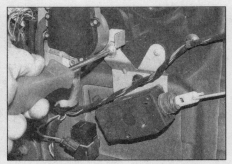

15.6a Undo the retaining bolt......

15.6b ...and remove the wiper motor

5 Disconnect the wiring plug connectors from the wiper motor **(see illustration)**.
6 Undo the bolt that also secures the door locking solenoid to the tailgate, then manoeuvre the wiper motor from the tailgate **(see illustrations)**.

Refitting

7 Refitting is a reversal of removal.

16 Windscreen/tailgate washer system components – removal and refitting

Note: *On models with headlight washers, an additional reservoir may also be fitted in the left-hand rear corner of the engine compartment.*

Washer system reservoir

1 Remove the left-hand headlight as described in Section 7.
2 Undo the screws and remove the heater intake grille from the left-hand wing.
3 Undo the 2 screws securing the heater intake ducting to the wing, and the 2 bolts securing the ducting retaining bracket **(see illustrations)**. Manoeuvre the ducting from under the wing.
4 Undo the 4 screws, release the clips and manoeuvre the left-hand wheel arch liner to gain access to the nuts on the underside of the reservoir retaining screws.
5 Undo the 3 screws and remove the reservoir from the inner wing **(see illustrations)**. Disconnect the hoses from the washers pump(s). Mark each hose for identification

purposes, to avoid the possibility of reconnecting the hoses incorrectly on refitting. Disconnect the pump wiring connector(s), and remove the reservoir from the vehicle.
6 Refitting is a reversal of removal.

Washer pump

7 Remove the left-hand headlight as described in Section 5, then undo the screws and remove the headlight shell from the wing.
8 Note their fitted positions, and disconnect the wiring plug and washer hose from the pump **(see illustration)**.
9 Pull the pump from the sealing grommet on the reservoir. Be prepared for fluid spillage.
10 Refitting is a reversal of removal.

Non-return valves

11 A non-return valve is fitted to both the windscreen and tailgate washer hoses.
12 To remove the valve, trace the hose back from the relevant pump to the valve, then disconnect the hoses and remove the valve from the vehicle.
13 On refitting, ensure that the valve is fitted the correct way around.

Windscreen washer jet

14 To gain access to the rear of the jet, remove the relevant parts of the facia panel as described in Chapter 12 Section 24.
15 Disconnect the washer hose from the jet, then unscrew the retaining nut and washer,

16.3a Undo the ducting retaining screws in the grille recess (arrowed) ...

16.3b ... and the bracket screws (arrowed)

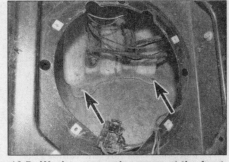

16.5a Washer reservoir screws at the front (arrowed) ...

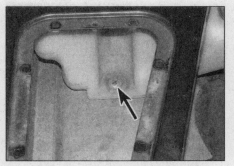

16.5b ... and at the rear (arrowed)

16.8 Disconnect the wiring plug(s) and washer hose(s) from the pump(s)

16.15 Nut securing washer jet to front panel

16.17 Carefully prise off the window surround trims each side

16.19 The trim panel above the tailgate is secured by 4 studs (2 right-hand ones arrowed)

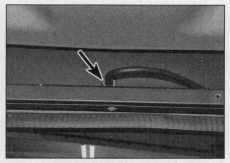

16.21 Undo the jet retaining nut (arrowed)

17.4a Release the securing clips...

17.4b ...and withdraw the radio/CD player

and remove the jet from the front of the vehicle **(see illustration)**.

16 On refitting, refit the washer and retaining nut, tightening it securely then reconnect the washer hose. Check the operation of the jet. If necessary, adjust the nozzle using a pin, aiming the spray to a point slightly above the centre of the swept area.

Tailgate washer jet

17 Carefully prise off the rear window surround trims on both sides **(see illustration)**.

18 Prise open the caps and undo the screws and remove both rear grab handles.

19 Release the 4 studs and remove the trim panel above the rear door **(see illustration)**.

20 Disconnect the hose from the washer jet. Be prepared for fluid spillage.

21 Undo the retaining nut and remove the washer jet **(see illustration)**.

22 On refitting, securely tighten the retaining

nut, then reconnect the washer hose. Check the operation of the jet and, If necessary, adjust the nozzle using a pin, aiming the spray to a point slightly above the centre of the swept area.

17 Radio/CD player and speakers – removal and refitting

Note: *The following removal and refitting procedure is for the radio/cassette units and speakers which Land Rover fit as an optional extra. Removal and refitting procedures of non-standard units may differ slightly.*

Removal

Radio/CD player

1 Most of the radio/cassette players fitted by Land Rover have DIN standard fixings. Two special tools, obtainable from most car

accessory shops, are required for removal. Alternatively, suitable tools can be fabricated from 3 mm diameter wire, such as welding rod. Some 'low-line' models are fitted with units released using 2.5 mm Allen keys.

2 Disconnect the battery negative lead as described in Chapter 5.

3 Unclip the small access covers (where fitted) from either side of the radio/cassette unit, to reveal the fixing holes.

4 Insert the tools into the holes, and push them until they snap into place. The radio/ CD player can then be slid out of the facia, and the aerial lead and wiring connectors disconnected **(see illustrations)**.

Speakers

5 Undo the retaining screws then withdraw the speaker, disconnecting its wiring connectors as they become accessible **(see illustrations)**. Small speakers are also fitted to the top of the facia (depending on model).

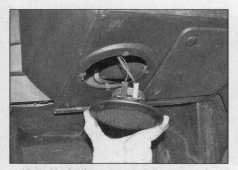

17.5a Undo the screws and remove the front speaker...

17.5b ... and rear speakers

17.5c Unclip the speaker from the top of the facia

18.3 Unclip the link rod from the door lock ...

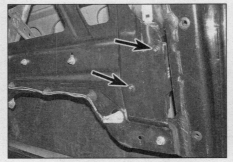

18.4a ...undo the securing screws...

18.4b ...then remove the solenoid and disconnect the wiring connector

Refitting

Radio/CD player

6 To refit the radio/CD player, reconnect the aerial lead and wiring connectors, then push the unit into the facia until the retaining lugs snap into place.

7 Reconnect the battery.

Speakers

8 Refitting is the reverse of removal.

18 Central locking components – general information, removal and refitting

General information

1 The system operates on the front and rear passenger doors, and on Station Wagon and County Station Wagon models it also operates on the rear tailgate.

Removal

Front door lock solenoid

2 Remove the door inner trim panel and weathershield as described in Chapter 12 Section 11.

3 Unclip the lock solenoid link rod from the door lock (see illustration).

4 Undo the 2 screws and remove the solenoid form the mounting panel (see illustrations). Disconnect the solenoid wiring plug as it is withdrawn.

Rear door lock solenoid

5 Remove the door inner trim panel as described in Chapter 12.

6 Unclip the lock solenoid link rod.

7 Unclip the interior release handle link rod from the lock mechanism.

8 Undo the 3 bolts at the rear of the mounting panel (see illustration). Slacken the remaining nuts and bolts, then pull the mounting panel

away from the door sufficiently to gain access to the lock solenoid.

9 Disconnect the solenoid wiring plug, then undo the 2 retaining bolts, and manoeuvre the solenoid from position (see illustration). Disconnect the solenoid link rod as it is withdrawn.

Tailgate lock solenoid

10 Remove the tailgate trim panel as described in Chapter 12 Section 15.

11 Disconnect solenoid wiring plug, and disconnect the wiring securing clip from the mounting bracket (see illustrations).

12 Undo the retaining screws and disconnect the solenoid link rod as the solenoid is withdrawn (see illustrations).

13 If required, undo the two screws and separate the solenoid from the mounting bracket.

Refitting

14 Refitting is a reversal of removal.

18.8 Undo the 3 bolts at the rear of the mounting panel (arrowed)

18.9 Door lock solenoid retaining bolts (arrowed)

18.11a Disconnect the wiring connector...

18.11b ...and release the wiring securing clip

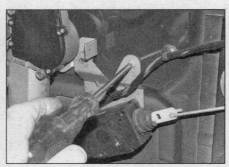

18.12a Undo the retaining screws......

18.12b ...and disconnect the linkage rod

SECONDARY FUSE BOX FROM 2007 TO 2011

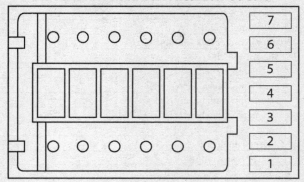

FUSE/RELAY	VALUE	DESCRIPTION
F1	30 A	Anti-lock braking
F2	20 A	Accessory socket
F3	20 A	Headlamp flash / horn
F4	-	Not used
F5	30 A	Main relay
F6	15 A	Alarm system
F7	20 A	Alarm system

MAIN FUSE BOX FROM 2007 TO 2011

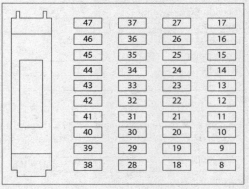

FUSE/RELAY	VALUE	DESCRIPTION
F8	10 A	Alarm system
F9	15 A	Front wipers/wash
F10	10 A	Rear wipers/wash
F11	10 A	Anti-lock brakes
F12	10 A	Speed transducer
F13	10 A	Brake lamps
F14	10 A	Reverse lamps
F15	5 A	Ignition
F16	-	Not used

Fuses and relays

F17	-	Not used
F18	10 A	Side lamps (left)
F19	10 A	Side lamps (right)
F20	10 A	Illumination/clock illumination
F21	10 A	Hazard switch
F22	10 A	Headlamp dipped beam (right)
F23	10 A	Headlamp dipped beam (left)
F24	10 A	Headlamp main beam (right)
F25	10 A	Headlamp main beam (left)
F26	10 A	Rear fog lamps
F27	10 A	Alarm sounder
F28	20 A	Heated rear window
F29	20 A	Cooling fan/A/C clutch link
F30	10 A	Audio/clock/diagnostic socket
F31	15 A	Hazard switch
F32	-	Not used
F33	20 A	Seat heater
F34	20 A	Electric window right
F35	20 A	Electric window left
F36	30 A	Heated front screen
F37	30 A	Spare fuse
F38	10 A	Engine ECU/PCM
F39	5 A	Engine ECU/PCM
F40	-	Not used
F41	5 A	Engine ECU/PCM
F42	10 A	Air conditioning switch
F43	20 A	Cigar lighter
F44	5 A	Audio unit
F45	30 A	Blower motor
F46	-	Not used
F47	-	Not used

No location information is available for the following fuses
SECONDARY FUSE BOX FROM 2012 TO 2016

FUSE/RELAY	VALUE	DESCRIPTION
F1	15 A	Fuel pump
F2	20 A	Heated rear screen
F3	30 A	Starter motor
F4	30 A	Engine ECU/PCM
F5	20 A	Accessory socket
F6	20 A	Air conditioning
F7	30 A	Heated front screen
F8	30 A	Anti-lock Braking System (ABS)
F9	5 A	Engine ECU/PCM
F10	10 A	Reverse lights
F11	10 A	Instrument panel
F12	15 A	Windscreen washers / wipers (front only)

Fuses and relays (continued)

F13	-	Spare fuse
F14	5 A	Air conditioning
F15	5 A	Engine ECU/PCM
F16	5 A	Engine ECU/PCM
F17	-	Not used
F18	-	Not used
F19	-	Not used
F20	-	Not used
F21	-	Not used
F22	-	Not used
F23	-	Not used
F24	-	Not used

MAIN FUSE BOX FROM 2012 TO 2016

FUSE/RELAY	VALUE	DESCRIPTION
F1	10 A	Alarm system
F2	10 A	Hazard warning lights
F3	15 A	Brake lights
F4	5 A	Ignition supply. Instrument panel, electric windows, headlights, heated front screen, heated rear screen
F5	5 A	Engine ECU/PCM
F6	10 A	Anti-lock Braking System (ABS)
F7	10 A	Air conditioning
F8	15 A	Alarm system
F9	20 A	Alarm system
F10	20 A	Horn
F11	10 A	Left-hand side light
F12	10 A	Right-hand side light
F13	10 A	Headlamp levelling, switch illumination
F14	10 A	Rear screen washer and wiper
F15	10 A	Right-hand headlamp (dipped beam)
F16	10 A	Left-hand headlamp (dipped beam)
F17	10 A	Right-hand headlamp (main beam)
F18	10 A	Left-hand headlamp (main beam)
F19	10 A	Rear fog lamp
F20	10 A	Alarm system
F21	-	Spare fuse
F22	10 A	Right-hand heated seat
F23	10 A	Left-hand heated seat
F24	20 A	Right-hand electric window
F25	20 A	Left-hand electric window
F26	20 A	Cigar lighter
F27	5 A	Entertainment system
F28	30 A	Blower motor
F29	10 A	Diagnostic socket, clock, entertainment system
F30	15 A	Hazard warning lights

Fuses and relays (continued)

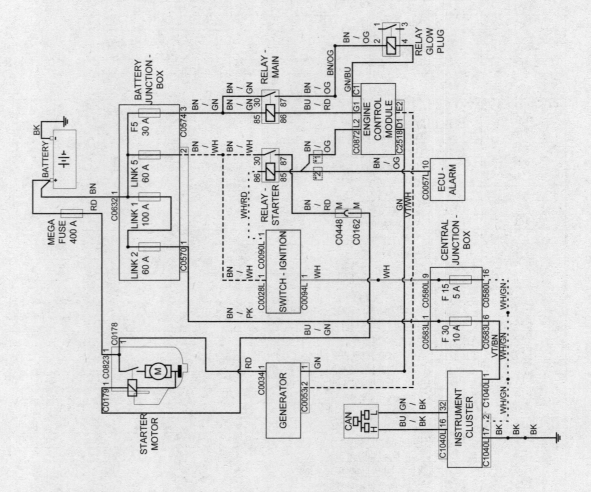

Starting and charging – from 2007 to 2011

*1 Without alarm
*2 With alarm

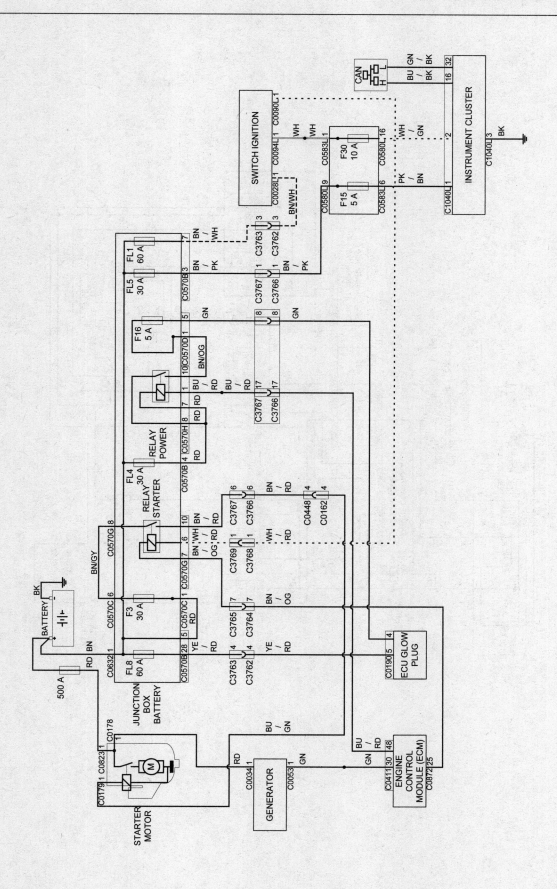

Starting and charging – from 2012 to 2016

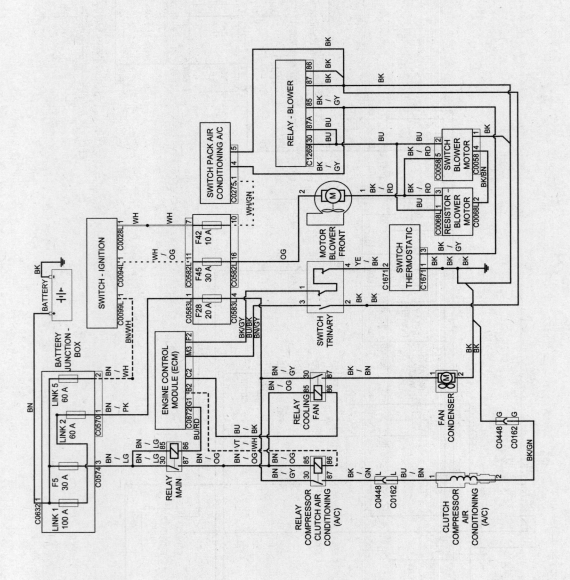

Air conditioning, heating & cooling – from 2007 to 2011

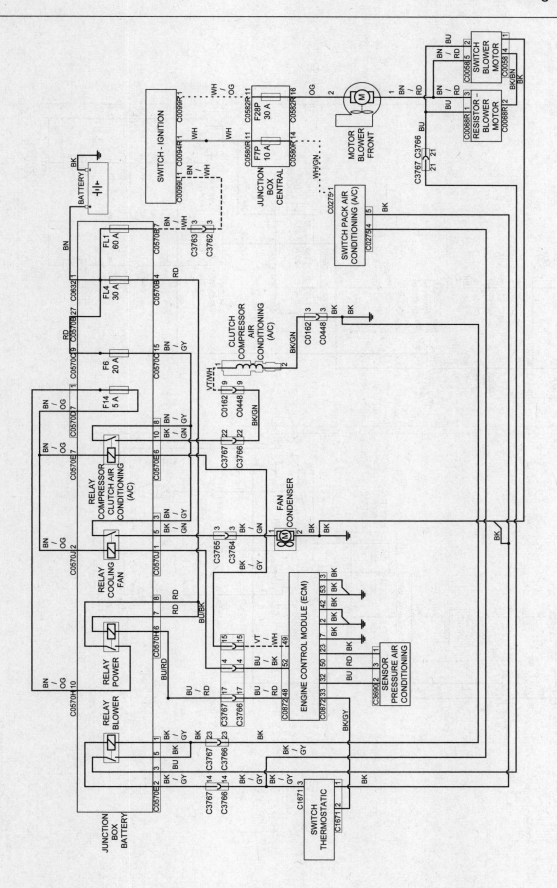

Air conditioning, heating & cooling – from 2012 to 2016

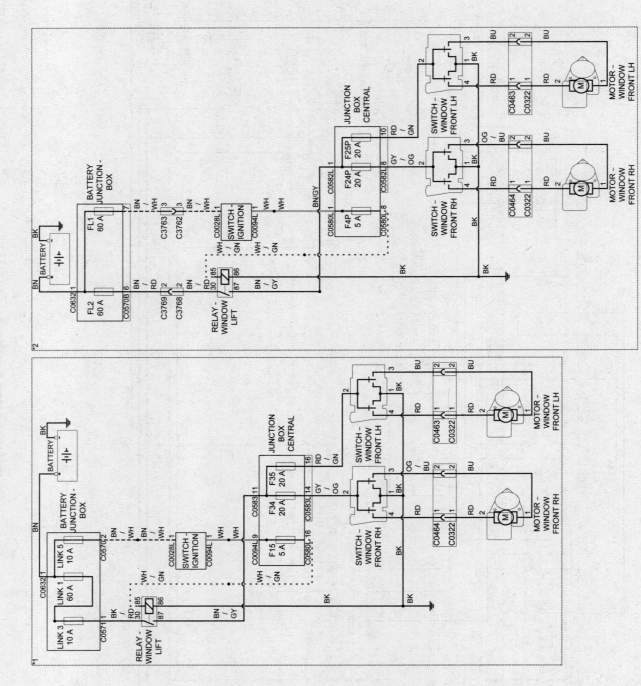

Power windows

*1 Up to 2012
*2 From 2012 From VIN **********412051

Power door locks

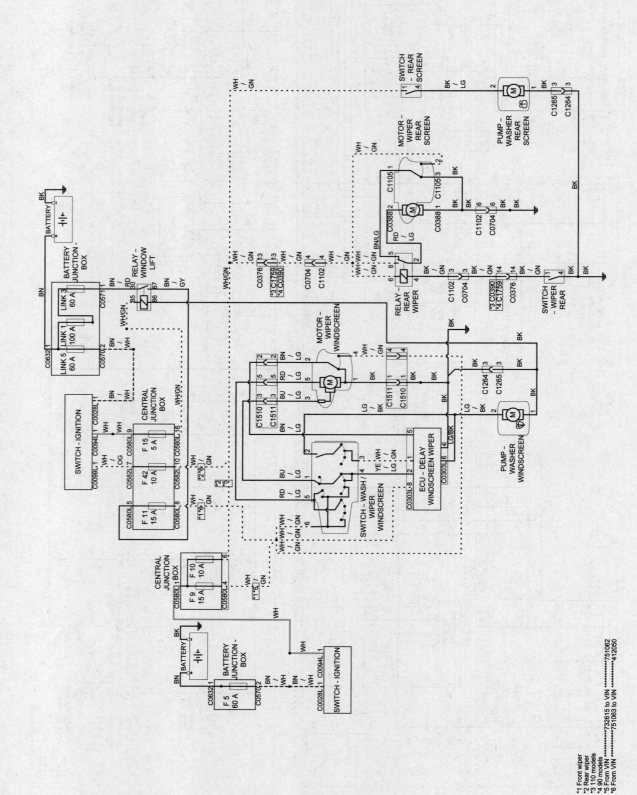

Wiper/washer – from 2007 to 2011

*1 Front wiper
*2 Rear wiper
*3 110 models
*4 90 models
*5 From VIN ···········732615 to VIN ···········751062
*6 From VIN ···········751063 to VIN ···········412050

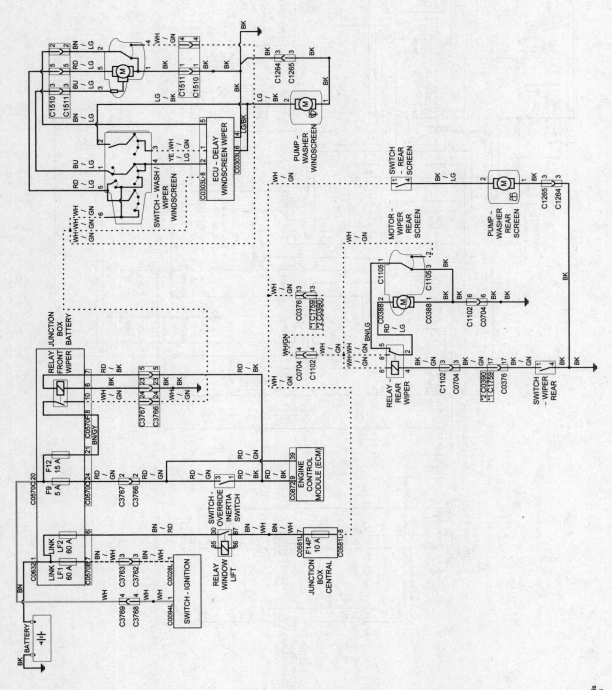

Wiper/washer – from 2012 to 2016

*1 110 models
*2 90 models

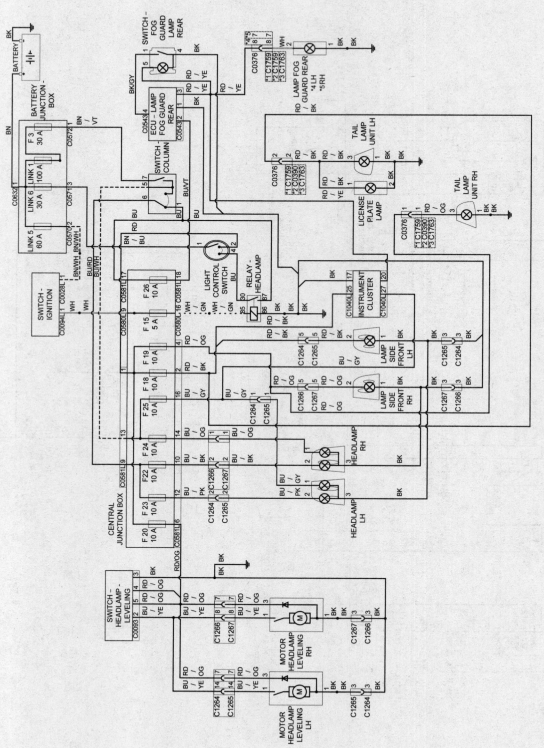

Exterior Lights – from 2007 to 2011 (1 of 2)

*1 110 models
*2 90 models
*3 HCPU, for 110 and 130 models
*4 LHD models
*5 RHD models

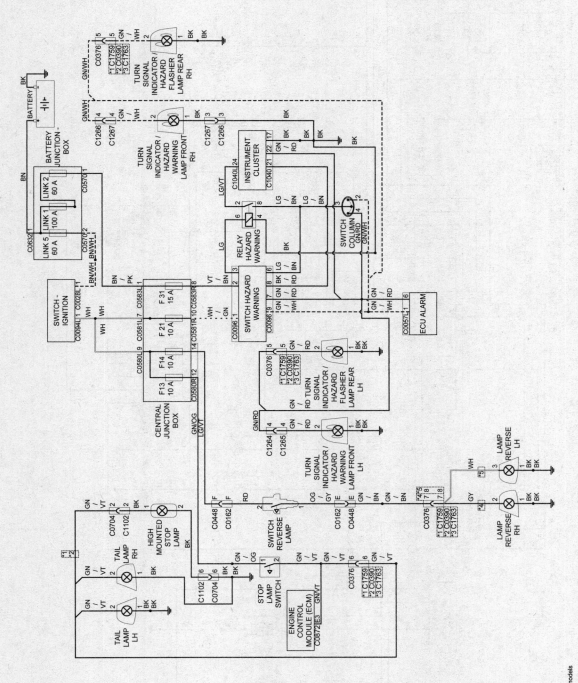

Exterior Lights – from 2007 to 2011 (2 of 2)

*1 110 models
*2 90 models
*3 HCPU, for 110 and 130 models
*4 LHD models
*5 RHD models

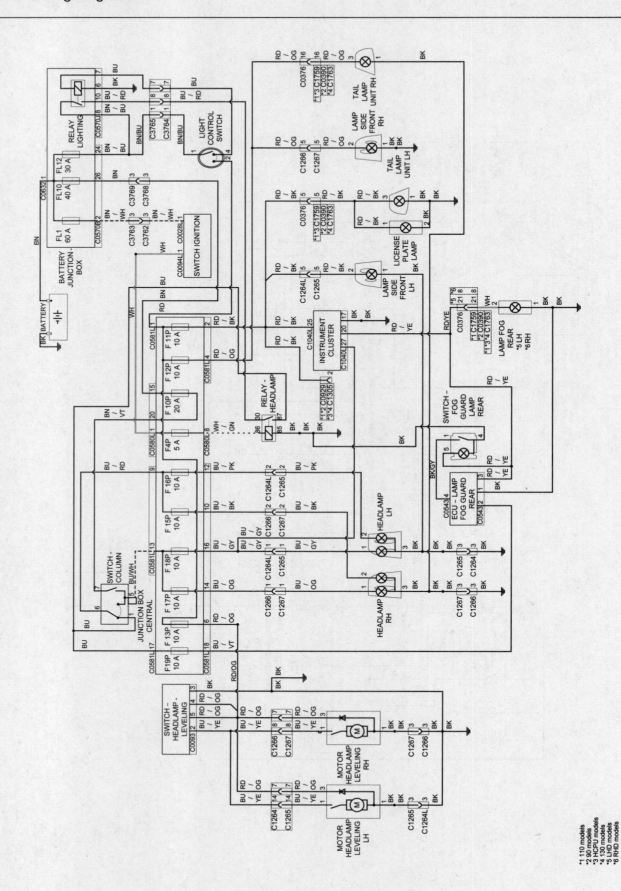

Exterior Lights – from 2012 to 2016 (1 of 2)

*1 110 models
*2 90 models
*3 HCPU models
*4 130 models
*5 LHD models
*6 RHD models

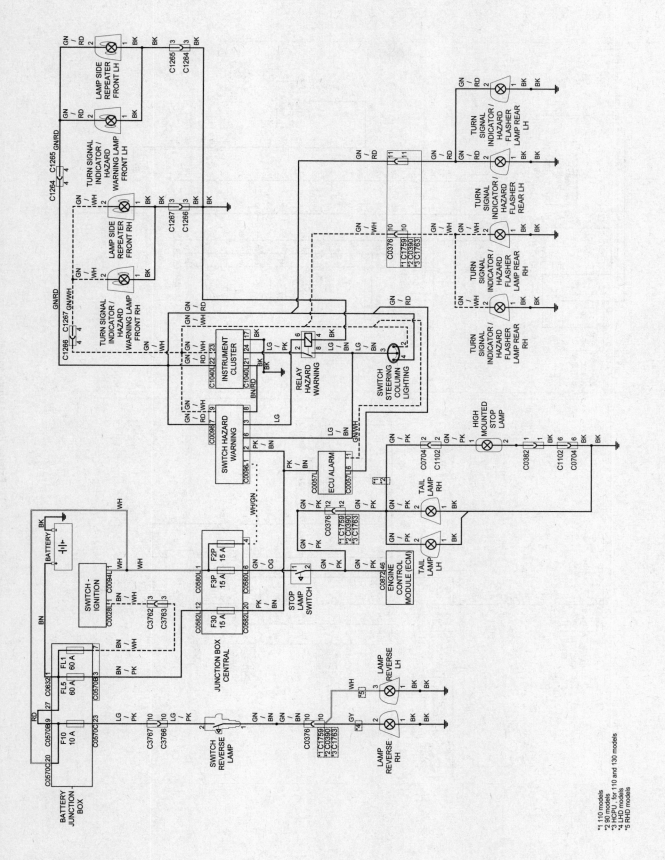

Exterior Lights – from 2012 to 2016 (2 of 2)

*1 110 models
*2 90 models
*3 HCPU, for 110 and 130 models
*4 LHD models
*5 RHD models

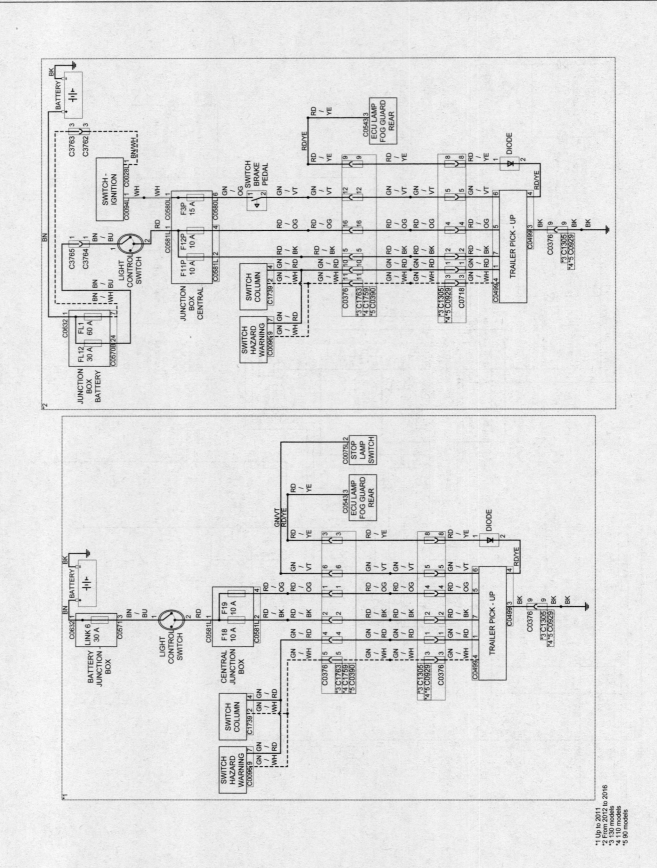

Exterior lights – trailor socket

*1 Up to 2011
*2 From 2012 to 2016
*3 130 models
*4 110 models
*5 90 models

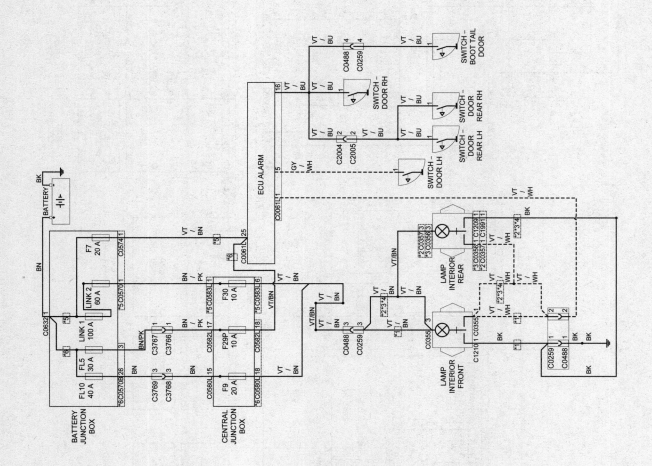

Interior lights

*1 Front lamp only
*2 90 models
*3 110 models
*4 With rear lamp
*5 From 2007 to 2011
*6 From 2012 to 2016

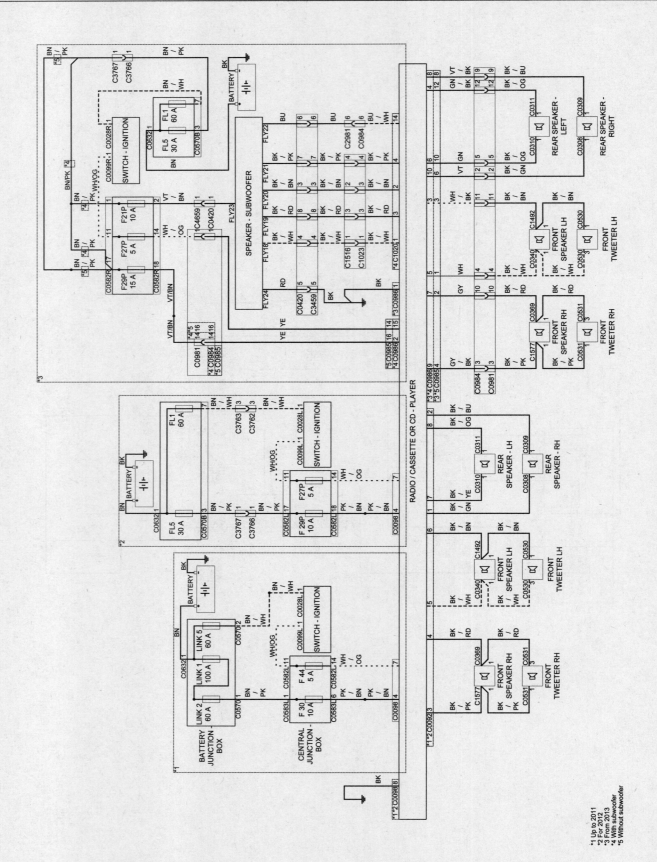

Sound system

*1 Up to 2011
*2 For 2012
*3 From 2013
*4 With subwoofer
*5 Without subwoofer

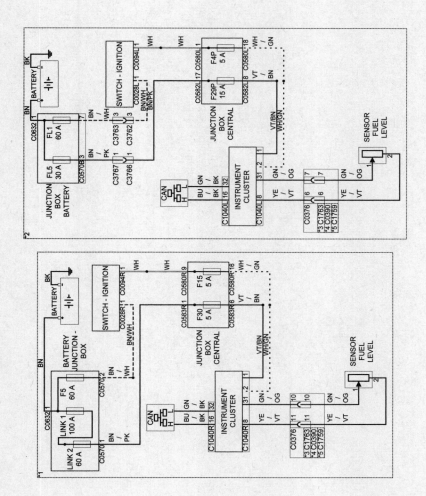

Fuel pump

Notes

Dimensions and weights

Note: *All figures and dimensions are approximate and may vary according to model. Refer to manufacturer's data for exact figures.*

Dimensions

Overall length:
  90 models:
    Soft-Top and Pick-Up models . . . . .3722 mm
    Hard-Top and Station Wagon models . . . . .3883 mm
  110 models:
    Soft-Top and Pick-Up models . . . . .4438 mm
    Hard-Top and Station Wagon models . . . . .4599 mm
    High Capacity Pick-Up models . . . . .4631 mm
  130 models. . . . . .5132 mm
Overall width (all models) . . . . .1790 mm
Overall height*:
  90 models. . . . . 1965 to 2000 mm
  110 models. . . . . 2035 to 2079 mm
  130 models. . . . . .2035 mm
Wheelbase:
  90 models. . . . . .2360 mm
  110 models. . . . . .2794 mm
  130 models. . . . . .3226 mm
Front and rear track . . . . .1486 mm
Turning circle (between kerbs)
  90 model:
    265/75 x 16 tyres . . . . 12.65 m (41.5 ft)
    All other tyre sizes . . . . 11.70 m (38.4 ft)
  110 model:
    7.50 x 16 tyres. . . . . .13.41 m (44 ft)
  130 model:
    750 x 16 tyres . . . . .15.24 m (50 ft)
* Overall height depends on suspension specification and load.

Weights

Kerb weight (approximate weights without options):
  90 models:
    Soft-Top . . . . .1643 kg
    Pick-Up. . . . . .1661 kg
    Hard-Top. . . . . .1685 kg
    Station Wagon . . . . .1727 kg
  110 models:
    Soft-Top . . . . .1742 kg
    Pick-Up. . . . . .1743 kg
    Hard-Top. . . . . .1796 kg
    Station Wagon . . . . .1906 kg
    High Capacity Pick-Up . . . . .1859 kg
  130 models:
    High capacity Pick-up . . . . .2120 kg
Maximum axle weights:
  Front axle:
    90 and 110 models. . . . . .1200 kg
    130 models. . . . . .1580 kg
  Rear axle:
    90 models:
      Standard suspension . . . . .1380 kg
      High-load suspension. .1500 kg
    110 models:
      Standard suspension . . . . .1750 kg
      High-load suspension. .1850 kg
    130 models. . . . . .2200 kg
Maximum gross vehicle weight:
  90 models:
    Standard suspension . . . . .2400 kg
    High-load suspension. . . . . .2550 kg
  110 models:
    Standard suspension . . . . .2950 kg
    High-load suspension. . . . . .3050 kg
  130 models. . . . . .3500 kg
Maximum roof load (including roof rack) . . . . .75 kg
Maximum towing weight:
  On-road:
    Unbraked trailer . . . . .750 kg
    Trailer with overrun brakes . . . . .3500 kg
    Fully-braked trailer*:
      Non-turbo models. . . . . .3500 kg
      Turbo models . . . . .4000 kg
  Off-road:
    Unbraked trailer . . . . .500 kg
    Trailer with overrun brakes . . . . .1000 kg
    Fully-braked trailer . . . . .1000 kg
* Only applies to vehicles modified to accept coupled brakes.

Fuel economy

Although depreciation is still the biggest part of the cost of motoring for most car owners, the cost of fuel is more immediately noticeable. These pages give some tips on how to get the best fuel economy.

Working it out

Manufacturer's figures

Car manufacturers are required by law to provide fuel consumption information on all new vehicles sold. These 'official' figures are obtained by simulating various driving conditions on a rolling road or a test track. Real life conditions are different, so the fuel consumption actually achieved may not bear much resemblance to the quoted figures.

How to calculate it

Many cars now have trip computers which will

display fuel consumption, both instantaneous and average. Refer to the owner's handbook for details of how to use these.

To calculate consumption yourself (and maybe to check that the trip computer is accurate), proceed as follows.

1. Fill up with fuel and note the mileage, or zero the trip recorder.
2. Drive as usual until you need to fill up again.
3. Note the amount of fuel required to refill the tank, and the mileage covered since the previous fill-up.
4. Divide the mileage by the amount of fuel used to obtain the consumption figure.

For example:

Mileage at first fill-up (a) = 27,903
Mileage at second fill-up (b) = 28,346
Mileage covered (b - a) = 443
Fuel required at second fill-up = 48.6 litres

The half-completed changeover to metric units in the UK means that we buy our fuel in litres, measure distances in miles and talk about fuel consumption in miles per gallon. There are two ways round this: the first is to convert the litres to gallons before doing the calculation (by dividing by 4.546, or see Table 1). So in the example:

48.6 litres ÷ 4.546 = 10.69 gallons
443 miles ÷ 10.69 gallons = 41.4 mpg

The second way is to calculate the consumption in miles per litre, then multiply that figure by 4.546 (or see Table 2).

So in the example, fuel consumption is:

443 miles ÷ 48.6 litres = 9.1 mpl
9.1 mpl x 4.546 = 41.4 mpg

The rest of Europe expresses fuel consumption in litres of fuel required to travel 100 km (l/100 km). For interest, the conversions are given in Table 3. In practice it doesn't matter what units you use, provided you know what your normal consumption is and can spot if it's getting better or worse.

Table 1: conversion of litres to Imperial gallons

litres	1	2	3	4	5	10	20	30	40	50	60	70
gallons	0.22	0.44	0.66	0.88	1.10	2.24	4.49	6.73	8.98	11.22	13.47	15.71

Table 2: conversion of miles per litre to miles per gallon

miles per litre	5	6	7	8	9	10	11	12	13	14
miles per gallon	23	27	32	36	41	46	50	55	59	64

Table 3: conversion of litres per 100 km to miles per gallon

litres per 100 km	4	4.5	5	5.5	6	6.5	7	8	9	10
miles per gallon	71	63	56	51	47	43	40	35	31	28

Maintenance

A well-maintained car uses less fuel and creates less pollution. In particular:

Filters

Change air and fuel filters at the specified intervals.

Oil

Use a good quality oil of the lowest viscosity specified by the vehicle manufacturer (see *Lubricants and fluids*). Check the level often and be careful not to overfill.

Spark plugs

When applicable, renew at the specified intervals.

Tyres

Check tyre pressures regularly. Under-inflated tyres have an increased rolling resistance. It is generally safe to use the higher pressures specified for full load conditions even when not fully laden, but keep an eye on the centre band of tread for signs of wear due to over-inflation.

When buying new tyres, consider the 'fuel saving' models which most manufacturers include in their ranges.

Driving style

Acceleration

Acceleration uses more fuel than driving at a steady speed. The best technique with modern cars is to accelerate reasonably briskly to the desired speed, changing up through the gears as soon as possible without making the engine labour.

Air conditioning

Air conditioning absorbs quite a bit of energy from the engine – typically 3 kW (4 hp) or so. The effect on fuel consumption is at its worst in slow traffic. Switch it off when not required.

Anticipation

Drive smoothly and try to read the traffic flow so as to avoid unnecessary acceleration and braking.

Automatic transmission

When accelerating in an automatic, avoid depressing the throttle so far as to make the transmission hold onto lower gears at higher speeds. Don't use the 'Sport' setting, if applicable.

When stationary with the engine running, select 'N' or 'P'. When moving, keep your left foot away from the brake.

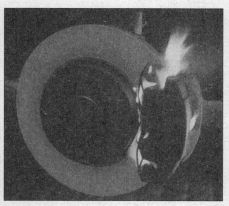

Braking

Braking converts the car's energy of motion into heat – essentially, it is wasted. Obviously some braking is always going to be necessary, but with good anticipation it is surprising how much can be avoided, especially on routes that you know well.

Carshare

Consider sharing lifts to work or to the shops. Even once a week will make a difference.

Electrical loads

Electricity is 'fuel' too; the alternator which charges the battery does so by converting some of the engine's energy of motion into electrical energy. The more electrical accessories are in use, the greater the load on the alternator. Switch off big consumers like the heated rear window when not required.

Freewheeling

Freewheeling (coasting) in neutral with the engine switched off is dangerous. The effort required to operate power-assisted brakes and steering increases when the engine is not running, with a potential lack of control in emergency situations.

In any case, modern fuel injection systems automatically cut off the engine's fuel supply on the overrun (moving and in gear, but with the accelerator pedal released).

Gadgets

Bolt-on devices claiming to save fuel have been around for nearly as long as the motor car itself. Those which worked were rapidly adopted as standard equipment by the vehicle manufacturers. Others worked only in certain situations, or saved fuel only at the expense of unacceptable effects on performance, driveability or the life of engine components.

The most effective fuel saving gadget is the driver's right foot.

Journey planning

Combine (eg) a trip to the supermarket with a visit to the recycling centre and the DIY store, rather than making separate journeys.

When possible choose a travelling time outside rush hours.

Load

The more heavily a car is laden, the greater the energy required to accelerate it to a given speed. Remove heavy items which you don't need to carry.

One load which is often overlooked is the contents of the fuel tank. A tankful of fuel (55 litres / 12 gallons) weighs 45 kg (100 lb) or so. Just half filling it may be worthwhile.

Lost?

At the risk of stating the obvious, if you're going somewhere new, have details of the route to hand. There's not much point in achieving record mpg if you also go miles out of your way.

Parking

If possible, carry out any reversing or turning manoeuvres when you arrive at a parking space so that you can drive straight out when you leave. Manoeuvering when the engine is cold uses a lot more fuel.

Driving around looking for free on-street parking may cost more in fuel than buying a car park ticket.

Premium fuel

Most major oil companies (and some supermarkets) have premium grades of fuel which are several pence a litre dearer than the standard grades. Reports vary, but the consensus seems to be that if these fuels improve economy at all, they do not do so by enough to justify their extra cost.

Roof rack

When loading a roof rack, try to produce a wedge shape with the narrow end at the front. Any cover should be securely fastened – if it flaps it's creating turbulence and absorbing energy.

Remove roof racks and boxes when not in use – they increase air resistance and can create a surprising amount of noise.

Short journeys

The engine is at its least efficient, and wear is highest, during the first few miles after a cold start. Consider walking, cycling or using public transport.

Speed

The engine is at its most efficient when running at a steady speed and load at the rpm where it develops maximum torque. (You can find this figure in the car's handbook.) For most cars this corresponds to between 55 and 65 mph in top gear.

Above the optimum cruising speed, fuel consumption starts to rise quite sharply. A car travelling at 80 mph will typically be using 30% more fuel than at 60 mph.

Supermarket fuel

It may be cheap but is it any good? In the UK all supermarket fuel must meet the relevant British Standard. The major oil companies will say that their branded fuels have better additive packages which may stop carbon and other deposits building up. A reasonable compromise might be to use one tank of branded fuel to three or four from the supermarket.

Switch off when stationary

Switch off the engine if you look like being stationary for more than 30 seconds or so. This is good for the environment as well as for your pocket. Be aware though that frequent restarts are hard on the battery and the starter motor.

Windows

Driving with the windows open increases air turbulence around the vehicle. Closing the windows promotes smooth airflow and reduced resistance. The faster you go, the more significant this is.

And finally . . .

Driving techniques associated with good fuel economy tend to involve moderate acceleration and low top speeds. Be considerate to the needs of other road users who may need to make brisker progress; even if you do not agree with them this is not an excuse to be obstructive.

Safety must always take precedence over economy, whether it is a question of accelerating hard to complete an overtaking manoeuvre, killing your speed when confronted with a potential hazard or switching the lights on when it starts to get dark.

Conversion factors

Length (distance)
Inches (in)	x 25.4	= Millimetres (mm)	x 0.0394	= Inches (in)
Feet (ft)	x 0.305	= Metres (m)	x 3.281	= Feet (ft)
Miles	x 1.609	= Kilometres (km)	x 0.621	= Miles

Volume (capacity)
Cubic inches (cu in; in³)	x 16.387	= Cubic centimetres (cc; cm³)	x 0.061	= Cubic inches (cu in; in³)
Imperial pints (Imp pt)	x 0.568	= Litres (l)	x 1.76	= Imperial pints (Imp pt)
Imperial quarts (Imp qt)	x 1.137	= Litres (l)	x 0.88	= Imperial quarts (Imp qt)
Imperial quarts (Imp qt)	x 1.201	= US quarts (US qt)	x 0.833	= Imperial quarts (Imp qt)
US quarts (US qt)	x 0.946	= Litres (l)	x 1.057	= US quarts (US qt)
Imperial gallons (Imp gal)	x 4.546	= Litres (l)	x 0.22	= Imperial gallons (Imp gal)
Imperial gallons (Imp gal)	x 1.201	= US gallons (US gal)	x 0.833	= Imperial gallons (Imp gal)
US gallons (US gal)	x 3.785	= Litres (l)	x 0.264	= US gallons (US gal)

Mass (weight)
Ounces (oz)	x 28.35	= Grams (g)	x 0.035	= Ounces (oz)
Pounds (lb)	x 0.454	= Kilograms (kg)	x 2.205	= Pounds (lb)

Force
Ounces-force (ozf; oz)	x 0.278	= Newtons (N)	x 3.6	= Ounces-force (ozf; oz)
Pounds-force (lbf; lb)	x 4.448	= Newtons (N)	x 0.225	= Pounds-force (lbf; lb)
Newtons (N)	x 0.1	= Kilograms-force (kgf; kg)	x 9.81	= Newtons (N)

Pressure
Pounds-force per square inch (psi; lbf/in²; lb/in²)	x 0.070	= Kilograms-force per square centimetre (kgf/cm²; kg/cm²)	x 14.223	= Pounds-force per square inch (psi; lbf/in²; lb/in²)
Pounds-force per square inch (psi; lbf/in²; lb/in²)	x 0.068	= Atmospheres (atm)	x 14.696	= Pounds-force per square inch (psi; lbf/in²; lb/in²)
Pounds-force per square inch (psi; lbf/in²; lb/in²)	x 0.069	= Bars	x 14.5	= Pounds-force per square inch (psi; lbf/in²; lb/in²)
Pounds-force per square inch (psi; lbf/in²; lb/in²)	x 6.895	= Kilopascals (kPa)	x 0.145	= Pounds-force per square inch (psi; lbf/in²; lb/in²)
Kilopascals (kPa)	x 0.01	= Kilograms-force per square centimetre (kgf/cm²; kg/cm²)	x 98.1	= Kilopascals (kPa)
Millibar (mbar)	x 100	= Pascals (Pa)	x 0.01	= Millibar (mbar)
Millibar (mbar)	x 0.0145	= Pounds-force per square inch (psi; lbf/in²; lb/in²)	x 68.947	= Millibar (mbar)
Millibar (mbar)	x 0.75	= Millimetres of mercury (mmHg)	x 1.333	= Millibar (mbar)
Millibar (mbar)	x 0.401	= Inches of water (inH₂O)	x 2.491	= Millibar (mbar)
Millimetres of mercury (mmHg)	x 0.535	= Inches of water (inH₂O)	x 1.868	= Millimetres of mercury (mmHg)
Inches of water (inH₂O)	x 0.036	= Pounds-force per square inch (psi; lbf/in²; lb/in²)	x 27.68	= Inches of water (inH₂O)

Torque (moment of force)
Pounds-force inches (lbf in; lb in)	x 1.152	= Kilograms-force centimetre (kgf cm; kg cm)	x 0.868	= Pounds-force inches (lbf in; lb in)
Pounds-force inches (lbf in; lb in)	x 0.113	= Newton metres (Nm)	x 8.85	= Pounds-force inches (lbf in; lb in)
Pounds-force inches (lbf in; lb in)	x 0.083	= Pounds-force feet (lbf ft; lb ft)	x 12	= Pounds-force inches (lbf in; lb in)
Pounds-force feet (lbf ft; lb ft)	x 0.138	= Kilograms-force metres (kgf m; kg m)	x 7.233	= Pounds-force feet (lbf ft; lb ft)
Pounds-force feet (lbf ft; lb ft)	x 1.356	= Newton metres (Nm)	x 0.738	= Pounds-force feet (lbf ft; lb ft)
Newton metres (Nm)	x 0.102	= Kilograms-force metres (kgf m; kg m)	x 9.804	= Newton metres (Nm)

Power
Horsepower (hp)	x 745.7	= Watts (W)	x 0.0013	= Horsepower (hp)

Velocity (speed)
Miles per hour (miles/hr; mph)	x 1.609	= Kilometres per hour (km/hr; kph)	x 0.621	= Miles per hour (miles/hr; mph)

Fuel consumption*
Miles per gallon, Imperial (mpg)	x 0.354	= Kilometres per litre (km/l)	x 2.825	= Miles per gallon, Imperial (mpg)
Miles per gallon, US (mpg)	x 0.425	= Kilometres per litre (km/l)	x 2.352	= Miles per gallon, US (mpg)

Temperature

Degrees Fahrenheit = (°C x 1.8) + 32   Degrees Celsius (Degrees Centigrade; °C) = (°F - 32) x 0.56

It is common practice to convert from miles per gallon (mpg) to litres/100 kilometres (l/100km), where mpg x l/100 km = 282

Spare parts are available from many sources, including maker's appointed garages, accessory shops, and motor factors. To be sure of obtaining the correct parts, it will sometimes be necessary to quote the vehicle identification number (see Vehicle identification). If possible, it can also be useful to take the old parts along for positive identification. Items such as starter motors and alternators may be available under a service exchange scheme – any parts returned should always be clean.

Our advice regarding spare part sources is as follows.

Officially-appointed garages

This is the best source of parts which are peculiar to your car, and which are not otherwise generally available (eg badges, interior trim, certain body panels, etc). It is also the only place at which you should buy parts if the car is still under warranty.

Accessory shops

These are very good places to buy materials and components needed for the maintenance of your car (oil, air and fuel filters, spark plugs, light bulbs, drivebelts, oils and greases, brake pads, touch-up paint, etc). Components of this nature sold by a reputable shop are of the same standard as those used by the car manufacturer.

Besides components, these shops also sell tools and general accessories, usually have convenient opening hours, charge lower prices, and can often be found not far from home. Some accessory shops have parts counters where the components needed for almost any repair job can be purchased or ordered.

Motor factors

Good factors will stock all the more important components which wear out comparatively quickly, and can sometimes supply individual components needed for the overhaul of a larger assembly (eg brake seals and hydraulic parts, bearing shells, pistons, valves, alternator brushes). They may also handle work such as cylinder block reboring, crankshaft regrinding and balancing, etc.

Tyre and exhaust specialists

These outlets may be independent, or members of a local or national chain. They frequently offer competitive prices when compared with a main dealer or local garage, but it will pay to obtain several quotes before making a decision. When researching prices, also ask what 'extras' may be added – for instance, fitting a new valve and balancing the wheel are both commonly charged on top of the price of a new tyre.

Other sources

Beware of parts or materials obtained from market stalls, car boot sales or similar outlets. Such items are not invariably sub-standard, but there is little chance of compensation if they do prove unsatisfactory. In the case of safety-critical components such as brake pads, there is the risk not only of financial loss but also of an accident causing injury or death.

Second-hand components or assemblies obtained from a car breaker can be a good buy in some circumstances, but this sort of purchase is best made by the experienced DIY mechanic.

Vehicle identification numbers

Modifications are a continuing and unpublicised process in vehicle manufacture, quite apart from major model changes. Spare parts manuals and lists are compiled upon a numerical basis, the vehicle identification numbers being essential to correct identification of the component concerned.

When ordering spare parts, always give as much information as possible. Quote the vehicle model, year of manufacture, body and engine numbers as appropriate.

The Vehicle Identification Number (VIN) plate is riveted to the top of the brake pedal box in the engine compartment, and can be viewed once the bonnet is open**(see illustration)**. The plate carries the VIN number, vehicle weight information, and paint and trim colour codes.

The Vehicle Identification Number (VIN) is also stamped into front right-hand side of the chassis, forward of the coil spring mounting and on a plate at the lower left-hand side of the windscreen **(see illustrations)**.

The engine number is stamped into the cylinder block, and is located on a machined surface on the right-hand side of the engine, at the transmission end.

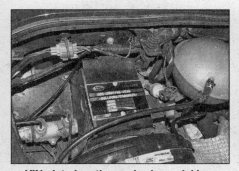

VIN plate location on brake pedal box

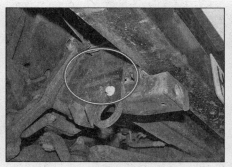

VIN stamped on right-hand side of chassis

VIN stamped on a plate in the lower part of the screen

Whenever servicing, repair or overhaul work is carried out on the car or its components, observe the following procedures and instructions. This will assist in carrying out the operation efficiently and to a professional standard of workmanship.

Joint mating faces and gaskets

When separating components at their mating faces, never insert screwdrivers or similar implements into the joint between the faces in order to prise them apart. This can cause severe damage which results in oil leaks, coolant leaks, etc upon reassembly. Separation is usually achieved by tapping along the joint with a soft-faced hammer in order to break the seal. However, note that this method may not be suitable where dowels are used for component location.

Where a gasket is used between the mating faces of two components, a new one must be fitted on reassembly; fit it dry unless otherwise stated in the repair procedure. Make sure that the mating faces are clean and dry, with all traces of old gasket removed. When cleaning a joint face, use a tool which is unlikely to score or damage the face, and remove any burrs or nicks with an oilstone or fine file.

Make sure that tapped holes are cleaned with a pipe cleaner, and keep them free of jointing compound, if this is being used, unless specifically instructed otherwise.

Ensure that all orifices, channels or pipes are clear, and blow through them, preferably using compressed air.

Oil seals

Oil seals can be removed by levering them out with a wide flat-bladed screwdriver or similar implement. Alternatively, a number of self-tapping screws may be screwed into the seal, and these used as a purchase for pliers or some similar device in order to pull the seal free.

Whenever an oil seal is removed from its working location, either individually or as part of an assembly, it should be renewed.

The very fine sealing lip of the seal is easily damaged, and will not seal if the surface it contacts is not completely clean and free from scratches, nicks or grooves. If the original sealing surface of the component cannot be restored, and the manufacturer has not made provision for slight relocation of the seal relative to the sealing surface, the component should be renewed.

Protect the lips of the seal from any surface which may damage them in the course of fitting. Use tape or a conical sleeve where possible. Where indicated, lubricate the seal lips with oil before fitting and, on dual-lipped seals, fill the space between the lips with grease.

Unless otherwise stated, oil seals must be fitted with their sealing lips toward the lubricant to be sealed.

Use a tubular drift or block of wood of the appropriate size to install the seal and, if the seal housing is shouldered, drive the seal down to the shoulder. If the seal housing is unshouldered, the seal should be fitted with its face flush with the housing top face (unless otherwise instructed).

Screw threads and fastenings

Seized nuts, bolts and screws are quite a common occurrence where corrosion has set in, and the use of penetrating oil or releasing fluid will often overcome this problem if the offending item is soaked for a while before attempting to release it. The use of an impact driver may also provide a means of releasing such stubborn fastening devices, when used in conjunction with the appropriate screwdriver bit or socket. If none of these methods works, it may be necessary to resort to the careful application of heat, or the use of a hacksaw or nut splitter device. Before resorting to extreme methods, check that you are not dealing with a left-hand thread!

Studs are usually removed by locking two nuts together on the threaded part, and then using a spanner on the lower nut to unscrew the stud. Studs or bolts which have broken off below the surface of the component in which they are mounted can sometimes be removed using a stud extractor.

Always ensure that a blind tapped hole is completely free from oil, grease, water or other fluid before installing the bolt or stud. Failure to do this could cause the housing to crack due to the hydraulic action of the bolt or stud as it is screwed in.

For some screw fastenings, notably cylinder head bolts or nuts, torque wrench settings are no longer specified for the latter stages of tightening, "angle-tightening" being called up instead. Typically, a fairly low torque wrench setting will be applied to the bolts/nuts in the correct sequence, followed by one or more stages of tightening through specified angles.

When checking or retightening a nut or bolt to a specified torque setting, slacken the nut or bolt by a quarter of a turn, and then retighten to the specified setting. However, this should not be attempted where angular tightening has been used.

Locknuts, locktabs and washers

Any fastening which will rotate against a component or housing during tightening should always have a washer between it and the relevant component or housing.

Spring or split washers should always be renewed when they are used to lock a critical component such as a big-end bearing retaining bolt or nut. Locktabs which are folded over to retain a nut or bolt should always be renewed.

Self-locking nuts can be re-used in non-critical areas, providing resistance can be felt when the locking portion passes over the bolt or stud thread. However, it should be noted that self-locking stiffnuts tend to lose their effectiveness after long periods of use, and should then be renewed as a matter of course.

Split pins must always be replaced with new ones of the correct size for the hole.

When thread-locking compound is found on the threads of a fastener which is to be re-used, it should be cleaned off with a wire brush and solvent, and fresh compound applied on reassembly.

Special tools

Some repair procedures in this manual entail the use of special tools such as a press, two or three-legged pullers, spring compressors, etc. Wherever possible, suitable readily-available alternatives to the manufacturer's special tools are described, and are shown in use. In some instances, where no alternative is possible, it has been necessary to resort to the use of a manufacturer's tool, and this has been done for reasons of safety as well as the efficient completion of the repair operation. Unless you are highly-skilled and have a thorough understanding of the procedures described, never attempt to bypass the use of any special tool when the procedure described specifies its use. Not only is there a very great risk of personal injury, but expensive damage could be caused to the components involved.

Environmental considerations

When disposing of used engine oil, brake fluid, antifreeze, etc, give due consideration to any detrimental environmental effects. Do not, for instance, pour any of the above liquids down drains into the general sewage system, or onto the ground to soak away, as this is likely to pollute your local environment. Many local council refuse tips provide a facility for waste oil disposal, as do some garages. You can find your nearest disposal point by calling the Environment Agency on 03708 506 506 or by visiting www.oilbankline.org.uk.

Note: It is illegal and anti-social to dump oil down the drain. To find the location of your local oil recycling bank, call 03708 506 506 or visit www.oilbankline.org.uk.

Warning: *The handbrake acts on the transmission, not the rear wheels, and may not hold the vehicle stationary when jacking, unless the following procedure is followed precisely. If one front wheel and one rear wheel are raised, no vehicle holding or braking effect is possible using the handbrake, therefore the wheels must always be chocked (using the chock supplied in the tool kit). If the vehicle is coupled to a trailer, disconnect the trailer from the vehicle before commencing jacking. This is to prevent the trailer pulling the vehicle off the jack and causing personal injury.*

Note: *To raise the vehicle, a hydraulic jack with a minimum load capacity of 1500 kg must be used. Never work under a vehicle supported solely by a hydraulic jack – always supplement the jack with axle stands.*

The jack supplied with the vehicle tool kit should only be used for changing the roadwheels – see Wheel changing later in this Section. When carrying out any other kind of work, raise the vehicle using a hydraulic jack, and always supplement the jack with axle stands positioned under the axles or the chassis sidemembers **(see illustration)**. Do not jack the vehicle, or position axle stands under any of the following components:

a) Body structure.
b) Bumpers.
c) Underbody pipes and hoses.
d) Suspension components.
e) Gearbox/transfer gearbox housings.
f) Engine sump.
g) Fuel tank.

2 To raise the front or the rear of the vehicle, chock the appropriate roadwheels, then position the jack head under the front or rear differential casing, as appropriate **(see illustration)**. **Note:** *The differential casing is not in the centre of the axle, and the vehicle will tilt when jacked under the differential*

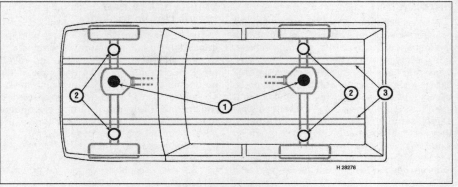

Vehicle jacking points

1 Jacking points for use with hydraulic jack (under differential housing)
2 Support points for use with axle stands (under axle tubes)
3 Chassis side members

Jack positioned under front differential casing

Axle stand positioned under right-hand end of front axle

casing. This is particularly noticeable when jacking up the front of the vehicle.
3 Operate the jack to raise the vehicle, then position an axle stand under the right-hand end of the axle **(see illustration)**.
4 Position an axle stand under the left-hand end of the axle, then carefully lower the

jack until the axle is supported by both axle stands.
5 Position axle stands under the appropriate axle tubes, or under the chassis, as required. Never work under, around, or near a raised vehicle, unless it is adequately supported in at least two places **(see illustration)**.

Radio/cassette unit anti-theft system – precautions

The radio/CD unit fitted as standard equipment by Land Rover may be equipped with a built-in security code, to deter thieves. If the power source to the unit is cut, the anti-theft system will activate. Even if the power source is immediately reconnected, the radio/CD unit will not function until the correct security code has been entered. Therefore,

if you do not know the correct security code for the radio/CD unit, do not disconnect the battery negative terminal of the battery, nor remove the radio/CD unit from the vehicle.

To enter the correct security code, follow the instructions provided with the radioCD player handbook.

If an incorrect code is entered, the unit will become locked, and cannot be operated.

If this happens or if the security code is lost or forgotten, seek the advice of your Land Rover dealer. On presentation of proof of ownership, a Land Rover dealer will be able to unlock the unit, and provide you with a new security code.

Introduction

A selection of good tools is a fundamental requirement for anyone contemplating the maintenance and repair of a motor vehicle. For the owner who does not possess any, their purchase will prove a considerable expense, offsetting some of the savings made by doing-it-yourself. However, provided that the tools purchased meet the relevant national safety standards and are of good quality, they will last for many years and prove an extremely worthwhile investment.

To help the average owner to decide which tools are needed to carry out the various tasks detailed in this manual, we have compiled three lists of tools under the following headings: *Maintenance and minor repair*, *Repair and overhaul*, and *Special*. Newcomers to practical mechanics should start off with the *Maintenance and minor repair* tool kit, and confine themselves to the simpler jobs around the vehicle. Then, as confidence and experience grow, more difficult tasks can be undertaken, with extra tools being purchased as, and when, they are needed. In this way, a *Maintenance and minor repair* tool kit can be built up into a *Repair and overhaul* tool kit over a considerable period of time, without any major cash outlays. The experienced do-it-yourselfer will have a tool kit good enough for most repair and overhaul procedures, and will add tools from the *Special* category when it is felt that the expense is justified by the amount of use to which these tools will be put.

Maintenance and minor repair tool kit

The tools given in this list should be considered as a minimum requirement if routine maintenance, servicing and minor repair operations are to be undertaken. We recommend the purchase of combination spanners (ring one end, open-ended the other); although more expensive than open-ended ones, they do give the advantages of both types of spanner.

☐ *Combination spanners:*
  Metric - 8 to 19 mm inclusive
☐ *Adjustable spanner - 35 mm jaw (approx.)*
☐ *Spark plug spanner (with rubber insert) - petrol models*
☐ *Spark plug gap adjustment tool - petrol models*
☐ *Set of feeler gauges*
☐ *Brake bleed nipple spanner*
☐ *Screwdrivers:*
  Flat blade - 100 mm long x 6 mm dia
  Cross blade - 100 mm long x 6 mm dia
  Torx - various sizes (not all vehicles)
☐ *Combination pliers*
☐ *Hacksaw (junior)*
☐ *Tyre pump*
☐ *Tyre pressure gauge*
☐ *Oil can*
☐ *Oil filter removal tool (if applicable)*
☐ *Fine emery cloth*
☐ *Wire brush (small)*
☐ *Funnel (medium size)*
☐ *Sump drain plug key (not all vehicles)*

Repair and overhaul tool kit

These tools are virtually essential for anyone undertaking any major repairs to a motor vehicle, and are additional to those given in the *Maintenance and minor repair* list. Included in this list is a comprehensive set of sockets. Although these are expensive, they will be found invaluable as they are so versatile - particularly if various drives are included in the set. We recommend the half-inch square-drive type, as this can be used with most proprietary torque wrenches.

The tools in this list will sometimes need to be supplemented by tools from the *Special* list:

☐ *Sockets to cover range in previous list (including Torx sockets)*
☐ *Reversible ratchet drive (for use with sockets)*
☐ *Extension piece, 250 mm (for use with sockets)*
☐ *Universal joint (for use with sockets)*
☐ *Flexible handle or sliding T "breaker bar" (for use with sockets)*
☐ *Torque wrench (for use with sockets)*
☐ *Self-locking grips*
☐ *Ball pein hammer*
☐ *Soft-faced mallet (plastic or rubber)*
☐ *Screwdrivers:*
  Flat blade - long & sturdy, short (chubby), and narrow (electrician's) types
  Cross blade – long & sturdy, and short (chubby) types
☐ *Pliers:*
  Long-nosed
  Side cutters (electrician's)
  Circlip (internal and external)
☐ *Cold chisel - 25 mm*
☐ *Scriber*
☐ *Scraper*
☐ *Centre-punch*
☐ *Pin punch*
☐ *Hacksaw*
☐ *Brake hose clamp*
☐ *Brake/clutch bleeding kit*
☐ *Selection of twist drills*
☐ *Steel rule/straight-edge*
☐ *Allen keys (inc. splined/Torx type)*
☐ *Selection of files*
☐ *Wire brush*
☐ *Axle stands*
☐ *Jack (strong trolley or hydraulic type)*
☐ *Light with extension lead*
☐ *Universal electrical multi-meter*

Sockets and reversible ratchet drive

Brake bleeding kit

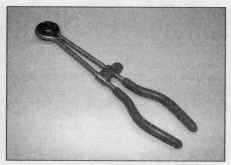
Hose clamp

Torx key, socket and bit

Angular-tightening gauge

Special tools

The tools in this list are those which are not used regularly, are expensive to buy, or which need to be used in accordance with their manufacturers' instructions. Unless relatively difficult mechanical jobs are undertaken frequently, it will not be economic to buy many of these tools. Where this is the case, you could consider clubbing together with friends (or joining a motorists' club) to make a joint purchase, or borrowing the tools against a deposit from a local garage or tool hire specialist.

The following list contains only those tools and instruments freely available to the public, and not those special tools produced by the vehicle manufacturer specifically for its dealer network. You will find occasional references to these manufacturers' special tools in the text of this manual. Generally, an alternative method of doing the job without the vehicle manufacturers' special tool is given. However, sometimes there is no alternative to using them. Where this is the case and the relevant tool cannot be bought or borrowed, you will have to entrust the work to a dealer.

- ☐ Angular-tightening gauge
- ☐ Valve spring compressor
- ☐ Valve grinding tool
- ☐ Piston ring compressor
- ☐ Piston ring removal/installation tool
- ☐ Cylinder bore hone
- ☐ Balljoint separator
- ☐ Coil spring compressors (where applicable)
- ☐ Two/three-legged hub and bearing puller
- ☐ Impact screwdriver
- ☐ Micrometer and/or vernier calipers
- ☐ Dial gauge
- ☐ Tachometer
- ☐ Fault code reader
- ☐ Cylinder compression gauge
- ☐ Hand-operated vacuum pump and gauge
- ☐ Clutch plate alignment set
- ☐ Brake shoe steady spring cup removal tool
- ☐ Bush and bearing removal/installation set
- ☐ Stud extractors
- ☐ Tap and die set
- ☐ Lifting tackle

Buying tools

Reputable motor accessory shops and superstores often offer excellent quality tools at discount prices, so it pays to shop around.

Remember, you don't have to buy the most expensive items on the shelf, but it is always advisable to steer clear of the very cheap tools. Beware of 'bargains' offered on market stalls, on-line or at car boot sales. There are plenty of good tools around at reasonable prices, but always aim to purchase items which meet the relevant national safety standards. If in doubt, ask the proprietor or manager of the shop for advice before making a purchase.

Care and maintenance of tools

Having purchased a reasonable tool kit, it is necessary to keep the tools in a clean and serviceable condition. After use, always wipe off any dirt, grease and metal particles using a clean, dry cloth, before putting the tools away. Never leave them lying around after they have been used. A simple tool rack on the garage or workshop wall for items such as screwdrivers and pliers is a good idea. Store all normal spanners and sockets in a metal box. Any measuring instruments, gauges, meters, etc, must be carefully stored where they cannot be damaged or become rusty.

Take a little care when tools are used. Hammer heads inevitably become marked, and screwdrivers lose the keen edge on their blades from time to time. A little timely attention with emery cloth or a file will soon restore items like this to a good finish.

Working facilities

Not to be forgotten when discussing tools is the workshop itself. If anything more than routine maintenance is to be carried out, a suitable working area becomes essential.

It is appreciated that many an owner-mechanic is forced by circumstances to remove an engine or similar item without the benefit of a garage or workshop. Having done this, any repairs should always be done under the cover of a roof.

Wherever possible, any dismantling should be done on a clean, flat workbench or table at a suitable working height.

Any workbench needs a vice; one with a jaw opening of 100 mm is suitable for most jobs. As mentioned previously, some clean dry storage space is also required for tools, as well as for any lubricants, cleaning fluids, touch-up paints etc, which become necessary.

Another item which may be required, and which has a much more general usage, is an electric drill with a chuck capacity of at least 8 mm. This, together with a good range of twist drills, is virtually essential for fitting accessories.

Last, but not least, always keep a supply of old newspapers and clean, lint-free rags available, and try to keep any working area as clean as possible.

Micrometers

Dial test indicator ("dial gauge")

Oil filter removal tool (strap wrench type)

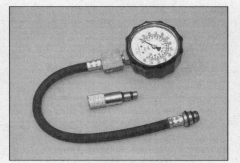

Compression tester

Bearing puller

This is a guide to getting your vehicle through the MOT test. Obviously it will not be possible to examine the vehicle to the same standard as the professional MOT tester. However, working through the following checks will enable you to identify any problem areas before submitting the vehicle for the test.

It has only been possible to summarise the test requirements here, based on the regulations in force at the time of printing. Test standards are becoming increasingly stringent, although there are some exemptions for older vehicles.

An assistant will be needed to help carry out some of these checks.

The checks have been sub-divided into four categories, as follows:

1 Checks carried out **FROM THE DRIVER'S SEAT**

2 Checks carried out **WITH THE VEHICLE ON THE GROUND**

3 Checks carried out **WITH THE VEHICLE RAISED AND THE WHEELS FREE TO TURN**

4 Checks carried out on **YOUR VEHICLE'S EXHAUST EMISSION SYSTEM**

---

1 Checks carried out **FROM THE DRIVER'S SEAT**

Handbrake (parking brake)

☐ Test the operation of the handbrake. Excessive travel (too many clicks) indicates incorrect brake or cable adjustment.
☐ Check that the handbrake cannot be released by tapping the lever sideways. Check the security of the lever mountings.

☐ If the parking brake is foot-operated, check that the pedal is secure and without excessive travel, and that the release mechanism operates correctly.
☐ Where applicable, test the operation of the electronic handbrake. The brake should engage and disengage without excessive delay. If the warning light does not extinguish when the brake is disengaged, this could indicate a fault which will need further investigation.

Footbrake

☐ Depress the brake pedal and check that it does not creep down to the floor, indicating a master cylinder fault. Release the pedal,

wait a few seconds, then depress it again. If the pedal travels nearly to the floor before firm resistance is felt, brake adjustment or repair is necessary. If the pedal feels spongy, there is air in the hydraulic system which must be removed by bleeding.

☐ Check that the brake pedal is secure and in good condition. Check also for signs of fluid leaks on the pedal, floor or carpets, which would indicate failed seals in the brake master cylinder.
☐ Check the servo unit (when applicable) by operating the brake pedal several times, then keeping the pedal depressed and starting the engine. As the engine starts, the pedal will move down slightly. If not, the vacuum hose or the servo itself may be faulty.

Steering wheel and column

☐ Examine the steering wheel for fractures or looseness of the hub, spokes or rim.
☐ Move the steering wheel from side to side and then up and down. Check that the steering wheel is not loose on the column, indicating wear or a loose retaining nut. Continue moving the steering wheel as before, but also turn it slightly from left to right.

☐ Check that the steering wheel is not loose on the column, and that there is no abnormal movement of the steering wheel, indicating wear in the column support bearings or couplings.
☐ Check that the ignition lock (where fitted) engages and disengages correctly.
☐ Steering column adjustment mechanisms (where fitted) must be able to lock the column securely in place with no play evident.

Windscreen, mirrors and sunvisor

☐ The windscreen must be free of cracks or other significant damage within the driver's field of view. (Small stone chips are acceptable.) Rear view mirrors must be secure, intact, and capable of being adjusted.

☐ The driver's sunvisor must be capable of being stored in the "up" position.

Seat belts and seats

Note: *The following checks are applicable to all seat belts, front and rear.*

☐ Examine the webbing of all the belts (including rear belts if fitted) for cuts, serious fraying or deterioration. Fasten and unfasten each belt to check the buckles. If applicable, check the retracting mechanism. Check the security of all seat belt mountings accessible from inside the vehicle, ensuring any height adjustable mountings lock securely in place.

☐ Seat belts with pre-tensioners, once activated, have a "flag" or similar showing on the seat belt stalk. This, in itself, is not a reason for test failure.

☐ The front seats themselves must be securely attached and the backrests must lock in the upright position.

Doors

☐ Both front doors must be able to be opened and closed from outside and inside, and must latch securely when closed.

Bonnet and boot/tailgate

☐ The bonnet and boot/tailgate must latch securely when closed.

2 Checks carried out WITH THE VEHICLE ON THE GROUND

Vehicle identification

☐ Number plates must be in good condition, secure and legible, with letters and numbers correctly spaced – spacing at (A) should be 33 mm and at (B) 11 mm. At the front, digits must be black on a white background and at the rear black on a yellow background. Other background designs (such as honeycomb) are not permitted.

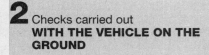

☐ The VIN plate and/or homologation plate must be permanently displayed and legible.

Electrical equipment

☐ Switch on the ignition and check the operation of the horn.

☐ Check the windscreen washers and wipers, examining the wiper blades; renew damaged or perished blades. Also check the operation of the stop-lights.

☐ Check the operation of the sidelights and number plate lights. The lenses and reflectors must be secure, clean and undamaged.

☐ Check the operation and alignment of the headlights. The headlight reflectors must not be tarnished and the lenses must be undamaged.

☐ Switch on the ignition and check the operation of the direction indicators (including the instrument panel tell-tale) and the hazard warning lights. Operation of the sidelights and stop-lights must not affect the indicators - if it does, the cause is usually a bad earth at the rear light cluster. Indicators should flash at a rate of between 60 and 120 times per minute – faster or slower than this could indicate a fault with the flasher unit or a bad earth at one of the light units.

☐ Check the operation of the rear foglight(s), including the warning light on the instrument panel or in the switch.

☐ The warning lights must illuminate in accordance with the manufacturer's design. For most vehicles, the ABS and other warning lights should illuminate when the ignition is switched on, and (if the system is operating properly) extinguish after a few seconds. Refer to the owner's handbook.

Footbrake

☐ Examine the master cylinder, brake pipes and servo unit for leaks, loose mountings, corrosion or other damage. If ABS is fitted, this unit should also be examined for signs of leaks or corrosion.

☐ The fluid reservoir must be secure and the fluid level must be between the upper (**A**) and lower (**B**) markings.

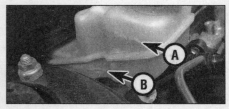

☐ Inspect both front brake flexible hoses for cracks or deterioration of the rubber. Turn the steering from lock to lock, and ensure that the hoses do not contact the wheel, tyre, or any part of the steering or suspension mechanism. With the brake pedal firmly depressed, check the hoses for bulges or leaks under pressure.

Steering and suspension

☐ Have your assistant turn the steering wheel from side to side slightly, up to the point where the steering gear just begins to transmit this movement to the roadwheels. Check for excessive free play between the steering wheel and the steering gear, indicating wear or insecurity of the steering column joints, the column-to-steering gear coupling, or the steering gear itself.

☐ Have your assistant turn the steering wheel more vigorously in each direction, so that the roadwheels just begin to turn. As this is done, examine all the steering joints, linkages, fittings and attachments. Renew any component that shows signs of wear or damage. On vehicles with power steering, check the security and condition of the steering pump, drivebelt and hoses.

☐ Check that the vehicle is standing level, and at approximately the correct ride height.

Shock absorbers

☐ Depress each corner of the vehicle in turn, then release it. The vehicle should rise and then settle in its normal position. If the vehicle continues to rise and fall, the shock absorber is defective. A shock absorber which has seized will also cause the vehicle to fail.

Exhaust system

☐ Start the engine. With your assistant holding a rag over the tailpipe, check the entire system for leaks. Repair or renew leaking sections.

3 Checks carried out WITH THE VEHICLE RAISED AND THE WHEELS FREE TO TURN

Jack up the front and rear of the vehicle, and securely support it on axle stands. Position the stands clear of the suspension assemblies. Ensure that the wheels are clear of the ground and that the steering can be turned from lock to lock.

Steering mechanism

☐ Have your assistant turn the steering from lock to lock. Check that the steering turns smoothly, and that no part of the steering mechanism, including a wheel or tyre, fouls any brake hose or pipe or any part of the body structure.

☐ Examine the steering rack rubber gaiters for damage or insecurity of the retaining clips. If power steering is fitted, check for signs of damage or leakage of the fluid hoses, pipes or connections. Also check for excessive stiffness or binding of the steering, a missing split pin or locking device, or severe corrosion of the body structure within 30 cm of any steering component attachment point.

Front and rear suspension and wheel bearings

☐ Starting at the front right-hand side, grasp the roadwheel at the 3 o'clock and 9 o'clock positions and rock gently but firmly. Check for free play or insecurity at the wheel bearings, suspension balljoints, or suspension mount-ings, pivots and attachments.

☐ Now grasp the wheel at the 12 o'clock and 6 o'clock positions and repeat the previous inspection. Spin the wheel, and check for roughness or tightness of the front wheel bearing.

☐ If excess free play is suspected at a component pivot point, this can be confirmed by using a large screwdriver or similar tool and levering between the mounting and the component attachment. This will confirm whether the wear is in the pivot bush, its retaining bolt, or in the mounting itself (the bolt holes can often become elongated).

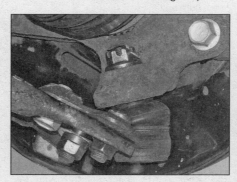

☐ Carry out all the above checks at the other front wheel, and then at both rear wheels.

Springs and shock absorbers

☐ Examine the suspension struts (when applicable) for serious fluid leakage, corrosion, or damage to the casing. Also check the security of the mounting points.

☐ If coil springs are fitted, check that the spring ends locate in their seats, and that the spring is not corroded, cracked or broken.

☐ If leaf springs are fitted, check that all leaves are intact, that the axle is securely attached to each spring, and that there is no deterioration of the spring eye mountings, bushes, and shackles.

☐ The same general checks apply to vehicles fitted with other suspension types, such as torsion bars, hydraulic displacer units, etc. Ensure that all mountings and attachments are secure, that there are no signs of excessive wear, corrosion or damage, and (on hydraulic types) that there are no fluid leaks or damaged pipes.

☐ Inspect the shock absorbers for signs of serious fluid leakage. Check for wear of the mounting bushes or attachments, or damage to the body of the unit.

Driveshafts (fwd vehicles only)

☐ Rotate each front wheel in turn and inspect the constant velocity joint gaiters for splits or damage. Also check that each driveshaft is straight and undamaged.

Braking system

☐ If possible without dismantling, check brake pad wear and disc condition. Ensure that the friction lining material has not worn excessively, (A) and that the discs are not fractured, pitted, scored or badly worn (B).

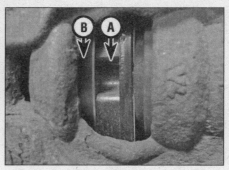

☐ Examine all the rigid brake pipes underneath the vehicle, and the flexible hose(s) at the rear. Look for corrosion, chafing or insecurity of the pipes, and for signs of bulging under pressure, chafing, splits or deterioration of the flexible hoses.

☐ Look for signs of fluid leaks at the brake calipers or on the brake backplates. Repair or renew leaking components.

☐ Slowly spin each wheel, while your assistant depresses and releases the footbrake. Ensure that each brake is operating and does not bind when the pedal is released.

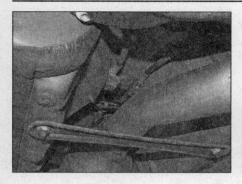

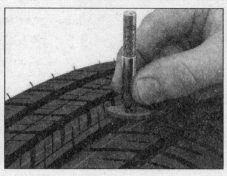

☐ Examine the handbrake mechanism, checking for frayed or broken cables, excessive corrosion, or wear or insecurity of the linkage. Check that the mechanism works on each relevant wheel, and releases fully, without binding.

☐ It is not possible to test brake efficiency without special equipment, but a road test can be carried out later to check that the vehicle pulls up in a straight line.

Fuel and exhaust systems

☐ Inspect the fuel tank (including the filler cap), fuel pipes, hoses and unions. All components must be secure and free from leaks. Locking fuel caps must lock securely and the key must be provided for the MOT test.

☐ Examine the exhaust system over its entire length, checking for any damaged, broken or missing mountings, security of the retaining clamps and rust or corrosion.

Wheels and tyres

☐ Examine the sidewalls and tread area of each tyre in turn. Check for cuts, tears, lumps, bulges, separation of the tread, and exposure of the ply or cord due to wear or damage. Check that the tyre bead is correctly seated on the wheel rim, that the valve is sound and properly seated, and that the wheel is not distorted or damaged.

☐ Check that the tyres are of the correct size for the vehicle, that they are of the same size and type on each axle, and that the pressures are correct.

☐ Check the tyre tread depth. The legal minimum at the time of writing is 1.6 mm over the central three-quarters of the tread width. Abnormal tread wear may indicate incorrect front wheel alignment or wear in steering or suspension components.

☐ If the spare wheel is fitted externally or in a separate carrier beneath the vehicle, check that mountings are secure and free of excessive corrosion.

Body corrosion

☐ Check the condition of the entire vehicle structure for signs of corrosion in load-bearing areas. (These include chassis box sections, side sills, cross-members, pillars, and all suspension, steering, braking system and seat belt mountings and anchorages.) Any corrosion which has seriously reduced the thickness of a load-bearing area (or is within 30 cm of safety-related components such as steering or suspension) is likely to cause the vehicle to fail. In this case professional repairs are likely to be needed.

☐ Damage or corrosion which causes sharp or otherwise dangerous edges to be exposed will also cause the vehicle to fail.

Towbars

☐ Check the condition of mounting points (both beneath the vehicle and within boot/hatchback areas) for signs of corrosion, ensuring that all fixings are secure and not worn or damaged. There must be no excessive play in detachable tow ball arms or quick-release mechanisms.

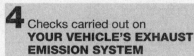

4 Checks carried out on **YOUR VEHICLE'S EXHAUST EMISSION SYSTEM**

Petrol models

☐ The engine should be warmed up, and running well (ignition system in good order, air filter element clean, etc).

☐ Before testing, run the engine at around 2500 rpm for 20 seconds. Let the engine drop to idle, and watch for smoke from the exhaust. If the idle speed is too high, or if dense blue or black smoke emerges for more than 5 seconds, the vehicle will fail. Typically, blue smoke signifies oil burning (engine wear); black smoke means unburnt fuel (dirty air cleaner element, or other fuel system fault).

☐ An exhaust gas analyser for measuring carbon monoxide (CO) and hydrocarbons (HC) is now needed. If one cannot be hired or borrowed, have a local garage perform the check.

CO emissions (mixture)

☐ The MOT tester has access to the CO limits for all vehicles. The CO level is measured at idle speed, and at 'fast idle' (2500 to 3000 rpm). The following limits are given as a general guide:

At idle speed – Less than 0.5% CO
At 'fast idle' – Less than 0.3% CO
Lambda reading – 0.97 to 1.03

☐ If the CO level is too high, this may point to poor maintenance, a fuel injection system problem, faulty lambda (oxygen) sensor or catalytic converter. Try an injector cleaning treatment, and check the vehicle's ECU for fault codes.

HC emissions

☐ The MOT tester has access to HC limits for all vehicles. The HC level is measured at 'fast idle' (2500 to 3000 rpm). The following limits are given as a general guide:

At 'fast idle' – Less then 200 ppm

☐ Excessive HC emissions are typically caused by oil being burnt (worn engine), or by a blocked crankcase ventilation system ('breather'). If the engine oil is old and thin, an oil change may help. If the engine is running badly, check the vehicle's ECU for fault codes.

Diesel models

☐ The only emission test for diesel engines is measuring exhaust smoke density, using a calibrated smoke meter. The test involves accelerating the engine at least 3 times to its maximum unloaded speed.

Note: *On engines with a timing belt, it is VITAL that the belt is in good condition before the test is carried out.*

☐ With the engine warmed up, it is first purged by running at around 2500 rpm for 20 seconds. A governor check is then carried out, by slowly accelerating the engine to its maximum speed. After this, the smoke meter is connected, and the engine is accelerated quickly to maximum speed three times. If the smoke density is less than the limits given below, the vehicle will pass:

Non-turbo vehicles: 2.5m-1
Turbocharged vehicles: 3.0m-1

☐ If excess smoke is produced, try fitting a new air cleaner element, or using an injector cleaning treatment. If the engine is running badly, where applicable, check the vehicle's ECU for fault codes. Also check the vehicle's EGR system, where applicable. At high mileages, the injectors may require professional attention.

Engine

- ☐ Engine fails to rotate when attempting to start
- ☐ Starter motor turns engine slowly
- ☐ Starter motor spins without turning engine
- ☐ Starter motor noisy or excessively-rough in engagement
- ☐ Engine rotates, but will not start
- ☐ Engine fires, but will not run
- ☐ Engine difficult to start when cold
- ☐ Engine difficult to start when hot
- ☐ Engine idles erratically
- ☐ Engine misfires at idle speed
- ☐ Engine misfires throughout the driving speed range
- ☐ Engine stalls
- ☐ Engine lacks power
- ☐ Oil pressure warning light illuminated with engine running
- ☐ Engine runs-on after switching off
- ☐ Engine noises

Cooling system

- ☐ Overheating
- ☐ Overcooling
- ☐ Corrosion
- ☐ External coolant leakage
- ☐ Internal coolant leakage

Fuel and exhaust systems

- ☐ Excessive fuel consumption
- ☐ Fuel leakage and/or fuel odour
- ☐ Excessive noise or fumes from exhaust system

Clutch

- ☐ Pedal travels to floor – no pressure or very little resistance
- ☐ Clutch fails to disengage (unable to select gears)
- ☐ Clutch slips (engine speed increases, with no increase in vehicle speed)
- ☐ Judder as clutch is engaged
- ☐ Noise when depressing or releasing clutch pedal

Manual gearbox

- ☐ Noisy in neutral with engine running
- ☐ Noisy in one particular gear
- ☐ Difficulty engaging gears
- ☐ Jumps out of gear
- ☐ Vibration
- ☐ Lubricant leaks

Transfer gearbox

- ☐ Noisy in neutral with engine running
- ☐ Noisy in Low or High positions
- ☐ Difficulty engaging ranges
- ☐ Jumps out of gear
- ☐ Vibration
- ☐ Lubricant leaks

Propeller shafts

- ☐ Knock or clunk when taking up drive
- ☐ Metallic grating sound consistent with vehicle speed
- ☐ Vibration

Front and rear axles

- ☐ Vibration
- ☐ Noise on drive and overrun
- ☐ Noise consistent with road speed
- ☐ Knock or clunk when taking up drive
- ☐ Oil leakage

Braking system

- ☐ Vehicle pulls to one side under braking
- ☐ Noise (grinding or high-pitched squeal) when brakes applied
- ☐ Excessive brake pedal travel
- ☐ Brake pedal feels spongy when depressed
- ☐ Excessive brake pedal effort required to stop vehicle
- ☐ Judder felt through brake pedal or steering wheel when braking
- ☐ Brakes binding
- ☐ Rear wheels locking under normal braking

Suspension and steering systems

- ☐ Vehicle pulls to one side
- ☐ Wheel wobble and vibration
- ☐ Excessive pitching and/or rolling around corners, or during braking
- ☐ Wandering or general instability
- ☐ Excessive play in steering
- ☐ Excessively-stiff steering
- ☐ Lack of power assistance
- ☐ Tyre wear excessive

Electrical system

- ☐ Battery will not hold a charge more than a few days
- ☐ Ignition/no-charge warning light remains illuminated with engine running
- ☐ Ignition/no-charge warning light fails to come on
- ☐ Lights inoperative
- ☐ Instrument readings inaccurate or erratic
- ☐ Horn inoperative, or unsatisfactory in operation
- ☐ Wash/wipe inoperative, or unsatisfactory in operation

Introduction

The car owner who does his or her own maintenance according to the recommended service schedules should not have to use this section of the manual very often. Modern component reliability is such that, provided those items subject to wear or deterioration are inspected or renewed at the specified intervals, sudden failure is comparatively rare. Faults do not usually just happen as a result of sudden failure, but develop over a period of time. Major mechanical failures in particular are usually preceded by characteristic symptoms over hundreds or even thousands of miles. Those components which do occasionally fail without warning are often small and easily carried in the car.

With any fault-finding, the first step is to decide where to begin investigations. Sometimes this is obvious, but on other occasions, a little detective work will be necessary. The owner who makes half a dozen haphazard adjustments or replacements may be successful in curing a fault (or its symptoms), but will be none the wiser if the fault recurs, and ultimately may have spent more time and money than was necessary. A calm and logical approach will be found to be more satisfactory in the long run. Always take into account any warning signs or abnormalities that may have been noticed in the period preceding the fault – power loss, high or low gauge readings, unusual smells, etc – and remember that failure of components such as fuses may only be pointers to some underlying fault.

The pages which follow provide an easy reference guide to the more common problems which may occur during the operation of the car. These problems and their possible causes are grouped under headings denoting various components or systems, such as Engine, Cooling system, etc. The Chapter and/or Section which deals with the problem is also shown in brackets. Whatever the fault, certain basic principles apply. These are as follows:

Verify the fault. This is simply a matter of being sure that you know what the symptoms are before starting work. This is particularly important if you are investigating a fault for someone else, who may not have described it very accurately.

Don't overlook the obvious. For example, if the car won't start, is there fuel in the tank? (Don't take anyone else's word on this particular point, and don't trust the fuel gauge either!) If an electrical fault is indicated, look for loose or broken wires before using the test gear.

Cure the disease, not the symptom. Substituting a flat battery with a fully-charged one will get you off the hard shoulder, but if the underlying cause is not attended to, the new battery will go the same way.

Don't take anything for granted. Particularly, don't forget that a 'new' component may itself be defective (especially if it's been rattling around in the boot for months), and don't leave components out of a fault diagnosis sequence just because they are new or recently fitted. When you do finally diagnose a difficult fault, you'll probably realise that all the evidence was there from the start.

Consider what work, if any, has recently been carried out. Many faults arise through careless or hurried work. For instance, if any work has been performed under the bonnet, could some of the wiring have been dislodged or incorrectly routed, or a hose trapped? Have all the fasteners been properly tightened? Were new, genuine parts and new gaskets used? There is often a certain amount of detective work to be done in this case, as an apparently-unrelated task can have far-reaching consequences.

Diesel fault diagnosis

The majority of starting problems on small diesel engines are electrical in origin. The mechanic who is familiar with petrol engines but less so with diesel may be inclined to view the diesel? injectors and pump in the same light as the spark plugs and distributor, but this is generally a mistake.

When investigating complaints of difficult starting for someone else, make sure that the correct starting procedure is understood and is being followed. Some drivers are unaware of the significance of the preheating warning light ?many modern engines are sufficiently forgiving for this not to matter in mild weather, but with the onset of winter problems begin.

As a rule of thumb, if the engine is difficult to start but runs well when it has finally got going, the problem is electrical (battery, starter motor or preheating system). If poor performance is combined with difficult starting, the problem is likely to be in the fuel system. The low pressure (supply) side of the fuel system should be checked before suspecting the injectors and injection pump. The most common fuel supply problem is air getting into the system, and any pipe from the fuel tank forwards must be scrutinised if air leakage is suspected. Normally the pump is the last item to suspect, since unless it has been tampered with there is no reason for it to be at fault.

Engine

Engine fails to rotate when attempting to start

- [ ] Battery terminal connections loose or corroded (Chapter 5 Section 4).
- [ ] Battery discharged or faulty (Chapter 5 Section 3).
- [ ] Broken, loose or disconnected wiring in the starting circuit (Chapter 5 Section 2).
- [ ] Defective starter solenoid or switch (Chapter 5 Section 2).
- [ ] Defective starter motor (Chapter 5 Section 9).
- [ ] Starter pinion or flywheel ring gear teeth loose or broken (Chapter 5 Section 9, Chapter 2A Section 16 or Chapter 2B Section 16).
- [ ] Engine earth strap broken or disconnected (Chapter 5 Section 2).

Starter motor turns engine slowly

- [ ] Partially-discharged battery (recharge, or use jump leads) (Chapter 5 Section 3).
- [ ] Battery terminals loose or corroded (Chapter 5 Section 4).

- [ ] Battery earth to body defective (Chapter 5 Section 2).
- [ ] Engine earth strap loose (Chapter 5 Section 2).
- [ ] Starter motor (or solenoid) wiring loose (Chapter 5 Section 9).
- [ ] Starter motor internal fault (Chapter 5 Section 10).

Starter motor spins without turning engine

- [ ] Starter motor reduction gears stripped (Chapter 5 Section 10).
- [ ] Starter motor mounting bolts loose (Chapter 5 Section 9).

Starter motor noisy or excessively-rough in engagement

- [ ] Starter pinion or flywheel ring gear teeth loose or broken (Chapter 5 Section 9).
- [ ] Starter motor mounting bolts loose or missing (Chapter 5 Section 9).
- [ ] Starter motor internal components worn or damaged (Chapter 5 Section 10).

Engine (continued)

Engine rotates, but will not start

☐ Fuel tank empty.Battery discharged (engine rotates slowly) (Chapter 5 Section 3).
☐ Battery terminal connections loose or corroded (Chapter 5 Section 4).
☐ Air in fuel (Chapter).
☐ Wax formed in fuel (in very cold weather).
☐ Faulty inertia/stop solenoid (Chapter 5 Section 16).
☐ Low cylinder compressions (Chapter 2A Section 2 or Chapter 2B Section 2).
☐ Fuel system or preheating system fault (Chapter 4A Section 2 and Chapter 5 Section 13).
☐ Major mechanical failure (eg camshaft drive) (Chapter 2A Section 1 or Chapter 2B Section 1).

Engine fires, but will not run

☐ Preheating system fault (Chapter 5 Section 13).
☐ Air in fuel (Chapter 4A Section 3).
☐ Wax formed in fuel (in very cold weather).
☐ Other fuel system fault (Chapter 4A Section 2).
☐

Engine difficult to start when cold

☐ Battery discharged (Chapter 5 Section 3).
☐ Battery terminal connections loose or corroded (Chapter 5 Section 4).
☐ Air in fuel (Chapter 4A Section 3).
☐ Air filter element dirty or clogged (Chapter 4A Section 4).
☐ Wax formed in fuel (in very cold weather).
☐ Preheating system fault (Chapter 5 Section 13).
☐ Other fuel system fault (Chapter 4A Section 2).
☐ Low cylinder compressions (Chapter 2A Section 2 or Chapter 2B Section 2).

Engine difficult to start when hot

☐ Battery discharged (Chapter 5 Section 3).
☐ Battery terminal connections loose or corroded (Chapter 5 Section 9).
☐ Air filter element dirty or clogged (Chapter 1 Section 24).
☐ Air in fuel (Chapter 4A Section 3).
☐ Low cylinder compressions (Chapter 2A Section 2 or Chapter 2B Section 2).

Engine idles erratically

☐ Air filter element clogged (Chapter 1 Section 24).
☐ Uneven or low cylinder compressions (Chapter 2A Section 2 or Chapter 2B Section 2).
☐ Camshaft lobes worn (Chapter 2A Section 9 or Chapter 2B Section 9).
☐ Timing chain/belt incorrectly tensioned (Chapter 2A Section 8 or Chapter 2B Section 8).

Engine misfires at idle speed

☐ Air in fuel (Chapter 4A Section 3).
☐ Wax formed in fuel (in very cold weather).
☐ Other fuel system fault (Chapter 4A Section 2).
☐ Uneven or low cylinder compressions (Chapter 2A Section 2 or Chapter 2B Section 2).
☐ Disconnected, leaking or perished crankcase ventilation hoses (Chapter 1 Section 11).

Engine misfires throughout the driving speed range

☐ Fuel filter choked (Chapter 1 Section 23).
☐ Fuel tank vent blocked or fuel pipes restricted (Chapter 4A Section 6).
☐ Uneven or low cylinder compressions (Chapter 2A Section 2 or Chapter 2B Section 2).

Engine stalls

☐ Fuel filter choked (Chapter 1 Section 23).
☐ Fuel tank vent blocked or fuel pipes restricted (Chapter 4A Section 6).

Engine lacks power

☐ Air in fuel (Chapter 4A Section 3).
☐ Timing chain/belt incorrectly fitted or tensioned (Chapter 2A Section 8 or Chapter 2B Section 8).
☐ Fuel filter choked (Chapter 1 Section 23).
☐ Uneven or low cylinder compressions (Chapter 2A Section 2 or Chapter 2B Section 2).
☐ Brakes binding (Chapter 10 Section 1).
☐ Clutch slipping (Chapter 6 Section 5, 6).

Oil pressure warning light illuminated with engine running

☐ Low oil level or incorrect grade (Chapter 1 Section 5).
☐ Faulty oil pressure switch (Chapter 5 Section 12).
☐ Worn engine bearings and/or oil pump (Chapters 2A, 2B, 2C).
☐ High engine operating temperature (Chapter 3 Section 1).
☐ Oil pressure relief valve defective (Chapter 2A or 2B).
☐ Oil pick-up strainer clogged (Chapter 2A Section 11 or Chapter 2B Section 11).

Note: *Low oil pressure in a high-mileage engine at tickover is not necessarily a cause for concern. Sudden pressure loss at speed is far more significant. In any event, check the gauge or warning light sender before condemning the engine.*

Engine runs-on after switching off

☐ Faulty inertia/stop solenoid – 2.2 litre engines (Chapter 5 Section 16).

Engine noises

☐ Note: To inexperienced ears, the diesel engine can sound alarming even when there is nothing wrong with it, so it may be prudent to have an unusual noise expertly diagnosed before making renewals or repairs.

Whistling or wheezing noises

☐ Leaking manifold gasket (Chapter 4A Section 15, 16).
☐ Leaking vacuum hose (Chapters 1, 4A, 4B).
☐ Blowing cylinder head gasket (Chapter 2A Section 2 or Chapter 2B Section 2).

Tapping or rattling noises

☐ Worn valve gear or camshaft (Chapter 2A Section 9 or Chapter 2B Section 9).
☐ Broken piston ring (ticking noise) (Chapter 2C Section 9).
☐ Ancillary component fault (water pump, alternator, etc) (Chapters 3, 5).
☐ Worn timing chain – where applicable (Chapter 2A Section 8 or Chapter 2B Section 8).

Knocking or thumping noises

☐ Air in fuel (Chapter 4A Section 3).
☐ Worn timing chain (Chapter 2A Section 7 or Chapter 2B Section 7).
☐ Fuel injector(s) leaking or sticking (Chapter 4A Section 11).
☐ Worn big-end bearings (regular heavy knocking, perhaps less under load) (Chapter 2C Section 12).
☐ Worn main bearings (rumbling and knocking, perhaps worsening under load) (Chapter 2C Section 12).
☐ Piston slap (most noticeable when cold) (Chapter 2C Section 9).
☐ Ancillary component fault (alternator, water pump etc) (Chapters 3 and 5).

Cooling system

Overheating

☐ Insufficient coolant in system (Chapter 1).
☐ Thermostat faulty (Chapter 3).
☐ Radiator core blocked or grille restricted (Chapter 3).
☐ Cooling fan faulty (Chapter 3).
☐ Pressure cap faulty (Chapter 3).
☐ Inaccurate temperature gauge sender unit (Chapter 3).
☐ Airlock in cooling system (Chapter 1).

Overcooling

☐ Thermostat faulty (Chapter 3).
☐ Inaccurate temperature gauge sender unit (Chapter 3).

Corrosion

☐ Infrequent draining and flushing (Chapter 1).
☐ Incorrect antifreeze mixture or inappropriate type (Chapter 1).

External coolant leakage

☐ Deteriorated or damaged hoses or hose clips (Chapter 1).
☐ Radiator core or heater matrix leaking (Chapter 3).
☐ Pressure cap faulty (Chapter 3).
☐ Water pump seal leaking (Chapter 3).
☐ Boiling due to overheating (Chapter 3).
☐ Core plug leaking (Chapter 2C Section 2).

Internal coolant leakage

☐ Leaking cylinder head gasket (Chapter 2A Section 2 or Chapter 2B Section 2).
☐ Cracked cylinder head or cylinder bore (Chapter 2A Section 2 or Chapter 2B Section 2).

Fuel and exhaust systems

Excessive fuel consumption

☐ Air filter element dirty or clogged (Chapter 1).
☐ Preheating system fault (Chapter 5).
☐ Brakes binding (Chapter 9).
☐ Tyres under-inflated (Chapter 1).

Fuel leakage and/or fuel odour

☐ Damaged or corroded fuel tank, pipes or connections (Chapter 4A Section 6).

Excessive noise or fumes from exhaust system

☐ Leaking exhaust system or manifold joints (Chapter 4A Section 16, 18).
☐ Leaking, corroded or damaged silencers or pipe (Chapter 4A Section 18).
☐ Broken mountings causing body or suspension contact (Chapter 4A Section 18).

Clutch

Pedal travels to floor – no pressure or very little resistance

☐ Leak in clutch hydraulic system (Chapter 6).
☐ Faulty hydraulic master or slave cylinder (Chapter 6).
☐ Broken clutch release bearing or fork (Chapter 6).
☐ Broken diaphragm spring in clutch pressure plate (Chapter 6).

Clutch fails to disengage (unable to select gears)

☐ Leak in clutch hydraulic system (Chapter 6).
☐ Faulty hydraulic master or slave cylinder (Chapter 6).
☐ Clutch disc sticking on gearbox input shaft splines (Chapter 6).
☐ Clutch disc sticking to flywheel or pressure plate (Chapter 6).
☐ Faulty pressure plate assembly (Chapter 6).
☐ Clutch release mechanism worn or incorrectly assembled (Chapter 6).

Clutch slips (engine speed increases, with no increase in vehicle speed)

☐ Clutch disc linings excessively worn (Chapter 6).

☐ Clutch disc linings contaminated with oil or grease (Chapter 6).
☐ Faulty pressure plate or weak diaphragm spring (Chapter 6).

Judder as clutch is engaged

☐ Clutch disc linings contaminated with oil or grease (Chapter 6).
☐ Clutch disc linings excessively worn (Chapter 6).
☐ Clutch cable sticking or frayed (Chapter 6).
☐ Faulty or distorted pressure plate or diaphragm spring (Chapter 6).
☐ Worn or loose engine or gearbox mountings (Chapter 2A Section 17 or Chapter 2B Section 17).
☐ Clutch disc hub or gearbox input shaft splines worn (Chapter 6).

Noise when depressing or releasing clutch pedal

☐ Worn clutch release bearing (Chapter 6).
☐ Worn or dry clutch pedal bushes (Chapter 6).
☐ Faulty pressure plate assembly (Chapter 6).
☐ Pressure plate diaphragm spring broken (Chapter 6).
☐ Broken clutch disc cushioning springs (Chapter 6).

Manual gearbox

Noisy in neutral with engine running

☐ Input shaft and/or mainshaft bearings worn (noise apparent with clutch pedal released, but not when depressed).*
☐ Clutch release bearing worn (noise apparent with clutch pedal depressed, possibly less when released) (Chapter 6 Section 3).

Noisy in one particular gear

☐ Worn, damaged or chipped gear teeth.*

Difficulty engaging gears

☐ Clutch fault (Chapter 6 Section 2).
☐ Worn or damaged gear linkage.
☐ Worn synchroniser units.*

Jumps out of gear

☐ Worn or damaged gear linkage.

☐ Incorrectly-adjusted gear linkage.
☐ Worn synchroniser units.*
☐ Worn selector forks.*

Vibration

☐ Lack of oil (Chapter 1 Section 13).
☐ Worn bearings.*

Lubricant leaks

☐ Leaking oil seal.
☐ Leaking housing joint.*

Although the corrective action necessary to remedy the symptoms described is beyond the scope of the home mechanic, the above information should be helpful in isolating the cause of the condition, so that the owner can communicate clearly with a professional mechanic.

Transfer gearbox

Noisy in neutral with engine running

☐ Worn mainshaft or output shaft bearings (Chapter 7B).*

Noisy in Low or High positions

☐ Worn, damaged or chipped gear teeth (Chapter 7B).*

Difficulty engaging ranges

☐ Clutch fault (Chapter 6).
☐ Main gearbox fault.Worn selector fork (Chapter 7B).*

Jumps out of gear

☐ Worn or damaged gear linkage (Chapter 7B).*
☐ Worn selector fork (Chapter 7B).*

Vibration

☐ Lack of oil (Chapter 1).
☐ Worn bearings (Chapter 7B).*

Lubricant leaks

☐ Leaking oil seal (Chapter 7B).*
☐ Leaking housing joint (Chapter 7B).*

* Although the corrective action necessary to remedy the symptoms described is beyond the scope of the home mechanic, the above information should be helpful in isolating the cause of the condition, so that the owner can communicate clearly with a professional mechanic.

Propeller shafts

Knock or clunk when taking up drive

☐ Worn universal joint bearings (Chapter 8).
☐ Worn axle drive pinion splines (Chapter 9).
☐ Loose drive flange bolts (Chapter 8).
☐ Excessive backlash in axle gears (Chapter 9).

Metallic grating sound consistent with vehicle speed

☐ Severe wear in universal joint bearings (Chapter 8).

Vibration

☐ Wear in sliding sleeve splines (Chapter 8).
☐ Worn universal joint bearings (Chapter 8).
☐ Propeller shaft out of balance (Chapter 8).

Front and rear axles

Vibration

- [ ] Propeller shaft out of balance (Chapter 8).
- [ ] Worn hub bearings (Chapter 9).
- [ ] Wheels out of balance.Propeller shaft or halfshaft joints worn (Chapters 8 and 9).
- [ ] Suspension or steering fault (Chapter 11).

Noise on drive and overrun

- [ ] Worn crownwheel and pinion gears (Chapter 9).
- [ ] Worn differential bearings (Chapter 9).
- [ ] Lack of lubrication in axle or swivel pin housings (Chapters 9 and 11).
- [ ] Manual gearbox or transfer gearbox fault.

Noise consistent with road speed

- [ ] Worn hub bearings (Chapter 9).
- [ ] Worn differential bearings (Chapter 9).

- [ ] Lack of lubrication in axle or swivel pin housings (Chapters 9 and 11).
- [ ] Manual gearbox or transfer gearbox fault.

Knock or clunk when taking up drive

- [ ] Excessive crownwheel and pinion backlash (Chapter 9).
- [ ] Worn propeller shaft or halfshaft joints (Chapters 8 and 9).
- [ ] Worn halfshaft splines (Chapter 9).
- [ ] Halfshaft bolts or roadwheel nuts loose (Chapter 9).
- [ ] Broken, damaged, or worn suspension components or axle mountings (Chapters 11 and 9).
- [ ] Manual gearbox or transfer gearbox fault.

Oil leakage

- [ ] Faulty differential pinion or halfshaft oil seals (Chapter 9).
- [ ] Blocked axle breather valve (Chapter 9).
- [ ] Damaged swivel pin housing or oil seal (Chapter 11).

Braking system

Vehicle pulls to one side under braking

Note: *Before assuming that a brake problem exists, make sure that the tyres are in good condition and correctly inflated, the front wheel alignment is correct, and the vehicle is not loaded with weight in an unequal manner.*

- [ ] Worn, defective, damaged or contaminated front or rear brake shoes/pads on one side (Chapter 10).
- [ ] Seized or partially-seized front or rear brake wheel cylinder or caliper piston (Chapter 10).
- [ ] A mixture of brake lining materials fitted between sides (Chapter 10).
- [ ] Brake caliper mounting bolts loose (Chapter 10).
- [ ] Worn or damaged steering or suspension components (Chapter 11).

Noise (grinding or high-pitched squeal) when brakes applied

- [ ] Brake friction lining material worn down to metal backing (Chapter 10).
- [ ] Excessive corrosion or wear of brake drum – where applicable (Chapter 10).
- [ ] Excessive corrosion of brake disc – where applicable. (May be apparent after the vehicle has been standing for some time (Chapter 10).

Excessive brake pedal travel

- [ ] Faulty master cylinder (Chapter 10).
- [ ] Air in hydraulic system (Chapter 10).
- [ ] Faulty vacuum servo unit (Chapter 10).
- [ ] Faulty brake vacuum pump (Chapter 10).

Brake pedal feels spongy when depressed

- [ ] Air in hydraulic system (Chapter 10).
- [ ] Deteriorated flexible rubber brake hoses (Chapter 10).
- [ ] Master cylinder mountings loose (Chapter 10).
- [ ] Faulty master cylinder (Chapter 10).

Excessive brake pedal effort required to stop vehicle

- [ ] Faulty vacuum servo unit (Chapter 10).
- [ ] Disconnected, damaged or insecure brake servo vacuum hose (Chapters 1 and 10).
- [ ] Faulty brake vacuum pump (Chapter 10).
- [ ] Primary or secondary hydraulic circuit failure (Chapter 10).
- [ ] Seized brake wheel cylinder or caliper piston(s) (Chapter 10).
- [ ] Brake shoes or pads incorrectly fitted (Chapter 10).
- [ ] Incorrect grade of brake shoes/pads fitted (Chapter 10).
- [ ] Brake shoes/pads contaminated (Chapter 10).

Judder felt through brake pedal or steering wheel when braking

- [ ] Excessive run-out or distortion of brake drum(s)/disc(s) (Chapter 10).
- [ ] Brake friction material worn (Chapter 10).
- [ ] Brake caliper mounting bolts loose – where applicable (Chapter 10).
- [ ] Wear in suspension or steering components or mountings (Chapter 11).
- [ ] ABS normal operation.

Brakes binding

- [ ] Seized brake wheel cylinder(s) or caliper piston(s) (Chapter 10).
- [ ] Faulty master cylinder (Chapter 10).

Rear wheels locking under normal braking

- [ ] Faulty brake pressure regulator (Chapter 10).

Suspension and steering systems

Vehicle pulls to one side

Note: *Before diagnosing suspension or steering faults, be sure that the trouble is not due to incorrect tyre pressures, mixtures of tyre types, or binding brakes.*

- [ ] Defective tyre (Chapter 1).
- [ ] Excessive wear in suspension or steering components (Chapter 11).
- [ ] Incorrect front wheel alignment (Chapter 11).
- [ ] Accident damage to steering/suspension components (Chapter 11).

Wheel wobble and vibration

- [ ] Front roadwheels out of balance (vibration felt mainly through the steering wheel) (Chapter 11).
- [ ] Rear roadwheels out of balance (vibration felt throughout the vehicle) (Chapter 11).
- [ ] Roadwheels damaged or distorted (Chapter 1).
- [ ] Faulty or damaged tyre (Chapter 1).
- [ ] Worn steering or suspension joints, bushes or components (Chapter 11).
- [ ] Wheel nuts loose (Chapter 11).

Excessive pitching and/or rolling around corners, or during braking

- [ ] Defective shock absorbers (Chapter 11).
- [ ] Broken or weak coil spring and/or suspension component (Chapter 11).
- [ ] Worn or damaged anti-roll bar or mountings (Chapter 11).

Wandering or general instability

- [ ] Incorrect front wheel alignment (Chapter 11).
- [ ] Worn steering or suspension joints, bushes or components (Chapter 11).
- [ ] Roadwheels out of balance (Chapter 11).
- [ ] Faulty or damaged tyre (Chapter 1).
- [ ] Roadwheel nuts loose (Chapter 11).
- [ ] Defective shock absorbers (Chapter 11).

Excessive play in steering

- [ ] Worn steering column universal joint(s) or intermediate coupling (Chapter 11).
- [ ] Worn steering track-rod end balljoints (Chapter 11).
- [ ] Worn steering box (Chapter 11).
- [ ] Worn steering/suspension joints, bushes or components (Chapter 11).

Excessively-stiff steering

- [ ] Lack of steering gear lubricant (Chapter 11).
- [ ] Seized track-rod end balljoint (Chapter 11).
- [ ] Broken or incorrectly-adjusted power steering pump drivebelt (Chapter 1).
- [ ] Incorrect front wheel alignment (Chapter 11).
- [ ] Steering box or column damaged (Chapter 11).

Lack of power assistance

- [ ] Broken or incorrectly-adjusted power steering pump drivebelt (Chapter 1).
- [ ] Incorrect power steering fluid level (Chapter 1).
- [ ] Restriction in power steering fluid hoses (Chapter 1).
- [ ] Faulty power steering pump (Chapter 11).
- [ ] Faulty steering box (Chapter 11).

Tyre wear excessive

Tyre treads exhibit feathered edges"

- [ ] Incorrect toe setting (Chapter 11).

Tyres worn in centre of tread"

- [ ] Tyres over-inflated (Chapter 1).

Tyres worn on inside or outside edges"

- [ ] Tyres under-inflated (wear on both edges) (Chapter 1).
- [ ] Incorrect camber or castor angles (wear on one edge only) (Chapter 11).
- [ ] Worn steering or suspension joints, bushes or components (Chapter 11).
- [ ] Excessively hard cornering.Accident damage.

yres worn on inside and outside edges"

- [ ] Tyres under inflated (Chapter 1).
- [ ] Worn shock absorbers (Chapter 11).

Tyres worn unevenly"

- [ ] Tyres out of balance (Chapter 1).
- [ ] Excessive wheel or tyre run-out (Chapter 1).
- [ ] Worn shock absorbers (Chapter 11).
- [ ] Faulty tyre (Chapter 1).

Electrical system

Battery will not hold a charge more than a few days

Note: *For problems associated with the starting system, refer to the faults listed under 'Engine' earlier in this Section.*

☐ Battery defective internally (Chapter 5).
☐ Battery electrolyte level low – where applicable (Chapter 1).
☐ Battery terminal connections loose or corroded (Chapter 1).
☐ Alternator drivebelt worn or incorrectly adjusted (Chapter 1).
☐ Alternator not charging at correct output (Chapter 5).
☐ Alternator or voltage regulator faulty (Chapter 5).
☐ Short-circuit causing continual battery drain (Chapter 5).

Ignition/no-charge warning light remains illuminated with engine running

☐ Alternator drivebelt broken, or incorrectly adjusted (Chapter 1).
☐ Alternator brushes worn, sticking, or dirty (Chapter 5).
☐ Alternator brush springs weak or broken (Chapter 5).
☐ Internal fault in alternator or voltage regulator (Chapter 5).
☐ Disconnected, or loose wiring in charging circuit (Chapter 5).

Ignition/no-charge warning light fails to come on

☐ Warning light bulb blown (Chapter 13).
☐ Disconnected or loose wiring in warning light circuit (Chapter 13).
☐ Alternator faulty (Chapter 5).

Lights inoperative

☐ Bulb blown (Chapter 13).
☐ Corrosion of bulb or bulbholder contacts (Chapter 13).
☐ Blown fuse (Chapter 13).
☐ Faulty relay (Chapter 13).
☐ Broken, loose, or disconnected wiring (Chapter 13).
☐ Faulty switch (Chapter 13).

Instrument readings inaccurate or erratic

Instrument readings increase with engine speed"

☐ Faulty voltage regulator (Chapter 13).

Fuel or temperature gauge gives no reading"

☐ Faulty gauge sender unit (Chapters 3 or).
☐ Wiring open-circuit (Chapter 5).
☐ Faulty gauge (Chapter 13).

Fuel or temperature gauge gives continuous maximum reading"

☐ Faulty gauge sender unit (Chapters 3 or).
☐ Wiring short-circuit (Chapter 5).
☐ Faulty gauge (Chapter 13).

Horn inoperative, or unsatisfactory in operation

Horn operates all the time"

☐ Horn push either earthed or stuck down (Chapter 13).
☐ Horn cable to horn push earthed (Chapter 13).

Horn fails to operate"

☐ Blown fuse (Chapter 13).
☐ Cable connections loose, broken or disconnected (Chapter 13).
☐ Faulty horn (Chapter 13).

Horn emits intermittent or unsatisfactory sound"

☐ Cable connections loose (Chapter 13).
☐ Horn mountings loose (Chapter 13).
☐ Faulty horn (Chapter 13).

Wash/wipe inoperative, or unsatisfactory in operation

Wipers fail to operate, or operate very slowly"

☐ Wiper blades stuck to screen, or linkage seized or binding (Chapters 1 and 13).
☐ Blown fuse (Chapter 13).
☐ Cable connections loose, broken or disconnected (Chapter 13).
☐ Faulty relay (Chapter 13).
☐ Faulty wiper motor (Chapter 13).

Wiper blades sweep over too large or too small an area of the glass

☐ Wiper arms incorrectly positioned on spindles (Chapter 13).
☐ Excessive wear of wiper linkage (Chapter 13).
☐ Wiper motor or linkage mountings loose or insecure (Chapter 13).

Wiper blades fail to clean the glass effectively

☐ Wiper blade rubbers worn or perished (Chapter 1).
☐ Wiper arm springs broken, or arm pivots seized (Chapter 13).
☐ Insufficient windscreen washer additive to adequately remove road film (Chapter 1).

One or more washer jets inoperative

☐ Blocked washer jet (Chapter 13).
☐ Disconnected, kinked or restricted fluid hose (Chapter 13).
☐ Insufficient fluid in washer reservoir (Chapter 1).

Washer pump fails to operate

☐ Broken or disconnected wiring or connections (Chapter 13).
☐ Blown fuse (Chapter 13).
☐ Faulty washer switch (Chapter 13).
☐ Faulty washer pump (Chapter 13).

Washer pump runs for some time before jets operate

☐ Faulty one-way valve in fluid supply hose (Chapter 13 Section 16).

A

ABS (Anti-lock brake system) A system, usually electronically controlled, that senses incipient wheel lockup during braking and relieves hydraulic pressure at wheels that are about to skid.

Air bag An inflatable bag hidden in the steering wheel (driver's side) or the dash or glovebox (passenger side). In a head-on collision, the bags inflate, preventing the driver and front passenger from being thrown forward into the steering wheel or windscreen.

Air cleaner A metal or plastic housing, containing a filter element, which removes dust and dirt from the air being drawn into the engine.

Air filter element The actual filter in an air cleaner system, usually manufactured from pleated paper and requiring renewal at regular intervals.

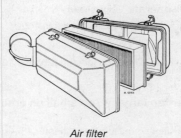

Air filter

Allen key A hexagonal wrench which fits into a recessed hexagonal hole.

Alligator clip A long-nosed spring-loaded metal clip with meshing teeth. Used to make temporary electrical connections.

Alternator A component in the electrical system which converts mechanical energy from a drivebelt into electrical energy to charge the battery and to operate the starting system, ignition system and electrical accessories.

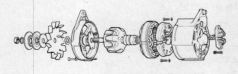

Alternator (exploded view)

Ampere (amp) A unit of measurement for the flow of electric current. One amp is the amount of current produced by one volt acting through a resistance of one ohm.

Anaerobic sealer A substance used to prevent bolts and screws from loosening. Anaerobic means that it does not require oxygen for activation. The Loctite brand is widely used.

Antifreeze A substance (usually ethylene glycol) mixed with water, and added to a vehicle's cooling system, to prevent freezing of the coolant in winter. Antifreeze also contains chemicals to inhibit corrosion and the formation of rust and other deposits that would tend to clog the radiator and coolant passages and reduce cooling efficiency.

Anti-seize compound A coating that reduces the risk of seizing on fasteners that are subjected to high temperatures, such as exhaust manifold bolts and nuts.

Anti-seize compound

Asbestos A natural fibrous mineral with great heat resistance, commonly used in the composition of brake friction materials. Asbestos is a health hazard and the dust created by brake systems should never be inhaled or ingested.

Axle A shaft on which a wheel revolves, or which revolves with a wheel. Also, a solid beam that connects the two wheels at one end of the vehicle. An axle which also transmits power to the wheels is known as a live axle.

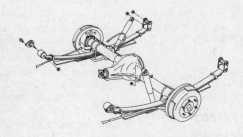

Axle assembly

Axleshaft A single rotating shaft, on either side of the differential, which delivers power from the final drive assembly to the drive wheels. Also called a driveshaft or a halfshaft.

B

Ball bearing An anti-friction bearing consisting of a hardened inner and outer race with hardened steel balls between two races.

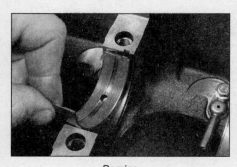

Bearing

Bearing The curved surface on a shaft or in a bore, or the part assembled into either, that permits relative motion between them with minimum wear and friction.

Big-end bearing The bearing in the end of the connecting rod that's attached to the crankshaft.

Bleed nipple A valve on a brake wheel cylinder, caliper or other hydraulic component that is opened to purge the hydraulic system of air. Also called a bleed screw.

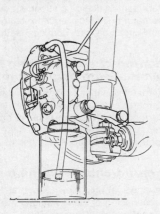

Brake bleeding

Brake bleeding Procedure for removing air from lines of a hydraulic brake system.

Brake disc The component of a disc brake that rotates with the wheels.

Brake drum The component of a drum brake that rotates with the wheels.

Brake linings The friction material which contacts the brake disc or drum to retard the vehicle's speed. The linings are bonded or riveted to the brake pads or shoes.

Brake pads The replaceable friction pads that pinch the brake disc when the brakes are applied. Brake pads consist of a friction material bonded or riveted to a rigid backing plate.

Brake shoe The crescent-shaped carrier to which the brake linings are mounted and which forces the lining against the rotating drum during braking.

Braking systems For more information on braking systems, consult the *Haynes Automotive Brake Manual*.

Breaker bar A long socket wrench handle providing greater leverage.

Bulkhead The insulated partition between the engine and the passenger compartment.

C

Caliper The non-rotating part of a disc-brake assembly that straddles the disc and carries the brake pads. The caliper also contains the hydraulic components that cause the pads to pinch the disc when the brakes are applied. A caliper is also a measuring tool that can be set to measure inside or outside dimensions of an object.

Camshaft A rotating shaft on which a series of cam lobes operate the valve mechanisms. The camshaft may be driven by gears, by sprockets and chain or by sprockets and a belt.

Canister A container in an evaporative emission control system; contains activated charcoal granules to trap vapours from the fuel system.

Canister

Carburettor A device which mixes fuel with air in the proper proportions to provide a desired power output from a spark ignition internal combustion engine.

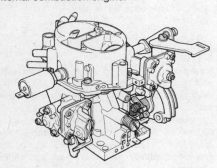

Carburettor

Castellated Resembling the parapets along the top of a castle wall. For example, a castellated balljoint stud nut.

Castellated nut

Castor In wheel alignment, the backward or forward tilt of the steering axis. Castor is positive when the steering axis is inclined rearward at the top.

Catalytic converter A silencer-like device in the exhaust system which converts certain pollutants in the exhaust gases into less harmful substances.

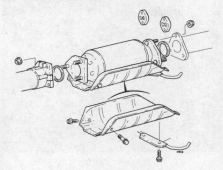

Catalytic converter

Circlip A ring-shaped clip used to prevent endwise movement of cylindrical parts and shafts. An internal circlip is installed in a groove in a housing; an external circlip fits into a groove on the outside of a cylindrical piece such as a shaft.

Clearance The amount of space between two parts. For example, between a piston and a cylinder, between a bearing and a journal, etc.

Coil spring A spiral of elastic steel found in various sizes throughout a vehicle, for example as a springing medium in the suspension and in the valve train.

Compression Reduction in volume, and increase in pressure and temperature, of a gas, caused by squeezing it into a smaller space.

Compression ratio The relationship between cylinder volume when the piston is at top dead centre and cylinder volume when the piston is at bottom dead centre.

Constant velocity (CV) joint A type of universal joint that cancels out vibrations caused by driving power being transmitted through an angle.

Core plug A disc or cup-shaped metal device inserted in a hole in a casting through which core was removed when the casting was formed. Also known as a freeze plug or expansion plug.

Crankcase The lower part of the engine block in which the crankshaft rotates.

Crankshaft The main rotating member, or shaft, running the length of the crankcase, with offset "throws" to which the connecting rods are attached.

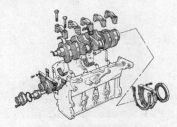

Crankshaft assembly

Crocodile clip See Alligator clip

D

Diagnostic code Code numbers obtained by accessing the diagnostic mode of an engine management computer. This code can be used to determine the area in the system where a malfunction may be located.

Disc brake A brake design incorporating a rotating disc onto which brake pads are squeezed. The resulting friction converts the energy of a moving vehicle into heat.

Double-overhead cam (DOHC) An engine that uses two overhead camshafts, usually one for the intake valves and one for the exhaust valves.

Drivebelt(s) The belt(s) used to drive accessories such as the alternator, water pump, power steering pump, air conditioning compressor, etc. off the crankshaft pulley.

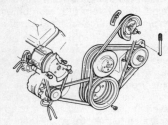

Accessory drivebelts

Driveshaft Any shaft used to transmit motion. Commonly used when referring to the axleshafts on a front wheel drive vehicle.

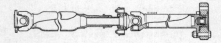

Driveshaft

Drum brake A type of brake using a drum-shaped metal cylinder attached to the inner surface of the wheel. When the brake pedal is pressed, curved brake shoes with friction linings press against the inside of the drum to slow or stop the vehicle.

Drum brake assembly

E

EGR valve A valve used to introduce exhaust gases into the intake air stream.

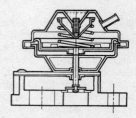

EGR valve

Electronic control unit (ECU) A computer which controls (for instance) ignition and fuel injection systems, or an anti-lock braking system. For more information refer to the *Haynes Automotive Electrical and Electronic Systems Manual*.

Electronic Fuel Injection (EFI) A computer controlled fuel system that distributes fuel through an injector located in each intake port of the engine.

Emergency brake A braking system, independent of the main hydraulic system, that can be used to slow or stop the vehicle if the primary brakes fail, or to hold the vehicle stationary even though the brake pedal isn't depressed. It usually consists of a hand lever that actuates either front or rear brakes mechanically through a series of cables and linkages. Also known as a handbrake or parking brake.

Endfloat The amount of lengthwise movement between two parts. As applied to a crankshaft, the distance that the crankshaft can move forward and back in the cylinder block.

Engine management system (EMS) A computer controlled system which manages the fuel injection and the ignition systems in an integrated fashion.

Exhaust manifold A part with several passages through which exhaust gases leave the engine combustion chambers and enter the exhaust pipe.

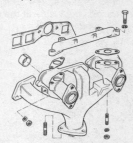

Exhaust manifold

F

Fan clutch A viscous (fluid) drive coupling device which permits variable engine fan speeds in relation to engine speeds.

Feeler blade A thin strip or blade of hardened steel, ground to an exact thickness, used to check or measure clearances between parts.

Feeler blade

Firing order The order in which the engine cylinders fire, or deliver their power strokes, beginning with the number one cylinder.

Flywheel A heavy spinning wheel in which energy is absorbed and stored by means of momentum. On cars, the flywheel is attached to the crankshaft to smooth out firing impulses.

Free play The amount of travel before any action takes place. The "looseness" in a linkage, or an assembly of parts, between the initial application of force and actual movement. For example, the distance the brake pedal moves before the pistons in the master cylinder are actuated.

Fuse An electrical device which protects a circuit against accidental overload. The typical fuse contains a soft piece of metal which is calibrated to melt at a predetermined current flow (expressed as amps) and break the circuit.

Fusible link A circuit protection device consisting of a conductor surrounded by heat-resistant insulation. The conductor is smaller than the wire it protects, so it acts as the weakest link in the circuit. Unlike a blown fuse, a failed fusible link must frequently be cut from the wire for replacement.

G

Gap The distance the spark must travel in jumping from the centre electrode to the side

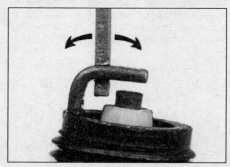

Adjusting spark plug gap

electrode in a spark plug. Also refers to the spacing between the points in a contact breaker assembly in a conventional points-type ignition, or to the distance between the reluctor or rotor and the pickup coil in an electronic ignition.

Gasket Any thin, soft material - usually cork, cardboard, asbestos or soft metal - installed between two metal surfaces to ensure a good seal. For instance, the cylinder head gasket seals the joint between the block and the cylinder head.

Gasket

Gauge An instrument panel display used to monitor engine conditions. A gauge with a movable pointer on a dial or a fixed scale is an analogue gauge. A gauge with a numerical readout is called a digital gauge.

H

Halfshaft A rotating shaft that transmits power from the final drive unit to a drive wheel, usually when referring to a live rear axle.

Harmonic balancer A device designed to reduce torsion or twisting vibration in the crankshaft. May be incorporated in the crankshaft pulley. Also known as a vibration damper.

Hone An abrasive tool for correcting small irregularities or differences in diameter in an engine cylinder, brake cylinder, etc.

Hydraulic tappet A tappet that utilises hydraulic pressure from the engine's lubrication system to maintain zero clearance (constant contact with both camshaft and valve stem). Automatically adjusts to variation in valve stem length. Hydraulic tappets also reduce valve noise.

I

Ignition timing The moment at which the spark plug fires, usually expressed in the number of crankshaft degrees before the piston reaches the top of its stroke.

Inlet manifold A tube or housing with passages through which flows the air-fuel mixture (carburettor vehicles and vehicles with throttle body injection) or air only (port fuel-injected vehicles) to the port openings in the cylinder head.

J

Jump start Starting the engine of a vehicle with a discharged or weak battery by attaching jump leads from the weak battery to a charged or helper battery.

L

Load Sensing Proportioning Valve (LSPV) A brake hydraulic system control valve that works like a proportioning valve, but also takes into consideration the amount of weight carried by the rear axle.

Locknut A nut used to lock an adjustment nut, or other threaded component, in place. For example, a locknut is employed to keep the adjusting nut on the rocker arm in position.

Lockwasher A form of washer designed to prevent an attaching nut from working loose.

M

MacPherson strut A type of front suspension system devised by Earle MacPherson at Ford of England. In its original form, a simple lateral link with the anti-roll bar creates the lower control arm. A long strut - an integral coil spring and shock absorber - is mounted between the body and the steering knuckle. Many modern so-called MacPherson strut systems use a conventional lower A-arm and don't rely on the anti-roll bar for location.

Multimeter An electrical test instrument with the capability to measure voltage, current and resistance.

N

NOx Oxides of Nitrogen. A common toxic pollutant emitted by petrol and diesel engines at higher temperatures.

O

Ohm The unit of electrical resistance. One volt applied to a resistance of one ohm will produce a current of one amp.

Ohmmeter An instrument for measuring electrical resistance.

O-ring A type of sealing ring made of a special rubber-like material; in use, the O-ring is compressed into a groove to provide the sealing action.

O-ring

Overhead cam (ohc) engine An engine with the camshaft(s) located on top of the cylinder head(s).

Overhead valve (ohv) engine An engine with the valves located in the cylinder head, but with the camshaft located in the engine block.

Oxygen sensor A device installed in the engine exhaust manifold, which senses the oxygen content in the exhaust and converts this information into an electric current. Also called a Lambda sensor.

P

Phillips screw A type of screw head having a cross instead of a slot for a corresponding type of screwdriver.

Plastigage A thin strip of plastic thread, available in different sizes, used for measuring clearances. For example, a strip of Plastigage is laid across a bearing journal. The parts are assembled and dismantled; the width of the crushed strip indicates the clearance between journal and bearing.

Plastigage

Propeller shaft The long hollow tube with universal joints at both ends that carries power from the transmission to the differential on front-engined rear wheel drive vehicles.

Proportioning valve A hydraulic control valve which limits the amount of pressure to the rear brakes during panic stops to prevent wheel lock-up.

R

Rack-and-pinion steering A steering system with a pinion gear on the end of the steering shaft that mates with a rack (think of a geared wheel opened up and laid flat). When the steering wheel is turned, the pinion turns, moving the rack to the left or right. This movement is transmitted through the track rods to the steering arms at the wheels.

Radiator A liquid-to-air heat transfer device designed to reduce the temperature of the coolant in an internal combustion engine cooling system.

Refrigerant Any substance used as a heat transfer agent in an air-conditioning system. R-12 has been the principle refrigerant for many years; recently, however, manufacturers have begun using R-134a, a non-CFC substance that is considered less harmful to the ozone in the upper atmosphere.

Rocker arm A lever arm that rocks on a shaft or pivots on a stud. In an overhead valve engine, the rocker arm converts the upward movement of the pushrod into a downward movement to open a valve.

Rotor In a distributor, the rotating device inside the cap that connects the centre electrode and the outer terminals as it turns, distributing the high voltage from the coil secondary winding to the proper spark plug. Also, that part of an alternator which rotates inside the stator. Also, the rotating assembly of a turbocharger, including the compressor wheel, shaft and turbine wheel.

Runout The amount of wobble (in-and-out movement) of a gear or wheel as it's rotated. The amount a shaft rotates "out-of-true." The out-of-round condition of a rotating part.

S

Sealant A liquid or paste used to prevent leakage at a joint. Sometimes used in conjunction with a gasket.

Sealed beam lamp An older headlight design which integrates the reflector, lens and filaments into a hermetically-sealed one-piece unit. When a filament burns out or the lens cracks, the entire unit is simply replaced.

Serpentine drivebelt A single, long, wide accessory drivebelt that's used on some newer vehicles to drive all the accessories, instead of a series of smaller, shorter belts. Serpentine drivebelts are usually tensioned by an automatic tensioner.

Serpentine drivebelt

Shim Thin spacer, commonly used to adjust the clearance or relative positions between two parts. For example, shims inserted into or under bucket tappets control valve clearances. Clearance is adjusted by changing the thickness of the shim.

Slide hammer A special puller that screws into or hooks onto a component such as a shaft or bearing; a heavy sliding handle on the shaft bottoms against the end of the shaft to knock the component free.

Sprocket A tooth or projection on the periphery of a wheel, shaped to engage with a chain or drivebelt. Commonly used to refer to the sprocket wheel itself.

Starter inhibitor switch On vehicles with an automatic transmission, a switch that prevents starting if the vehicle is not in Neutral or Park.

Strut See MacPherson strut.

T

Tappet A cylindrical component which transmits motion from the cam to the valve stem, either directly or via a pushrod and rocker arm. Also called a cam follower.

Thermostat A heat-controlled valve that regulates the flow of coolant between the cylinder block and the radiator, so maintaining optimum engine operating temperature. A thermostat is also used in some air cleaners in which the temperature is regulated.

Thrust bearing The bearing in the clutch assembly that is moved in to the release levers by clutch pedal action to disengage the clutch. Also referred to as a release bearing.

Timing belt A toothed belt which drives the camshaft. Serious engine damage may result if it breaks in service.

Timing chain A chain which drives the camshaft.

Toe-in The amount the front wheels are closer together at the front than at the rear. On rear wheel drive vehicles, a slight amount of toe-in is usually specified to keep the front wheels running parallel on the road by offsetting other forces that tend to spread the wheels apart.

Toe-out The amount the front wheels are closer together at the rear than at the front. On front wheel drive vehicles, a slight amount of toe-out is usually specified.

Tools For full information on choosing and using tools, refer to the *Haynes Automotive Tools Manual*.

Tracer A stripe of a second colour applied to a wire insulator to distinguish that wire from another one with the same colour insulator.

Tune-up A process of accurate and careful adjustments and parts replacement to obtain the best possible engine performance.

Turbocharger A centrifugal device, driven by exhaust gases, that pressurises the intake air. Normally used to increase the power output from a given engine displacement, but can also be used primarily to reduce exhaust emissions (as on VW's "Umwelt" Diesel engine).

U

Universal joint or U-joint A double-pivoted connection for transmitting power from a driving to a driven shaft through an angle. A U-joint consists of two Y-shaped yokes and a cross-shaped member called the spider.

V

Valve A device through which the flow of liquid, gas, vacuum, or loose material in bulk may be started, stopped, or regulated by a movable part that opens, shuts, or partially obstructs one or more ports or passageways. A valve is also the movable part of such a device.

Valve clearance The clearance between the valve tip (the end of the valve stem) and the rocker arm or tappet. The valve clearance is measured when the valve is closed.

Vernier caliper A precision measuring instrument that measures inside and outside dimensions. Not quite as accurate as a micrometer, but more convenient.

Viscosity The thickness of a liquid or its resistance to flow.

Volt A unit for expressing electrical "pressure" in a circuit. One volt that will produce a current of one ampere through a resistance of one ohm.

W

Welding Various processes used to join metal items by heating the areas to be joined to a molten state and fusing them together. For more information refer to the *Haynes Automotive Welding Manual*.

Wiring diagram A drawing portraying the components and wires in a vehicle's electrical system, using standardised symbols. For more information refer to the *Haynes Automotive Electrical and Electronic Systems Manual*.

Note: *References throughout this index are in the form* "**Chapter number**" • "**Page number**". *So, for example, 2C•15 refers to page 15 of Chapter 2C.*

Note: *References throughout this index are in the form* **"Chapter number"** • **"Page number"**. *So, for example, 2C•15 refers to page 15 of Chapter 2C.*

Note: *References throughout this index are in the form* **"Chapter number"** • **"Page number"**. *So, for example, 2C•15 refers to page 15 of Chapter 2C.*

Preserving Our Motoring Heritage

< The Model J Duesenberg Derham Tourster. Only eight of these magnificent cars were ever built – this is the only example to be found outside the United States of America

Almost every car you've ever loved, loathed or desired is gathered under one roof at the Haynes Motor Museum. Over 300 immaculately presented cars and motorbikes represent every aspect of our motoring heritage, from elegant reminders of bygone days, such as the superb Model J Duesenberg to curiosities like the bug-eyed BMW Isetta. There are also many old friends and flames. Perhaps you remember the 1959 Ford Popular that you did your courting in? The magnificent 'Red Collection' is a spectacle of classic sports cars including AC, Alfa Romeo, Austin Healey, Ferrari, Lamborghini, Maserati, MG, Riley, Porsche and Triumph.

A Perfect Day Out

Each and every vehicle at the Haynes Motor Museum has played its part in the history and culture of Motoring. Today, they make a wonderful spectacle and a great day out for all the family. Bring the kids, bring Mum and Dad, but above all bring your camera to capture those golden memories for ever. You will also find an impressive array of motoring memorabilia, a comfortable 70 seat video cinema and one of the most extensive transport book shops in Britain. The Pit Stop Cafe serves everything from a cup of tea to wholesome, home-made meals or, if you prefer, you can enjoy the large picnic area nestled in the beautiful rural surroundings of Somerset.

> John Haynes O.B.E., Founder and Chairman of the museum at the wheel of a Haynes Light 12.

< Graham Hill's Lola Cosworth Formula 1 car next to a 1934 Riley Sports.

The Museum is situated on the A359 Yeovil to Frome road at Sparkford, just off the A303 in Somerset. It is about 40 miles south of Bristol, and 25 minutes drive from the M5 intersection at Taunton.
Open 9.30am - 5.30pm (10.00am - 4.00pm Winter) 7 days a week, *except Christmas Day, Boxing Day and New Years Day*
Special rates available for schools, coach parties and outings Charitable Trust No. 292048